Portrait of Lionardo Salviati as a Knight of St. Stephen, artist unknown
By kind permission of the Accademia della Crusca, Florence

LIONARDO SALVIATI

A Critical Biography

BY

PETER M. BROWN

OXFORD UNIVERSITY PRESS

1974

Oxford University Press, Ely House, London W. 1

GLASGOW NEW YORK TORONTO MELBOURNE WELLINGTON
CAPE TOWN IBADAN NAIROBI DAR ES SALAAM LUSAKA ADDIS ABABA
DELHI BOMBAY CALCUTTA MADRAS KARACHI LAHORE DACCA
KUALA LUMPUR SINGAPORE HONG KONG TOKYO

ISBN 0 19 815523 9

Printed in Great Britain
at the University Press, Oxford
by Vivian Ridler
Printer to the University

TO
ROGER REES
IN AFFECTIONATE AND
GRATEFUL MEMORY

PREFACE

IN late sixteenth-century Florence creative writers of lasting reputation and significance are rare. The autobiography of the comparatively unlettered Cellini has more life for us today than the sonnets, discourses, and dialogues of the learned Academicians in whose state-controlled institution so much of the literary activity of the city was concentrated. Unlike Ferrara, Florence produced no great creative literary genius in this period. Yet we must not imagine that she was devoid of spiritual life. On the contrary, despite a general shrinking of cultural horizons, the activity of the Florentine Academy, as implied in its declared aims, represents an intellectual ferment of a nature, and with a direction, which maintain Florence in the forefront of the development of Italian thought. Basically, the aim of the Academy was to substitute the national for the classical standard, and this principle dominated its every activity. It is in this context, itself of European significance, that the Florentine figures of the period acquire their importance.

The more one examines this context the more one figure stands out, namely Lionardo Salviati. He stands out for two reasons. Amongst such individuals as Varchi, Gelli, Grazzini, all of them valid representatives of some of the many aspects of contemporary thought, Salviati alone emerges as a monolithic figure whose output reveals itself to be the completely homogeneous expression of a single guiding idea. There is virtually no aspect of his work which is not inspired and dominated by that principle which gave the Academy's activity its chief importance. Secondly he was an outstandingly effective spokesman of that principle. It was he who embodied it with lasting influence in his *Vocabolario*, in the *Avvertimenti*, in his contributions to the disputes over the *Gerusalemme Liberata*, and in his *Orazioni*. This he did also with a power and a coherence appreciated by his contemporaries whom evidence shows us to have been well aware of his importance and his stature.

After a long period of neglect recent years have witnessed a revival of interest in the late sixteenth century. Inevitably, given
what has already been said of him, Salviati is beginning to emerge
as a key figure. Yet whoever wishes to investigate further his
activities and his production will look in vain for any biographical
or critical work which might represent a point of departure.
Although he enters indirectly into numerous lengthy studies—
Crescini investigating Jacopo Corbinelli, or Trabalza writing the
history of Italian grammar—there is hardly a handful of articles
devoted to him or his works. His life, apart from what is revealed
by scanty collections of his letters and faulty editions of his
Rime and minor prose works, has remained completely unexplored,
his manuscripts unexamined. Even his relations with other men of
letters, despite the importance conceded to him in his own times,
have attracted virtually no attention. What references to him are
to be found generally perpetuate a tissue of accumulated errors.

The aim of the present work is to begin at least to remedy this
state of affairs. For this purpose a biography is obviously the first
essential. Consequently the book has been given a biographical
basis which integrates Salviati's literary and other cultural activities, including those of his early and less fruitful years, into
his movements and into his relationships with the Medici court,
with the Academy, and with other men of letters. If the work was
to serve as a much needed initial source for work on Salviati it
had also to provide as much factual information (including bibliographical information) on the subject as could be assembled,
and indicate in the fullest practicable manner the sources of further
information of this kind. The notes in particular have been designed with this aim in mind. Finally the book embodies a personal
interpretation of Lionardo Salviati and an attempt to assess his
position in Florentine (and Italian) culture and thought in the
late sixteenth century.

Throughout it has been deliberate policy to cut inessential
detail down to a minimum. Discussions better suited to the
periodical article have been omitted, only their conclusions being
incorporated. Similarly the temptation to include more information
of a 'background' character has been firmly resisted. Whilst the

main determining consideration here has been one of space it is
hoped that one compensation of the concentration on Salviati
himself will be his emergence in clearer relief.

Future study of Salviati cannot but be fruitful for the understanding of Florence and Italy in the late Renaissance. The present
book will have achieved its aims in proportion to its usefulness
in facilitating that study.

Hull, January 1972

ACKNOWLEDGEMENTS

I N writing this book I owe a great debt to many institutions and individuals. I would like to thank first the Carnegie Trust for the Universities of Scotland, the Sir John Cassell Trust, and the Italian Government, all of whom have given generous financial assistance towards the expenses of long periods of research in Italy; secondly the courteous and helpful staffs of many libraries and archives both in Britain and in Italy, particularly those of King's College Library, Aberdeen, the British Museum, the Biblioteca Nazionale Centrale and the Archivio di Stato of Florence, the Archivio Vaticano and the Biblioteca Apostolica Vaticana, Rome, the Archivi di Stato of Pisa, Modena, and Parma, the Biblioteca Palatina of Parma, and the Biblioteca Estense of Modena; I wish to thank thirdly those friends and colleagues who have made so many helpful contributions and suggestions, especially Professor Carlo Dionisotti, Professor C. Grayson, Professor C. P. Brand, Dr. J. Woodhouse, and Dr. D. E. Rhodes. Finally I am grateful to the Accademia della Crusca in Florence for permission to reproduce the portrait of Salviati in the frontispiece.

CONTENTS

ABBREVIATIONS

Ab. inc.	Ab incarnatione (Florentine-style dating)
A.Bu.	Archivio Buoncompagni (Archivio Vaticano)
Ambr.	Ambrosiano (Biblioteca Ambrosiana, Milan)
A.S.	Archivio di Stato
A.S.St.	Archivio di Santo Stefano (Archivio di Stato, Pisa)
Aut.	Autografo
A.V.	Archivio Vaticano
Bib.	Biblioteca
B.M.	British Museum
B.N.C.	Biblioteca Nazionale Centrale
C.A.F.	Cancelleria, Ambasciatori, Firenze (Archivio di Stato, Modena)
Cod.	Codex
Cons. (S.St.)	Consiglio (di Santo Stefano, Pisa)
Ded. lett.	Dedicatory letter
F.L.O.	Filze di lettere originali
F.Med.	Filze Medicee (Archivio di Stato, Florence)
G.S.L.I.	*Giornale storico della letteratura italiana*
Inc.	*Incipit*
Lett.	Letter
Magl.	Fondo Magliabechiano (manuscripts in the Biblioteca Nazionale Centrale, Florence)
Misc.	Miscellanea
M.L.R.	*Modern Language Review*
Nap.	Napoletano (manuscripts in the Biblioteca Nazionale Centrale Vittorio Emanuele II, Naples)
Pal.	Fondo Palatino (manuscripts in the Biblioteca Nazionale Centrale, Florence)
Repr.	Reprint
Ricc.	Riccardiano (manuscripts in the Biblioteca Riccardiana, Florence)
R.L.M.	Registri di lettere missive

S.St.   Santo Stefano

St. com.   Common Style (in dating)

U.   Unpublished

Dates are given in the Common Style unless otherwise indicated. In the notes publication details are normally given in English, but on occasion, in the case of older books, the form as printed has been retained, e.g. 'In Firenze per i Figliuoli di Luigi Torrentino e Carlo Pettinari, Con licenza e Privilegio, 1566'.

I

THE SALVIATI

AT five o'clock in the morning on 27 June 1539 in the Quartiere di San Pier Maggiore, Florence, a son was born to Ginevra (*née* Corbinelli) and Giovambattista di Lionardo Salviati. That same day they had him baptized 'Lionardo et Romolo'. In sixteenth-century Florence the family of the newly born child could claim to have few equals. Their genealogy was traceable with certainty back to one Gottifredo in the middle of the twelfth century through an impressive line of merchant-nobles who had played a prominent part in the political, social, and commercial life of both their own city and that of numerous others in central Italy.[1]

In the Salviati family Lionardo was a traditional name, and particularly in the Prato branch of it to which belonged Giovambattista, father of the newly born child. The latter's grandfather was Lionardo di Ruberto Salviati, and he, after a term in 1472 as one of the priors of the city of Florence, had married a certain Madonna Polissena Ambrogini. By Florentine standards Madonna Polissena was a foreigner. Her father, Piero di Jacopo Ambrogini, came from the city of Iesi in the Marche, and the high standing which he had reached in his native city is revealed in a letter written by the *Gonfaloniere* and Priors of Iesi at the request of the Council of the Order of St. Stephen thirty years later when Lionardo et Romolo, by then thirty years old, was invested with the order.[2] The *Auditore* Domenico Bonsi (one of the new and

---

[1] The most useful genealogical works on the Salviati family are: G. Passerini, *MS. collezione genealogica Passerini*, 203, 12, Salviati, B.N.C., Florence; E. Gamurrini, *Istoria generale delle famiglie nobili toscane ed umbre*, 5 vols. (Florence, 1679), iv. 170; J. W. Imhof, *Genealogiae viginti illustrium in Italia familiarum* (Amsterdam, 1710); S. Ammirato, *Delle famiglie nobili fiorentine* (Florence, Giunti, 1615); G. M. Mecatti, *Istoria genealogica della nobiltà e cittadinanza di Firenze divisa in tre parti* (Napoli, Simione, 1753–4); P. Mini, *Discorso della nobiltà di Firenze e de' Fiorentini* (Florence, Manzani, 1593).

[2] The letter (Pisa, A.S., A.S.St., 'Provanze di nobiltà', Filza 7, Parte prima, N. 3, Lionardo Salviati), runs: 'Noi Gonfalonieri e Priori della città di Iesi attestiamo come M. Piero di Iacopo Ambrogini da Iesi, il quale all'età de nostri

powerful figures of Duke Cosimo's reformed administration), called to testify on that occasion to Lionardo's noble birth, had known Piero Ambrogini personally, and was able to produce documentary evidence to the effect that he had come to Florence as 'podestà' and was an 'huomo famoso di lettere'. Piero's daughter Polissena and Lionardo the elder had three sons, Giovambattista, Diamante, and Pietro, and no fewer than three witnesses at the 'provanza' had known personally the eldest of these, Giovambattista, born in 1477. In due course Giovambattista himself married, into the prominent Corbinelli family, taking as his wife Ginevra, daughter of Carlo di Vincenzo Corbinelli and Caterina di Vincenzo Zati. To this couple were born at least three sons and at least one daughter. First came Giuliano, then Silvestro, followed by a girl whose name we do not know; and finally in 1539, when Giovambattista had reached the age of sixty-two, Lionardo.[3] His birth, and his baptism on the same day, are registered in the Opera di Santa Maria del Fiore.[4] The choice of a second Christian name (though Romolo was by no means uncommon in Florence, being the name of San Romolo, erstwhile Bishop of Fiesole) may not have been altogether unconnected

avoli se impatriò in Firenze, et i suoi antenati furono gentiluomini et nobili di questa città et goderno, e furono habili a godere, tutti i supremi gradi e honori, ch'erano soliti a godere i più nobili della detta nostra città e vissero senza macchia, e, non hebbero origine da infedeli, e, di tanto ricerchi per la verità, havemo fatto far la presente di mano dell'infrascritto nostro cancelliere, e, sigillata col nostro solito sigillo, in Iesi, questo dì xxii di Luglio 1569.'

[3] Passerini, op. cit., who gives the fullest table, notes three sons, Giuliano, Silvestro, and Lionardo. In his will (Florence, A.S., Notarile moderno, 10 [also marked 1149], 'Protocolli di Ser Francesco Parenti'), Salviati has the following item: 'Item iure legati reliquit et legavit sorori Angelae de Salviatis moniali in Monasterio sancti Johannis de Florentia ordinis Hierosolimitani unam Pietantiam faciendam quolibet anno cum illa impensa videbitur infrascriptis eius heredibus.' There is no indication that the lady referred to is his own sister, though she may well be, as the fact that he had at least one sister, and quite possibly two, is confirmed by the sum total of the references to members of his family in his own correspondence.

[4] The certificate of birth, containing information taken from the sixteenth-century registers in the Opera di Santa Maria del Fiore, reads: 'Certificasi dal sottoscritto come dai registri di quest'archivio, risulta che l'anno 1539, a dì 27 del mese di giugno è stato battezzato Lionardo et Romolo di Gio. Battista di Lionardo Salviati, nato il dì 27 di Giugno 1539 a ore 5 nel popolo di S. Pier Maggiore.' 'Lionardo' was thus the name given to him at birth, and Calzabigi was quite wrong when in his celebrated letter to Alfieri he wrote: '. . . sotto la bandiera del signor Lionardo, non Leonardo Salviati (per maggior pretesa eleganza di lingua) . . .'.

with an event scheduled to take place two days later and for which all Florence was busily preparing, namely the marriage of Duke Cosimo and Donna Eleonora di Toledo. For Cosimo, too, had been christened 'Cosimo et Romolo'.

Nothing could have symbolized more tellingly than this almost royal wedding between a Duke of Florence (a title which still could not have rolled easily off Florentine tongues) and the daughter of a Spanish Viceroy the fundamental transformation which had taken place in Florence in the preceding generation, a transformation which produced the forces operating on the generation of Lionardo and gave rise to the tensions and the pressures which moulded them and determined their development.

For in no period of her long history had the City of the Red Lily undergone more profound and far-reaching changes. Throughout this history three things had remained dear to the hearts of her citizens—independence, a free republican constitution, and the French alliance. Now all three were things of the past. Falling under Medici rule again in 1512 after eighteen years as a revived Republic, Florence had for the next fifteen years been virtually governed from Rome by the Medici Popes Leo X and Clement VII. Her period of renewed liberty after the sack of Rome in 1527 had been short-lived, for by the Treaty of Barcelona between Clement and the Emperor Charles V the latter promised to deliver Florence once again into the hands of the Medici and to marry his own illegitimate daughter Margaret of Austria to Alessandro de' Medici, a bastard son of Lorenzo de' Medici Duke of Urbino.

The fall of Florence to the Papal–Imperialist forces in 1530 after a long and valiant resistance led by Francesco Ferrucci does indeed mark a turning-point in her history. As one eminent historian puts it: 'con la caduta della Repubblica la storia di "Firenze" è finita . . . l'anima stessa di Firenze è morta, con i suoi impeti, i suoi abbandoni, le sue collere, le sue iniquità, i suoi eroismi, le sue audacie: le sue caratteristiche tipiche sono cancellate quasi completamente.'[5] The changes now introduced affected in the profoundest possible manner the climate in the city, the outlook of the citizens in general, and its men of letters in particular.

In the new constitution of 1532 Alessandro as 'duca della repubblica Fiorentina' replaced the *Gonfaloniere:* the two

[5] R. Caggese, *Firenze dalla decadenza di Roma al Risorgimento d'Italia*, 3 vols. (Florence, Bemporad, 1912–21), iii. 1.

legislative assemblies—the Council of Two Hundred and the Senate (or Council) of Forty-eight—were created, and four Senators, changing every three months, replaced the Priors as aids to the Duke in governing.[6] Disillusionment overtook the great Florentine families (who had hoped that the government would in practice revert to the old oligarchical system with the Duke as a mere figurehead) as Alessandro's rule acquired a steadily more tyrannical character, and in an ever-increasing flood they left the city in protest. To list the exiles or *fuorusciti* is to compile a funerary monument to any power or consistency in the Florentine aristocracy.

Snubbed by the Emperor the exiles allied themselves to the anti-Medicean pope Paul III and the throne of France, and great was the rejoicing amongst them when Alessandro was assassinated in 1537. Their hopes were quickly dashed, for no popular uprising followed this event and the initiative passed quickly from the king-making *ottimati* led by Guicciardini, Rucellai, and Vettori, who aspired to restore an oligarchical regime, to the imperial faction and to the young Cosimo de' Medici, whom they themselves had appointed head of state to succeed Alessandro. With the Hispano-Imperialist forces poised for action at the slightest sign of disaffection (whereupon Florence would almost certainly have become a Spanish province like Milan or Naples), the city had no choice but to throw in her lot with the Emperor.

Helped by Spanish arms Cosimo defeated the forces of the invading French-assisted exiles at Montemurlo, and Charles was sufficiently convinced of his loyalty and the stability of his state to recognize him as Alessandro's legitimate successor. Normality was restored by the young Duke with astonishing rapidity and efficiency. By 1538 he succeeded in having the Spanish garrisons withdrawn and was master of his own state.[7] He did not succeed in persuading Charles to give him Alessandro's widow Margaret, however, and took to wife instead Eleanora di Toledo, daughter of Don Pedro di Toledo, Viceroy of Naples. Eleanora left Naples with seven galleys on 11 June 1539, and

[6] Amongst the first members of the Consiglio dei Quarantotto on its inauguration, all of them loyal to the house of Medici, there figures Lorenzo Salviati representing the Quartiere di Santa Croce; see E. Repetti, *Compendio storico della città di Firenze* (Florence, Tofani, 1849), p. 148.

[7] See G. Spini, *Cosimo I de' Medici e l'indipendenza del principato medíceo* (Florence, 1945).

on Sunday 29 June she arrived in Florence, where a spectacle-loving populace in festive mood had excelled itself in preparing a sumptuous welcome in a gaily decorated city. Not that the good citizens had been given complete licence to express their spontaneous delight as the fancy took them. A single theme was chosen to predominate, and that was the harmonious conjunction of Florence and Empire, represented respectively by Cosimo de' Medici and the daughter of the Emperor Charles V's viceroy in Naples. In the Palazzo Medici itself, the final goal of an itinerary which led through an unbroken succession of decorative paintings and groups of sculpture produced by such artists as Bronzino and Battista Franco,[8] there was an imperial eagle embracing the inter-twined arms of Medici and Toledo.

In the decorations of the interior of the ducal palace in Via Larga the family of the child newly born to Giovambattista and Ginevra was not neglected. The Salviati coat of arms, linked with that of the Medici, took its due place on the walls of the famous loggia, which was the scene of the festivities (including the inevitable comedy) held exactly a week later to celebrate the wedding.

But to be born a Salviati in June 1539 was not the unmixed blessing which it might at first sight appear. There must have been few members of the Florentine oligarchy who boasted an escutcheon entirely free from anti-Medicean blots, but in this respect the Salviati family had acquired a somewhat unfortunate distinction. In the first place, comparatively early in the history of Medici dominance in Florence, they had played a principal role in the ill-fated Pazzi conspiracy of 1478, losing an archbishop and two other prominent members of their family in the subsequent hangings from the windows of the Palazzo Vecchio. In 1485 (and not for the first time) Salviati allied with Medici in the marriage of Jacopo Salviati the elder, head of the house, and Lucrezia de' Medici, daughter of Lorenzo de' Medici il Magnifico, a union of which the very numerous offspring (there were eleven in all who survived) were to play a prominent if occasionally unfortunate and anything but concerted role in Florentine affairs as well as

[8] See especially L. Cantini, *Storia di Cosimo de' Medici primo Granduca di Toscana* (Pisa, 1805), and P. F. Giambullari, *Apparato et feste nelle nozze dello illustrissimo Signor Duca di Firenze, e della Duchessa sua consorte, con le sue stanze, madrigali, comedia, e intermedii in quella recitati* (Florence, 1539).

in the life of Lionardo himself. Their son Giovanni, thanks to his mother's brother Leo X, became the family's first cardinal, and some years later Giovanni's brother Berardo was also raised to the purple. Alamanno, the third son, was Captain of Pisa in 1509 when the city came once again under Florentine control, and founded the line which produced the Dukes of Giuliano. Their daughter Francesca married Ottaviano de' Medici.

But it was their plain, white-faced little daughter Maria who took the prize, as it turned out, when she married the soldier Giovanni de' Medici, better known as Giovanni delle Bande Nere, of the junior line of the Medici of Cafaggiolo. Giovanni's father was the grandson of Lorenzo the founder of the line, and his mother was the fiery Caterina Sforza of Forlì. In 1519, seven years before the death of Giovanni delle Bande Nere fighting for the French at Mantua, Maria Salviati gave birth to the future Duke Cosimo whose marriage was now being celebrated in June 1539. There was thus good reason why the Medici and Salviati arms should find themselves together in the wedding decorations.

Despite this windfall, however, even the more recent record of the Salviati, taken all round, could hardly be considered totally satisfactory. Leaving aside the political manœuvres of the lesser members of the family the whole progeny of Jacopo, despite its half-Medici ancestry, was split neatly into two camps over the main political issue of the Medici versus the *fuorusciti*. Two of Cosimo's most active and unrelenting opponents were Jacopo's cardinal sons Giovanni and Berardo. Of these the former was humiliatingly driven from Florence in 1537 along with his fellow cardinals Gaddi and Ridolfi ('come mosche senza capo' as Varchi later contemptuously wrote) when as representatives of the exiles they attempted to cow the young Cosimo into submission. Students of Italian literature, however, will remember Cardinal Giovanni Salviati best as he emerges from the autobiography of Benvenuto Cellini, who describes a heated altercation between himself and 'questo cardinale bestia . . . che avea più viso di asino che di uomo'. The second, Berardo, narrowly missed the gruesome fate of many of his colleagues at Montemurlo by arriving at the scene of battle too late. Firmly anchored to the Medici cause, on the other hand, were old Jacopo himself and his third son Alamanno, both of whom, and especially the former, had played a considerable role in the upbringing of young 'Cosimino'

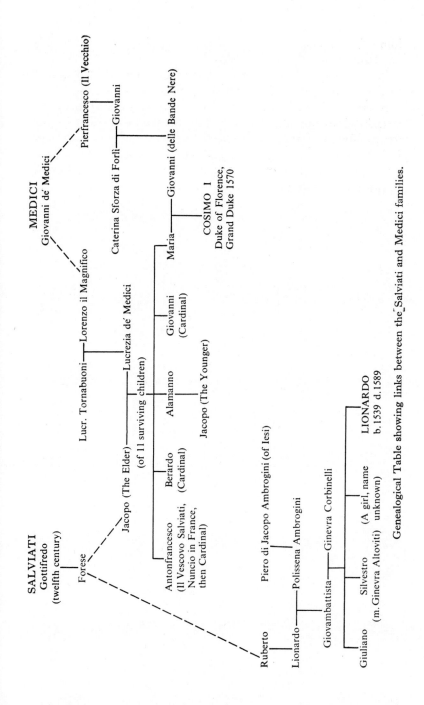

Genealogical Table showing links between the Salviati and Medici families.

himself, as the new Duke was wont to be called during his child-
hood and youth.

Like the city of Florence the Salviati family was divided against
itself. It had a past to live down and a future to search for. When
Lionardo et Romolo became a Florentine in June 1539 to the
sounds of feasting and merry-making the past was still too near
for comfort, and the future uncertain. But he himself would at
least have the advantage of being one of the 'new' citizens, for
whom the Florentine Republic, and all it had stood for, belonged
to the history books.

II

FLORENCE: THE POLITICAL AND SOCIAL SCENE

O F Lionardo's early life little can be learnt, for he was far too unimportant a unit in the vast complex of the Salviati family to make any impression on Florentine society. That he was even a frequent visitor to the sumptuous Palazzo Salviati, with its acanthus-capitalled colonnades, built to designs by Bramante Lazzeri, and in which Cosimo himself was born in 1519, is very unlikely.

It is also improbable that he entered into the more strenuous activities—the football games between teams of young nobles for example, of which contemporary diarists speak so much—which still characterized festive occasions in a city whose tradition made any occasion an excuse for merry-making, bonfires, and fireworks. Indeed if anything these celebrations became even more splendid than before, and full honour was done to the birth of the eleven children, seven males and four females, who were born to the ducal couple between 1540 and 1554. But Lionardo et Romolo appears to have been a weakling from birth. According to Pierfrancesco Cambi, who had known him all his life, he was 'grazioso e giocondo d'aspetto' as a boy, excelling in particular as an actor, when in keeping with the tradition for Florentine youths he took part in the public performances of plays as part of his education. In this pastime of acting, which was also designed to equip youths for public speaking, Lionardo, so Cambi tells us, took a passionate interest, being outstanding amongst his companions for his clear voice, his fine enunciation, and the gracefulness of his movements.[1]

Cambi's information on the youth of Lionardo is tantalizingly limited, yet what little he does tell us in his funeral oration has the ring of authenticity. For in these histrionic propensities and delight in public applause we see foreshadowed much of the future

[1] See P. F. Cambi, *Orazione funebre di Pierfrancesco Cambi: delle lodi del cavalier Lionardo Salviati* (Florence, Padovani, 1590).

Lionardo, characterized by an oratorical instinct, a desire to attract attention (as in the polemics over the *Gerusalemme Liberata*), and that predilection for acting a double part which led to his writing under a string of false names. Moreover, the incompatibility of certain of his actions in later life with his constant outward exaltation of friendship, the nonchalance with which he warmly assured his associates of his unshakeable friendship, and loyalty whilst betraying them in secret without a qualm, all suggest that he was an enthusiastic and consummate actor throughout his life to the extent of being virtually incapable of spontaneity except when uncontrollably angry.

All witnesses agree on his delicate health, further confirmed by frequent periods of incapacity through sickness at all stages of his life, to which his own letters, and those of his friends, bear abundant testimony. What few reliable facts can be accumulated, apart from the very definite information on his final illness and his own references specifically to recurrent malaria, seem to indicate an extreme general constitutional weakness.

Around him in these first formative decades of his life there was growing a new Florence in more senses than one; and feeling himself from the very first a Florentine, he must have followed with interest the progress of the many projects initiated by Cosimo for the beautification of his capital city. There was the Mercato Nuovo, designed by Giovambattista Tasso, of which the foundations were laid in 1546; the new Uffizi begun by Vasari in 1560; and the new bridges of Carraia and Santa Trinita, the latter destined to become one of the glories of Florence and created by Bartolommeo Ammannati after the flood of 1557. In 1554 Cellini's *Perseus* was erected under the Loggia dei Lanzi, and Pontormo, Bronzino, and in particular Vasari were busy transforming and decorating the ducal palaces for which Niccolò del Tribolo laid out the gardens and fountains. And if, taken together, the statues and kindred works of art with which Cosimo ennobled his capital have a somewhat inflated and rhetorical character, with more than a touch of humourless pomposity about them, they are not for this any less representative of the regime.

In 1540 the Duke and his family had moved to the Palazzo Vecchio, redesigned and redecorated for the purpose by Vasari. The reasons for the move may well have been, as the historian Adriani suggests, that Cosimo wished to identify himself and his family even more with the government of the state. For the outward change in the city, its acquisition of a certain regal grandeur, was but a true reflection of an even more epoch-making internal transformation.

Duke Cosimo, in whose hands for good or ill the destinies of Florence lay, was a remarkable person, who from the very moment of his election in 1537 seemed to be in possession of fully matured plans for his dominions from which he never for one instant swerved, and in the implementation of which he displayed a skill, tenacity, firmness of purpose—and ruthlessness—which made him one of the outstanding figures of his century. He was a man whose contemporaries, whilst stressing his combination of patience, cunning, and guile, and his exceptional capacity for dissimulation, nevertheless insist to have been a just man by his own lights, neither greedy nor mercenary.[2]

Under Cosimo's early rule a vast programme of reform, with centralization and unification as its main aims, welded the hitherto chaotic and heterogeneous elements of the Florentine state into a coherent whole. An administrative hierarchy of professional civil servants was created, culminating in the *Pratica Segreta* or inner cabinet, which co-ordinated the work of the various *Auditori*, the high-ranking ministers invested with wide powers in the fields of civil and criminal justice, finance, and relations with the Church. Hand in hand with centralization and unification went the establishment of absolute rule, in which the Duke alone exercised the ultimate authority in every field.[3]

All this was not without effect on the social structure of Florence. Whilst a more impartial justice was enjoyed by the mass of the populace and the lowly were protected against the strong, the death-blow was delivered to a nobility already weakened by the mass exodus under Alessandro. When one remembers the fierce exclusive jealousy with which the metropolitan Florentine nobles

[2] See particularly D. Mellini, *Ricordo intorno ai costumi, azioni e governo del sereniss. Gran Duca Cosimo I* (Florence, Maghera, 1820); B. Baldini, *Vita di Cosimo I Granduca di Toscana scritta da Baccio Baldini, suo protomedico* (Florence, Sermartelli, 1578); A. Manuzio, *Vita di Cosimo de' Medici primo Granduca di Toscana* (Pisa, 1823); G. B. Cini, *Vita del serenissimo Sig. Cosimo de' Medici primo Granduca di Toscana* (Florence, 1611).

[3] For accounts of Cosimo's rule and his reforms see L. A. Ferrai, *Cosimo de' Medici duca di Firenze* (Bologna, 1882): A. Anzilotti, *La costituzione interna dello stato fiorentino sotto il Duca Cosimo I de' Medici* (Florence, Lumachi, 1910): C. Booth, *Cosimo I de' Medici* (Cambridge, 1921).

had always reserved for themselves the privilege of government, the *Pratica Segreta* (of which Averardo Salviati was from the outset a member, and whose members eventually represented all areas of the Florentine dominion) seems to symbolize the bodily removal of the Florentine aristocracy as such from the government of the state and their new equality *before* their Prince rather than *with* him as had been the case in the old regime. In the Florence of Cosimo a man such as Lelio Torelli, *Primo Segretario e Primo Auditore* wielded more power than a Salviati or a Strozzi. The days of the oligarchy were indeed over.

In this sense, too, the move to the Palazzo Vecchio when Salviati was one year old was significant, for it symbolized the identification of the state with the 'court', rather than with the *arti* and the old merchant bourgeoisie who in the great days of the republic had been its very soul, but who were now reduced to an ineffectual petty bourgeoisie no longer constituting a significant social force. Stripped of both political and economic power the merchant bourgeoisie developed into a court nobility in keeping with the familiar pattern of absolutism, whilst the court itself became increasingly aristocratic and aloof.

It was in this climate of the new principate that Lionardo Salviati, born only two years after Cosimo's election, spent his formative years, and the policies of Cosimo, which canalized the energies of the citizens into the one direction of the service of the state as epitomized in its Duke, were having their effect on the constitution of the class with which he was to be primarily associated, namely the men of letters. In their case, too, no activity, literary or artistic, was considered extraneous to the purposes of the state, and no activity was willingly tolerated which went counter to the latter or even which made no contribution to it. This is particularly evident in Cosimo's procedure in the readmission of exiles with whom, whatever their category, he only took good risks, keeping a close eye on them once they were back in the fold, cautiously rewarding and encouraging good behaviour by financial assistance, lucrative commissions, or posts of prestige, until the process of rehabilitation was complete.

This is what happened to one individual destined to play a significant part in Salviati's career, namely Giovanni Battista Adriani, a soldier and man of letters, the republican ardour of whose youth kept him suspect long after his approaches to the

Medici had tentatively been received with favour. By degrees—admission to the Florentine Academy in 1541, the post of historio-grapher at the court, the Chair of Eloquence at the Studio in 1549 —he slowly regained his respectability, and eventually so succeeded in living down his past that he was commissioned by Cosimo, on the death of Varchi, to write the history of Cosimo's rule. On occasion, as with Benedetto Varchi, the Duke would consider reconcilia-tion so desirable that he himself would take the initiative. Nor was this principle of absorption into the state limited to individuals. Institutions, and even cultural movements, were directed along lines which allowed Cosimo to exploit them for the greatest possible benefit of the state.

It is important to bear this climate in mind in judging the behaviour of Lionardo when he strikes out on his own, for he was surrounded by individuals who combined exaggerated demon-strations of loyalty (not infrequently prompted by the skeletons in their cupboards) with a smouldering inner resentment. More-over, they represented the privileged who had been screened by Cosimo and not found wanting, conscious that their activities were being observed with interest and aware that to conform, at least outwardly, was the only means of survival.

But if Cosimo has been blamed (largely by Romantic historians such as Botta) for reducing the once independent-minded Floren-tines to a spiritless band of yes-men, puppets who jumped when he pulled the strings, and for stifling whatever genius or originality might still be lingering on in the Florentine spirit, the effective-ness of that policy was not entirely due to one-sided pressure on his part. It has been rightly observed that 'the atmosphere in which republics thrive was no longer to be encountered in the Cinquecento, and . . . not only in Italy, but everywhere in Europe the stage was set for the absolute monarchy'.[4] This truth the Florentine *letterati* dimly perceived and whilst vaguely frustrated by their imposed role they saw the movement of history personified in their Duke and suffered from a split personality in that they could not but identify themselves with him in this sense, and could not but take a pride in what appeared to be the 'modern' achievements of Florence. In this dichotomy is to be found the key to the person-ality of Lionardo Salviati, and to the tragedy of his personal life.

4 F. Schevill, *History of Florence in the Middle Ages and Renaissance* (London, Bell, 1937), p. 315.

As a result of the conflicting forces outlined, Cosimo exercised over Florentines a little older than Lionardo a compulsive attraction, often stronger than the resentment with which it was combined. Cosimo's almost unbroken success in domestic and foreign policy, his successful reform of internal administration and justice, his apparent restoration of commercial and industrial prosperity, the very fact of his ruling over an independent state where in his place there might have been a Spanish viceroy, and the territorial expansion he achieved (Siena was captured when Salviati was sixteen, avenging Montaperti after three centuries almost to the year) enabled him to command the respect, if not the affection, of much of the generation which had opposed him decades earlier at Montemurlo.

The newer generation represented by Lionardo, nurtured from birth under the new regime, could not feel as acutely even as their immediate predecessors the loss of a liberty which they had never known. They saw Cosimo as the first prince of Italy in the eyes of foreign powers. Florence once again appeared to be a force to be reckoned with, counting for something even in European politics. They were full of enthusiasm for Florentine—and Italian—achievements.

III

EARLY YEARS AND
FIRST LITERARY SUCCESSES

BEING apparently too delicate to take part in the commercial activities of his family (his father was a businessman in Florence) Lionardo seems to have dedicated himself from the first, and with great determination, to academic studies. No evidence points to his having participated in his early youth in the meetings of any of the minor academies then flourishing in Florence, though he cannot fail to have come into contact with their activities and to have been influenced by the increasingly parochial character which they were assuming in this period.[1]

On the whole the literary scene was a sad one. Florentine horizons were fast shrinking, and the *letterati* of the time are interesting or important largely in a Florentine context. They wrote 'Florentine' histories (with the exception of the learned Giambullari, who had extended his field of vision to Europe); their poetry turned all too frequently on Florentine allusions, and its appeal was based largely on linguistic *proprietà* fully appreciated only by fellow Florentines. Increasingly their subject-matter concerned events of no interest beyond the city walls of Florence, dominated by Alessandro's Fortezza da Basso.

It is significant that the brightest stars in the Florentine firmament in the years of Lionardo's youth are the most essentially

---

[1] At this period the Accademia del Piano was holding its meetings on the Piano di Ripoli just outside Florence. S. Salvini, *Fasti consolari dell'Accademia Fiorentina* (Florence, 1717), pp. 198–9 (Consolato di Jacopo Pitti), quotes the MS. Strozzi RRR (B.N.C., Florence) in which the names of the members were listed, transformed into Roman names or otherwise camouflaged. Salvini asserts that the Plutonei in one such list, where the false and real names are given side by side, represent the Salviati. This manuscript is now the Cod. Magl. Cl. IX, 18, B.N.C., Florence, and the 'Plutonei' is in fact the pseudonym of the Salviati. Agrippa Plutonei, however, behind which name Salvini believes Lionardo Salviati to be hidden, does not figure in the list. And neither in this list nor in others in the B.N.C. which deal with the Accademia del Piano (Magl. VIII, 38; VIII, 47; VII, 343) is there anything to suggest that Lionardo participated in its activities.

'Florentine' amongst the men of letters. Typical is Antonfrancesco Grazzini, commonly called 'Il Lasca', the nickname he
assumed as a founder member of the Accademia degli Umidi.
This body, to which we shall have to return, was in its aims,
purposes, and programme an exaltation of 'Florentinity'. Grazzini
himself excelled in the typical Florentine wit, improvisation,
burlesque debate, and poetry, and it is significant also that the
most outstanding constant feature of both his comedies and his
short stories is their intensely Florentine character in setting,
allusion, and language. From the sights, sounds, and speech of
Florence they draw their life-blood. Nor is it any accident that
Lasca's reputation was first established by, and long rested on, his
editions of *poesie burlesche* mainly by Florentine authors, and of
the 'trionfi, carri, mascherate o canti carnascialeschi' seen or
heard in Florence since the days of Lorenzo de' Medici.

When the last-mentioned work came out Lionardo was twenty.
The generation amongst whom Salviati grew up, dominated by
such men as Grazzini and Varchi, represents the degeneration of
the Florentine spirit from universal to local proportions, its forced
insertion into the moulds of the academies, its exhaustion in an
ever-narrowing circle of parochial standards. All of which is not
to say that activity, of a kind, was not intense, or even, as we shall
see, that Florence did not have an interesting and significant
contribution to make to the development of Cinquecento culture.
With a quasi-feudal attachment to their lords the academies,
the Florentines gushed forth an unceasing stream of comedies,
orations, poems petrarchesque and burlesque, academic lectures,
histories, discourses, polemical works on critical theory, and other
matters of current fashion. But if one feature can be singled out as
characterizing Florentine literary activity during this period it is
the narcissistic contemplation of their own image by the Florentine men of letters, the acceptance of Florentine standards as an
absolute, and the progressive loss of contact with the wider stream
of Italian culture.

Whatever Salviati's participation in these activities in his earlier
years, he was certainly one of the many Florentines, young and
old, nobles and academics, who sat at the feet of Pier Vettori,
lecturer in the Studio di Firenze since 1538, though from 1563
onwards he had been giving classes mainly in his own home.
Amongst his pupils were many who were later to be numbered

amongst Salviati's friends—Lorenzo Lenzi, Lorenzo Giacomini, Giovanni Rondinelli, Francesco Buonamici, and Baccio Valori the younger. Lionardo, in his funeral oration for Vettori, tells how he was one of the latter's pupils, and in 1575 spoke of his 'singolar osservanza e riverenza verso l'Eccellentissimo e Nobilissimo M. Pier Vettori suo onorandissimo precettore'.[2] The two were to maintain a lifelong friendship and Salviati makes frequent allusions, over many years, to his revered master.

Lionardo was thus yet another product of that school of Vettori which had an almost inestimable influence on the course and development of classical studies in Florence and indeed in the whole of Italy. It is certainly to Vettori that Lionardo owes not only the philological bias of his activities, and his early training in method, but also the orientation towards Greek scholarship which was to make him outstanding amongst his contemporaries.

Whatever his first training there is no doubt about the early literary direction of his interests for by 1560—that is to say at the age of twenty-one—he had embarked on an ambitious literary programme, the writing of a series of *Dialoghi dell amicizia*. The work was scarcely under way, however, when Salviati suffered a number of misfortunes described as 'travagli domestici' by his friend Alessandro Canigiani, who also tells of his heroic struggle to complete at least the first part of the projected programme. The first and only dialogue, which the author described as the 'first-fruit, or flower, of his youth', is of a compendiary character, adequately summed up by Canigiani himself who writes in connection with it that Salviati's intention was, and is: 'di fare della Amicizia uno intero e compiuto trattato: cioè fare opera di scriverne quel che se ne può dire, raccogliendo ciò che da' Greci e da' Latini, o da altri ne fosse mai scritto, ed aggiungendovi quello che la natura sua, e 'l suo ingegno, alla Amicizia oltre ogni umana credenza mirabilmente inclinato, gli venisse somministrando.'[3]

Depending, like many a contemporary dialogue, primarily on

[2] For details of the Florentines who studied with Vettori, see F. Niccolai, *Pier Vettori* (Florence, Seeber, 1912), especially Ch. VI, 'Gli scolari suoi, Fiorentini i più, nello studio.' This reference to Vettori (one of many in Salviati's works and correspondence) is to be found in Razzi's presentation of Salviati's translation of Vettori's oration in praise of Joan of Austria (Salviati, *Opere*, Milan, Classici italiani, 1910, v. 295).

[3] Lett. A. Canigiani to Don Silvano Razzi, published first with the *Primo libro delle orazioni* (Florence, Giunti, 1575). The letter dates from December 1563.

Cicero, it is a hotch-potch of borrowed views, put together with all the ingenuous zeal of youth. As much ancient wisdom on the subject as possible is crammed into the dialogue (the occasion is the death of Pico della Mirandola in 1494, and the interlocutors are the neoplatonist Girolamo Benivieni, Piero Ridolfi, and Jacopo Salviati the elder), and the whole, shot through with a superficial neoplatonism, is held together only by Salviati's oft-repeated zeal for friendship. The work conforms to an established sixteenth-century pattern; but in the absence of other evidence it does give us some idea of the direction in which he was developing, especially as regards linguistic theory and practice. By this time he was evidently a knowledgeable classical scholar, devoted to Cicero (as indeed he remained), with a keen interest in moral philosophy. He is clearly a convinced Bembist archaist in language (of no small significance when one takes into account the more modern orientation of many of his contemporary Florentines—and Gelli was still alive at this point), and perhaps the most significant aspect of the work for us is that its language and content are characterized by Boccaccian imitation of a most pedestrian kind. A glance at the opening words—'Convenevol cosa è lo ingegnarsi di giovare ad altrui, e come che il giovar grandemente sia conceduto a pochi, pochi eziandio si ritruovano, che pure in qualche parte far nol possono alcuna volta'—is sufficient to permit the reader to take rapid and accurate stock of the linguistic and stylistic model of the youthful Salviati. At the same time a marked oratorical tendency colours the tone and style of his prose and prepares us for future developments.

As a result of the mysterious *travagli domestici* the work was halted at the end of the first dialogue, which was promptly sent off to Alamanno Salviati, son of Jacopo the Elder, whom we have seen to be one of the most influential members of the Salviati family, and close to Cosimo. This is Lionardo's first recorded approach to the richer branch of the family, though the wording of the letter of dedication reveals that he has already had some sign of favour from his wealthy but distant relation.[4]

---

[4] Ded. lett., 18.8.61, of the *Dei dialoghi dell'amicizia, libro primo* (Florence, Eredi di Bernardo Giunti, 1564). Canigiani states in the letter to Razzi that Lionardo sent the manuscript to Alamanno 'tre anni sono', which takes us back to 1560, but this is probably a slip of the memory on the part of Canigiani. Alamanno Salviati was the son of Lorenzo il Magnifico's daughter Lucrezia and Jacopo Salviati the Elder, whom she married in 1485. He, Alamanno, was brother

It is paradoxical that this, the earliest work of Salviati (unless some of the undated poems are anterior to it), should have been constructed round this concept of friendship which he declared at all times to be his ideal, yet which was so completely at odds with his behaviour. There were, however, at this period a number of individuals whom Lionardo considered his friends, for at the same time as the first copy of the *Dialogo* was sent to Alamanno it was also circulated to a number of intimates including Giovambattista Adriani, Tommaso Ferrini, Francesco Buonamici, and Alessandro Canigiani.

This list of Florentines given a preview of Lionardo's work, whilst including some fellow pupils of his, indicates that he was moving at this period in the Florentine literary circle which centred on the Accademia Fiorentina, and there is every reason to believe that until the completion of the *Dialogo dell'amicizia* Lionardo lived in his birthplace, Florence, with periods at Prato and at the University of Pisa. Canigiani, who was in a position to know, reproduces without demur the Giunti's description of the *Dialogo* as a 'cosa generata da un Fiorentino in Firenze'. Ferrini was the current Consul of the Accademia Fiorentina, a position which Buonamici, philosopher and future Archbishop of Pisa, had held in the previous year. The presence of Adriani in the list is interesting, for he was now incumbent of the Chair of Eloquence in Florence and was much esteemed and courted by many of the prominent *letterati* of the city, though not so much as later when as official historian he had a certain control over their image for posterity.

Immediately after completion of this first *Dialogo*, Canigiani tells us, 'gli sopravvennero di poi accidenti ai quali gli fu forza d'arrendersi'. The *Dialoghi* were set aside, Lionardo was obliged for the moment to 'turn to other occupations', and not until 1563 are we able to take up the threads once again. In the meantime, though widening his circle of acquaintances, Lionardo cannot have been very conspicuous in Florentine literary circles, since Borghini and Varchi, men destined to have a profound effect on him,

---

to the two cardinals, Berardo and Giovanni Salviati, and founder of the line which produced the Dukes of Giuliano (extinct 1704). He was therefore probably the most powerful of the Salviati, a prominent Florentine figure with an impressive political and diplomatic past. Alamanno was a common name in the family.

are absent from the list of those privileged to see the 'first fruit' of his youthful genius, and Canigiani expressly states that they read it only a year later, 'per non avere avanti avuta con esso loro Messer Lionardo alcuna dimestichezza'. But even if they were not on intimate terms it is unlikely that Lionardo's path had never crossed that of Messer Benedetto.

On Benedetto Varchi we might do well to pause for a moment, since he is in many respects the perfect representative of that late sixteenth-century Florentine literary world into which Lionardo was entering, his career from an intensely republican youth to a comfortable post as court historian following a typical pattern. Yet he, too, was characteristically attracted by the achievements of Cosimo, and collaboration with the regime seemed to cause him little heartache, even if he had once fought against it at Montemurlo. His circle of friends was wide, including such disparate characters as Tribolo, Bronzino, Cellini, and Michelangelo; the men of letters Caro, Bembo, Speroni, and Borghini; and the scourge of princes himself, Pietro Aretino, whose stand in refusing to be bribed into attacking Varchi when he was publicly disgraced suggests that whilst basically a weak and spineless character, made to measure for the regime, Varchi had an attractive personality.

Whatever relationship existed, if any, between Varchi and Salviati before the *Dialogo*, Benedetto and his voluminous works must have been well known to the young Lionardo. Since being received into the Accademia Fiorentina in 1543 Varchi had on innumerable occasions addressed it on subjects of interest to Lionardo: he was its Consul in 1553, and he therefore moved in close company with those academicians with whom Salviati appears to have been on sufficiently close terms of friendship to send them his manuscript. As he was official Lecturer on Petrarch for the Academy and had also delivered funeral orations in public on two of Cosimo's daughters, Maria in 1557 and Lucrezia in May 1561, it is in the highest degree improbable that Salviati had not heard him perform on numerous occasions. However the case may be, it is significant that Lionardo's youthful model should be one who had an interest in ostentatious outward conformism. If Salviati was not on terms of close friendship with Varchi it is nevertheless no negligible coincidence that the former's first work should be devoted to 'friendship', a subject close also to

the heart of Varchi, who unlike his emulator had a record of stead-
fast loyalty to his friends and seemed to command a similar degree
of loyalty in them.

The immediate and most prominent source of Salviati's *Dialogo*,
as was seen, is Cicero's *De Amicitia*. Now it was Varchi who said
that this latter work should be written up in letters of gold and
that all men should learn it by heart. Yet Canigiani, as we have
seen, insists that late in 1561 Lionardo had not yet become friendly
with Varchi, and that the latter did not read the dialogue until
about a year after it was first circulated. Canigiani's letter is not
altogether above suspicion, but Varchi was still very much alive
when it was written, and it is improbable in the extreme that if
Canigiani knew the nature of the work to have been personally
prompted by Varchi he would deliberately have denied the fact.

Probably, in fact, the choice of subject-matter was no coincidence, nor yet does it necessarily point to an established acquaintance. Lionardo's choice of subject for his first literary work of
any scale may well have been determined by undeclared admiration
for Varchi.[5] The tremendous influence which the latter exercised
on every aspect of Lionardo's thought in the space of three short
years reveals such an affinity of vision that we should not be
surprised to find the young Salviati a disciple of the great
Messer Benedetto whilst the latter is yet but dimly aware of his
existence.

All available information connects him at this point with the
Florentine scene. One of Lionardo's close acquaintances in this
early period, for example, was Jacopo Corbinelli, whom we have
already encountered as a fellow pupil of Vettori. At this time they
were on terms of close friendship, holding long intimate discussions on literary and cultural topics, in which Corbinelli, always ready to talk about himself, bared his soul—rather unwisely
perhaps—to his friend. And though even at this stage they held
profoundly differing views, particularly on language, there does
seem to have been a close bond of friendship between them.
Combining his irrepressible conceit with a certain nostalgia, the
exiled Corbinelli was to look back on this period over twenty
years later and say that Lionardo was 'quasi mio scolaro a Firenze,

---

[5] Unless, taking into account his future attitude to the *volgare*, we see him as
inspired by Alberti's bold and calculated action in choosing that selfsame theme
for the *Certame coronario* of 1441.

havendo il medesimo homore da giovinetti'[6]—though this was by no means how Salviati conceived the relationship.

Certainly Lionardo had a very detailed knowledge of his companion's mannerisms, of his student career at Pisa (where Corbinelli graduated in law in 1558), and of his activities, particularly literary. Already an accomplished Greek scholar himself, he acted as tutor to Corbinelli in Greek (this being *his* conception of the relationship), and lent a hand in his work on Demetrius Falereus. It is particularly noteworthy that Lionardo's classical (especially Greek) scholarship, and his *volgare* scholarship, of both of which he was already proud, merge precisely in connection with this work: for he assisted his friend in finding suitable Tuscan passages to substitute for the Greek examples in Demetrius' text. Already he considered himself an authority on language and style in Tuscan old and modern, and in his co-operation with Corbinelli it is interesting to see combined with this enthusiasm for his native tongue an interest in the current topic of poetic theory.[7] One cannot imagine that he was ever altogether enthusiastic about the notions and methods of the somewhat unorthodox Corbinelli, but the association, in retrospect a somewhat odd one, seems to have lasted until shortly before Corbinelli's exile in 1562.[8] There is no documentary evidence, in the University archives or elsewhere, that Lionardo ever graduated at the Studio di Pisa as did his friend, or even frequented it. But he was certainly familiar with the background of the Studio and in early life he was to be closely connected with the city itself, where were to be found many of those who had been his fellow pupils under Vettori, such as Baccio Valori.

For Salviati, a Tuscan born and bred under the new regime, Pisa must have epitomized the triumphal rebirth of Tuscany and increased his already powerful enthusiasm for contemporary Florentine achievement. Indeed, it is in precisely these terms that

---

[6] Lett. Corbinelli to Pinelli, 29.9.84, quoted by V. Crescini, 'Jacopo Corbinelli nella storia degli studi romanzi', *Per gli studi romanzi* (ed. Crescini; Padua, Draghi, 1892), p. 194.

[7] This information is contained in a letter from Lionardo to Jacopo Corbinelli, probably dating to early 1563, for which see Ch. IV, n. 7.

[8] For the trial and exile of Jacopo Corbinelli see M. Battistini, 'La condanna di Jacopo Corbinelli', *Archivio storico italiano*, lxxii, Serie V, 1, Dispensa prima (1914), pp. 61–3. Also R. Calderini De Marchi, *Jacopo Corbinelli et les érudits français* (Milan, Hoepli, 1914), especially pp. 28–30.

he speaks of the city in an oration many years later.[9] Cosimo had revitalized the city industrially and commercially, promoted a bold programme of public works, and restored life and vigour to the Studio. Pisa was, moreover, to be the starting-point of an episode which brought Lionardo at one stroke from comparative obscurity to celebrity. It all began with the peregrinations of the ducal household.

Fond at all times of Pisa, which suited his wife's delicate health, Cosimo set out with his family in the autumn of 1562 through the Tuscan Maremma on a pleasure trip planned to end in Pisa, where Eleonora intended to pass the winter. By mid December Eleonora and her two sons, the Cardinal Giovanni and Don Garzia, were all dead, probably of a virulent fever. Lionardo Salviati immediately recognized a unique opportunity to bring himself before the public—and ducal—eye in this triple domestic tragedy which had aroused the greatest possible public interest in Florence, not only because it was a major disaster to the Medici house, but because unsavoury rumours were abroad as to the circumstances of the deaths. A strange discrepancy between the honours paid to Giovanni—a lying in state in the Cathedral of Pisa and the Chiesa del Carmine, burial in San Lorenzo, and a funeral oration by Pier Vettori—and the secret and hasty night burial of Garzia, 'senza pompa alcuna' as Lapini commented, further fed the suspicion and curiosity of the Florentines. A diabolical role in the triple death was quickly and characteristically attributed to Cosimo by the *fuorusciti*.[10]

Whatever the truth may be, all Florence was agog. Assured of

[9] In the *Orazione intorno all'incoronazione del serenissimo Cosimo de' Medici* (Florence, Sermartelli, 1570). He praises Cosimo for founding and fostering the Order of St. Stephen. And how marvellous Cosimo's achievement was, he says, 'lo sa la nobile città di Pisa, lo mostra quel real palagio, lo testifica quel magnifico tempio, ne fanno fede quegli opportuni edifici, ce ne chiarisce la dote di tante e sì ampie commende, ce lo 'nsegnano le sontuose fabbriche degli strumenti, de' navigli, e de' legni.'

[10] Majority opinion now tends to deny authenticity to the rumours, which were supported by M. Rastrelli, *Illustrazione storica del Palazzo della Signoria* (Florence, 1782), and denied principally by R. Galluzzi, *Istoria del Granducato di Toscana* (Florence, Cambiagi, 1781). Amongst modern writers G. E. Saltini, *Tragedie medicee domestiche* (Florence, Barbera, 1898), purports to destroy the legend completely, as does G. Pieraccini, *La stirpe dei Medici di Cafaggiolo* (Florence, 1924). But A. Baja, *Eleonora di Toledo* (Todi, 1907), and G. O. Corazzini, in notes to the *Diario fiorentino di Agostino Lapini* (Florence, Sansoni, 1900), are by no means convinced. The *Diario* of Lapini clearly reveals the extent of contemporary suspicion.

an interested public—and possibly prince—Lionardo set to work, and in the first two months of 1563[11] there appeared his three 'orazioni confortatorie' on the death of Garzia, dedicated respectively to Paolo Giordano Orsini, Giulio de' Medici and the 'valorosissimi cavalieri di Santo Stefano', and to Jacopo Salviati the younger, son of that Alamanno to whom Lionardo had dedicated the *Dialogo dell'amicizia*.

Even when one makes due allowance for contemporary manners it is impossible not to be struck by the tone of subservience in these, the first dedicatory letters of Lionardo, of which the central, obsessive theme throughout is servile adulation of the Medici. It is significant that he appears completely untouched either by republican nostalgia or by any trace of independence of thought. The finest compliment he invents for Jacopo is a reminder of his ties of kinship and upbringing with the Medici, particularly through his illustrious grandfather Jacopo the Elder: in extolling Giulio de' Medici (bastard son of Alessandro), who had been placed in command of the fleet of the newly created Order of St. Stephen, Lionardo does not blush to describe the young man's late detested father as 'lo specchio de' valorosi prencipi'. Taking cover under the figure of reticence he refers to Jacopo's noble lineage 'della quale io non potrei per aventura con modestia parlare', revealing already the snobbery which led him at all times to vaunt his extremely tenuous family connections with Cosimo's mother Maria Salviati, and which was throughout his life one of the strongest influences determining his judgements of men.

If the letters to Jacopo Salviati and Giulio de' Medici give us a glimpse into the character of Salviati, the dedication to Paolo Giordano Orsini, Duke of Bracciano, has greater interest biographically, being Lionardo's first recorded contact with a family with whom he was to be linked, sometimes too closely for comfort, over a number of years. Paolo had married Cosimo's daughter Isabella in 1557 (Jacopo Salviati was prominent at the wedding), both parties envisaging therein their mutual advantage. Now, in Michelozzo's old Medici Palace in Via Larga, given to the Medici–Orsini by Cosimo, Isabella held splendid court, deservedly

---

[11] Not 1562 as is often erroneously stated (e.g. by C. Marconcini, *L'Accademia della Crusca dalle origini alla prima edizione del 'Vocabolario'* (Pisa, Valenti, 1910)). The date on the title-pages and letters of dedication are *ab inc*. Garzia died on 6 December 1562. Giovanni had died on 12 November, and Eleonora was to die on 18 December 1562.

acquiring a reputation for gaiety and extravagance. Paolo was often absent for long periods in Rome or Bracciano, but the couple frequently spent the winter in Pisa, where they were notorious for their sumptuous entertaining and the festivities they promoted. The most memorable occasion was a party given in that City towards the end of January 1561 lasting a full twenty days.[12] Isabella and her retinue were thus familiar sights in both the cities in which Lionardo spent his late teens and early twenties, and if he was aware that Isabella's ever-wilder parties and rash nocturnal escapades were in part self-consolation for her husband's absences and gallant adventures, he no doubt kept the facts discreetly to himself.

To Isabella the death of her brother Giovanni, with whom she had been on terms of close and affectionate friendship, was a sad blow, and her husband Paolo, who with his retinue had followed immediately behind the bier in the procession from the Carmine to S. Lorenzo, was called from Giovanni's funeral service by the news that his wife had collapsed from grief.[13] (Varchi, with characteristic tact, wrote her a sonnet as a perpetual reminder of the incident.) With great tactical skill Lionardo at once recognized the appropriateness of the dedication of one of his orations to one so intimately connected with the ducal court and who along with his wife had associated himself so closely with the mourning for Garzia's brother. He lost no time, for the date of the dedicatory letter is 1 January 1563 (1562 *ab inc.*), considerably less than a month after the death of Garzia. Penetrating the smoke-screen of vague and ambiguous terminology characterizing this letter, which declares Lionardo's undying devotion to the husband of Isabella, we are probably justified in interpreting it as an attempt to bring the author to the benevolent notice of the Duke of Bracciano, whom he informs of his 'infino a hora oziosa, e tacita servitù', of which the present composition is the first tangible but apparently unsolicited manifestation.

The dedications indicate that in the practical sphere Lionardo is courting influential patrons. The texts reveal certain characteristics of the man and his writings which were to remain constant, whilst others show progress along the literary road which was to

---

[12] See F. Winspeare, *Isabella Orsini e la corte medicea* (Florence, Olschki, 1961), for details of the career of Isabella and Paolo.

[13] G. B. Adriani, *Istoria dei suoi tempi* (Florence, 1583), libro xvi, p. 637.

lead to the *Avvertimenti* and the correction of the *Decameron*. Much in evidence in particular is that lack of a sense of proportion which was Salviati's besetting vice. In the orations he is particularly prone, as a result of this curious flaw in his capacity for judgement, to be drawn by the attraction of the figure or the image into the most staggering absurdities and exaggerations. The manner in which he attributes to the small boy Garzia all the moral and intellectual qualities of Cosimo the Elder, Lorenzo il Magnifico, Clement VII, and Giovanni delle Bande Nere rolled together, whilst basically in the tradition of the *orazione in lode*, oversteps the bounds between acceptable hyperbole and nonsense. In the same oration we are treated to a description of a vision, enjoyed by the writer, of Paradise, in which he saw: 'Pure allora ricevuto il giovine Don Garzia, raccolto spezialmente e con maggior diletto da due santissime e beatissime damigelle, le quali per lo corpo di suprema bellezza, e per lo ammanto di materia celeste, mi sembravano la più stupenda cosa' (I).[14] That Salviati, even at the tender age of twenty-three, could be capable of such a grotesque parody of the Christian heaven, into which Botticelli, Poliziano, and the Mohammedan paradise are indiscriminately lumped together, almost defies credibility. This remarkable performance, however, was matched in oration after oration, until at an advanced stage in his career he reaches the point of declaring (drawing on Aristotle and Pliny) that there is no need to be surprised that religion is natural to man, when a religious inclination even amongst animals is clearly shown by the behaviour of the elephant towards the moon (XIV).

Linked with this phenomenon is a similarly extraordinary lack of taste and tact of which he did not rid himself with the years. Justly Marconcini observes that these orations are 'confortatorie da far ridere chi non fosse tocco di dolore, e da mover parole di vituperio in chi fosse stato intimamente colpito'.[15] Their unvarying theme is summed up in the words 'Io niuna cosa più richiedersi in questo tempo che gioia, che riso, e che letizia vi manifesto'(I) and the working-out of this theme is a monument of bad taste. Salviati's aim is to combat those who weep for Garzia ('they weep', he says, 'and invite others to weep, whilst I, rejoicing, invite the world to

---

[14] The Roman numerals following quotations from, or references to, passages in the *Orazioni* refer to the numbering of the orations as listed in Appendix B.

[15] Marconcini, *L'Accademia*, p. 119.

rejoice') and to banish misguided sorrow. He aims, so he declares, to present the situation in such a way 'che giocondissima resti la rimembranza del prossimo avvenimento' (I)—and this at a moment when the grief-stricken Duke was writing to his own son Francesco (now completing his education with a spell at the court of Spain) moving letters expressing his anguish at the loss of his wife and sons.[16]

A complicated tissue of conceits forms the substance of the orations. Fearful portents mark the event. But these manifestations of cosmic mourning occur merely because the heavenly bodies are concerned (paradoxically enough) only with the purely terrestrial implications of the event, not the eternal: and because of these strict limitations on their sphere of interest the elements and the stars are often known to show signs of sorrow for occurrences which, when seen in a proper, eternal light, are 'a valid reason for rejoicing and joy, as is the case with the departure of Don Garzia' (I).

Fortunately Salviati was quick to abandon the style of these first orations. There is a perceptible and swift development from these orations *In morte di Don Garzia* to those of later periods. The former are packed tight with rhetorical figures of every description, used with almost disarming ingenuousness. There is a plethora of exclamation, apostrophe, hyperbole, periphrasis, antithesis, reticence. The whole of the first oration I, moreover, is constructed as a complicated web of paradoxes: the stars (as we have seen), in spite of their appearance (which is one of mourning), call on us to rejoice: to weep for Don Garzia is selfish indulgence in our own sorrow for our loss, because he is now better off than ever he was, and it could only mean that we grudged him his beatitude: yet, even more than that, to mourn for him is self-pity misplaced, since Garzia, amongst the celestial elect, is now well positioned to afford us help.

Such are the *orazioni confortatorie*. In his dedicatory letter to Alamanno Salviati of the *Primo libro delle orazioni* the editor Don Silvano Razzi declares that Salviati was reluctant to have the 'Garzia' orations republished because they were 'di stile da quello, ch'egli ha oggi, molto diverse', and certainly in a very short time

---

[16] See G. Spini (ed.), *Cosimo I de' Medici: lettere* (Florence, Vallecchi, 1940) (published by the Centro Nazionale di Studi sul Rinascimento), especially pp. 180–7 (letters of 21.11.62 and 18.12.62 to his son Francesco).

Lionardo developed a style in which the rhetorical figures are infinitely less obtrusive, the prose depending much more on repetition, inversion, and those figures which principally affect the balance and structure of the period. The result is immediately more sophisticated and sheds the character of a schoolboy exercise.

In general the artificiality of the sentiments, the obvious exclusive concern with formal elegance, the absence of any shred of real feeling about the tragic event, and the monstrous lack of taste make these 'Garzia' orations offensive, and when Salviati, pursuing with blundering insensitivity the same theme in the second of them, condemns the feelings and the whole attitude of those who sympathize with the Duke over the loss of his child, declaring that he has no reason not to be joyful since 'se uno n'è gito, ne sono rimasi due' (II), we once again cannot avoid a poignant contrast with the tone of the letters of Cosimo himself. The Duke declares that, humbly acquiescing in the will of God, he consoles himself by the presence of his other children: and we can only stand amazed that the power over Salviati's contemporaries of the external form of this series of orations was such as to mask the pretentious nonsense of the content and bring him fame almost overnight.

Yet in praising the small boy Garzia the fact is that Salviati had not been aiming merely at a literary and oratorical triumph. At the same time the lack of any emotional motivation for the choice of Garzia as his subject-matter is revealed quite clearly by the character of the orations themselves. A third, even more powerful motive governed his choice. Rumours circulating about the death of Garzia had it that the boy was in some way responsible for the death of Giovanni, and that Cosimo in turn had killed him in rage. By extolling Garzia, Lionardo became the self-appointed advocate of the boy's innocence and, by implication, of the innocence of Cosimo. He no doubt calculated that the advantages to be reaped from this bold move would by no means be confined, in Florence, to the world of letters.

IV

THE QUARREL WITH CORBINELLI

THE oration being an art form typical of the times, and competent orators in high esteem, Salviati's success in this competitive field destined him to come constantly before the public eye, both literally and figuratively. From this point onwards his progress in the Florentine literary world was swift, arousing among his fellow *letterati* reactions of dislike and affection of roughly equal proportions and intensity. If we give credence to Cambi, Lionardo seems to have been well fitted by nature for success within the type of literary society to which he was now committing himself (albeit not without aspirations, shortly to emerge, of a different nature).

Allowance must be made for the recognized vagaries of funeral orators, the conventional assertions about Lionardo's universal popularity for example being provably untrue. Nevertheless the account given by Cambi of Salviati's social accomplishments is on the whole convincing in so much as it corresponds to a realistic streak in the oration. It tells us that Lionardo had a clear enunciation and a soft, gentle voice more fitted for prayer than for commanding, but which nevertheless exerted a strange fascination over whoever heard him speak. In addition he was gifted with great clarity of mind, which added force to his arguments and gave him remarkable powers of persuasion. If the characteristics here enumerated did not necessarily serve to endear Lionardo to his fellow citizens, one can imagine that they were tolerably effective in enabling him to perform the formidable task of rendering acceptable some of the more preposterous passages of later orations delivered orally.

But there was in Florence a long tradition of frivolity, wit, and humour which did not die out simply because the 'New Prince' was no longer of a stamp to descend into the public square and join in the festivities as one of the citizens. In this aspect of Florentine life Lionardo was equally a success, and a favourite in festive company, so Cambi relates, for his witticisms, his repartee, his *bons mots*, and a capacity for poking fun without giving offence.[1] This averred quality of *esprit* accords badly with the heavy-handedness of Lionardo's humorous poetry, but when Cambi adds to these accomplishments an extreme adaptability which, combined with his knowledge and love of all aspects of Florentine life, enabled him to adjust his tone, manner, and even subject-matter to suit any company, we are tempted to see the apparent contradictions reconciled in the picture of Salviati the actor skil-fully playing out his lifelong role on the stage of Florentine society.

Of this society Adriani, Ferrini, and Buonamici were already his intimates. By the time of the publication of the first *Garzia* oration his relationship with Varchi is such that the latter can append a Latin epigram ('Garsias Medices iacet hic: qui corde parentem / Vix puer: & dextra iam referebat Avum'), whilst the printed edition of the second oration carries an exchange of sonnets between them, Varchi adding yet another epigram.[2] The *Orazione terza*, which followed a month later, bore ten more sonnets, eight by Salviati and two by Varchi. Almost all fall into the category of adulatory verse, since even some of those written ostensibly in self-defence (in circumstances shortly to be con-sidered) contain sly flattering references, appeals, and tributes, to the judgement of the dead prince, combined with reminders of the selfless Medicean devotion of the author.

The themes of the *Garzia* poems are those of the orations them-selves. In addition to fulsome praise of Garzia—and, of course, his family—they express the 'intimate conflict' which this and any other occasion demanded in the times. On the one hand they vie

[1] Marconcini, op. cit., p. 69 n. 3, mentions a 'motto di spirito' attributed to Salviati to be found in the Carte Dei of the A.S., Florence, adding 'che forse il tacere è bello'. Apart from the *poesie in burla* (see Ch. V) and brief flashes of wit in the polemical works, the *Avvertimenti* and, of course, the comedies, the only extant example of Salviati's 'social' humour is an unpublished letter written from Rome on 8 December 1578 to a certain cavalier Paciotto, commenting on the 'Bicchierografia' he had received from the latter and asking him to answer the query 'onde avviene, che comunemente più si rompe de' bicchieri tondi, che de' quadri, o angulari' (U. lett., Pesaro, Bib. Oliveriana, Cod. 338, vol. ii, fol. 380).

[2] The sonnets are: Sal. to Varchi, *inc.* 'Aura che 'n picciol cerchio asconde, e serra' (3): Varchi to Sal., *inc.* 'Quanto ride hora il ciel, tanto la terra'. The epi-gram is: 'Garsias iacet hic: quem si fata non tulissent: atque patrem, atque invictum exsuperasset Avum.' The bracketed numbers following quotations from poems by Salviati refer to the numbering of these poems in Appendix C.

with one another in exaggerated expressions of grief, as in Salviati's first: 'Pioggia, che nella fronte humida guerra / Fai giorno, e notte, il tuo crudo veneno / Caccia fuor tutto . . .', to which Varchi replies telling of a grief and despair such as would have driven him to suicide 'se ragion non mi tenesse a freno'. On the other hand they, too, strive to convince the reader that the occasion is one for joy and celebration, since, as Lionardo puts it, Garzia is in heaven with 'mille attorno angelici messaggi, / Celesti canti, angeliche carole'.[3]

Like the orations which they accompany, these sonnets show a truly astonishing degree of bad taste. Blatantly profiting from a domestic tragedy Salviati cheapens both the private grief of Cosimo and the mourning of the general public. The insincerity of the sentiments expressed is further thrown into relief by the obtrusive artificiality of the Petrarchan conceits on which many of the poems rely. Even making full allowance for contemporary taste and customs these sonnets are distasteful.

One of them, however, the first of those appended by Varchi to the *Orazione terza*, has a curious beginning which runs: 'Seguite pur, Salviati mio la vostra / Arditissima impresa: e non curate / L'altrui lingue mordaci: ch'ogni etate / Hebbe sempre i suoi Momi: e più la nostra.' It is plain that Salviati's efforts to exalt Don Garzia had been subjected to some form of attack. The attacker, as it turned out, was none other than that Jacopo Corbinelli who had been a co-pupil with Lionardo of Pier Vettori and the companion of his youth. Since the days in which Corbinelli could claim, as he later did, to have had Lionardo 'quasi mio scolaro a Firenze' there had been swift and dramatic developments. On 21 March 1562 Corbinelli was called upon to appear before the Magistrato degli Otto 'in fra 20 dì sotto pena di scudi 1000 e arbitrio'. This he failed to do, and although eventually given until the end of September to put in an appearance, he preferred voluntary exile abroad to the doubtful political justice of ducal Florence. By 1563, a declared rebel, he was over the Alps in France. What his 'crime' was has never been established with certainty— even the Florentine authorities were unable to find out in 1607 when Jacopo's sons applied for a pardon and permission to return— but as his brother Bernardino was deeply implicated in the conspiracy of Pandolfo Pucci in 1559 (and eventually murdered

---

[3] The three extracts are from (i) No. 3, (ii) Varchi, 'Quanto ride hora il ciel, tanto la terra', (iii) No. 3, respectively.

for it) it is more than likely that some suspicion in the same connection had fallen on him.[4]

Indeed his presence in Rome since early in 1562 seeking a post commensurate with his social status and native abilities may well have been prompted by doubts about the healthiness of his native Florentine air. Wherever he was by early 1563, information had reached him on Salviati's current literary activities inspired by the death of Don Garzia, and it is quite clear from subsequent developments that he proceeded to subject that activity to the kind of attack to which he was temperamentally disposed. Of this attack the one existing piece of evidence is a series of uncomplimentary marginal annotations to Salviati's *Orazione seconda* in praise of Don Garzia.[5]

It would be true to say that the remarkable episode arising from these marginal notes is the first great landmark in Lionardo's career, the first occasion in which we see him acquiring a distinct physiognomy and a certain stature. Although he liked to think that Corbinelli's aggressive notes constituted a betrayal of their former friendship and an unprovoked act of aggression, this is only partly true. Indeed in the fact that it is not the whole truth lies the importance of the episode. The seeds of the clash lay in the provocative nature of the *Orazione seconda* itself. In it the dead prince's supposed views on language and literature had been held up as an example of his infinite wisdom and virtue. These views Lionardo describes as follows:

Percioche Egli haveva in somma venerazione & grado questo nostro

---

[4] For the biography of Corbinelli and for all further information on him and his connections with Salviati, see particularly R. Calderini De Marchi, *Jacopo Corbinelli*, and the review of this work by V. Crescini in *G.S.L.I.* lxviii. 395–434, along with his reviews of R. Calderini De Marchi and A. Calderini, *Autori greci nelle epistole di J. Corbinelli* (Milan, Hoepli, 1915), and A. Calderini, *A proposito di una gita di J. Corbinelli a Épernay nel 1576* (Milan, Scuola tipo-litogr., 'Figli della Provvidenza', 1916). Also see Crescini, 'Jacopo Corbinelli nella storia degli studi romanzi', pp. 181–222, (a reprint with only minor alterations of his article 'Lettere di Jacopo Corbinelli', *G.S.L.I.* ii (1883), 303–33). For the documents relating to the sentence pronounced against Jacopo Corbinelli, see M. Battistini, *La condanna*.

[5] The comments are autograph marginal notes to a copy of Lionardo's *Orazione seconda in lode di Don Garzia de' Medici* (Florence, Giunti, 1562, i.e. '63 st. com.) now in the Biblioteca Comunale Ariostea, Ferrara, Misc. Est. 343, 2. The margins also bear a series of counter-annotations, critical of the Corbinelli originals, in an unknown hand. There is a transcription, also in an unknown hand, of these notes and the counter-notes in the Ambrosiana, Milan, in Cod. D. 191 inf., fols. 98ʳ–99ʳ (see my article 'Jacopo Corbinelli and the Florentine "Crows"', *Italian Studies*, xxvi (1971), 68–89.

parlare: et spesse volte ne' suoi ragionamenti non dubitava a' piu perfetti, et piu antichi linguaggi paragonarlo. et ben mostrava d'haverci maraviglioso gusto, percioche poneva sempre in esso nel primo grado la Comedia di Dante; il quale egli non istimava lasciarsi punto sopraffare da Homero. ma di esso per riverenza non osava parlare. Celebrava per tanto le Rime del Petrarca, et quel suo moralissimo, et leggiadrissimo Canzoniere, & il suo nome riveriva come si sogliono le memorie de' Santi; et ponendolo innanzi a Horazio, et a Pindaro, et a quanti Amorosi Poeti, et Lirici furon mai; ne' suoi Sonetti, et nelle sue Canzoni si beatificava, et affermava sentire, leggendole, un non so che divino, che pareva rapirlo da queste basse cose a fruire la dolcezza della Celeste gioia. Hor che gusti esquisiti; che giudicij perfetti; che concetti mirabili direm' noi, che sian questi, non pur 'nun giovinetto, che non ha pieno il corso del quindicesimo anno, ma 'nuno huomo maturo, 'nun ch'habbia speso nella scrittura le lunghezze degli anni?[6]

On this a brief but illuminating comment is made by Corbinelli, who, it must be borne in mind, had been closely associated with the orator until but a year or two earlier. 'Questo è detto più per oppenione del dicitore', he observes, 'ma in un medesimo tempo biasima luj e se. E non s'ha a scherzar co' santi. Lasciarle dire al Varchi queste pazzie.'

From this verbal encounter there emerges a valuable picture of the Florentine scene as it was still vividly remembered by Corbinelli. What he remembers is a literary circle dominated by Varchi, and including Salviati, in which certain ideas were held on the relationship of the Italian national tradition to the classical; and in Salviati's attribution of pronounced views on the subject to Don Garzia he recognizes Salviati as indulging in direct and undisguised propaganda for these ideas. The comment is most enlightening, especially the suggestion that Salviati should leave such 'pazzie' to Benedetto Varchi, for in addition to revealing that the two, as Corbinelli remembers it, were hand-in-glove, it may also indicate that he had some acquaintance with the unpublished *Ercolano* in which Varchi states most vigorously the very point which is Salviati's main point here, namely the superiority of the Italian tradition over the classical, not least because it represented a 'moral' Christian tradition.

It is particularly interesting that the comment should be made by one who had such a first-hand knowledge of the cultural climate

[6] *Orazione seconda in lode di Don Garzia de' Medici* (Florence, Giunti, 1562, i.e. 1563 st. com.), p. 6.

in Florence. It makes it almost certain that the relative merits of 'classical' and 'Italian' had been the subject of discussion between Corbinellli, Varchi, and Salviati, and the importance which Corbinelli obviously attributes to this whole subject in the economy of Lionardo's thought at the time—'più per oppenione del dicitore', he says—tells us a great deal about Lionardo's early development in what was to be his main direction.

Here in this *Garzia* oration (otherwise devoted almost exclusively to lengthy praise of Garzia and various other Medici) the theme is not given a further elaboration which would distinguish it, other than in emphasis, from similar scattered pronouncements in the past by others over several generations. Only later—though not very much later—and by degrees, is it brought to fruition, so as to constitute Salviati's main contribution to the thought and culture of his times. Nevertheless the present provocative and polemical thrust is the first recorded blow struck openly by Salviati in a campaign which was to engage him all his life.

Corbinelli, however, did not restrict himself to criticism of Lionardo's views on the relationship between the classical and the Italian national traditions. He criticized the inevitable concomitant, which he found manifested everywhere in the oration, namely the imitation of the style of the great Italian authors. In addition he ridiculed the content, the style, and the language of the work, finally advising Salviati, who already considered himself a writer as accomplished and polished as any in Florence, to improve himself by reading Tacitus, 'il quale estirpa le pedanterie'. In all this ridicule Lionardo was associated with Varchi, whom Corbinelli treated as a figure of fun throughout. Finally Corbinelli mocked the Medici, showing scant respect for their bereavement.

On reading these comments Lionardo lost all control. First of all he rushed to show the offensive notes to his literary friends, including Varchi, to whom he was already close, and Grazzini who had an immediate interest in them, and at this point in his life was close to Varchi. Subsequent events prove beyond doubt that they at once read the comments for themselves. All of them, Salviati himself tells us, judged them 'worthy of Corbinelli', which for him was enough to damn them. In the heat of his anger he composed a letter which far surpassed in violence of vituperation anything else he ever produced, incidentally supplying for posterity a notable amount of information about both his own and Corbinelli's early years. Amongst other things he makes a point of dissociating himself from the ideas which Corbinelli had held during their period of intimacy and sets out, not so much to defend his own views as to blacken Corbinelli's character, belittle his classical scholarship, and ridicule his taste and literary abilities in general, with the overall aim of denying him the authority to pronounce an opinion on anything at all. The letter ends threatening a thunderbolt in the form of a dialogue 'il quale tosto che sia stampato vi si manda volando'.[7]

But the promised revenge was achieved in another manner. The offence Corbinelli had given in appending his notes to the *Orazione seconda* was by no means limited to Salviati, for the comments ridiculed a whole institution, and that institution was Florence, where Medici and men of letters were one. Here was a devastating attack on the parts and on the whole. Looking at the Florentine scene in perspective from his transalpine exile, and inspired by an oration which he considered its perfect representative, Corbinelli had found that scene ridiculous, and had voiced his impressions in satirical comments in which the Florentine men of letters, their Duke and his family, the Academicians' self-importance and their pomposity, their literary and linguistic notions and practices, were all subjected to merciless ridicule. The Florentines well knew, moreover, that this was Corbinelli's attitude and purpose. Their reaction was expressed in what Lorenzoni called 'un coro di male lingue'. The 'chorus' was the collective voice of the Florentine men of letters and it took a curious form.

It was in a sonnet to Varchi—'Varchi, Margite, e chi con esso giostra' (*printed with the Orizione terza*)—that, in addition to appealing to the now deified Garzia, Lionardo had expressed his confidence in Varchi's ability to protect him against all comers: 'Nè di Momi temendo, i vanni tuoi / Avrò per saldo scudo', he chanted. He was not disappointed. Those same friends who in recognition of Salviati's eloquence in the *Garzia* orations had referred to him as the 'Cigno gentil d'Etruria e d'Arno', and the 'Tuscan swan' (in both Latin and Italian),[8] now marshalled

---

[7] See supplementary note 1, p.245.

[8] Two Latin compositions by Varchi to Don Silvano Razzi and Lionardo respectively, begin: 'Quid Racti mirare Cycnum tam dulce loquentem', and 'Te vivente suum Leonarde habet Arnus olorem.'

disciplined, and generalled by Varchi, rallied round their 'swan' to encourage him, and heaped abuse on his infamous detractor. Thus was Salviati's faith rewarded, for his friends contributed a total of thirty-two poems in his defence.[9]

All the authors were quick to grasp the verbal potentialities of the antithesis *corbo–cigno*. Grazzini sets the tone: 'Fra tutti gli altri uccei tristo, e maligno / Fu sempre il corbo: hor non so come è stato / Semplice e goffo sì, ch'egli ha sfidato / A cantar seco un bianco, e dolce Cigno'—and the same theme is taken up with many, if not very subtle, variations by the rest.

In fact Varchi's 'Seguite pur . . .' was the first of these 'Corbi', as they came to be known, following a facetious reference to them as a 'nidiata di corbi' in a manuscript letter in which Lionardo dedicates them to Annibale Caro, and the tone and content of the poetic exchanges which followed, exchanges in which Salviati expresses his admiration for Varchi's virtue, thanks for his assistance, and absolute confidence in his protector (whom in keeping with the ornithological trend of the compositions he calls his 'fenice'), confirm the closeness of the association between the two in these early months of 1563.[10]

Varchi in particular felt offended. He had helped Corbinelli in the past, as it appears, by drawing the favourable attention of the Duke to him, and by speaking up for him against Cosimo's anger. Even during Corbinelli's Roman sojourn he had assisted him unsparingly, giving him letters of introduction to Caro and writing strongly in his favour to persons of rank and influence until a matter of weeks before his summons to appear before the Otto.[11]

---

[9] Contributors were: (i) Varchi (25 sonnets, 2 Latin epigrams); (ii) Gherardo Spini (1 *sonetto caudato*); (iii) Grazzini (3 *sonetti caudati*); (iv) anonymous author (1 sonnet). The originals are in the B.N.C., Florence, Cod. Magl. VII, 306, fols. 196^r–211^r (pp. 387–417). The three Grazzini sonnets were published by C. Verzone, *Le rime burlesche edite e inedite di Antonfrancesco Grazzini, detto Il Lasca* (Florence, Sansoni, 1882), pp. 96–8, in the section 'Sonetti', as Nos. CXX, CXXI, and CXXII. All the 'Corbi' poems were published, with an introduction, by A. Lorenzoni, *Un coro*.

[10] The exchanges consist of the two sonnets already mentioned, plus the sonnets: (a) Varchi: (i) *inc.* 'Non fia, se ben dal manco lato viene; (ii) *inc.* 'A tutti gli altri, gentil Cigno, aggrada'; and (iii) *inc.* 'Me forse con ragion, voi certo a torto'; (b) Salviati's respective replies, Nos. 76, 9, and 68. (The exchanges all have the traditional formal features of the *tenzone di sonetti*.)

[11] See especially Crescini, review, pp. 405–8, in which he gives a copious bibliography on the subject, including indications of the relevant sections of R. Calderini De Marchi, *Jacopo Corbinelli*.

His sonnet, however, in which he writes of Corbinelli '. . . non pur a me scortese, e fello / Ma guerra a tutti i più lodati indice', shows that he has fully understood how Corbinelli's notes transcend the purely individual and personal, and constitute an attack on the Florentine men of letters and all they stand for in the new state of Cosimo.

So the literary broadside fired by the Florentines against Corbinelli is not merely a gesture of support for a wronged colleague, or colleagues. By their action they raise Salviati to the status of a symbol of Florentine, and particularly Florentine Academic, literary society—which in a way is what Corbinelli had already done in his comments. In his notions on language, on the relationship of the Italian tradition to the classical, in his literary practices, even in his attitude to the Medici, he is accepted as their representative and their spokesman. This is why, in addition to the fact that as we have seen he uses the *Orazione seconda* as a vehicle for the first substantial expression of his cultural vision, this episode of the quarrel with Corbinelli is a landmark in Salviati's life.

No less significant is the status which Salviati acquired as a result of these poems within the socio-political framework of Florence. Since Corbinelli happened by a stroke of good fortune to embody a rich combination of qualities—literary, political, and possibly religious—undesirable to the regime, his attackers stood to reap a rich reward for the comparatively little effort which participation demanded of them. Moreover, the victim was too far away to fight back effectively in this field. Thus the poems were not by any means restricted to a defence of Salviati and a condemnation of Corbinelli's bad manners. Accusations were extended to those spheres in which reason was least likely to prevail over passion. In so much as they contain all the stock charges of immorality, heresy, disloyalty to the Medici, inseparable from late sixteenth-century Florentine witch-hunting, they seem to symbolize all the mighty forces of religious, social, and political conformism in counter-reformation Medici Florence.

Now this socio-political aspect of the 'Corbi' acquires its importance in the career of Salviati from the fact that the supposition basic to the whole collection is that Salviati, whom they hold up as the ideal, is a selfless, right-minded, loyal, and enlightened citizen, unjustly and gratuitously attacked in the loving expression of his feelings by an unscrupulous evil-doer devoid of wisdom or decency and an ungrateful blackguard into the bargain. Absurdly hyperbolic eulogies of the prince Garzia ('Al terzo del gran duca inclito figlio, / Ch'era per trapassar gl'antichi Eroi', sings Varchi) and of the Medici in general (countering the anti-Medicean sentiments of the notes), coupled with praise and encouragement for the 'swan' who rightly and spontaneously sings their praises, alternate with venomous abuse of the pitiful, deluded, and altogether contemptible 'crow' whose meagre talents have been misdirected. Corbinelli was reminded that he was a rebel against the best of all possible regimes. He was also, said Varchi, 'al ciel rubelle', to which Spini added that he was such as 'da sindacare il credo e le tanie'. Such accusations were profitable at this time, for Cosimo's counter-reformation zeal is well known.

This was the climate in which Salviati was coming to maturity, and which his own works were to document. The fact that he emerges at this time as the ideal representative of the regime in this sense, too, is the direct consequence of the quarrel. Within the context of this quarrel, the emergence of Grazzini as a friend and ally of Lionardo has its own considerable interest. From this time onwards Grazzini looms ever larger in the life of Lionardo Salviati, and the importance of their relationship in the development of the latter's outlook is probably much greater, even from a very early stage, than the comparatively few surviving documents of their acquaintance would suggest.

The 'Corbi' are the first of these documents. With them Salviati emerged triumphant from what was destined to be only the first recorded bout in a lifelong enmity between the two philologists.[12] Though Corbinelli was the more gratuitously aggressive of the two, Salviati's behaviour throughout reveals his usual extreme sensitivity to any slight, and a malicious delight in vengeance. By throwing out the handy accusation of immorality in his letter—he charges him with taking pleasure in 'così sporchi e così disonesti versi'—and reproaching Corbinelli with the fact that in his literary and linguistic tastes he differs from the 'opinion of the majority', Salviati reveals that he, too, is willing to become, for his own

---

[12] For documentation of this enmity, and especially the constant stream of adverse comment on Salviati's linguistic and literary activities put out by the exiled Corbinelli (found chiefly in the Corbinelli–Pinelli correspondence in the Bib. Ambr., Cods. T. 167 sup. and B. 9 inf.), see particularly Crescini, 'Jacopo Corbinelli', and Soldati, 'Jacopo Corbinelli'.

purposes, the instrument of growing political, religious, and moral conformism, and to give it thereby added strength.

Nothing could have given Salviati more effective, or more favourable, publicity than he received from the quarrel with Corbinelli. The 'image' of Salviati which emerged from the orations, the poems, and the 'Corbi' which followed, of a pious, moral, loyal, patriotic, and conformist Salviati, dedicated heart and soul to the Medici through choice and not through necessity, a prop of the established social, religious, and political order, left nothing to be desired. By the spring of 1563 Salviati could be said, even if in a limited sense and without any distinctive physiognomy such as he was later to acquire, to have 'arrived' in Florentine literary society.

V

PISA: THE POEMS

IN the course of this successful year 1563 Salviati transferred his residence to Pisa, probably as a result, direct or indirect, of his having attracted the attention of Cosimo. This latter development can safely be dated between the composition of the last *Garzia* oration, with its dedicatory letter of February 1563 (which makes no mention of it), and December of the same year, when Alessandro Canigiani states explicitly that Salviati had not resumed work on his *Dialoghi* because he had now put aside his own business in order to attend to Cosimo's, into whose service he had been 'ultimamente con inaudita benignità ricevuto.'[1] In view of Lionardo's own reference, in a letter to Cosimo of 1564, to 'rescripts' from Cosimo, and interviews with him, a year earlier, in which the Duke showed him such favour and gave him such hope for the future, that he was beside himself with joy,[2] the appointment, whatever it was, probably dates back to about October 1563. And we might mention in passing that in July of this same year there died an Academician whose passing can be said to symbolize the end of the generation of Florentine men of letters which preceded Lionardo's. That man was Giovambattista Gelli.

About this time Cosimo de' Medici himself fell victim to an illness which may have been an important factor in the eventual decision to delegate powers to his son Francesco who now, in the late summer of 1563, came back from the court of Spain. There he had lavished such vast sums of hard-earned Medicean money in a show of splendour aimed at dazzling and humiliating his rival Alessandro Farnese (with whom he had been engaged in a perpetual undignified wrangle over precedence) that Cosimo had found it necessary on at least one occasion to refuse part of the allowance requested, and give his first-born at the same time a lesson on the duties of a ruler. On this latter point Francesco's

---

[1] Lett. Alessandro Canigiani to Don Silvano Razzi, 19.12.63, prefaced to *Il primo libro delle orazioni del cav. Lionardo Salviati* (Florence, Giunti, 1575).
[2] See Lett. Salviati to Cosimo, 12.10.64, Contin, *Lettere edite e inedite*, No. 3.

sojourn in Madrid seems to have done disappointingly little for him, though perhaps the fault here did not lie with the Spanish side.

In a *tenzone di sonetti* inspired by the Duke's illness, Varchi for his part begged Lionardo to pray for Cosimo's health (son. *inc.* 'Salviati mio, se voi sapete quanto'), whilst Salviati in his reply does as he is bid, describing Cosimo as seeking to fly away to heaven 'leaving the earth desolate', and praying also that should Cosimo die he, Lionardo, might end with him 'il mondo e i giorni e l'hore' (25, 'Dunque è pur ver, che 'l più gradito e santo'). The fact that Cosimo is referred to as being in Florence (during this illness he was in fact at Poggio a Caiano), that Varchi addresses Lionardo with the 'Corbi' epithet of 'cigno immortal', and the obvious intimacy between the two—who seem to be genuinely convinced that Cosimo is on the point of death—excludes the possibility of the occasion being any other recorded malady of the Duke.

But Medicean domestic tragedies seemed destined to bring out Salviati's worst characteristics of tastelessness and insensitivity, manifested now in a second sonnet on a similar theme, 'Saggio signor, cui ne' primi anni elesse' (61). After praise of Cosimo's achievements, including the conquest of Siena, he tells how the whole citizenry of Florence are 'pale and white' in sympathy with their lord, for is it not right 'Se 'l capo il fe, che indebolisce il fianco?' This tissue of absurdities culminates in the question: 'Ma quale è in me Signor chiusa cagione / Che tosto, che languite io vengo manco, / Nè durar posso a più pungente sprone?'

His words were prophetic. For by the time we have further news of him he is lying ill at Pisa in such a state that his doctors consider it unwise to disturb him even to discuss the possible publication of his own book. In his illness he was cared for by Alessandro Canigiani, assisted possibly by Filippo Spadini. In the meantime a manuscript copy of the *Dialogo dell'amicizia* had fallen into the hands of the publishers in Venice who decided, now that the author had rocketed to fame with his *Garzia* orations, that it was worth publishing. When this came to the ears of the Giunti, Salviati's own publishers in Florence, they hastened to write begging Salviati's permission to print the *Dialogo* in Florence, considering, as Canigiani put it, that it was 'ufizio di buoni compatrioti (così dicono) e d'amorevoli stampatori' to see to the publication in Florence of a work produced there by a Florentine, rather than have it handled by foreign publishers who had neither the author's permission nor his advice and assistance during the printing.

Salviati was in any case in Pisa, not in Florence. Canigiani felt that he was too ill to be disturbed. He had not even dared to convey to Lionardo the previous day certain news (evidently bad) of his mother. Now he found himself in a moral dilemma. For he felt also that as one of Salviati's most intimate friends he must take some decision. This dilemma he finally resolved by writing to Don Silvano Razzi on 19 December, passing on to him everything he knew of Salviati's opinions and wishes concerning the *Dialogo*, and leaving the decision on publication to Razzi, as being the author's most intimate and trusted friend and possibly also (he suspected) the 'persona, alla quale dicono che porta messer Lionardo affezione grandissima e riverenza' who had supplied the Giunti of Florence with a reliable copy of the *Dialogo* to serve as the basis for an edition.

The main concern of the publishers was to know if the author required any corrections or alterations to the original version, on which topic Canigiani was in a position to say that Salviati had often told him that he no longer approved of the style (especially of 'clausule intere o poco rimutate del Boccaccio') or of the order of the work. But he also pointed out that Salviati had always refused to alter it, since presented as the 'parto nei suoi primi anni generato da lui' it was acceptable, but revised and pretending to be a mature work, never.

All the same, Canigiani insisted somewhat contradictorily, Lionardo still had hopes of finishing the work, principally because he was such a devotee of friendship. Leaving aside the question of the authorship of the letter in its published form (and it is not unlikely that Lionardo had a hand in it), its contents reveal a number of interesting facts. First, Canigiani's account of Lionardo's attitude to the *Dialogo* accords with what Razzi himself in the 1575 edition says of the *Garzia* orations, where he writes that being a product of the author's youth they were 'di stile da quello, ch'egli ha oggi, molto diverse'. Both authorities thus agree on the early change of views on Boccaccian imitation, and in fact Salviati never again produced prose quite like that of these earlier works. Of this change of attitude, which condemned the copying or borrowing of phrases and imagery from the *Decameron*, the significance was shortly to be brought out in the oration on the Florentine language.

Secondly, Salviati's refusal to alter, or be ashamed of, a work which was the mirror of his juvenile mind, indicates self-confidence in progress towards a goal which would itself justify the stages along the way towards it. And if, as is not improbable, the letter expresses the views of the author of the *Dialogo* no less than those of the ostensible writer Canigiani, it is also the first instance of Lionardo's predilection for hiding behind a mask, that reluctance to speak out under his own name, which was to lead to such pseudonyms as the Infarinato, Carlo Fioretti, and perhaps others.

This winter of 1563-4 was a fatal one for Florence. It was in December 1563 that a young Venetian girl Bianca Cappello, destined to control the future Grand Duke body and soul and eventually become Grand Duchess of Tuscany, married in a house overlooking San Marco the young Florentine Piero Bonaventuri with whom she had eloped. As for Salviati, he was undoubtedly on the brink of death in Pisa. It had been his expectation that he would serve Cosimo with his pen, and we have his word for it (in circumstances which leave no doubts as to reliability, since it is in a letter to Cosimo himself) that the Duke, both by letter and by word of mouth, promised to give him 'materia da scrivere'.[3] But it is possible that he was on some minor ducal business of a non-literary nature in Pisa when he fell so seriously ill that those around him despaired of his life.

Fortunately for him he had influential connections. His doctors declared that if he were to survive he must get back to his 'native' air of Florence, but at that particular moment there was in Pisa neither a suitable litter nor suitable bearers to whom Salviati, in the heart of winter, with bad roads and incessant rain could, as he put it, 'senza grave pericolo commettere la vita mia'. Salvation came in the form of the Medici–Orsini, then busy enlivening Pisa with their winter season of entertainments and festivities. Salviati must have made some progress in furthering his relationship with them since the dedication of the first *Garzia* oration to Paolo if in the midst of their merry-making they were aware of his plight. At all events Isabella—at no small inconvenience to

---

[3] Salviati to Cosimo, 12.10.64, Contin, *Lettere edite e inedite*, No. 3.

herself, Salviati tells us—put at his disposal her best litter and
bearers. By this time Salviati's close relationship with the couple
was common knowledge, and he himself indicates that they were
already his patrons to whom he was tied by bonds of affection,
obligation, and gratitude.[4] Whether, in view of her new passion
for that latest extravagance the *cocchio*, Isabella's sacrifice was
quite what Salviati makes it out to be is more doubtful.

Back in his native Florence Lionardo rallied. The coming of
spring witnessed a return of strength and vigour, and full of delight
in his recovery he wrote two sonnets to the friend who had cared
for him, Alessandro Canigiani, the theme of both being the joy
he feels on regaining life and hope. In one of them, 'Scrolli pur,
se gli aggrada, e sfrondi, e schianti' (63), he likens his recovery
to the calm, the renewal of life and growth, which follow a storm,
whilst in the other, 'Questa, ch'alfin, dopo dannoso, e rio' (53), he
equates his own emergence from the shadow of illness with the
coming of spring. In these sonnets he succeeds in capturing a spirit
of exultation in triumph over darkness: 'ecco, dico cantando, ecco
ch'al gielo / Pur succedono i fior, dell'aspra, e ria / Tempesta
è fine un più benigno cielo' (53).

On reading these sonnets we feel that in the spring of 1564
life must have seemed full of promise to the young Salviati, who
regained strength rapidly, though in March he was once again
made ill by the cold winds blowing down from the Apennines on
Florence and the Arno basin. When Varchi, solicitous for his
health, urged him to set aside study for a few weeks, Lionardo,
compelled by circumstances, reluctantly agreed. The friendship
between the two appears complete, and Salviati ends a letter
written to Varchi at this time with the words 'Di Vostra Signoria,
come figlio . . .'. Yet to this period relates the one recorded quarrel
which disturbed the otherwise unruffled serenity of Lionardo's
relations with Messer Benedetto, to whose villa La Topaia, given
him by the Duke as part of the price of his services and of the
intellectual prestige which he was considered to bring to Cosimo's
capital, Lionardo appears to have had free access, possibly for the
purpose of consulting Varchi's library, or possibly to do some
work for him. At the beginning of March Varchi himself was not at

---

[4] See ded. lett. (2.2.64, i.e. '65 st. com.) of Salviati's edition of Gerolamo
Razzi's *La Gostanza* (Florence, Giunti, 1565), in which Salviati relates the
episode.

La Topaia. Worried by the fact that his absent friend's books were dispersed throughout the villa and thus vulnerable to the attentions of visitors less trustworthy than himself (and no doubt anxious to avoid the shadow of doubt falling upon him should any in fact go astray), Lionardo wrote to Varchi asking for the key to the *anticamera*, intending to lock the books up there. Varchi seems to have in some way misunderstood this request as meaning that the present arrangement was inconvenient, whereas Salviati had only made it, as he himself says, 'per soddisfazione di V. S. [i.e. Varchi], se per aventura ella non havesse voluto che detti libri stessero altrimenti che sotto la sua chiave'. Varchi's suggestion, if Salviati's reaction was to write eventually 'Hora mi trovo soprapreso da tanta liberalità che io non posso', seems to have been to give his protégé even greater freedom, in all probability permission to take books away at his convenience. All the same, Lionardo declared his intention of making a complete inventory of the books, indicating their exact whereabouts.

Yet within three weeks the two were at daggers-drawn. Varchi, perhaps facetiously, made some slighting comment on Salviati to their mutual friend Don Silvano Razzi, implying it appears that Salviati, in debt, was up to some kind of dishonest manœuvre. The books may well have played some part in it all. Stung to the quick by the real or imagined slight, Lionardo composed another of his indignant letters. His only desire, in his blind rage, is to hurt in return for the hurt received, which he does by suggesting that it is perhaps fortunate for him that he has witnesses to his having lent Varchi certain books, of which he now demands the return, and by insinuating that he has not only been of greater service to Varchi in the past than Varchi to him, but has also had plenty of cause to be dissatisfied with his friend's past behaviour. In evidence again are the morbid sensitiveness, the intolerance of criticism, and the vicious temper. But in his world, and amongst his contemporaries, such storms were commonplace, and no more importance is to be attached to this one than to the exaggerated sentiments of the sonnets.[5]

[5] Certainly one cannot accept this letter, dated 24.3.63 (i.e. '64 st. com.), as proof (as one authority would have us do) that Salviati's subsequent oration on the death of Varchi was a masterpiece of hypocrisy, and that Salviati, despite his outward partisanship for Dante, wrote the *Discorso* of Castravilla against Dante with the express purpose of spiting the dead Varchi and contradicting his *Ercolano*. For this thesis see M. Rossi, 'Il discorso di Ridolfo Castravilla contro

That the quarrel did not mark a definitive break—though the friendship of the two was by no means so complete and devoted as some of their contemporaries liked to make out (see Ch. VIII, n. 8)—is confirmed beyond doubt by further affectionate and congratulatory poetic exchanges between the two later that year. This seems in fact to have been the period in which Lionardo was most active poetically, and the list of those to whom he addressed poems, or from whom he received them, tells us who were his friends, colleagues, and patrons.

Of those poems to which a definite or approximate date can be assigned, the bulk fall into this early period of Salviati's life.[6] Many of them are directly or indirectly adulatory, with the Medici receiving most attention. Flattery is meted out directly in nine poems, including two sonnets to Cosimo, one of which ('Saggio Signor, cui ne' primi anni elesse') we have already seen. In another such poem beginning 'Non per sottrarmi al dolce peso ond'io' (43) Salviati also justifies a desire to leave Florence for a more cloistered existence. Others similarly praised directly are Francesco de' Medici, Jacopo Salviati, Giacomo Buoncompagni, Lodovico Beccadelli. More frequently, as in the case of the *Garzia* sonnets, adulation is achieved indirectly. This is done in at least fifteen poems, abject flattery of Cosimo being expressed in conventional terms in the poems to Vettori, 'Se di senno, e virtù, Vettorio quanto' (64), and to Varchi, 'Dunque è pur ver, che 'l più gradito e santo' (25), whilst in a sonnet to Tommaso del Nero, 'Nero ch'al nome tuo contrario chiudi' (42), the same theme is treated in a more restrained and one might say almost grateful manner.

Given the social and governmental structure of Florence at this time, where individual and state patronage played such a vital part in the life of the *letterato*, verses addressed to, and in praise

Dante', *Giornale Dantesco*, v (Florence, Olschki, 1897), Quad. 1-2, pp. 1 ff. One would be inclined to doubt the authenticity of the letter (published by Manzoni and Contin), if it were not extant in the A.S. Florence, Filza 139, (A. 133), fols. 133-5. Manzoni, however, wrongly prints the date of the letter as 24.3.68, two-and-a-half years after the death of Varchi. Further information on Varchi's relations with Salviati in this period is found in a letter from Salviati to Varchi dated 4.3.63 (i.e. 1564 st. com.; unnumbered manuscript in the Archivio della Crusca, Florence), published by Severina Parodi in 'Una lettera inedita del Salviati', *Studi di filologia italiana*, xxvii (1969), 147-8. Marconcini, op. cit., refers to this letter but gives the year as 1553.

[6] See supplementary note 2, p. 245.

of, one's betters and benefactors were part and parcel of the man of letters' daily routine. Taken as a whole the twenty-four adulatory sonnets are typical in conception, attitude, content, theme, and approach, of their genre and their times, and fit unobtrusively into the *lirica cortigiana* of which the sixteenth century has left us such an overwhelming volume. But as poems these are often clumsy: they lack in particular (as did most of Salviati's literary works) a sense of proportion, as a result of which they are frequently ridiculous, and the exaggerated praises they contain are rarely redeemed by any truly poetic qualities, or even adequate mastery of technique, which might have raised them above the status of crudely expressed adulation.

Little more can be claimed for the numerous poems which Salviati, in the contemporary manner, addressed to friends, expressing admiration, affection, loyalty, gratitude, or any other emotion which the occasion demanded. Their tone and character naturally varies. Sometimes the dedication is secondary, the main purpose being praise of a third party, or even an exercise in the Italian poetic tradition. Salviati's closest friends at this time would seem from these poems to have been Canigiani, Varchi, Razzi, and Orazio Urbani who, on the retirement of Bernardo Canigiani in 1575, became Florentine ambassador to Ferrara and thus another valuable link in the chain with which Salviati eventually attempted to bind himself to that city. Other friendships poetically documented were with Ascanio da Ripa (another pupil of Vettori),[7] Prospero Mannelli, Lodovico Beccadelli, and Laura Battiferra degli Ammannati, the poetess friend and correspondent of Annibale Caro and Varchi. Tommaso del Nero, Frosino Lapini, and Giovambattista Adriani also receive poems about this time, from which it is clear that Salviati's Florentine connections are already with Varchi and the Accademia, whilst the link eventually formed with the Florentine Monastero degli Angeli of the Order of Camaldoli is represented not only by Don Silvano Razzi but by Don Antonio da Pisa Camaldolese and Don Lorenzo Camaldolese.

Apart from brief flashes such as in the sonnet, 'Lappole a i

---

[7] For the unpublished correspondence between Vettori and Ascanio da Ripa see B.M. Additional MSS. 10272, 10278, and 10281, and for the list of these letters, see C. Roth, 'I carteggi volgari di Piero Vettori nel British Museum', *Rivista storica degli archivi toscani*, i, pt. 3 (1929), 1 ff.

vaghi fiori, a i giorni gai' (37), addressed to Prospero Mannelli, which in the lines 'Quanto di bello e di vezzoso un Sole / Accolse, un punto scioglie, e spesso resta / Per breve ombra di vita, eterna morte' treats the stock Renaissance theme of the transience of life, and whilst not wholly immune from incipient *secentismo* in its verbal and conceptual patterns gives it the more deeply weary tone of the late Cinquecento, the chief interest of these poems is undoubtedly biographical. In particular they shed important light on the esteem in which Lionardo was held by his contemporaries, for it is to be noted that the extant poems *to* Salviati far outweigh in number those composed *by* him, even if Salviati himself does account for this by the unlikely tale that he did not possess copies of some of his own poems to friends.[8]

One group of poems is more homogeneous than the others, namely the seven *Rime in burla*, two of which enjoyed widespread and long-lasting celebrity, quite unjustified in the case of the ode in *terzine* to Filippo Spadini, *In lode del piatire* (45), and merited only by its gross obscenity in the case of the *canto carnascialesco: In lode delpino* (19). Two others, 'Come all'hor ch'al gran Rio germe novello' (8) and 'D'Ostro tirio fulgente' (24), styled as parodies of the works of 'un poeta ridicolo', are barely distinguishable from Salviati's own attempts at serious verse. Yet another, a madrigal beginning 'Dunque il mio ricco, antico' (26), to Frosino Lapini 'in nome del Buonanni sopra l'orazione delle lingue fatta nell'Accademia Fiorentina da Lionardo Salviati' is in a mock-pompous, pseudo-elevated style, full of classical allusions, as befits its recipient. Although the last two, a *capitolo* 'Quando e' s'udì, che Maestro Maccario' (49) ridiculing a certain Maccario whose lecture disappointed his eager listeners[9] and 'Buonanni,

---

[8] This he says in the Ded. lett., to Lodovico Capponi, which accompanies his poems in the MSS. Ricc. and Nap. Poems addressed to, or principally about, Lionardo number at least 87. The list of their authors, with the number of compositions in this category securely attributable to each is: G. B. Adriani (1), Baldello Baldelli (1), Laura Battiferra (1); Lodovico Beccadelli (1), Angelo Bronzino (1), Aless. Canigiani (17), Ascanio da Ripa (3); Giulio de' Libri (1), Anton Francesco Grazzini (6), Benedetto Macci (1), Prospero Mannelli (1), Giuseppe Nozzolini (1), Camillo Pellegrino (1), Gherardo Spini (2), Piero Stufa (1), Orazio Urbani (1), Benedetto Varchi (44) (i.e. 41 to Salviati, 2 to Razzi, and 1 to Aloisio Spadino), uncertain author (2).

[9] The fact that both Salviati and Grazzini wrote poems ridiculing this same Maestro Maccario is not likely to be a coincidence, and may be taken as a possible further indication of acquaintance at an early stage. Grazzini wrote on the subject three *stanze* of single *ottave*, two ironically praising, 'In lode di

questo è stato un passerotto' (4) which pokes fun at a recently performed *mascherata* of Vincenzo Buonanni (commentator of Dante and familiar of both Salviati and Grazzini), are moderately witty and amusing, Lionardo's touch was not light enough, and he lacked the concision and incisive turn of phrase needed to put real punch and zest into compositions of this kind, in which wide use is made of colloquial language and various jargons. Salviati was no Grazzini—manifestly his model in these *poesie in burla*. As a result the two parodies are dull, the humour of *In lode del piatire* is heavy-handed, and the clumsy, gross obscenity of the *In lode del pino* remains offensive.

In his theoretical works Lionardo says little about the lyric, treating the subject only incidentally in discussing language. His lavish praise of Bembo in his *Orazione in lode della fiorentina favella* and whenever he mentions lyric poetry seems to indicate that he does not consider Bembo's theories on lyric composition in their narrower interpretation to conflict with his own present views on language in general.[10] Whoever wishes to excel in the composition of lyric poetry, he consistently repeats, has little alternative but to emulate Petrarch. As early as the letter to Corbinelli he states: 'chi non imita in questa maniera di componimenti il Petrarca, lo fa per non poter far altro, e perchè si dispera di poter mai in quel divino stile conseguire alcuna mezzana lode.' He is thinking here, in 1563, exclusively in terms of style, as he was twenty years later when he wrote that the language of the *Canzoniere* was 'quasi una favella fatta dall'autore, ma bellissima a maraviglia, e maestrevole in tanto, che altra non possa forse imitarsi da chi lodevolmente esercitar si debba, in quella guisa di poesia.'[11] This being so it is not surprising that his own serious

Maestro Maccario' ((i) *inc*. 'Alla presenza proprio, od alla vista' and (ii) *inc*. 'L'aria di ebreo, il nome di Maccario'), and one ironically repentant, 'Al medesimo' *inc*. 'Dico mia colpa, e mi dolgo, e mi pento'; see Verzone, *Le rime burlesche*, *Ottave* Nos XCIX, C, CI respectively.

[10] In his oration *In lode della fiorentina favella* Salviati clearly echoes Varchi, who in the *Ercolano* wrote that Bembo was 'il primo, il quale osservando le regole della grammatica, e mettendo in opera gli ammaestramenti del bene, e artificiosamente scrivere l'imitò daddovero [i.e. Petrarch], e rassomigliando a lui mostrò la prima, e diritta via del leggiadramente comporre nella lingua *fiorentina*' (italics mine), *Ercolano* (Padua, Comino, 1747), p. 87.

[11] Salviati, *Avvertimenti della lingua sopra 'l Decamerone* (Raillard, Naples, 1712), Vol. I, Bk. ii, p. 106. *Avvertimenti* references will henceforth be to this edition and the volume, book and page reference will be given in brackets, e.g. in this case (I. ii. 106).

lyrics hold closely, linguistically and stylistically, to the model set by the *Canzoniere*, especially as they are mostly youthful compositions. Metre, form, vocabulary, word-forms, and constructions are dictated by Petrarch, whose cadence and musicality are everywhere imitated. Some poems, in content as well as style, are out-and-out Petrarchan exercises. In others the content, which may be adulation, protestations of friendship, or comment on some recent event, merely finds a Petrarchan expression.

But by 1563 Salviati had renounced—and denounced—the practice of incorporating into his own work phrases from his models, substituting for this the kind of imitation which he outlines in his letter to Borghini of 1576, involving the reproduction of the style of the model 'in un cotal generale, cioè nella dolcezza del suono, nella purità delle voci, nella agevolezza della disposizione, nella leggiadria, nella vaghezza, e nell'armonia convenevole'.[12]

Though we do not find whole lines or phrases lifted bodily from Petrarch we do find many passages which come perilously near to this, as well as many more in which the *Canzoniere* is echoed. Even in poems which are not exclusively or even principally Petrarchan exercises we find passages such as:

> Mentr'io per luoghi inabitati e crudi
> Erro solingo, e di concetti amari
> Mi vo pascendo, e vuol Amor, ch'io impari
> Nuovi schermi a' suoi colpi, e nuovi scudi. (42)

or

> Più d'altro fugge, e non val dietro ad esso
> Pentir profondo (37)

and

> E del tardo pentir m'affliggo solo (28)

in all of which Petrarch is distinctly echoed, through cadence and the suggestiveness of vocabulary, as much for sound as for concept, without being anywhere exactly reproduced.

Dull though most of the Petrarchist poems are it is, nevertheless, interesting to find in them distinct symptoms of the late

---

[12] Lett. Salviati to Vincenzo Borghini, 7.8.76, published by F. S. Zambrini, *Lettere di uomini illustri del sec. XVI* (Lucca, 1853). Salviati is in this particular instance referring to the imitation of Boccaccio.

Cinquecento cult of sound. The Petrarchan conceits undergo a
subtle change which shifts the accent from content heavily on to
the musical sound. Typical is the sonnet 'Come languendo all'hor
pietade e zelo' (11):

> Ed io, poich'a me stesso il ver non celo
> Come pur or facea, m'allegro e sdegno
> Meco in un tempo, anzi a me stesso insegno
> Ardere insieme, e provar freddo, e gielo.

where the concept loses any force or vitality in the rhythmic lilt
and the musical, madrigalesque quality of the verse. This feature
is most outstandingly present in other pseudo-Petrarchan passages
such as:

> Così fia vostro riso senza pianto
> E vostro dolce d'ogni amaro scarso   (11)

or

> Come il duolo è piacere, e 'l danno aita ...
> Come si speri il male, e 'l ben si tema;
> Come si pianga il riso, e 'l pianto rida;
> Come 'l più lento e lieve astringa e prema   (13)

Here the play on words, the creation of verbal and conceptual
patterns is a game to which the verse-form is a musical accompaniment. Almost all the *Garzia* sonnets are constructed on these
lines—a series of extended conceits which it is almost impossible
to take seriously.

It is, therefore, not surprising that the most successful of these
poems are the madrigals. A detailed examination of Salviati's
poems would be out of place here, where it must suffice to repeat
that behind the overwhelming influence of Petrarch, and the
quite manifest imitation of Dante, Michelangelo, and Della Casa,
some characteristics are discernible which give the poems a limited
historical interest in the context of their times.

Though Lionardo's poetic production was considerable, and
apparently appreciated by his contemporaries,[13] he himself seems

---

[13] Most significant in this respect is the evidence given by Pier Vettori at
the so-called 'Provanza di nobiltà' a few years later, when Lionardo was being
screened for acceptance into the Order of St. Stephen. Vettori said Lionardo
was: 'di gran dottrina et elegantia et ingegni sublimi sì nelli studii come nella
poesia' (Pisa, A.S., A.S.St., 'Provanze di nobiltà', Filza 7, Parte prima, No. 3,
Lionardo Salviati).

to have had the good sense to realize his lack either of inspiration or of any of the technical ability of Della Casa (his chief model in respect of formal innovation against a Petrarchesque ground as well as for a number of structural and lexical features) which might have taken its place, and to have begun very early to give his poems a purely practical or recreational role, using them either as an elegant means of communication or vehicle of adulation, or alternatively as an amusement. Only twenty-two of his seventy-six poems—and those twenty-two include the *intermedii* for his comedy *Il Granchio*, the five *mascherate*, and a madrigal group—are not in direct address.

There is little doubt that Lionardo very soon ceased to take himself seriously as a poet, never agreeing to the publication of his verses (the exceptions are the handful of sonnets published at a very early age with the *Garzia* orations), with which he remained thoroughly dissatisfied.[14] In 1585 he speaks as one who considers without emotion that his poetic aspirations were to be numbered amongst the follies of his youth,[15] and his compositions, even at their best, are a confirmation, and an exemplification, of the bulk of late Cinquecento lyric poetry as 'l'imitazione petrarchesca, lo sfoggio dell'erudizione, l'abilità nel verseggiare'.[16]

[14] Cf. Cambi, *Orazione*. N.B. also that the quotation given by Manzoni, *Rime inedite*, pp. xiii–xv, from Annibale Caro's letter of 20.7.66 gives Caro's opinion, not on Salviati's verse, as we might be led to believe by the way in which Manzoni used the quotation, but of his prose, and to be exact of the prose of Lionardo's funeral oration for Varchi.

[15] See Lett. Salviati to Pellegrino, Florence, 2.1.86, printed with the *Infarinato secondo* (Padua, 1588).

[16] E. M. Fusco, *La lirica* (Milan, 1950), p. 273.

VI

A CALL TO REBELLION:
THE *ORAZIONE IN LODE DELLA FIORENTINA FAVELLA*

'I LETTERATI del secolo XVI', writes Manacorda, 'non amavano troppo vivere nell'isolamento.' Varchi, who was certainly one of the Academy's most indefatigable members, was one of Salviati's intimates: numerous other Academicians, including such ex-consuls as Ferrini, Adriani, Buonamici, but above all Grazzini, were already closely associated with him and his works: for some time he had participated in activities which it was the Academy's special task to foster. Salviati was not likely to remain long aloof from it.

Early in 1564 he was invited by Baccio Valori, the current Consul, to become a member. An erudite scholar and writer, a great patron of the arts, and one of the most influential men of letters in contemporary Florence (with an unfortunate anti-Medicean ancestry to live down), Valori seems to have been one of the first persons to recognize Lionardo's talents. He remained a constant friend to him throughout his life, and at this point considered that the young Salviati, with his passion for the *volgare* of which he himself was a strong supporter (he also had a collection of old Italian manuscripts which was to prove invaluable to his protégé), would be an asset to the institution whose highest office Valori now occupied.

In view of the importance of this institution, and the part it was to play in Salviati's life, a glance back at its birth in the early days of Cosimo's rule will be both opportune and illuminating. Though few documents give reliable information, the early history of the Academy is exceptionally revealing of the relationship of culture and politics in Medicean Florence.

Here, on 1 November 1540, one year after Lionardo's birth, a group of twelve young *letterati*, including Antonfrancesco Grazzini, Niccolò di Giovanni Martelli, and Filippo Salvetti, began to hold meetings in the Via San Gallo house of the eccentric Giovanni Mazzuoli—'Lo Stradino' so often good-humouredly teased by Lasca—and having fallen to discussing the Tuscan language, decided to form an Academy. Without delay they drew up rules and statutes, eventually dubbing themselves the Accademia degli Umidi, and taking individual names connected with water, according to the fashion of the times for facetious nomenclature.[1]

From the beginning the orientation of this body, which was joined in December by Cosimo Bartoli and Pierfrancesco Giambullari, and shortly afterwards by Giovambattista Gelli and Filippo del Migliore, was in general literary, though Grazzini and his intimates were in favour of the inclusion of a strong element of Florentine *piacevolezza*. Its serious side was directed entirely towards literature in *volgare* and particularly the great Florentine writers. Pride of place was given to Petrarch, whose perpetual study was made compulsory by the statutes, but the function of the Academy was to be a broader one, namely, 'che . . . si potesse leggere in Toscano ogni autor Latino, e chi leggesse, tenuto fosse a dare il testo tradotto, pensando, che da tal modo di operare, le scienze tutte si potessero a poco a poco vedere in lingua nostra.'[2]

This formulation of the Academy's policy clearly indicates that there had arisen in Florence, as a result of cultural exigencies and quite independently of any direct political influence, a society whose avowed purpose was the conscious furthering of a process now of long standing and great vigour in Italy, namely the transfer of culture and learning into the *volgare* medium and the fostering of the national tradition. Yet the development of the new Academy might not have been quite what it was, had it not attracted the vigilant eye of Cosimo de' Medici.

---

[1] The *Capitoli* were drawn up by Cosimo Bartoli and Giovanni Norchiati, and are to be found in Cod. Magl. II, IV, 1 (B.N.C., Florence) headed 'Libro di Capitoli, leggi e composizioni dell'Accademia degli Umidi di Firenze, creata l'anno del Signore 1540: regnante lo Ill.mo ad Ecc.mo Sig. D. Cosimo Medici, in casa il Padre Stradino.' For the history of the Umidi see also J. Rilli, *Notizie letterarie ed istoriche intorno agli uomini illustri dell'Accademia Fiorentina* (Florence, Martini, 1700), pp. xviii ff. and S. Salvini, *Fasti*. In addition to the above-mentioned *Capitoli*, etc. the chief manuscript sources of information on the Academy are: (i) *Atti dell'Accademia Fiorentina*, Florence, Bib. Marucelliana. 3 vols., Cods. B III, 52: B III, 53; B III, 54. (ii) *Costituzione dell'Accademia Fiorentina*, Florence, B.N.C., Cod. Pal. 1037.
[2] Rilli, *Notizie*, p. xix.

For the statutes had hardly been approved (on 11 February 1541), when Duke Cosimo ordered that the Accademia degli Umidi should henceforward be called the Accademia Fiorentina and be under ducal protection. This by no means signified unconditional favour and assistance, but rather that the new Academy was to be the servant of Cosimo. Significantly the instrument of this transformation was an Academician of comparatively short standing, Pirro Colonna, described as 'familiare e confidente' of Duke Cosimo, significantly because the situation symbolized the relationship which the Accademia was henceforward to have with the regime. Likewise, as Rilli says, the statutes were 'ordinati e compilati solennemente di volontà, ed espresso consentimento di quel buon Principe, a coll'assistenza e direzione di Mes. Lelio Torelli da Fano suo primo Auditore e Segretario.' After some short-lived resistance most of the Academicians, typically, capitulated and accepted their new status and that of their newly born and twice-christened Academy.

The edict dated 22 February 1542 officially establishing the new body is a particularly important document, illustrating a development destined to have far-reaching effects, namely the utilization for political purposes of a current which had led to the spontaneous emergence, in the Umidi, of a society to further the above-mentioned process of the transfer of culture into the *volgare*. Past members of the House of Medici, says Cosimo in the edict, have distinguished themselves by sponsoring the search for missing classics and contributing to the glory of the classical languages. But the time has now come for his subjects to become even richer: it is time that 'si onorino di quel buono, e bello, che Iddio Ottimo Massimo ha dato loro, cioè l'eccellenza della propria lingua.' The task of the Academicians is to 'seguitare i dotti loro esercizij interpretando, componendo, e da ogni altra lingua ogni bella Scienza in questa nostra riducendo'[3]—a task in which the Duke encourages them by transferring to their Consuls all the privileges of the Rector of the University of Florence.[4]

[3] Extracts from the edict, published by Rilli, *Notizie*, pp. xxi–xxii.
[4] For the relationship of the Academy to the Studio see M. Maylender, *Storia delle accademie d'Italia*, 5 vols. (Bologna, 1926–30), iii. 1–6, and also G. Prezziner, *Storia del pubblico studio e delle società scientifiche e letterarie di Firenze*, 2 vols. (Florence, 1810). A good, and fairly detailed study of the origins of the Academy, its early development, its aims, and its relationship to the state,

No less important, however, is that whilst the *volgare* is firmly indicated as the language of the future, that same *volgare* is equally firmly identified with the tongue of the city of Florence. The document states plainly that the activities of the Academicians in promoting the Florentine language are aimed at the 'Gloria di S. E. . . ., onore alla patria' no less than the 'esaltazione di se stessi', and it is made unequivocally clear that the glory and honour derive from the fact that 'patria' and 'lingua volgare' are one and indivisible. The Proemio to the statutes, repeating that the function of the Academy is the glorification of the Florentine language, lists the favours which await those who adequately perform the will of the Prince in this respect. Thus, as one historian of the Italian academies states, as a result of this ducal 'privilege' (without equal in the history of those Italian academies) the Accademia Fiorentina became 'quasi una corporazione dello stato'.[5] The interests of the *volgare* (considered purely and wholly Florentine) and the interests of the state now coincide.

This intensely pro-Florentine orientation of the Academy, and the stress which Cosimo placed on its duties, is repeated over and over again by contemporary historians. A scrutiny of the officials of the Academy in its first decades suffices to demonstrate the intense compenetration of Academy and administration. The censors were drawn by lot, but the statutes decreed that the *Consiglieri*—counsellors—of which each new Consul took two, should be from the *Magistrato*. In the function of Counsellor there appear in the early years such stars of the administrative firmament as Francesco Campana, Pirro Colonna, Pierfrancesco Ricci da Prato 'Segretario e Majordomo del Duca Cosimo' (and his one-time tutor), Stefano Colonna, Giovanni Battista Ricasoli, and the great Lelio Torelli himself. Though the stipends themselves were not very high, it was made clear that the favour of the Duke, on whom depended all privileges and prospects of advancement, could well be determined by the manner in which the Academicians performed their allotted task of furthering the cause of

accompanied by an analysis of its activities and a discussion of its significance in sixteenth-century culture is to be found in A. De Gaetano, 'The Florentine Academy and the Advancement of Learning through the Vernacular: the Orti Oricellari and the Sacra Accademia', *Bibliothèque d'Humanisme et Renaissance*, xxv (1968), 19–52.

[5] Maylender, *Storia delle accademie*, iii. 4.

the *volgare* and its tradition. Hence the tradition (to which as we shall see Salviati himself subscribed) whereby a new Consul spoke to his colleagues in the name of the Duke, exhorting them as the latter's servants to apply themselves with zeal to their appointed mission, reminding them of the rewards which awaited the obedient, and hinting at the displeasure which would follow on lukewarmness. Other forms of control, numerous and effective, are reflected in the statutes and in various 'reforms' which were from time to time found necessary. The approval of the Duke's *Auditore*, Lelio Torelli, was needed for any public or private lecture, and the so-called *specchio* kept the register of an Academician's record, balancing his industry against any short-comings. Eligibility for office required a favourable balance. In addition Cosimo himself maintained certain controls over printing and publication.

Beyond question the role which Cosimo imposed on the Academy in his greater design for the Florentine state significantly influenced its attitude to certain urgent questions of the day. At the same time the particular cultural orientation of the Academy, its Florentine-Italian drive, was there as we have seen long before Cosimo's interference, which served first and foremost to reinforce that drive. Furthermore, an important fact to recognize and take due account of, despite the parochial element in this orientation, is the importance of the phenomenon of the Florentine Academy within Italian culture as a whole. Like the Infiammati of Padua, which despite significant differences in attitude to such matters as translations and rhetoric was likewise dedicated to the spread of the *volgare* and fostered intense study of Petrarch and Boccaccio, it represented within that culture, in its quality as the promoter of Italian studies and hence of the *volgare*, the spearhead of a rapidly growing national consciousness which sought the rehabilitation of the national tradition and indeed saw the latter as taking over from the classics the function which they had enjoyed throughout the preceding stages of humanism.

But returning to the narrower, Florentine expression of all this, too much stress cannot be laid on the complete identification of Salviati's close friend Grazzini with this movement. Indeed it would not be going too far to say that in the older man's vision of the *volgare* and the national culture is to be found virtually all the raw material which Salviati later developed into a programme. Grazzini's *stanze A' riformatori della lingua toscana*,[6] for example, written on the occasion of the appointment, in 1550, of a commission to formulate the rules of Tuscan, express a view which coincides almost completely with the cause which Salviati was to make his own. Florentine, Grazzini asserts, is well worthy to take a place alongside Latin and Greek. Addressing Florence herself he says that for language and culture: 'dietro ti viene | L'invitta Roma e la superba Atene.'[7] Ariosto is praised for the pure Tuscan of his language, and one can see in embryo Salviati's (and Varchi's) thesis of the need to supplement a native knowledge of Florentine with 'art' and the study of the great authors, superimposing their discipline on to one's 'natural' sense of the language. Not without significance in an examination of the soil from which Salviati's theories grew are Lasca's call for more careful observance of linguistic propriety, his praise of Bembo, and his insistence on the potential of Florence to complete a linguistic conquest not only of Italy but of the world: ideas, all of them, which were to form, fourteen years later, the substance of Lionardo's *Orazione delle lingue*.

No wonder then, in view of the purpose of the Accademia degli Umidi as revealed by its statutes, and given its character as a spontaneous product of the Florentine currents of the times, that

[6] Verzone, *Ottave*, No. XIII, pp. 360–4, *inc.* 'Voi ch'a sì bella impresa e pellegrina'.

[7] *A' riformatori*, ll. 79–80. In view of future works by Salviati expressing identical sentiments, the following sections of the *stanze* in question deserve quotation in full.

> La lingua nostra è sì dolce e capace
> d'ogni soggetto, e così bene esprime
> gli affetti e gesti umani in guerra e in pace,
> che mettersi può ben tra le due prime.
> Nella prosa il Boccaccio tanto piace,
> tanto piace il Petrarca nelle rime,
> ch'a tutt'altri poeti vanno avante;
> ma finimondo è poi quando vien Dante.
>
> Questi tre degni e famosi scrittori
> ti danno tanta lode e tanta gloria,
> Fiorenza bella, che tra le maggiori
> città, sempre di te sarà memoria;
> onde carca ne vai di tanti onori,
> che di te fia ricordo in ogni storia:
> tal che, la lor mercè, dietro ti viene
> l'invitta Roma e la superba Atene.   (65–80).

Grazzini could later say of the Accademia Fiorentina into which it was transformed, 'Or non sa 'l mondo ch'ell'è mia figliuola?'[8] Grazzini did not long maintain control over his offspring. The ease of the takeover effected by the Grand Duke and the comparative zeal of the bulk of the Academicians in obeying him reveal the extent to which Cosimo's policy of harnessing all activity to the waggon of the state was accepted even at this early stage. Lasca grumbled and fumed, but eventually bent to his sovereign's will and vented his resentment on his colleagues.

Once established, however, the Academy prospered. Though occasionally its members had to be reminded quite sharply (as in the 'reform' of 1549 which made compulsory the submission of all works in *volgare* to the Censors) that they were paid to further the cause of the Florentine language: and though frequently torn by a singularly sterile brand of internal strife, they maintained a fairly high rate of production in the form of lectures and commentaries on the great Italian authors, translations of the classics, and original compositions in the *volgare*. Therefore, in assessing Lionardo Salviati's position in, and contribution to, Florentine culture, it would be a grave error to overlook this important element of the Accademia as we have seen it, its origins and its progress hitherto, and to forget how thoroughly the ground had been prepared for him by Grazzini's 'daughter'. In the Academy's programme from the outset one recognizes the main features of Salviati's future campaign. Like him the Academy promoted the replacement of Latin by the *volgare* as the medium for the transmission and advancement of knowledge, and consequently encouraged translation from the classics. Just as in his later years he attached more importance to the production of original works in, and translations into, the vernacular, than to theoretical works on its use, so the Academy saw its many *lezioni* and other practical activities in Italian as the most effective contributions towards the achievement of its ultimate aim.

Of recent years, however, the Academy had languished somewhat. But with the election of Baccio Valori as thirty-seventh Consul in 1564, appointed in the hope that he would revitalize a lethargic organism, the Academy took on a new lease of life. G. B. Adriani, Antonio Benivieni, Agnolo Segni, Baccio Baldini,

---

[8] Sonnet, *inc.* 'Se nel fin ch'io stia cheto a voi pur piace', addressed to Duke Cosimo; Verzone, No. LXXXIV, p. 70.

Benedetto Varchi, and Piero Rucellai all gave lectures covering a wide range of topics from the 'Essenza del fato' (Baldini) to 'Giustizia' (Rucellai) and 'Amore' (Varchi, of course). But if any performance could be pinpointed as the highlight of the consulship it was undoubtedly a lecture given by Lionardo Salviati, his choice as lecturer at a moment, when offers to speak exceeded the demand, being a tribute to Valori's firm faith in his value and promise for the future.[9] The invitation came at the beginning of March, via Varchi. Lionardo was flattered, and felt the consulship of Valori was the ideal moment for him to show his mettle. Yet one thing worried him. Whereas lecturers could normally refer to their script, he was already so short-sighted that he would find it difficult to consult a written text if his memory momentarily failed him. Torn between enthusiasm and fear he referred the decision on the wisdom of his lecturing to Varchi, who must have decided in favour, for by the end of April Lionardo was ready to deliver his lecture, a landmark in the cultural history of Florence and Italy, in the history of the language question, and in the career of Salviati himself. He entitled it: *Orazione nella quale si dimostra esser la fiorentina favella e i fiorentini autori superiori a tutte le altre lingue, sì dell'antichità che moderne, e a tutti gli altri autori.*[10]

After numerous vicissitudes which had taken it from Michelozzo's Medici Palace in the Via Larga through a succession of seats including the Studio and the Sala del Papa in Santa Maria Novella, the Academy now held its public lectures—lectures, that is, to which the public were invited as distinct from private meetings—in the Sala de' Dugento in the Palazzo Vecchio. In this hall on 30 April 1564 the young Lionardo Salviati ascended the rostrum a comparatively obscure figure. Despite the publicity of the *Garzia* orations and the subsequent 'Corbi', and though probably regarded as one of Florence's bright hopes for the future, in Florentine academic waters he was still a small fish. Before the *Orazione in lode della fiorentina favella* there is no hint of active

---

[9] This information, and a good deal more on Salviati's relationship with Valori, is given by Salviati himself in the dedicatory letter to Baccio Valori of his edition of Passavanti's *Specchio di vera penitenza* (Florence, 1585).

[10] Florence, Giunti, 1564. The dating of the dedicatory letter to Don Francesco de' Medici raises a problem. Although its date is the same as the date of delivery of the oration (30.4.64), it includes the words 'lo essere le cose contenute nella presente orazione da diversi diversamente racconte, mi ha costretto finalmente a pubblicarla quasi contro mia voglia'. The letter must have been backdated.

participation by Salviati in the disputes, public or private, of his contemporaries, for they, not he, wrote the 'Corbi'. His bent had all been, as he himself and Alessandro Canigiani said, towards 'friendship'. Varchi had been his friend: so had Adriani, Grazzini, Ferrini, Valori, Buonamici. The audience in the Sala de Dugento on 30 April 1564 may well have had little inkling of what they were about to experience.

In a conventional introduction to the *Orazione* Salviati praises Valori and declares it natural that on first publicly addressing the Academy[11] he should make the Florentine language—'il general subbietto della loro Accademia'—his theme. What follows makes it a landmark in the history of Italian culture in the Cinquecento and a statement of principle which was to govern Lionardo's activity for the rest of his life.

Literary and linguistic studies, he begins, are the medium for the achievement of human perfection, and in this he echoes the humanistic conception of education.[12] The innovation appears when he states of the language 'most suited to bring the greatest perfection to literature' that 'Tale, senz'alcun fallo, Uditori nobilissimi, è la presente nostra Fiorentina favella. Questa favella, Uditori nobilissimi, che noi tutto giorno parliamo, ad apportare alle scritture maggior perfezione di tutte l'altre lingue principalmente è più atta.'[13] And in case his hearers, as he puts it, should

[11] He says 'la prima volta che mi conviene ai Fiorentini Accademici pubblicamente parlare'. It is difficult to know what importance to attach to the word 'pubblicamente' here, if any. It sometimes means that the speaker, who is now lecturing 'publicly', i.e. in public as a member of the Academy at one of its 'public' lectures, has lectured previously *privatamente*, i.e. either as a private individual invited to address the Academy in private session, or as an Academician at a private meeting of the Academy. No 'private' lecture by Salviati is recorded as having taken place. He was admitted to the Academy 18 March 1565, see Florence, Biblioteca Marucelliana, Cod. B III 54, fol. 14 v.

[12] The stages in this argument are in themselves of little consequence, and the material of his argumentation is conventional and hackneyed. The essential is that this introductory section is a significant and integral part of the work, whose whole conception depends on it. I cannot agree with B. T. Sozzi, *Aspetti e momenti della questione linguistica* (Padua, Liviani, 1955), p. 110, who dismisses it as 'un preambolo di maniera, in istile boccaccevole, prendendo le mosse da inutili generalità'. For a more detailed discussion of the significance of this aspect of the oration see P. M. Brown, 'A Significant Use of the Word "Umanista" in the Sixteenth Century', *M.L.R.* lxiv. 3 (July 1969), 565–75.

[13] *Orazione in lode della fiorentina favella*, in Salviati, *Opere*, 5 vols. (Milan, Classici Italiani, 1810), v. 61. Quotations from this oration or references to its content will henceforward be followed in the text by a capital 'F' and the number of the relevant page of this 1810 edition.

doubt if they have heard correctly, he repeats it with an assurance
that he means every word he says. For he is fully aware of its
implications.

To appreciate what these implications were we must recall the
virtual identification, in the early humanists, of the 'studies be-
fitting man' with the study not only of Classical Antiquity in
general, but more precisely with the study of classical literature
as the guide to life, and the intense study of the classical languages
as an inevitable concomitant.[14] This identification of the humanist
programme with the classics has to be presupposed in order to
understand the significance of Salviati's casting of Italian in what
had normally been considered the role of the classical languages
and literatures. Transferring that role to Florentine means
destroying this exclusive link between the *studia humanitatis* as
the implementation of a vision of the perfection of Man, and the
language and literature of Classical Antiquity.

We must proceed shortly to examine the implications for the
Florentine language itself, which Salviati sees to be contained in
his statement. But first let it be said that there is in embryo, in
that statement, virtually the whole of Salviati's later production,
which all develops, in the last analysis, from the conviction which
is here expressed. In the meantime we must follow briefly Salviati's
substantiation of what he has enunciated in general terms, a
substantiation which for him demands an examination of Florentine language and literature to prove them to be the most perfect
medium for the programme which he has outlined, and which we
have seen to be, in its essentials, 'humanistic'.

Some of his arguments, such as the importance he gives to the
fact of Florentine being a spoken, living language, and thus more
truly a 'language' than the classics, and the importance he gives to
its wider diffusion at the present time than the ancient languages,
belong more properly to a detailed consideration of Salviati's
linguistic theories.[15] More significant is the manner in which he

[14] See supplementary note 3, p. 246.

[15] On the question of the concept of 'dead' and 'living' languages, and of
the relationship of this concept both to the details of the linguistic disputes, the
development of the vernacular, and Renaissance attitudes towards it, see in
particular R. G. Faithfull, 'The Concept of "Living" Language in Cinquecento
Vernacular Philology', *M.L.R.* xlviii (1953), 278–92. The question is intimately
linked with that of the relationship of Latin to Greek (itself strongly present
in this oration) which affects contemporary ideas on the place and potential of
Italian: see C. Grayson, *A Renaissance Controversy, Latin or Italian?* (Oxford,

proceeds to justify, as a preliminary, his association of Florentine with Latin and Greek as media for the process of human perfection. Whatever his eventual claims for Florentine, he clearly cannot deny to these languages some part in that function of language and literature which he began by outlining. But the mere fact that he takes the trouble to explain why Florentine should be classed, in this respect, with them, is tantamount to stating that they are the languages normally associated with these functions, of which he now wishes to give the lion's share to Florentine.

The distinction between Florentine, Latin, and Greek on the one hand, and other languages, is that the three former are 'noble'; that is to say they are distinguished from the general mass of 'non-noble' languages and from the 'lingue barbare' (amongst which he includes all the other Italian dialects and possibly other European languages as well) in that they have certain inherent superior qualities which have been developed within the discipline of a distinguished literary tradition.[16] Latin and Greek, then, are 'noble' languages, noble both in potential and in having had that potential developed and 'illustrated', and thus able to fulfil the function of language as he has expounded it. The 'lingue barbare' (the 'non-noble' languages), though living languages, lack these qualities. They have 'Nè scrittori, nè gran fatto dolcezza, nè efficacia, nè gravità, nè grandezza, nè alcuna altra di quelle parti che sogliono comunemente perpetuare i linguaggi' (F. 65). There is both lack of potential and lack of development. Latin and Greek are another matter. In them the products of the intellect have found such expression as will enable them to be communicated to other minds in the most effective possible manner, and a vehicle to perpetuate them in time—the function of language and literature as he had defined it in the early part of his oration. No classicist humanist would have disagreed with him on matters of principle or of detail. His next step, however, carries him firmly away on a new path, for he states that everything he has said of Latin and Greek 'dell'idioma nostro per tutti i segni, che intorno a questo possano desiderarsi, parimente è da credere' (F. 65). And why is it that Florentine is to be included in the 'lingue nobili',

Clarendon Press, 1960): also M. Vitale, 'Le origini del volgare nelle discussioni dei filologi del '400', *Lingua nostra*, xiv (1953), 64–9: and for a general survey the same author's *La questione della lingua* (Palermo, Palumbo, 1960).

[16] See supplementary note 4, p. 246.

to which category Latin and Greek clearly belong? The answer is
given in an analysis of both Florentine language and Florentine
literature aimed at demonstrating both their potential and their
development. With regard to the former, Florentine has inherent
characteristics which even now are effectively drawing under its
spell the whole of the civilized world, and which mark it as the
ideal literary medium. These characteristics he sums up in the
word 'dolcezza', and by means of a comparison between Florentine and Greek (itself, he says, by the admission of the Romans
themselves, a more attractive language than Latin) claims to
prove that 'niun linguaggio fu mai, e per quanto può giudicarsi
delle cose avvenire, niuno ne sarà' (F. 67) which can be compared
in this respect to Florentine.

Potentially (and let us note in passing the interest within the
history of Cinquecento culture the fact that Salviati considers the
sound of a language to be the yardstick of its excellence) Florentine
is therefore greater than Latin and Greek. As regards development—what Florentine has to offer in the way of 'content'
within the 'humanistic' programme outlined—he believes that
here Florentine has already surpassed the classical languages.
Petrarch and Dante alone are together worth the whole of what
ancient Greece and Rome can boast. Boccaccio is compared
favourably with Cicero and Demosthenes, and Petrarch with
Pindar.[17] The way to the perfection of man is through the cultivation of the humanities. It follows from what Salviati has said
that for the fulfilment of this aim Florentine language and literature, though closely followed by Latin and Greek, stand supreme.[18]

---

[17] The following extracts from the *Ercolano* indicate the closeness of depen-
dence on Varchi on this point. '*V*. (referring to the Greeks having lyric poets)
Ebbergli già, se non gli hanno oggi, ma noi avemmo, e avemo, il Petrarca. *C*.
Domin, che voi vogliate che il Petrarca solo vi vaglia per tutti e nove. *V*. Voglio,
in quanto alla qualità' (pp. 390–1); and again on the subject of the epic: '*C*.
E nell'eroico, avete voi nessuno, non dico che vinca, ma che pareggi, Omero?
V. Uno, il quale non dico il pareggia, ma lo vince. *C*. Chi? *V*. Dante' (p. 391).
And the comparison, in both authors, embraces not only the *artistic* value of the
works, but also their *moral* content.

[18] This conception of the relationship of Latin and Greek to Florentine is
behind his later assertion: 'Avvengachè in ogni guisa, per quel che si presuma, sia
per fiorir lo studio, e per vivere il pregio, della Latina lingua, sì per la sua grandezza, e splendore, sì per la nobiltà, ed eccellenza de' suoi sovrani autori: non
pur delizie delle lettere umane, ma singolar tesoro, e conserva di tante notizie,
e dottrine. Senza la qual favella, e senza i quali Autori, assai sarebbe il Mondo
men felice da riputare: oltrechè, e per la chiarezza de' predetti Autori, e per

This is the basic message of the *Orazione in lode della fiorentina favella*, and everything else it contains springs from this
message.[19]

Its first implication is that in so much as it breaks the exclusive
link between the *studia humanitatis* and the classics it relegates
these latter to, at best, a relative rather than the absolute position
which they had enjoyed in the past. It marks the take-over, by
Florentine, of their educational function: and it is the first full
declaration by Salviati of the modernist-nationalist principle of
which he was to be the champion throughout his life. He sees
the national tradition as the one through which the stated aims of
the 'perfection of Man' are to be achieved. That the nature of
humanism in Florence from the early Quattrocento pointed to the
eventual vindication of the modernist and nationalist current is
a commonplace of recent scholarship.[20] To make it a conscious
programme, with a clear analysis of the relationship to the
humanist programme of both the classical and national traditions,
and to construct a defence of the latter on the basis of this analysis,
was Salviati's achievement.

In building this oration round his conviction of the need for the
national tradition to take over from Classical Antiquity, Salviati
is not an anachronism or a crank, nor is he an isolated revolutionary. He is the spokesman of a well-established movement of his
times, one to which more and more of his contemporaries were
subscribing, but which had perhaps never, until this moment,
received such coherent, forceful expression, or been given its
full significance in the context of the age.[21] Yet it was the natural
outcome of a movement practically as old as humanism itself,
manifested in a different way long before in the Quattrocento

diffondere i concetti nelle provincie più lontane, sarà lo scrivere latinamente,
necessario di tutti i tempi' (*Avvertimenti*, Vol. i, Bk. ii, Ch. vii, p. 77).

[19] As was recognized by J. E. Spingarn, *A History of Literary Criticism in the
Renaissance* (New York, Macmillan, 1899), p. 162 (see 'Conclusion').

[20] See especially H. Baron, 'The Querelle of the Ancients and Moderns as a
Problem for Renaissance Scholarship', *Journal of the History of Ideas*, xx
(1959), 3–22, and id., *The Crisis of the Early Italian Renaissance* (Princeton,
N.J., 1955), especially Pt. IV, pp. 249–312. Also G. Margiotta, *Le origini italiane
de 'la querelle des anciens' et des modernes* (Rome, Studium, 1953).

[21] Cf. C. Trabalza, *Storia della grammatica italiana* (Bologna, Forni, repr.
1963), p. 206, who, in reference to Salviati's claim that Florentine language and
literature were superior to all others, states that Salviati 'rappresentava, s'in-
tende, ed esprimeva, un'opinione ormai non solo largamente diffusa, ma trion-
fante'.

attempts to raise the *volgare* to the dignity of an adequate literary language, and to rehabilitate the *volgare* tradition.

But Salviati, in his first public declaration of principle, does not stop at the mere assertion of the superiority of the modern national tradition and the declaration of its role. He incorporates an attack on classicism as such. Following up the favourable comparison of Florentine with classical languages and literature he says: 'E dicano pure a loro senno ciò che più lor aggrada, coloro che mostrano di stemperarsi, e di venire quasi manco alla dolcezza dei cori d'Euripide. E Dio sa poi se come molti la vanno magnificando, così ancora molti sieno quelli che la sentono veramente' (F. 69). This is an accusation of hypocrisy, or at the very least of affectation. It is a repudiation of the classicist elements of the previous century by an age which no longer appreciates either the spirit of classicism or its positive value as a contribution to developments of which this later age is the natural product.[22] Classicism to Salviati means an affected and irresponsible subservience to Antiquity, seriously damaging to that very process of self-perfection in whose name it was practised.

The dominant sense of an Italian tradition, with its accompanying anti-classicism, inspires Salviati from now on. His linguistic theory springs from it.[23] One extremely important aspect of that theory, namely his anti-latinism, which is documented principally in the *Avvertimenti*, springs from an attitude more clearly stated in this oration than anywhere else. For in the *Avvertimenti* we find that in language, too, the Italian tradition has so completely replaced the classical one that Salviati's main concern is to maintain the 'purity' of the Tuscan language (in opposition to the Quattrocento principle of its enrichment through Latin), which for him means cleansing it of Latin contamination.[24]

---

[22] See also Salviati, *Avvertimenti* (I. ii. 76), where Salviati further documents the passing of the classicist spirit by attributing the Quattrocento latinization of the language to a kind of linguistic snobbery.

[23] For anti-classicism as the mainspring of Salviati's linguistic theory see P. M. Brown, 'The Conception of the Literary "Volgare" in the Linguistic Writings of Lionardo Salviati', *Italian Studies*, xxi (1966), 57–90.

[24] See Grayson, *A Renaissance Controversy*, p. 19. Despite this, Salviati (not contradictorily as has sometimes been supposed, but completely logically) is at great pains to stress that it is not his wish to turn his readers in any way against Latin or the study of it, provided the two languages are kept distinct. Dante, Petrarch, and Boccaccio have all illustrated, he says, how men 'involti nella Latina lingua' can avoid this danger of contamination when they want to. Indeed he considers, with considerable historical acumen, that it would be

Like the rebellious younger generation which he represents, Salviati undertakes in his orations—composed over several decades—a systematic devaluation of Antiquity, striking the first blow in this very *Orazione delle lingue* when he declares:

Io conosco di molti, e uomini di gran credito, e di gran riputazione nelle lingue, ai quali più che Omero, Virgilio, e le sue opere soddisfanno, e io in alcune parti (non so che efficacia mi si sia mostrato nelle ragioni di costoro) mi sono agevolmente lasciato persuadere. Nondimanco quando io risguardo l'opera di Virgilio, e alzo punto dall'altro canto gli occhi verso quella stupenda maraviglia di Dante, non voglio dire quello che m'avvenga per non essere tenuto più resoluto e più ardito, che non mi conviene. (F. 71)

Embodied in this mock confession is the implication that in looking to classical civilization, and particularly literature, instead of to the vastly more rewarding Italian tradition, Italians have been blindly facing the wrong direction for close on two hundred years. Similarly, although Salviati's references to ancient philosophers, for example, in other orations may appear at first sight to be conforming to a long-established pattern of admiration for their achievements without revelation, these achievements are in fact systematically played down, and the shortcomings of Antiquity equally insistently brought to the fore. Whilst their efforts receive generic praise, the tone is generally and overwhelmingly a patronizing one bordering on contempt for the general inadequacy of the civilization they represent, the 'vani misteri di quei loro falsi dii da trastullo, e da gioco', the 'tenebre della loro idolatria', and 'quella loro fallace superstizione' (XIV). They lived in the 'error di tutte le falsità, e quasi nella notte dell'idolatria' (II). This darkness is contrasted with the modern world, where men, in addition to all their other qualities and achievements are 'illuminati dallo splendor della fede e dalla luce della verità stessa e da Dio' (II).

Indeed, one of the arguments he adduces to prove the superiority of the national, i.e. *volgare*, tradition over the classical is that

difficult to imagine a person handling Italian adequately without a mastery of Latin, 'Perciocchè noi stimiamo allo 'ncontro, che chi non ha buon gusto nel latino idioma, e non ha per le mani gli scrittori suoi più solenni, in questo nostro piccolo spazio avanti proceder possa, ò nella prosa, ò nel verso. E perchè 'l gusto in quella guisa si fa migliore, e più fine; utilissima cosa, al dettar bene in toscano, reputiam senza fallo l'esercitarsi nello scriver latinamente' (*Avvertimenti*, I. ii. 80–1).

since the great Italian writers represent the Christian tradition
they have, by virtue of that fact alone, something relevant and
beneficial to offer which the classics could never have.[25] Even in
this present work the attack on Gelli, who right up to his death in
the previous year was anything but an opponent of the regime, and
who had basically a good deal in common with Salviati including
a passionate love of Florence and the Florentine tradition and
a fervent admiration for Dante, may have been not entirely uninfluenced by the fact that Gelli's *Capricci* were at this very
point being severely censured by the Inquisition.

Coupled with the assessment of the comparative value of the
classical and national traditions from the educational and moral
point of view is a reappraisal of the relationship between the
civilization of Tuscany (which Salviati frequently identifies with
Florence, and both with Italy) and that of Rome. The modern
superiority asserted is not limited to language and literature.
In civil life, in military achievement, in politics, in the conquest
of knowledge, the modern Tuscan has excelled his classical
counterpart. Classical civilization and culture are now themselves
being judged by the yardstick of modern achievement and found
distinctly wanting. One of the most interesting passages in this
connection, the first of a series, occurs in this very oration, where
Salviati proclaims: 'Non comincia pure ora questa nostra con-
trada a tenere principato di fiorito idioma. Sono più di due mila
anni che i Romani potentissimi a quella lingua che in questa
provincia si parlava in quel tempo pubblicamente attendevano'
(F. 71). This image of Rome as the pupil of Tuscany is one which
Salviati develops elsewhere with persistency and determination.
It was not only in matters of language that Rome had looked to

---

[25] He writes for example of Petrarch's lyrics: 'La qual guisa di poetare, dico
quella del Petrarca, parmi che agli antichi fusse ascosa del tutto, e credo che sia uno
degli speziali privilegi della nostra favella, prodotto massimamente dalla naturale onestà, e gravità, e grandezza che essa, siccome io stimo, ha prese della religione.
Perciocchè in queste parti la Fiorentina lingua vince senza contrasto la Latina e
la Greca [again the identification of language and content]. Il che altrui materia
essendo, e da altrui trattata, e stringendomi il tempo, altramente non proverò'
(F. 72). The 'altrui' in this case may again be Varchi, though the *Ercolano* was
still in manuscript. For not only is Varchi's favourable comparison of Italian
language and literature with the classical languages and literatures manifestly
the immediate model for Salviati's (see *Ercolano*, pp. 388–440), but Varchi, too,
goes on in a most important passage to stress the Christian and moral character
of the bulk of the Italian tradition, and the consequent superiority of the latter
over the classical tradition (pp. 451–4).

Tuscany: 'Perciocchè a cui non è noto che i Romani allora che tutto il mondo prendeva da loro leggi e governo, prendevano essi da' Toscani il governo e le leggi della religione? e i loro più nobili giovinetti nelle nostre contrade sotto la cura e disciplina de' Toscani uomini mandavano ad appararla e le sagrate cose e i misteri di quella in quell'antico idioma tuttavia conservarono, che in questa provincia si parlava in quel tempo' (X).

A sense of parity of achievement ('to put it mildly', using Salviati's own term) inspires the *Orazioni*. One cannot but feel an almost nineteenth- or twentieth-century nationalist note in his interpretation of the facts he adduces, as if they revolutionized the accepted view of the relationship between the two civilizations and were yet another proof of the primacy of Tuscany over Rome.

Salviati conceives himself throughout this oration and succeeding ones as the spokesman of a civilization which, having risen to even greater heights, looks down on Classical Antiquity, and whilst using the classics freely as rhetorical material he consistently stresses the superiority of the achievements of his own times, in every field, over those of Antiquity. Indicative of the belief in parity (if not more) of achievement is the reorientation of the educational function of the classics to which his *Orazione in lode della fiorentina favella* is the monument.

The oration is also of great importance, of course, as the first statement of Salviati's position in the linguistic disputes.[26] In this connection the oration is a revealing document in that it demonstrates the relationship of dependence between Salviati's overall interpretation of the position of the *volgare* in contemporary culture and his linguistic theories. We need not analyse in detail this polemical element, in which Salviati is transformed from the passive, uncommitted pupil of Varchi into a hard-hitting

---

[26] There is no room here for a detailed examination of the relationship of all Salviati's statements in this oration to the history of the *questione della lingua*. For an exhaustive analysis of the oration from this point of view, in which every position taken by Salviati, every allusion, and every reference is related to the history of that particular aspect of the linguistic disputes, see Sozzi, *Aspetti*, pp. 109–19. Of greater immediate importance is the fact that the oration reveals the underlying vision on which Salviati's principles in the linguistic debates depend, and which gives these latter their coherence. Nevertheless, it is important to remember that almost the whole of the oration is intensely polemical, hitting out hard not only at systems and principles, but at individuals whom the author makes identifiable to his audience without mentioning them by name.

polemicist. The basis of his attitude to language is to be found in his master Varchi, on the one hand the stress on the function and importance of living usage as an indispensable element in a language which is to fulfil the functions he has outlined, and on the other the acceptance of the normalizing role of the great writers. Here as elsewhere he takes from Varchi the definition of 'language' as spoken usage, as well as that very distinction between 'noble' and 'non-noble' languages on which so much of his thesis rests. At the same time he takes up Varchi's praise of Bembo, stating unequivocally that he approves of Messer Pietro because the latter considers the literary language to be Florentine, because his attempt to draw up rules for the language was healthy and, though only by implication, because he drew attention to the 'Golden Age' of Tuscan.

From praise of Bembo he proceeds to condemnation of those who have attacked him, and he has in mind the previous generation of Accademici, especially the 'Aramei', namely Gelli (scarcely cold in his grave), Lenzoni, and Giambullari, all sworn enemies, be it noted, of his bosom friend Grazzini. In doing so Salviati reveals that he belongs to a new generation in Florentine linguistic thought. For those he attacks opposed Bembo not only as a 'foreigner' but as one who took the writers of the Trecento as a model whilst they tended to see the language as still moving towards maturity, and consequently opposed any immediate attempt at legislation. It is clear that Salviati in contrast is already thinking in terms of that reconciliation between Bembist archaism on the one hand and Florentinism on the other which was to characterize his *Avvertimenti*.

Most important of all, however, in pinpointing his position is the insistence throughout on the identity of the old and modern languages, of the language of Boccaccio and the present spoken tongue of Florence. The ideal vehicle for the perfection of Man, of which he speaks in his introduction, is not the style of the great authors considered as an entity apart from the living language, but 'la presente nostra Fiorentina favella. Questa favella, Uditori nobilissimi, che noi tutto giorno parliamo' (F. 61), which for him is identical with the language of Dante, Petrarch, and Boccaccio. Though his overall linguistic position, heavily influenced by Varchi, emerges only indirectly, and his views on the subject are largely secondary to the main issues which we have considered, we find in embryo elements to be developed twenty years later in the *Avvertimenti*.

Salviati's conception of those main issues found a ready echo in his contemporaries, whose feelings he was crystallizing and conceptualizing. We have already seen how, as long ago as 1550, Grazzini had expressed, in his *A' riformatori della lingua toscana* (see Ch. vi, p. 58), identical views on the superiority of the Italian tradition to the classical, equating at all points that Italian tradition with Florentine. Likewise in his *stanze, Contro le commedie in versi*, he praises Ariosto for spurning the classics and imitating, as he sees it, the Boccaccesque tradition.[27] His *canto carnascialesco, De' poeti*, is based solidly on the two main principles contained in Lionardo's *Orazione delle lingue*, namely the literary and linguistic primacy of Tuscany over Rome and Greece, which we have examined, and the firm identification, in these spheres, of 'Italian' and 'Florentine', which we have yet to discuss, as is clearly shown when the non-Tuscan poets sing:

> Noi scriviam tutti nella dolce e bella
> Fiorentina favella
> che per tutto si vede oggi fiorire,
> mercè de' tre maggiori
> vostri eterni splendori,
> che le dier lume tal, ch'oggi a Fiorenza
> e Roma e Grecia fanno riverenza.[28]   (4–11)

Clearly the sentiments inspiring the *Orazione* were rampant amongst Salviati's contemporaries, clamouring for expression in the reasoned, clear-sighted manner which characterizes that work. No wonder then that on hearing Salviati's oration Grazzini burst into unrestrained jubilation, addressing to its author—'O dotto, o saggio, o leggiadro Salviati'—a *sonettessa* which sums up the content of the oration. Salviati's work—Grazzini even echoes the accusation of hypocrisy found in the oration—has his unqualified, unconditional support and approval, and he regards the oration as an overwhelming triumph for the cause.[29] There

---

[27] Verzone, *Le rime burlesche, Ottave*, No. XCV, *inc.* 'Apollo vuol che sempre un calzaiuolo', pp. 424–6.

[28] Ibid., *Canti carnascialeschi*, No. X, 'De' poeti' (*inc.* 'L'abito nostro, donne, e la corona'), pp. 178–80.

[29] Verzone, *Sonetti*, No. CXLIII (*inc.* 'Di questa opinion, che ve ne pare'), pp. 115–16. It is extremely significant that in this poem Grazzini refers to the fact that certain of the material of Salviati's *Orazione delle lingue*—and, to be

was certainly no doubt in *his* mind as to the significance of Salviati's address to the Accademia Fiorentina, or its timeliness.

Yet whilst stressing their common views over a wide field, we must beware of carrying the comparison too far and imagining that Salviati shared any part of the rebellious, anti-authoritarian current with which Grazzini, the 'arch-anti-pedant' was so closely associated. From this current, to which belonged the Bernis and the Aretinos, Salviati was, and remained, utterly alien; and his anti-classicism, whilst constituting a lifelong bond between him and Lasca, producing identical reactions on many matters, most emphatically did not owe its origins in the slightest degree to any anti-authoritarian, anti-imitation principle *per se*.

For this very reason the importance of Salviati's anti-classicism is historically much greater than it would have been had it been a mere facet of this rebellious current with its call for freedom, release from the restricting bonds of academic pedantry, liberty of invention, closer adherence to life, and originality rather than imitation. His quarrel was with a specific authority, not authority

exact, the assessment of the relationship of the Italian to the classical tradition— is to be the subject of an imment work of Varchi. The passage in question is worth quoting in full:

> Ma certo i lor migliori,
> Virgilio, Orazio, Pindaro e Omero,
> appetto a Dante non vagliono un zero.
>   Del Petrarca non chiero,
> nè del Boccaccio dir, che per mia fede,
> darien lor trenta e la caccia sul piede.
>   Ne 'l volgo anche s'avvede
> del suo gran danno, anzi chi manco intende,
> più meraviglia degli antichi prende:
>   e di qui si comprende
> che chi più chi meno ognun sel becca:
>   or questa grave pecca,
> questo atro velo e questi chiusi varchi
> fian tosto aperti dal gran padre Varchi.   (24–38)

A madrigal from Grazzini to Ser Frosino Lapini the classicist grammarian, also written in the moment of euphoria following Salviati's oration, is likewise a cry of triumph, celebrating a victory of *volgare* culture over classical, especially lines 3–7:

> O sfortunati Romani ed Achei
> O miseri Latini, o mesti Grai,
> Chi creduto aria mai
> ch'un Fiorentin bizzarro, ancor novizio,
> mandasse il Lazio e Grecia in precipizio.

(Verzone, *Madrigali*, No. I (*inc.* 'O sommi eterni dei'), p. 221.)

in itself: and what he opposed was the authority of the classics over a modern tradition and culture for which he desired independence.

It is in this sense that Salviati is one with Grazzini, who in his enthusiasm even takes up the theme of awakening from the darkness of blind attachment to Antiquity which figures in Lionardo's *Orazione delle lingue*. It is the theme of Grazzini's sonnet *Di questa opinion, che ve ne pare* (on the *Orazione*), and is developed extensively in his *madrigalessa, Nelle esequie di Michelagnolo Buonarroti* (1564), where he says:

> Se sono stati già gli uomini ciechi
> e vivuti di notte infino ad ora,
> venuto [sic] è l'aurora anzi il dì chiaro,
> che le tenebre e l'ombre ha già sgombrato.[30]

Here and elsewhere Grazzini seemed to find in Salviati an articulate formulator of ideas which governed his own thought and behaviour and figured in his compositions, though fitfully and never in such a compelling manner. However specious some of the logic of the *Orazione*, Salviati certainly is formulating something which his contemporaries vaguely feel and wish to hear confirmed, Grazzini amongst them. And although, amongst those of Salviati's fellow citizens who had in recent decades expressed themselves with vigour on the question of the *volgare* and its relationship to Latin, it was probably Varchi who was most strongly present in Salviati's mind, nevertheless Anton Francesco Grazzini was exerting a strong influence, as ever, behind the scenes.

Yet despite its identification with this unique historical moment the oration, and indeed the whole of Salviati's anti-classicist, modernist-nationalist campaign, acquires added interest when one traces back to its earliest origins this long-standing struggle, of which Salviati's campaign is but the most recent manifestation, between a native Italian culture on the one hand, and classicism on the other: back, that is, to the late fourteenth and early fifteenth centuries.

At this point the champions of the 'national' culture born of the communal revolution were fighting a rearguard action against the attacks of classicism. Francesco Landini, Cino Rinuccini, and their associates had made comparisons between the achievements of the

---

[30] Verzone, *Madrigalesse*, No. XLIII (*inc.* 'Dante e 'l Petrarca e 'l Boccaccio passati'), pp. 314-15.

native tradition and the classical, concluding in favour of the
former, as did Varchi and Salviati. Coluccio Salutati's defence of
Petrarch's superiority, on the grounds that he represents a superior
modern tradition, a Christian tradition, could without discord be
integrated into Lionardo's orations, as could much of the work
of the anti-humanist Benedetto Accolti, who in his *Dialogus de
Praestantia Virorum sui Aevi* covers much the same ground as
Salviati, affirming the superiority of his own times over Classical
Antiquity in virtually every respect.[31] But in the times of Accolti
the vigorous offensive of humanistic classicism was irresistible.
Salviati, on the other hand, is conscious of leading the massive
assault on the weakened ranks of classicism in decline—weakened
already by several decades of a process known as the 'Italianization
of humanism' in which such men as Salviati's friend Sperone
Speroni, with his *Dialogo delle lingue* in defence of the 'volgare'
and its culture, and even Bembo (whom Salviati defends vigorously in this very oration), with his substitution of Italian for
Latin, had played an important part. If Salviati's *Orazione delle
lingue* is a landmark, it is built on foundations laid steadily and
persistently through the century.

As it marks the culmination, the point of articulate self-awareness,
of a long-standing movement, so it is also a spring-board for
Salviati himself. The nationalist militancy first revealed in this
oration governs his attitude from now on to the critical, literary,
and linguistic questions of his times. When in the disputes over the
Gerusalemme Liberata in the eighties (see Ch. xiv) he declares the
superiority of Ariosto over Tasso, it is on the principle of Italian
modernism that he does so; and when he champions the language
of Petrarch and Boccaccio it is because that language represents
for him the touchstone of excellence in modern Italian undebased
by Latin contamination.

---

[31] So striking, in fact, is the resemblance in attitude between Salviati and
Accolti, so distant from each other in time, and at opposite ends of a historical
cycle, that a direct influence of the writings of Accolti on Salviati would be
worth investigating. For a discussion, and an analysis of the attitudes of early
anti-humanism, see Margiotta, *Le origini*, esp. Ch. v, pp. 65–77. On p. 75 Margiotta quotes Accolti, who leans heavily on the moral and religious superiority
of the national tradition and of his contemporaries 'apud quas maior cartias,
purior fides, minor nocendi cupiditas, minor avaritia et crudelitas, minus
crebra delicta omnia, et virtutes multae reperiuntur'. From B. Accolti, *Dialogus
de Praestantia Virorum sui Aevi* in Filippo Villani, *Liber de Civitatis Florentiae
Famosis Civibus* (Florence, 1847), p. 127.

Thus the *Orazione in lode della fiorentina favella* announces Salviati's future role as the champion of the modern tradition. But this is by no means all. This modern nationalism was an Italian phenomenon, not merely a Florentine one. Yet throughout the oration there is implied the firm identification of 'Italian' and 'Florentine', with no compromise even entertained. Even the inoffensive Tolomei, himself a Tuscan though not a Florentine, is attacked as one who with 'la bocca piena di vocaboli maremmani e maremmanamente parlando' had had the impertinence to suggest that the word 'Tuscan', accepted by Salviati himself as applicable to the literary language, might be considered to refer to anything but pure Florentine.

This identification had always been in some form a feature of the Florentine linguistic outlook from Machiavelli and Martelli through Lenzoni and Gelli to Borghini and Varchi, and in the context of the history of Italy and her language a clash between the two linguistic worlds of the Florentines, who were aware of the identity of the standard literary language with their native speech, and of the non-Florentines, who refused to accept the dictates of Florence in regard to what was now common property, was inevitable. But it is on this point of Florentinism that the worlds of language and politics, as clearly seen in Cosimo's edict establishing the Academy, came together in Florence. Thus, the second vital feature of the role which Salviati took on in this oration was that of the spokesman of the inextricable identity of linguistic and political nationalism in Florence. The role which Cosimo had cast for the Academy has already been touched upon: this oration serves as its policy-statement.

For the successful conclusion in 1555 of the War of Siena was the culmination of a process which had restored to Florence and Tuscany order, peace, justice, an appearance (however deceptive) of prosperity, and, most important of all, self-respect, and international prestige. By this war Florence fulfilled that aspiration to control all Tuscany which had characterized her political thinking since the fourteenth century. Only little Lucca remained independent. The background in the early days of Cosimo's rule had been a grim struggle for survival, in which the Florentines soon identified themselves and their state with the absolute ruler who at the same time was eliminating opposition internally and absorbing all activity into the service of the state. By the sixties

the erstwhile Florentine republicanism, particularly in intellectual
quarters, had been largely replaced by recognition of the regime
as an irreversible reality corresponding to the exigencies of the
times, and by a patriotic, rhetorical nationalism characteristic of
the absolute regime ancient or modern.

As a background feature to cultural activity in Florence this
fact is of great importance, for amongst its most damaging
concomitants was an accentuation of the process already in
motion of the narrowing of the Florentine outlook to a point
at which it was entirely circumscribed by its own standards,
judgements, and interests. It is this restricted Florentine nationalism which characterizes and determines the attitudes, reactions,
and behaviour of the Florentines in the face of the more pressing
cultural problems of the times. In an age when Florence herself
was moving, culturally, from the centre to the periphery, and when
an 'Italian' nationalism was rising which sought cultural unity in
the absence of political unity, this rabid Florentine nationalism,
inevitably fostered by the salient aspects of Cosimo's state,
exacerbated and exasperated an already unavoidable cultural
clash between Florence and the rest of Italy. Educated and
indoctrinated in the service of the state, the new Florentine was
virtually incapable of seeing beyond it. For him it was an absolute,
and its every trivial manifestation, setting its own standard and
never seen in perspective, represented a peak of achievement.

Salviati reflects this atmosphere of 'no compromise'. Conscious
of fulfilling the wishes of his Duke he enjoins the Academicians
to greater efforts in nurturing and improving their language.
Joining battle with Gelli, who had expressed doubts as to
whether, without the political backing enjoyed by Latin, Florentine
could impose itself as the latter had done,[32] Salviati counters sharply
that Florentine is backed by a far greater force—its *dolcezza*.
'Questa più che la Monarchia dell'Impero', he says, 'e più che
altra cosa non potrebbe giammai, della perpetuanza v'assicura
della vostra favella. Troppo maggior balìa, e troppo maggior

---

[32] At the same time, like most of his contemporaries, Gelli too championed
the beauty of the *volgare* in relation to the classical languages: this beauty he
said was such '. . . che tu non puoi in maniera alcuna credere, o immaginarti,
che e' fusse più bello udire, o Cesare, o Cicerone, o qual altro Romano che sia'.
From Gelli, 'Lettera sopra la difficultà di ordinare detta lingua', prefaced to
P. Giambullari, *De la lingua che si parla e scrive a Firenze* (Florence, 1551),
p. 11. And see pp. 11–12 in general.

imperio che i Romani mai non ebbero, sopra gli umani appetiti ha la dilettazione' (F. 69).

Speaking these words, which he knows represent the will of Cosimo, Salviati here becomes the very personification of both uncompromising Florentine nationalism and political conformism, as he is when he calls upon the Accademici to perfect their language and assert the supremacy of Florence as the ultimate linguistic authority in Italian. First of all, new works are needed: the Accademia must draw up the rules of the language. In keeping with the function imposed on it by Cosimo it must effect the 'Florentinization' of all culture, transferring into the (strictly Florentine) *volgare* all the philosophical, medical, legal, and theological works hitherto only existing in Latin and Greek, so that 'gli autori delle scienze, e dell'arti e delle professioni, nè più barbari, nè più barbaramente come oggi si leggeranno' (F. 78–9). For one moment Latin plumbs the depths of humiliation; for it, too, in the context of Salviati's humanistic vision, is classed amongst the *lingue barbare*.

The so-called 'divulgative' function of the Academy, into which this call for translations fits, as it does into Salviati's vision of the replacement of the classical languages by the *volgare* in the fullest and most comprehensive sense, had been a feature of the Academy from its earliest times, and one whose interpretation had had very varied nuances. Gelli, as is well known, saw this function within the context of a passionate humanistic belief in the morally uplifting nature of knowledge and in the duty of Man to benefit his neighbour by communicating this knowledge, including knowledge and understanding of the Christian faith. On such principles indeed many a Quattrocento humanist—and the most outstanding in this respect was probably Alberti—had based his defence of the use of the *volgare* rather than Latin. The argument had had a continuous history through to Sperone Speroni. In the latter's *Dialogo*, moreover, the philosopher Pomponazzi is made to say that only the lack of good translations into Italian, which lack obliges even the greatest intellects to waste their time on linguistic studies before they can read indispensable texts, prevents the 'moderns' from surpassing the scientists and philosophers of Antiquity.[33]

---

[33] 'Noi, vani più che la canna, pentiti quasi d'aver lasciato la cuna ed essere uomini divenuti, tornati un'altra volta fanciulli, altro non facciamo dieci o venti

Thus Salviati is within a well-established tradition of considerable strength and diffusion when he calls for this wholesale transfer of knowledge into the *volgare*. Yet he cannot be credited with any related *moral* vision such as characterized certain of his humanist predecessors. His aim is the glory of Florence within the overall victory of the modern standard through which he believes the humanist programme can be achieved. The crowning triumph will come, he says, when the position of Florence as the centre and universal point of reference is recognized by all institutions of learning in the civilized world, all of which 'riconosceranno questo luogo per capo, a questo luogo come le linee al cerchio, tutti si ridurranno' (F. 79).

In this remarkable first address to the Academy, then, the finest of his orations with a power, a punch, a close-knit coherence, and a perfection of construction corresponding to deep sincerity of sentiment passionately expressed, Salviati becomes the ideal mouthpiece of Florence under the regime. The Italian nationalist anti-classical revolt is not only sanctioned but fervently preached as a sacred duty: at the same time there is the total identification of 'Italian' with 'Florentine', the unyielding imposition of *fiorentinità* on *italianità*: finally there is the further identification of Florentine language and literature with the Florentine state, all corresponding perfectly to the Florentines' view of their position in Italy, a view fostered by the blind nationalism characterizing an absolute regime in which the Florentine Academy was doomed to exist for the greater glory of the State.

In an impassioned peroration Salviati brought together more firmly the two threads, the cultural and the political, reminding the Accademici that the idea of the Academy was in the first place Cosimo's, that it was his desire that they should devote all their efforts to the 'esaltazione di questo luogo', and calling upon the Accademici, in the name of Cosimo, in his (Salviati's) own name, and in that of the *Tre Corone* and their Mother Florence, to dedicate themselves to their great task.

With the applause of an enthusiastic public ringing in his ears

anni di questa vita, che imparare a parlare chi Latino, chi Greco, ed alcuno, come Dio vuole, Toscano.' It must be stressed that Pomponazzi's and Speroni's attitude to translations was by no means identical to that of the Florentines. But their belief in the need for them can nevertheless be integrated into the general movement of the transfer of culture into the *volgare*.

it was a new Salviati who stepped down from the rostrum in the Sala de' Dugento on the last day of April 1564. Friends, academicians, politicians, merchants, men of letters, and administrators rushed to congratulate him, for in the place of the turner of elegant phrases, the mere disciple of Varchi, there stood a man to be reckoned with, and whose friendship was to be sought, a man who was at once a revolutionary and yet the perfect representative and spokesman of the Establishment.

VII

BENEDETTO VARCHI

THIS eloquent championing of the *volgare* may well have enhanced Lionardo's credit with Cosimo. There is no doubt that amongst contemporaries it was considered to have done so. It therefore created a healthy respect for the author, who was now regarded as one of the foremost orators in the *volgare* and a contender for the crown of Varchi and Adriani. Indeed, it was chiefly on his orations that his reputation was still for some time to depend.

Salviati's services were constantly in demand, and his contemporaries who (Corbinelli excepted) spared these works no praises obviously derived considerable sincere pleasure from them, though ulterior motives for some of the praise are by no means to be excluded. Yet today the orations are quoted only to illustrate the corruption of taste by ephemeral fashion, atmosphere, and circumstances which we cannot recapture, or to ridicule the rhetorical excesses which at the time passed for eloquence. The modern reader, deriving little or no pleasure from them, appreciates with difficulty the enthusiasm they aroused in the author's own times.

Having acquired importance during the period of early humanism, the oration still enjoyed a tremendous vogue in the late sixteenth century within the context of academic society, of the linguistic disputes, and of the general upsurge of rhetoric. Yet despite its popularity it was thoroughly decadent, the plaything of erudition and of the pedestrian rhetoric of the *letterato*.[1] The form of eloquence most practised was the *orazione in lode* — *gratulatoria*, *apologetica*, or *funebre* — and it is to this category almost exclusively that Salviati's orations belong,[2] including

[1] See A. Galletti, *L'eloquenza italiana* (Milan, Vallardi, 1938), p. 592; E. Santini, *Storia dell'eloquenza italiana dal Concilio Tridentino ai nostri giorni*, 2 vols. (Palermo, Sandron, 1928), ii: *Gli oratori civili*, pp. 30–50.

[2] Those published are eighteen in number: nine funerary orations, six of them of a standard type for public delivery (*Michelangelo, Varchi, Cosimo de' Medici, Pier Vettori, Cardinal Luigi d'Este, Donno Alfonso d'Este*) and the other three *confortatorie* (Garzia I, II, and III); four are *apologetiche* (*Giustizia,*

a composition following close on the heels of the *Fiorentina favella*, namely the funeral oration for Michelangelo. This last colossus of the Italian Renaissance had died in Rome on 17 February 1564, and his body had arrived in Florence, in circumstances surrounded by mystery, on 10 March for burial in Santa Croce.

Michelangelo was one of the big fish who escaped Cosimo, despite the latter's persistent angling to get him back, and though he had been in his own fashion a republican it was typical of the regime that he should be honoured in Florence as no other artist ever had been, since he added lustre to the image of the city. Cosimo agreed to a funeral service in San Lorenzo requested by a delegation from the Accademia del Disegno including Bronzino, Vasari, Ammannati, and Borghini: he also agreed to appoint Salviati's friend and protector Varchi the funerary orator and to foot the bill himself for the magnificent catafalque and splendid decorations in the church.[3]

Varchi's official oration, delivered on 14 August, was printed almost immediately.[4] Grazzini, characteristically, praised it as yet another example of the literary and linguistic triumph of Florence over Athens and Rome.[5] In the meantime Salviati was busy producing his own oration for the occasion, in the accompanying dedication of which he tells us that he was 'commanded' to take upon himself the task, whilst discreetly omitting to mention

Religione, Religione militare, Fiorentina favella); one is an *orazione gratulatoria* (*Incoronazione di Cosimo de' Medici*); one is *apologetico-esortativa* (*Religione di Santo Stefano*); and the last three are formal addresses (though their content could on occasion justify the description *esortative*) (*Nel prendere il suo consolato* I and II; *Nel lasciare il suo consolato*). For a list of the orations see Appendix B. Large Roman numerals in the text refer to numbering in this list.

[3] See D. Moreni, *Pompe funebri celebrate nell'imp. e real. basilica di San Lorenzo* (Florence, Magheri, 1827), p. 79. See also Corazzini (ed.), *Diario*, p. 139, and Cosimo, *Lettere* (ed. Spini), pp. 197–9, letters to Borghini and Vasari of 12.11.64.

[4] B. Varchi, *Orazione funerale fatta, e recitata nell'esequie di Michelangelo Buonarroti in Firenze nella chiesa di San Lorenzo* (Florence, Giunti, 1564). The dedication is to Borghini. For a survey of all manifestations in Florence in favour of Michelangelo, and in particular a critical examination of the anonymous *Esequie* aimed at determining their authorship, see *The Divine Michelangelo: the Florentine Academy's Homage on his Death in 1564, a Facsimile Edition of Esequie del Divino Michelangelo Buonarroti Firenze 1564* introduced, translated and annotated by R. and M. Wittkower (London, Phaidon Press, 1964).

[5] *Nell'esequie di Michelagnol Buonarroti* (*inc.* 'Dante e 'l Petrarca e 'l Boccaccio passati', Verzone, op. cit., pp. 314–15).

whence the command emanated.[6] The work may well have been undertaken at the request of the Florentine Academy, since no other official contribution seems to have been made by them, the well-known *Esequie* being associated with the Accademia del Disegno. At all events the individual, or individuals, allowed him complete freedom in his dedication of the work, and his choice fell on the Apostolic Protonotary Piero Carnesecchi. Despite his shrewd opportunism, Salviati was pitifully unlucky in his dedications.

In this case one cannot help but wonder to what extent this was a calculated risk aimed at pleasing Cosimo, for however firmly Carnesecchi was at that moment ensconced in Florence enjoying ducal favour, the fact was that as an ecclesiastic associated with earlier reform movements in the days of Valdès, Pole, Contarini, he had twice been summoned to Rome to answer charges of heresy, once in 1546 when reaction was in its infancy, and again in 1556 in the very different religious climate of Paul IV. Discharged on the first occasion, the death of Paul IV had saved him the second, and throughout Cosimo had pleaded in his favour, grateful to him for remaining loyal despite tempting bait dangled by the *fuorusciti*, and perhaps convinced that whatever fanciful ideas he held they did not amount to heresy with which he, Cosimo, would have little truck. Indeed, Cosimo was proud to see himself as a promoter of counter-reformation activity.

Probably under the impression that the Apostolic Protonotary's doctrinal aberrations were a thing of the past, Salviati does not stint his praises. Some of them, such as his statement that Carnesecchi would have reached the pinnacle of his profession had he not preferred virtue to honours and glory to ambition, must have had an ironical ring when reread in the days of intensified religious intolerance, when Carnesecchi went to a martyr's death for what he believed to be the truth. There had been some previous contact between the two men, but even Salviati's ambiguous phraseology fails to hide the fact that it was of the slightest, consisting of Carnesecchi's 'honorata presenza in un solo giorno' and of a request to Salviati for a copy of the work. This latter request is the reason Lionardo gives for the dedication of the oration to Carne-

---

[6] L. Salviati, *Orazione in morte di Michelagnolo Buonarroti* (Florence, Figliuoli di Lorenzo Torrentino, 1564). Ded. lett. to P. Carnesecchi is dated 20. 9.64, and refers to 'coloro, per comandamento de' quali, già sono molti giorni, sopra le spalle questo carico m'arrecai'.

secchi, a dedication which must have appeared to him at the time wise and advantageous.

Probably Salviati's assertion in the dedication that he had been asked to write the oration some considerable time earlier is true, since the dedication consists mainly of a defence of the work itself (which makes only fleeting references to Michelangelo), probably against critical voices which had observed that 'it did not correspond to the subject which it was supposed to be praising'.[7] And if the oration was well known before it was printed, which it clearly was, it may well have been delivered before a private audience—perhaps the 'solo giorno' on which Carnesecchi had honoured Salviati by his presence?

Contemporaries seem to have murmured in private that this most recent product of Cosimo's protégé, in addition to being off the subject, was not quite up to his usual standard. It is indeed one of Salviati's most tedious compositions. A dull stylistic exercise drawing heavily on Varchi's *Della maggioranza delle arti* of 1549, it occupies a not very honourable place in the mass of sixteenth-century literature on the relationship of the arts, to which innumerable predecessors and contemporaries, artistic and otherwise, from Leon Battista Alberti and Leonardo da Vinci to Vasari, Cellini, Pontormo, Bronzino, Tribolo, and Varchi made contributions of widely varying interest and importance. Even Lionardo's friend Lasca disputed with Cellini on the subject, the former championing painting, the latter sculpture.[8]

Being sub-titled *In lode della pittura* it concludes with a judgement in favour of painting as the noblest of the arts, as the occasion presumably appeared to demand, despite the fact that Michelangelo himself had discreetly extricated himself from any commitment on the question by telling Varchi that in view of their common end the arts of painting and sculpture could be considered of equal nobility, and that people would do well to 'lassare tante dispute, perchè vi va più tempo che a far le figure'.[9] Yet

[7] For these criticisms see D. Moreni, op. cit., p. 84. Salviati may have been obliged to avoid material already in Varchi's and others' orations on the same subject.

[8] See P. Barocchi, *Trattati d'arte del Cinquecento* (Bari, Laterza, 1960); also C. Milanesi, *Trattati . . . di B. Cellini* (Florence, 1857), Preface, pp. xx-xxxv, and A. Mabellini, *Delle rime di B. Cellini* (Rome, 1885), pp. 25–77.

[9] See the letter from Michelangelo to Varchi, in *Due lezioni di M. Benedetto Varchi* (Florence, Torrentino, 1549). In the second 'si disputa quale sia più nobile arte, la Scultura, o la Pittura, con una lettera d'esso Michelagnolo'.

despite the dullness of the content, the dedication contains material
of prime importance for assessing Salviati's position, in the form
of a declaration of methods and principles in the composition of
orations. Especially important is his analysis of his own practice
in relation to the theory and practice of the ancients. At first sight
it might appear that in defending his own 'aim' and 'method' (the
two elements in which he considers an oration may be faulty)
he relies on the authority of the ancients entirely, especially in
justifying the way he uses the three *mezzi*, i.e. loosely, style,
construction, and subject-matter. It is their words and their theory
which permit him to stray from the strict limits of the subject
announced, and at the same time he is prepared to depart from
the traditional order of procedure precisely because they do not
condemn such a departure.[10] Thus he declares that he differs from
certain of his contemporaries as to the *interpretation* of the precepts
and the example of the ancient writers on rhetoric, and reserves
for himself considerable freedom of action.

If an examination of his statement of theory were concluded
at this point the impression would be that Salviati accepted
unconditionally and apparently uncritically, in a classicist–
humanist spirit, the authority of the ancients. But on the subject
of procedure, after saying that what his critics consider obligatory
is found neither in the theory nor in the practice of the ancients,
he adds (referring to Isocrates, Aristotle, and Cicero) that even
were it found there, 'ad ogni modo, non essendo su la ragione
appoggiata, per legge non la torrei'. And with this statement is to
be linked another. Though admitting that in the case of one of the
mezzi, namely style, he has not achieved the standard he might
have hoped for he adds: 'Nondimanco, se dietro a questo non son
degno di lode, non sono peravventura, secondo il moderno scrivere,
ne anco degno di gravissimo biasimo.' Modern composition, he
here states unequivocally, is not necessarily subject, in all its
aspects, to the dictates of ancient rhetoric.

Taken together, these two statements represent a miniature of
that outlook on literature, culture, and life, which we have seen
developing even in Salviati's early life. First there is the critical

---

[10] Salviati may be deliberately opposing the theory of Francesco Bonciani
(a friend nevertheless) who in a lecture to the Accademia degli Alterati had
laid down rigid laws for the minutest details of the composition of funeral
orations.

attitude towards the classics which, though representing a perhaps unrivalled body of information, advice, and example, invaluable for reference, are no more than this, and must yield in authority to the considered opinion of modern representatives of an Italian culture no less distinguished. The relationship of Italian culture to classical is at least a relationship of equals, with the bias, as was clearly and boldly stated in the *Fiorentina favella* oration, in favour of Italian. Quotation of the classics, as example or authority, remains only a habit of mind.

The second point is the stress on 'reason' as opposed to the mere 'example' of the classics. Classical examples may conveniently illustrate, and conform to, 'reason', but the latter is by no means circumscribed by them. They are, that is to say, themselves merely examples of a higher principle which can be found exemplified also (and perhaps even better) in Italian works differing substantially in outward character and representing another culture. Both points are illustrated fully in the text of the orations themselves, and eventually assume front-rank importance in the disputes over the *Gerusalemme Liberata*.

As a result of this firm belief in the equal authority of an established modern Italian tradition Salviati claims, and uses, freedom to accept or reject classical authority, both in language and style (though neither of these is discussed in detail) and in the 'ordinamento' or 'construction' of the oration, by which means Lionardo says he intends principally to achieve his aim. This stress on the importance of 'construction' is of particular interest. For he asserts that the legitimacy of the subject-matter depends entirely on the skill employed in this 'ordinamento', in the 'ragioni e argomenti' which can alone make the subject-matter relevant to the 'end'. It is the very soul of the oration, for, as he himself asks, 'quali cose sono tra loro sì diverse, che l'oratore in questa guisa non possa insiememente adattare?' Here he captures the spirit of much of his own writing, for it amounts to a defence of *form*. The subject-matter is not to be held together by an inner necessity brought out and thrown into relief by skilful construction. On the contrary, the orator may take any material whatsoever and 'con la parte principale annodarla e appicicarla convenientemente'. A composition without inner compulsion, depending for its very existence on formal unity in the narrowest sense, and delighting in its external harmoniousness: this is how Salviati conceives the oration, and nothing could be a more appropriate comment on the *Orazioni* as we see them today.[11]

Between theory and practice there is, moreover, a remarkable correspondence. So secondary a place does content take to 'la bella forma' that in matters which are of no real interest to him, basing his arguments on the same authorities, Salviati can contradict gaily in one oration what he had said in the last. In the *Fiorentina favella* oration, in which Salviati was deeply committed to the exposition of his commanding vision of the *volgare*, the great writers are proved to be the supreme guides to Man in his aim of earthly happiness, in the Michelangelo oration, where expediency governs his words, he is quite happy to place painters, who in reality mean little or nothing to him, at the pinnacle of a hierarchy of artistic nobility.

Yet despite these tributes (however contradictory) to writers and painters, when speaking to Cosimo's Knights of St. Stephen he declares that anyone comparing Homer, Cicero, Aristotle, and their ilk (universally regarded, he had previously said, as 'earthly Gods') to the Hannibals and Scipios of this world, i.e. the warriors such as formed his audience, would be laughed to scorn. In the *Fiorentina favella* he can tell us how the Greeks 'made Homer a God', but with equal conviction in speaking to the above-mentioned soldiers he can state that only men of their profession 'sono stati al mondo in vita come semidei adorati, e dopo morte come Dii adorati' (XV). Words, sounds, and constructional patterns were what interested Salviati in the orations as in the poems, and in general the content was dictated entirely by the occasion, formulated with the most complete independence from aspiration to truth or even consistency. Only when we transcend detail do we find anything approaching a coherent view of life or letters on the part of the author, and only within an extremely limited range, virtually all relating to that vision of contemporary culture of which the *Orazione in lode della fiorentina favella* was the manifesto.

Of very minor importance, therefore, is the bulk of the content of this, and in general of other, orations. But in his statements on

[11] Here, on the other hand, consciously or unconsciously, Salviati is much more in line with Bonciani, whose rules for the composition of funeral orations (though Salviati does not agree that they should be regarded as binding, see p. 84) are formulated with precisely this object in view, namely that of providing a 'form' when the orator has in fact nothing whatsoever to say.

the ordering of the material Salviati stresses the importance of *originality*,[12] seeing once again very closely into his own art. Three out of the preceding four orations were those in praise of Don Garzia, in which Lionardo seeks cleverness—'originality'— at all costs, relying in this case on the most outlandish paradoxes and antitheses. He displays great ingenuity in evolving a coherent pattern out of the extravagant ideas from which he begins, and one of the attractions of his orations, in an age increasingly spellbound by formal virtuosity and in this sense moving towards the baroque, must have been precisely Lionardo's skill in maintaining in patterned equilibrium the elements with which he juggled.

Yet despite this striving for formal novelty, the treatment strikes the modern reader as thoroughly stereotyped. Whatever the ostensible subject, the arguments proceed from the same *a priori* bases towards predetermined conclusions to which they are trimmed and adapted, and we are well aware that the same material, sources, and authorities could with little effort on the part of the author have been used to produce quite different conclusions had he had other ends in view. The process by which, in the Michelangelo oration, Salviati contrives to place painting firmly at the apex of a pyramidal hierarchy of works which enable Man to fulfil his earthly function by exhorting him to virtue, belittling successively as he does so both philosophical treatises and poetry (despite his impassioned reasoning to the contrary in the *Fiorentina favella* oration) is the supreme example of this technique.

The influence of Varchi, at its highest point generally in Salviati's production of 1564, is discernible throughout this oration on Michelangelo, and Messer Benedetto's presence can be discerned in the fact that when Salviati here for the first time manifests an interest in the current question of Poetics, his attitude to it bears the heavy moral emphasis characteristic of Varchi in general and *Lettura sulla poesia* in particular. Art, he repeats *ad nauseam*, exists for the moral purpose of inciting to virtue. His thesis is an adaptation of Varchi's with no sign of a personal direction, but given Salviati's vigour and determination in pursuing any line taken up it is no surprise to find that in December of the

---

[12] 'Essendo in ciò il fine dello Oratore il lodare: quanto ciascheduno ciò facendo dalla vulgata consuetudine si diparte, tanto merita al mio parere maggior commendazione e più lode. Et io in quelle poche, che ho fatte, ho sempre avuto davanti agli occhi questo proponimento.'

same year he delivered a lecture to the Florentine Academy entitled *Della poetica lezzion prima*. With the aid of the quasi-Aristotelian definition of poetry as 'habito d'operare in subbietto esteriore con ragione' he proceeds to demonstrate that poetry is 'arte', first proving by dint of quotations from the *Ethics*, the *Physics*, and the *Metaphysics* and other books of Aristotle (whose side he never for one moment leaves) that it is also a 'habito' and finally confuting the arguments which the Platonists, represented on this occasion by Bastiano Antinori,[13] had adduced to prove otherwise. Once having confirmed the definition he proceeds to develop the other themes he had proposed, namely the 'agente', 'fine', 'forma', and 'materia' of poetry.[14]

The openly polemical character of this work links it with the previous lectures given on the same subject, and so, though this work is of some minor interest within the framework of contemporary critical discussions,[15] it is primarily an intellectual exercise of an occasional nature, in which Salviati is not always on the surest of critical and philosophical ground, and not always as Aristotelian as he imagines himself to be.[16]The occasional character of the work explains the discrepancies between it and other compositions, likewise dictated by no inner necessity, on allied subjects, and particularly the 'paradosso' *Il Lasca*, written in 1583, of which the subject is the relationship between art and history,

[13] S. Salvini, *Fasti*, p. 170: 'Parlò ancora il Salviati [i.e. in the Consulship of Valori in 1564] in due lezioni della Poetica, come Peripatetico, avendone innanzi ragionato come Platonico, Bastiano Antinori.'

[14] The manuscript of this work, non-autograph, unpublished, is in the B.N.C., Florence, Cod. Magl. VII, 307: 'Della Poetica di Lionardo Salviati, allo Ill.mo ed Ecc.mo Sig.re Don Francesco de Medici, Principe di Firenze e di Siena suo Signore, Lezzion Prima, da lui pubblicamente recitata nella Fior. Accademia la iiia Dom.ca di dicembre nel Consolato di M. Baccio Valori nel MDLXIII.' For a description of the manuscript and of the relationship of the *Lezzion prima* to a *Lettura terza* sent by Salviati to the Cavalier Gaddi in 1566 (see p. 123) see P. M. Brown, 'L'edizione del 1873 delle "Prose inedite del cav. Leonardo Salviati" ', *Rinascimento*, viii, No. 1 (June 1957), 111–29. (Whilst this work was in the proof stage, the *Lezzion prima*, but not the dedicatory letter, has been published by B. Weinberg and its title is *Trattati di poetica e retorica del' 500*, Vol. 2, Bari, Laterza, 1970, pp. 585–611.)

[15] G. E. Spingarn, *Literary Criticism*, p. 88, pointed to Salviati's use in this work of the term 'umori' as being a possible critical precedent to Jonson's.

[16] See B. Weinberg, *A History of Literary Criticism in the Italian Renaissance* (Univ. of Chicago Press, Ill., 1961), especially i. 494–6. The author comes to this conclusion after his own careful examination of the content, and writes: 'Salviati finds no philosophical impropriety in considering a single element as now material, now instrument.'

and which consists at least in part of an attack on poetry, in favour of history, from an entirely Platonic point of view.

Time and the development of Salviati do not explain the discrepancies. The conclusion in the *Lasca*, that poetry is greatly inferior to history and to some extent a danger, flatly contradicts this lecture, along with all that Salviati had said in the Michelangelo orations, and examination of these works in the total context of Salviati's thought makes it quite obvious that they are works of linguistic and stylistic virtuosity only, presenting only an ingenious and superficially pleasing pattern of ideas. References are made in the *Lezzion prima* to Antinori's lectures, and internal evidence, as well as the explicit testimony of Salvini, who had before him the records of the Accademia, confirms that Salviati's lectures were at least two in number. Of a second or further lectures, intended to present conclusions for which the first is but a preliminary analysis, there is no trace.

Salviati sent Francesco a copy of this lecture before he delivered it. An accompanying letter indicates Salviati's interest in the matter generally, for he complains that the subject of Poetics has hitherto been treated only in a poor and unsatisfactory manner in Italian.[17] In view of the fact that in May 1582 he stated that he had been working for sixteen years on his own translation and paraphrase of Aristotle he must have begun work on it fairly soon after this, perhaps on the strength of encouragement, real or imagined, from Francesco.[18]

Yet this interest was still purely academic.[19] It was not until the polemics over the *Gerusalemme Liberata* fired him with a conviction

---

[17] The text of this letter, dated 12.12.64 and prefixed to the manuscript of the *Lezzion prima*, Florence, B.N.C., Cod. Magl. VII, 307, is published in the above-mentioned article 'L'edizione del 1873' of P. M. Brown.

[18] In the dedicatory letter of the *Decameron* (pub. Contin, op. cit., No. 40) (written in a different form originally in May 1582), Salviati writes: 'seconda questa mia voglia sarebbono già a questa hora pubblicate con lo stesso nome suo le mie fatiche della Poetica, le quali sedici anni hanno occupato della mia vita.' See P. M. Brown, 'I veri promotori della rassettatura del *Decameron* nel 1582', *G.S.L.I.* cxxiv (1957), especially p. 323.

[19] In his dedicatory letter to Isabella Orsini, dated 5.2.65, to his edition of Razzi's comedy *La Gostanza*, Lionardo does speak of 'il mio Trattato della Poetica: del quale ho già indiritto il principio allo Illustrissimo Principe mio Signore'. But it is clear from the character of the *Lezzion prima*, to which he is here quite clearly referring, that when writing it Salviati had not conceived it as part of a full translation, paraphrase, and commentary, which later occupied him for many years.

which brought the whole question of Poetics alive for him in the context of modern Italian culture and its relationship to Antiquity that he made his real contribution to the current discussions. In the meantime the *Lezzion prima* played its part in Salviati's manœuvres to secure patronage, for it was dedicated to Francesco, in whose favour Cosimo had abdicated in June of this year 1564. Several approaches had been made by him to the Medici in recent months, and we gather from a rather pathetic letter to Cosimo of October of that year that Salviati's jubilation the previous year had been a little premature. Lionardo was now experiencing some of the disappointments of the struggle between courtier men of letters for official recognition, for he had been manifestly neglected since the day Cosimo discussed with him how his talents might best be employed, and what was more, as Salviati subtly reminds him, committed the conclusions to paper.[20] Moreover, his life was embittered by professional jealousy. It was the general opinion amongst his intimates that someone had poisoned the Duke's mind against him suggesting, amongst other things, that the credit for his works was not due to his own native talents but to a person or persons unnamed who had assisted him in their composition. There seems to be only one person to whom these carefully framed accusations, once analysed, could refer, and that person is Benedetto Varchi who had in fact been the source and inspiration of some of Salviati's most significant compositions to date.[21] In defending himself Salviati reveals a good deal about his conception of his own abilities at this time. Certainly he does not fear competition with 'quel tale che havesse ciò fatto'. Let Cosimo give them both the same material to write about, he proposes, and he will soon see who is the more able. He points out that he is not speaking of the knowledge that can

[20] Lett. Salviati to Cosimo 12.10.64, Florence, A.S., Filza 509, fol. 81 (pub. Contin). Salviati speaks of 'li rescritti e risposte havute più d'una volta da V. E. I. sì favorevoli e sì benigni'. Research in the archives in what ought to be the appropriate records (especially Filze Med. 56–7; 497–502; 503–13) failed to reveal any trace either of the letters and replies mentioned (preserved as *minute di lettere*) or of the letters to which Salviati refers elsewhere in this same letter.

[21] The fact that the Michelangelo oration was the occasion of an affectionate exchange of sonnets initiated by Varchi with 'S'a noi diletto, a voi pregio alto e loda' in praise of Lionardo's oration, to which the orator replied with his 'Sì del mio buon voler s'appaghi, e goda' (69), means little in the context of the deceit of which both Varchi and Salviati were capable.

come only with maturity (an indication, probably, that his calumniator is an older man) but of matters in which at his age he can compete on equal terms, of the 'modo dello scrivere e della pulitezza e candore della lingua e dello stile e del numero'— driving home again the importance he attaches to form and style as distinct from content.

Considering himself second to none as a master of the *volgare* he proposes that he employ his full potential in translating into Tuscan, with commentaries, great works of Antiquity. His sense of the urgency of the work, his tone of sincerity here, and the encouragement he was to give throughout his life to those who undertook similar tasks, indicate that the sentiments expressed in the *Fiorentina favella* were no flash in the pan, and that whilst linked with Florentine nationalism and political conformism they corresponded to his basic conception of the position of modern Italian civilization as represented by the language, and a sincere desire to further the cause of modernist emancipation from Antiquity. He couples his request with an appeal to Cosimo's patriotism, his desire for glory, and his family pride, pointing out that the Duke, by encouraging this kind of translation, could endow Florentine with the only attributes lacking to make it greater than the languages of Greece and Rome. At the same time he reveals, discreetly, what he considers to be the ideal way of making his own contribution, for he says he would like to be employed on translations 'whilst Varchi is busy writing his history'. In other words, he aspires ideally to the post of official historian, fired perhaps by the publication, in precisely those years 1561–4, of Guicciardini's *Storia d'Italia*, This is but the first manifestation of a hankering which remained with him through his life.

Though in a difficult position, since he is attacking in the letter someone in whom the Duke has placed his trust, he is nevertheless determined to press his case with vigour. The missive breathes resentment, a sense of injustice, and an impotent frustration, and despite the writer's attempt to be discreet and respectful the wording on occasion comes dangerously near to impertinence, very unwise at this moment, for notwithstanding his proud boast to Varchi of March 1564 'io non ho debito un lupino, e ho tanto al sole che io potrei dare le spese a qualche compagno', he is in reality already in the throes of the losing financial struggle which was to continue for the rest of his life. Just a small grant at the moment, he begs, whilst Cosimo is deciding precisely how to employ his talents, will allow him to lead an honourable existence. And although, as he puts it, his tastes were 'reasonable and moderate', it was with some hope of escaping from the pressure of constant harrying poverty that twelve days later he wrote in haste to Cosimo asking him for a canonicate in the Propositura di Prato left vacant by the death of Giovanni Ronconcelli.[22] It is in this letter that we have the first documentation of his friendship with Lodovico Beccadelli, though there are also three extant sonnets to him by Salviati all addressing him as the 'Reverendissimo di Raugia', and thus dating to the period 1555–64 when he was bishop of Ragusa. Beccadelli spent the last four years of this period in Pisa and Florence and the near certainty is that the two struck an acquaintance then, though Beccadelli was so close to such intimates of Salviati as Varchi and Vettori that contact could easily have been established at any time. Beccadelli was to assume the Propositura of Prato in November of that year, and favoured Salviati's application. But he was mistaken in thinking the benefice was in the Pope's patronage,[23] and by the time Salviati wrote to Cosimo the usual mechanism for the election of Ronconcelli's successor was in motion, only Cosimo's approval of the nominee being awaited. Lionardo was to be disappointed, for the canonicate of Santo Stefano di Prato was conferred on another.[24]

Cosimo was in any case embroiled in the Corsican crisis, having been offered the crown of Corsica by the anti-Genoese faction in July of that year, the jealous opposition of Philip II and the Emperor again serving to emphasize his status and importance. By this time, however, Salviati's hopes are again rising, for by the time he comes to dedicate the previously mentioned *Lezzion prima* to Francesco, in the middle of December that same year, he

[22] Lett. Salviati to Duke Cosimo, 24.10.64, Florence, A.S., Filza 509, f. 80 Contin, No. 4).

[23] Beccadelli had advised Salviati to send a courier direct to Rome, which he did. The Vatican Archives being incomplete for original letters received during this period, it is not surprising that there is no record of Salviati's letter in the *Lettere di privati*. Nor is there any trace of an official *supplica* having been made by the Vatican *scriptores* from Salviati's letter.

[24] Salviati himself does not specify the canonicate. But in the A.V., Registri di brevi segreti, Armadio 42 n. 21, f. 395 r.e.v., there is a letter addressed to the Archbishop of Florence conferring the canonicate of Santo Stefano di Prato on one Simone Barbi.

is able to thank him for the 'singolar grazia ultimamente ricevuta da Lei', apparently a promise by Francesco, whom he now addresses as his 'Signore', to employ him. Ostensibly the *Lezzion prima* is for Francesco's entertainment in the interim period: on a more practical plane its purpose is to keep Salviati's memory alive in a young man who had many more appealing distractions. All the indications are that Salviati is hitching his waggon to the rising star of Francesco. He was to discover that Florence was on the verge of great changes, which were not for the better, and which were to have a profound effect on his life and fortunes.

VIII

CONSUL OF THE ACADEMY: THE FIRST
TASTE OF POWER

THE previous decade had not been a happy one for Cosimo personally. His eldest daughter Maria, promised to Alfonso son of Ercole d'Este, Duke of Ferrara, had died in 1557. Lucrezia, who took her place, who did marry Alfonso and was miserably neglected, died in April 1560. There followed the triple death of 1562. It may be that this succession of tragedies, aggravated by the evil rumours they aroused, was a significant factor in persuading Cosimo to withdraw in part from the active life in which he had so vigorously participated. At all events on 11 June 1564, Cosimo's birthday, the Duke formally abdicated in favour of his son Francesco, a move unexpected even to the Florentines, and interpreted by the *fuorusciti* and others averse to the regime as the prelude to some hidden but inevitably sinister political manœuvre. In fact Cosimo, whilst disburdening himself of administrative and other onerous responsibilities, retained the title of Duke and ultimate control in any sphere of consequence.

Unfortunately the political changes coincided with a moral deterioration in Cosimo which seemed to symbolize the end of an epoch. No efforts on the part of the exiles in his earlier years had succeeded in robbing his regime, autocratic though it undoubtedly was, of its positive character. Its image was one of defiance against hostility externally, of reconstruction, justice, and sober wisdom internally, and as such it had caught the imagination even of those amongst his compatriots who were by tradition and conviction republicans. Of this new Tuscany the figure and character of Cosimo himself, fair, stubborn, tenacious, with more than a touch of primitive austerity, and combining self-denial with unswerving determination, had been the symbol. The state was his creation and identified with him. The disintegration of moral standards now observable in Cosimo coincided with the beginning of the disintegration of the climate which he, single-handed, had created.

Freed of minor cares he threw himself into a dissolute life of love and pleasure, in which featured a sordid succession of mistresses and illegitimate children. A new phase was opening, one in which the insinuations, the accusations of the *fuorusciti* found more meat on which to feed. But for the time being the effects of the incipient moral rot were retarded by the initial impetus which the energy, vision, and purpose of Cosimo had given to his new state. Young men of Salviati's generation, impressed by the positive achievements of that state, believing in its solidity, its fibre, and its dynamism, had escaped the resentment of the older generation and were as yet not disillusioned.

Outwardly Florence was growing daily more impressive. In March of that year work had begun on the long overhead corridor connecting the Palazzo Vecchio to the Palazzo Pitti, and huge extensions and modifications had been made to the Palazzo Pitti itself by that same Bartolommeo Ammannati whose gigantic statue of Neptune was ready to be erected in the Piazza della Signoria. For the benefit of the courtiers, with whom he was at first tolerably popular, Francesco developed ever further the type of lavish and spectacular entertainment in which they took delight. It was natural that Salviati, immersed as he was in the life of his native city, should play his part in these activities rooted in Florentine tradition. He was in demand for the composition of heraldic mottoes, epigrams, and interludes, but it was in the Florentine world of the popular spectacle that his reputation was highest. So much so that in 1589, when Salviati was on his death-bed, Grand Duke Ferdinand believed that the show could only be a success if Salviati were available to supervise and direct operations in the masque which he was staging for the entry into Florence of the Grand Duchess.[1]

Cambi mentions in particular the 'suntuosa cavalcata degli Ermafroditi', the procession of the 'Tritoni', and the 'Mascherata degli Amorini'. No doubt such compositions provided Salviati with a pleasant respite from his philological labours, though the first of these spectacles, performed early in 1565, provoked a mild quarrel between the author and Pier Martelli, who had had the indiscretion to refer to the work as 'anzi scura che no', and was sharply rebuked for it by the author.[2] If there was some

[1] Lett. Ercole Cortile to Alfonso II, 24.3.89. Modena, A.S., C.A.F., 1589.
[2] Lett. Sal. to Piero Martelli, 24.2.65, published Manzoni, *Prose*, and Contin,

justification for the charge of obscurity in this case, the words at least
of the other *mascherate* are clear enough. These compositions are
amongst the most enjoyable of Salviati's works. He seems to be
relaxed and at ease, enjoying free rein for his imagination. All are
typical of the *mascherate* of the times, with their subjects
drawn from classical mythology, and in them figure tritons,
mermaids, hermaphrodites, Venus, and Orpheus. In the most
sumptuous of all, the *Mascherata dei Tritoni*, as in all the others
except that of Venus (which is interesting in that it has affinities
with the prologue of the *Aminta*) the allegorical element is strong.
The sea-monsters are not to be feared, for

> Non può fraude occultar mostro deforme
> che rado nuoce il reo, che fuor si mostra . . .

but the mermaids, who have

> sì dolce il guardo
> sì dolci gli atti e 'l riso
> che sembra ogni lor cosa un paradiso

have also, hidden out of sight, 'di vil membro il fine', and symbolize, like Geryon, fraud, deceit, and lies. Whilst not startlingly
original, these works show some degree of inventiveness. The
choruses flow with an easy, unstrained rhythm, and have a singable
quality which gives the necessary inconsequential character to
the verses and keeps them always within the limits of a game.
Sound and rhythm ensure that the drownings, the shipwrecks,
caused by the mermaids with their 'crudo ventre immondo', do not
horrify us, but only entertain.

If, as appears certain, Salviati did enjoy participation in these
entertainments, the years 1565 and 1566 must have been particularly memorable ones. The long train of public spectacle and
merriment was touched off by the engagement of Francesco to the
Archduchess Joan of Austria, on whose father G. B. Adriani had
delivered a funeral oration two months earlier in San Lorenzo.[3]

op. cit. (Manzoni, *Rime*, p. 126, states that the manuscript is in Florence, A.S.,
Filza 139, fols. 133–5, but this is not the case, and it is untraceable.) It is
accompanied by a letter from Maestro Daniello, who designed and produced
the *mascherata*, giving the correct interpretation of the allegories.

[3] See D. Moreni, *Pompe funebri*, p. 124. The oration, in Latin, was published
as *Oratio Habita Florentiae in Aede D. Laurentii in Funere Ferdinandi Impera-
toris Augusti*, an. 1564 XII Kal. Sept. (Florentiae, apud Iunctas, in 4).

Once the protracted negotiations were over (negotiations in which there arose the question of precedence between Medici and Este, later to bedevil Salviati's plans and to have a disastrous influence on his future) and the announcement made, Florence prepared to welcome the couple. The first party which met Joan at Trento included Salviati's patron Paolo Giordano Orsini who as a favourite of Francesco was playing an ever more prominent part in the affairs of the court. The second, which escorted the Archduchess to Cafaggiolo di Mugello, home of Cosimo's branch of the Medici, was led by Alamanno Salviati, Cosimo's uncle and Lionardo's distant kinsman. On the last stage of her journey she was received at the villa of Poggio a Caiano by that 'illustrissima signora di Piombino' to whom, as we shall see, Salviati was already beginning to turn some of his attention. Thus Lionardo himself was by no means out of contact with the proceedings.

Joan finally arrived in Florence, and to make room for the fifteen horses needed for her ceremonial entrance the luckless sculptures for Michelangelo's catafalque, which had been stored in a room behind the sacristy of San Lorenzo, were thrown out and never seen again. There was a feast of pageantry, ceremony, spectacle, dancing, banqueting, and entertainment on a scale, and of a richness, to make it memorable even in the annals of Florence.[4] Salviati's contribution to the happy occasion was a madrigal 'O di terrestri Dij', in which the wretchedly ill-fated marriage of convenience is exalted as a happy conjunction of 'terrestri Dij' and 'celesti eroi'. The 'celeste eroe' in question, Francesco de' Medici, was in fact already in the throes of that infatuation with Bianca Cappello which was to last all his life. By the time Lionardo was celebrating the Prince's wedding with the unattractive Joan, Bianca was already mistress of his heart and mind.

Lionardo had been fairly active poetically in this period. Apart from numerous sonnets to Varchi and an exchange with Laura Battiferra degli Ammannati he had addressed one sonnet to

[4] See D. Mellini, *Descrizione dell'entrata della Serenissima Reina Giovanna d'Austria et dell'apparato fatto in Fiorenza nella venuta, & per le felicissime nozze di S. Altezza et dell'Illustrissimo & Eccell.mo S. Don Francesco de' Medici, principe di Fiorenza e di Siena* (In Fiorenza, appresso i Giunti, MDLXVI): and by the same author *Descrizione dell'apparato della commedia et intermedii d'essa recitata in Firenze il giorno di Santo Stefano l'anno 1565 nella gran sala del palazzo di Sua Ecc. Illust. nelle reali nozze dell'Illust. & Eccell. S. il S. Don Francesco Medici, Principe di Fiorenza & di Siena & della Regina Giovanna d'Austria sua Consorte* (In Fiorenza, appresso i Giunti, MDLXVI).

Paolo Giordano Orsini ('Il cor doglioso e lagrimosi i rai') on the death of Guido Ascanio Sforza, the Cardinal di Santa Fiora who had negotiated the marriage between Paolo and Isabella. Obviously he was keen to maintain good relations with a couple whose fortunes at court seemed to be in the ascendant—Paolo had been a witness at the wedding of Francesco on 18 December. To Isabella herself he had dedicated his edition of Gerolamo Razzi's *La Gostanza* published in 1565, in whose dedicatory letter he makes the previously mentioned reference to his 'particolare servitù' with the couple, refraining from giving details, 'essendo cosa pur troppo nota horamai di quanto nodo io mi ritruovi con amendue obligato'.[5] And it was once again to Isabella that he dedicated the following year, though anonymously, his translation of an oration by Vettori in praise of Joan.[6]

The festivities lasted well into 1566 and included comedies, tournaments, mock battles, and fireworks, in all of which the presence, and the ostentatious spending, of Orsini were well in evidence. It was during the course of this prolonged merry-making that Lionardo's talents were given their full scope. The last day of the Carnival of 1566 saw the traditional *mascherate delle bufale* of which the most sumptuous and impressive was the one sponsored by Francesco. The author was Salviati and the work was his *Mascherata dei Tritoni*, a veritable orgy of coloured silk, rich embroidery, gold and silver cloth and thread; the ingenious costumes of the Tritons were ornamanted with a variety of marine motifs, some done in genuine pearls of great value, whilst the horses on which they rode were disguised to simulate reefs of coral.[7]

In the midst of all these celebrations, in December 1565, Benedetto Varchi died. That Salviati initially learnt much from him is beyond doubt: that his early years were strongly influenced by the older man is self-evident. What is less certain is the degree of friendship the two really felt for each other. At all events Lio-

---

[5] Ded. Let. (22.2.64, i.e. '65 st. com.) of Salviati's edition of *La Gostanza*.

[6] Presenting this translation in the *Primo libro delle orazioni* (1575), Razzi writes: 'Quantunque questa traduzione fosse pubblicata senza il nome dell'autore, e così fino a ora si sia stata . . .' (Salviati, *Opere*, Milan, 1810, v. 295). So far I have not succeeded in tracing the publication.

[7] D. Mellini, *Descrizione delle dieci mascherate delle bufale mandate in Firenze il giorno di Carnevale l'anno 1565* [i.e. '66] *con la descrizione di tutta la pompa delle Mascherate, ele loro invenzioni* (In Fiorenza, appresso i Giunti, MDLXVI).

nardo's contemporaries, sincerely or hypocritically, included in a
volume of poems composed on the death of Varchi eight addressed
to Salviati, commiserating with him. The whole was appropriately
enough dedicated to Varchi's friend Piero Stufa.[8]
Naturally, the Academy, of which Lionardo had been elected
a member on 18 March 1565, chose Salviati to deliver his funeral
oration, in the Chiesa degli Angeli where Varchi was buried. The
funeral, which was done in style, seems to have made an impression
on Salviati. Writing up the records of Antinori's consulship in the
Atti of the Accademia he told how Varchi 'fu lodato con orazione
funebre da Lionardo Salviati con universal concorso di tutti
i letterati e di tutta la nobiltà, et il mortal corpo portato alla
sepoltura sopra le spalle de' gentilhuomini dell'Accademia et
accompagnato per la città dalla medesima nobiltà con solenne
pompa, e magnifica.'[9] The oration had a success far beyond its
merits. Composed in a great hurry (Salviati was busy with his
mascherate) it has all the features of a mechanical stylistic
exercise, and its plethora of hyperbole fails to compensate for the
total absence of any ring of sincerity or throb of emotion. It is dedicated to Lorenzo Lenzi, Bishop of Fermo, *nipote* of one of
Varchi's patrons and Benedetto's long-standing friend whom he
made his executor and heir to his books.

One feature of this oration, however, confers on it a vital importance in the history of the expression of Salviati's thought,
making it the fourth significant document in his lifelong campaign.
Referring to Varchi's learning he says: 'Perciocchè chi può
mai dubitare che il *Varchi* ottimo umanista non fosse, avendo
egli le tre lingue più nobili, cioè la Fiorentina, la Latina, e la

---

[8] This is a very rare booklet entitled *Componimenti latini e toscani da diversi
suoi amici composti nella morte di M. Benedetto Varchi* (In Firenze, per i figliuoli
di Lorenzo Torrentino e Carlo Pettinari, Con Licenza e Privilegio, 1566).
Poems to Salviati (7 in Italian and 1 in Latin), were contributed by Anton
Ranieri, Baldello Baldelli, Antonfrancesco Grazzini, Gherardo Spini, Giulio
de' Libri, Bronzino (the painter), Benedetto Macci, and Piero Stufa. Honourable
mention was made of him in numerous others. See also Florence, B.N.C., Cod.
Magl. Cl. VIII, 600, *Carmi sacri d'occasione*, p. 314, an anonymous Latin
elegy 'Ad Leonardum Salviatium in Benedicti Varchi obitum'. On the subject
of personal relations between Varchi and Salviati see M. Rossi, 'Il discorso di
Ridolfo Castravilla'. The conclusions reached by Rossi are not persuasive.
[9] Salviati's account of the funeral is to be found in the Cod. B. III, 54 of the
Atti dell'Accademia Fiorentina, f. 20ᵛ. The oration is the *Orazione delle lodi di
Benedetto Varchi* (Florence, Giunti, 1565, i.e. 1566 st. com.).

Greca, ottimamente sapute?'[10] That this statement, in view of its implication, was deliberately provocative and polemical, cannot be doubted, once it is placed in the context of the cultural history of the previous two centuries. Whilst the term for the 'proper study of man', the *studia humanitatis*, probably suggested a whole range of disciplines, the term *(h)umanista* had a much narrower application. Since it had been coined in the early fifteenth century it had designated a teacher, or devotee, of classical language and literature, and particularly Latin. The reason is to be found in the influence of humanism proper; of humanism, that is to say, as a particular conception of the significance in the modern world of Classical Antiquity. A direct consequence of this conception was that classical language and literature occupied a special place as the *key* to those studies which perfect Man. It was to the person skilled in that language and literature that the title *(h)umanista* was precisely and exclusively applied. Likewise *umanità* denotes that language and literature itself.[11] It is clear from recorded uses of the word that the one and only valid qualification for the title *umanista* was skill in the classical languages and literatures. No other knowledge or competence could replace this qualification: no other achievement could enhance a claim to the title.

Yet Salviati classifies Varchi as an *umanista* because he was an expert in *Florentine*, Latin, and Greek. In so doing he completes a process he began two years earlier in the *Fiorentina favella* oration. There he had destroyed any exclusive link between the *studia humanitatis* as the implementation of a vision of the perfection of Man, and the study of the language and literature of Classical Antiquity. In addition he had pointed to Florentine language and literature as the ideal medium for the execution of this 'humanist' programme. A 'humanist' being one who contributes to man's realization of his full potential by the cultivation of the humanities, it follows—and thus Salviati has taken the wheel full circle—that Varchi's competence in Italian, the most 'noble' of all languages, is in its turn the supreme qualification for the title *umanista*.

The application of this title to Varchi, on these grounds, is not

[10] Salviati, *Opere*, v. 122–3.

[11] The most important work in which the meaning of the word *umanista* in the fifteenth and sixteenth centuries is discussed is A. Campana, 'The Origin of the Word "Humanist"', *Journal of the Warburg and Courtauld Institute*, lx (1946), 60–73.

merely a verbal innovation. It is a profoundly significant move because it is one more element in the accumulating evidence of an overall vision of human purpose behind Salviati's attitude to the *volgare* and to contemporary culture. It is in particular a further indication that the discussion of the means to human perfection, and the role of Florentine in this, which figured in the *Fiorentina favella* oration, was not merely conventional padding but the expression of a firm conviction inspiring Salviati's conception of the role of Italian (i.e. Florentine) culture.[12]

Apart from this one feature of front-rank importance, the Varchi oration has nothing to recommend it. In this oration, more perhaps than in any other, is manifested that lack of a sense of proportion which characterized Salviati as an orator. For even allowing for the declared aims of a funeral oration, to say that Varchi is the greatest poet who ever lived, the acknowledged master and object of study of the whole civilized world, that all Europe resounds with his name, that Varchi 'era a guisa d'uno oracolo celebratissimo e venerabilissimo divenuto' is evidence of a lack of common sense which takes the author far beyond the limits of permissible exaggeration. His insensitivity to the grotesque inappropriateness of his own images is manifested in his description of how Varchi (notoriously gross in build) 'ne' purissimi fonti della filosofia si tuffò'.

Nevertheless, Lionardo's orations, symphonies of pure archaic Tuscan yet animated by the Florentine contact with the living language, continued to delight and enrapture. Praise of the oration flowed in from all directions, and the would-be poets writing to console Salviati on his friend's death exalted the power of his eloquence to restore the ravages of time and death. Its fame spread beyond the boundaries of Tuscany, notably to Rome where lived Varchi's friend, consultant, and adviser, Annibale Caro. On learning of Varchi's death from Laura Battiferra, Caro asked her for a copy of Lionardo's oration. For the author, he said, he felt a deep affection, both for his links with Varchi and for his own

[12] For a more detailed consideration of this use of the word *umanista* in the Varchi oration, and its relationship to the thesis expounded in the *Fiorentina favella* oration (also for a bibliography on the history of the word), see P. M. Brown, 'A Significant Sixteenth-Century Use of the Word "Umanista" '. To the bibliography in this article now add: P. Grendler, 'The Concept of Humanist in Cinquecento Italy', in *Renaissance Studies in Honor of Hans Baron* (Florence, Sansoni, 1971), pp. 447–63.

merits, adding that he would be pleased if his feelings were made known to him.[13]

That there should have been no previous contact between them is surprising, for as long before as 1564, knowing of the friendship between Caro and Varchi, and how the latter had made the defence of Caro against Castelvetro his own cause, Salviati prepared a copy of the 'Corbi' to be sent to Caro, writing a letter to accompany it couched in the facetious style of the Florentine composition *in burla*.[14] Moreover, amongst Salviati's most intimate acquaintances were men of letters with whom Caro had close ties, Piero Stufa, for example, and Lorenzo Lenzi. Caro was, too, a great cultivator of the Italian tradition, and with his translations and his compositions corresponded to what was to be Lionardo's ideal of activity in the *volgare*. Yet contact does not seem to have taken place, for in January 1566 Caro describes a letter received from Salviati after Varchi's death as 'la prima lettera che ho veduto di vostro'. On 12 January Caro repeats his original request, this time to Piero Stufa. After this Salviati must have lost little time, for by 19 January Caro, in a letter concerned mainly with settling Varchi's affairs (including arrangements for the publication of the *Ercolano*), can mention a communication from him.[15] Salviati had obviously discussed with Caro his favourite subject, language, and had revealed his intention of writing a defence of the *Ercolano* against a person or persons who were preparing to attack it.[16] For his part Messer Annibale seems to be most solicitous of the

[13] Lett. Caro to Laura Battiferra, published in A. Caro, *Lettere familiari* (3 vols., Venezia, Remondini 1751), ii. 288. No date, but certainly January 1566.

[14] Prefatory letter to the *Corbi* in MS. Magl. VII, 306, B.N.C., Florence, published by Manzoni, *Rime*, and by Lorenzoni, *Un coro*.

[15] These two letters to Salviati (19.1.66) and Stufa (12.1.66) are in the *Let. fam.* ii. 279. Writing to Stufa Caro asks for 'L'Oration di M. Lionardo Salviati, il quale sento molto celebrare: di che ho dato impresa a Madonna Laura.'

[16] It is unlikely that this is Castelvetro, whose *Opposizioni* did not appear until 1572, after the publication of the *Ercolano*. We have no trace of a defence by Salviati, and this seems to have remained one of his numerous unfulfilled promises. On the other hand the person referred to may be Girolamo Muzio see Vivaldi, *La più grande polemica del cinquecento* (Catanzaro, Caliò, 1895, revised after original publication in *Studi letterari*, 1891, Naples, Morano), p. 23, quotes Apostolo Zeno, who 'nelle sue note al Fontanini ci apprende che il Salviati aveva promesso al Varchi di difenderlo dal Muzio: difesa, che poi, per la morte del Salviati, non vide la luce'. (On the grounds of this statement by Zeno, which may itself be based on the letter to Caro, Vivaldi identifies Orlando Pescetti, who makes frequent reference in his *Difesa* to his intended defence of the *Ercolano*, as Salviati.)

friendship and recognition of Salviati, on whose shoulders he apparently conceives the mantle of Varchi to have fallen, and whose oration reached him soon afterwards.

A cordial correspondence was then initiated, in which, as we gather from Caro's letter of 20 April, Lionardo had made two requests to his new friend. What the first of these was is revealed by Caro in a letter of 20 July. He had confidently asked Caro's opinion on his work, and in particular on the oration on Varchi.[17] It is unlikely that he envisaged the frankness of Caro's reply which, whilst attempting to convince Salviati of his approval, reveals in every word his distaste. Vague general expressions of commendation alternate with damning judgements on particulars, in which the glaring defects of Salviati's style are pinpointed with chilling inexorability. Following to the letter Salviati's request to comment on the 'cose', 'parole', and 'composizione', Caro criticizes the swollen bladder of hyperbole, which he points out makes the content less acceptable, not more; the duplication and repetition of words which robs them of their efficacy; the confusion caused by the lengthy and involved periods. The fact is that he has seen through the oration and been offended by it. Though he sugars the pill with expressions of encouragement, the judgement is virtually a condemnation and remains even today an acute and valid criticism of Salviati's early prose. Being now, for reasons not exclusively literary, a spoilt child of Florentine letters, the over-confident Lionardo must have found particularly galling Caro's semi-paternal attitude to a man whom he conceives as a young enthusiast eager for the guidance of his elders, but who in reality considered himself the equal of any man in Florence. Caro's advice to him to seek the art which conceals art, however carefully such advice was presented as the fruits of a desire to help; the patronizing attribution of Salviati's stylistic excesses to his 'fertility of mind'; and finally the picture of him as being full of good intentions, but clumsy, like a 'polledro, che per troppa gagliardia va continuamente in su la schiena', must have been an intolerable affront to his dignity.

In view of this, Caro's inability to come to Florence for a

---

[17] In a letter of 19.2.66 Caro asks Razzi to give his regards to Lionardo, and on 30.3.66 apologizes to the same person for delay in returning the oration, which he has lent to a friend (*Let. fam.* ii. 281 and 283 respectively; Caro's letter of 20.7.66 is on p. 289).

personal meeting cannot have been a great disappointment, nor can Caro's negative reply to his second request, namely that he should become a member of the Accademia. For Salviati was now an important figure of that institution, of which he had during the last two years been such an active and vigorous member. He and Varchi had accompanied Valori's successor in the consulship, Bastiano Antinori, as *Consiglieri* at his investiture, and during Antinori's period of office Salviati delivered a lecture on the fifth sonnet of Varchi.[18] He had given two lectures at least on *Poetics* and, of course, it was he whom the Academy chose to deliver Varchi's funeral oration.

It was this last-mentioned work which convinced the Academicians that Salviati must be their choice as leader, now that Varchi was gone. The hint had already been dropped. Baldello Baldelli speaks for all of them:

> Voi potrete fermar l'acerbo pianto
> Di FLORA, anzi d'Etruria, e 'l grave danno
> Ristorar solo, e del suo amato Lauro
> Ch'al vostro (o raro Cigno) dolce canto
> Queterà il duolo: e leverà l'affanno
> Tal del perduto ben presto restauro.[19]

Lasca, Bronzino, Del Libro, and others took up the chorus, and the Academicians were convinced. On 27 March Salviati was duly led to the consular chair by the *Consiglieri* Fra Paolo del Rosso and Francesco da Diacceto, with his friend Giovambattista Adriani as Censor and Domenico Mellini as Secretary.

So now, still officially too young for the post, Salviati found himself head of the Accademia Fiorentina and Rector of the Studio of Florence, the latter an office which had been one of the Consul's attributes for some time, and which itself carried some considerable authority. His precocious consulship he himself later attributed to the favour of Valori.[20] Of his two inaugural speeches the first was short, formal, and conventional. The second indicates once again how Salviati considers his functions as *letterato* and courtier to be indissoluble, seeing his literary and intellectual

---

[18] This information is given by Salvini, *Fasti*, pp. 180–1. The *Censore* was another friend of Lionardo, Tommaso Ferrini.

[19] *Componimenti latini e toscani.*

[20] See ded. lett. of his edition (1588) of Passavanti's *Specchio di vera penitenza.*

activities, and the Accademia itself, as being all servants of ducal policy. In this he is distinguished, at this youthful stage, by his whole-hearted zeal for collaboration. No shadow of suspicion, and no recalcitrant republican past, attaches to him. His undoubted early unpopularity with many of his contemporaries may well be due to the arrogance with which, under the safe protection of his master, he becomes Cosimo's priggish spokesman.

Here in this second oration he delivers to the Academicians a pointed reminder, by now a commonplace of the consul's inaugural lecture, of the purposes of their institution, and the possible consequences, including extreme ducal displeasure, of failure to fulfil them. The functions of the courtier and the Academician are combined when Salviati, pointing out that he speaks not as a private individual, but as the mouthpiece of the Duke, delivers with all the intolerable arrogance of the Jack in office the following half-threat: 'e restinvi nella memoria queste parole saldamente scolpite: perciocchè io ho da pubblicamente dirlevi, da chi può mantenerle, espresso comandamento.'[21] In the words to which he here refers, Salviati had stressed how princely favour towards the Academy would be in direct proportion to its usefulness. Here was a consul who intended to take his job seriously. It was Lionardo's first taste of the power reserved for devoted minor adherents of an autocratic regime.

[21] Salviati, *Orazione seconda nel prendere il suo consolato*, first published in a rare booklet *Primo libro delle orazioni di Lionardo Salviati* (Florence, Marco Peri e Valente Panizzi, 1567). This volume is not to be confused with the *Primo libro delle orazioni* of 1575. The oration is dedicated to Bernardo Vecchietti.

IX

THE COMEDIES: ANTONFRANCESCO GRAZZINI

ONCE Consul, Salviati acted swiftly on two counts. First of all he sent off a delegation composed of Mario Colonna and Domenico Mellini asking Cosimo and Francesco to try to prevent the printing by Paolo Manuzio in Venice of a revised version of the *Decameron* (now on the Index). He and his colleagues considered that the publication of such a work should be the prerogative of the Florentine Academy. Immediately after this he arranged for the readmission to the Academy of his friend and former defender Antonfrancesco Grazzini. With Salviati as anxious to have him back as Lasca was to be readmitted, it was agreed between them that this should be arranged under a provision made in 1553, which stipulated that anyone who had been expelled could be considered re-elected if they produced a work approved by the Censor. This office being held by his friend Giovanni Battista Adriani, Salviati sent off to him on 18 April ten eclogues by Grazzini, indicating the formula for readmission. On 1 May. Adriani gave his formal approval and on 6 May 1566 Grazzini was restored to full academic status.[1]

This is one of the most revealing actions of Salviati's life. Had it merely involved the readmission of one who had always been something of a firebrand—'alquanto risentito e satirico' Biscioni calls him in a classic understatement—not an eyebrow would have been raised. But Lasca's relationship with the Academy had not only a cultural and academic, but also a political aspect.

Proud of his creation, the Accademia degli Umidi, he took extremely ill to its being absorbed into the Medicean state machine

---

[1] See Lett. Salviati to Adriani, 18.4.66 (Aut.), Florence, A.S., Carte Strozzi, Serie I, xix, published by Verzone, *Le rime burlesche edite e inedite di Anton Francesco Grazzini*, p. lix. The eclogues, which A. Biscioni, as he states in his 'Vita del Lasca', prefaced to his *A. Grazzini, Novelle* (London, Rickardo Bancker, 1793), p. 29, believed were lost, were found by Domenico Moreni, and had been printed by Poggiali at Leghorn in 1799.

to which he, in 1541, was as yet by no means reconciled. It was he who kicked most strongly, but to no avail. The 'Umidi' became the 'Fiorentina'. But he continued to grumble about the new state of affairs, quarrelled about it with other academicians, and generally made himself a difficult and exasperating colleague. In 1542 he refused to give a lecture when drawn by lot to do so, and fostered strife within the Accademia by ridiculing the Aramei. It was these latter who contrived to have him expelled on a technicality in 1547, whereupon he expressed his disgust and fury in an indiscreet composition (unpublished then but known), entitled *Lamento dell' Accademia degli Umidi*. This *capitolo* depicts the Academy bewailing its prostitution:

> . . . d'imperatrice e regina
> son tornata fantesca e concubina   (ll. 111–12)

and compares the fate of itself and its members (some of whom also come in for individual attack) to that of the primitive Church which became corrupted by wealth. The allusions to the Academy's dependence on Cosimo (contrasted with its previous glorious freedom) and to the moral corruption of its members since they became the Duke's protégés are only too obvious, as is the resentment against the Duke which emanates from the whole composition.

To be thrown out of the Academy was tantamount to a fall from ducal grace. Nor was the position improved by Grazzini's subsequent behaviour, for there flowed from his pen an uninterrupted stream of satirical compositions directed against those whom he believed had betrayed the noble origins of the Academy. In vain he protested to Cosimo that he was basically devoted to the Academy and its patron.[2] He remained an academic exile for the best part of twenty years—until Lionardo Salviati took it upon himself to readmit him.

This action (repeated on 6 June for the artist Bronzino, one of the Florentines who had composed poems imploring Salviati to come to the rescue of the Academy after the death of Varchi), was a bold one, which tells us much, not only of Salviati's devotion

---

[2] See particularly Verzone, op. cit., *Sonetti*, No. LXXXIII, p. 69, 'Al duca di Firenze', (*inc.* 'Signor, da loro a loro una giornea') and No. LXXXIV, p. 70, 'Al medesimo' (*inc.* 'Se nel fin ch'io stia cheto a voi pur piace') and No. LXXXV, pp. 70–1, 'Al medesimo' (*inc.* 'Supplica umile alla vostra eccellenza').

to Grazzini, but also of Lionardo's position in the Florence of his
times. It tells us for example that the new Consul of the Florentine Academy felt himself in a sufficiently secure position to grant
favours to a man in ducal disfavour without prejudice to himself.
Whether or not it was necessary to consult Cosimo on this
action is immaterial. Even if we consider that the position of
Cosimo in Florence was now such as to allow Grazzini's reaction
to the transformation of the Umidi, and his subsequent behaviour, to be seen in a new perspective, the step is still one which
commands admiration and respect.

As for the two men concerned, they seem to have been aware
at all times that their differences on detail were negligible when
related to the common ground they shared. Even at this time the
influence of Grazzini was about to manifest itself again, this time
in the realm of comedy, in Salviati's comedy *Il Granchio*, whose
highly successful performance in carnival week 1567 was a fitting
sequel to a consulship which had proved lively and fertile for the
Academy. There had been many public lectures during the year,
speakers including Francesco Buonamici, Piero Caponsacchi (a
comparatively new Academician), Francesco Verini, and Lorenzo
Giacomini. Salviati himself had again given a public lecture on a
sonnet by Varchi. On 4 February 1567 the assembled Academicians
had discussed at length ways and means of putting on the comedy,
finally deciding to impose a levy of two scudi on members to
finance the production. Some were very slow to pay, and the
matter had to be brought to their attention several times, but
the then consul elect, Jacopo Pitti, made an immediate contribution of five scudi. The play itself was dedicated to Tommaso del
Nero, who in turn offered it to Francesco de' Medici.[3]

Given Salviati's previous experience of public spectacle, and given
the vogue of the genre, it was inevitable that he should graduate
to the pseudo-classical comedy. The *Granchio* was presented in
the Sala del Papa in Santa Maria Novella, which had special
connections with the Accademia, and where Grazzini's comedy
La gelosia had been performed in the corresponding week of 1550.
Tommaso del Nero and Cambi both insist that the Medici were
lavish with financial aid for the production, though neither the
play nor the *intermedii*, written on this occasion by Bernardo de'

[3] *Il Granchio, commedia in versi con gl'intermedii di Bernardo de' Nerli*
(Florence, Torrentino, 1566 i.e. '67 st. com.).

Nerli, seem to call for the '. . . apparato superbo' and the 'moventi e giranti e andanti macchine' which according to Cambi excited the wonder of the spectators and made a hole in Cosimo's pocket. Despite the play's continued high reputation only one further performance is recorded.[4]

Il Granchio was the first of two pseudo-classical plays written by Salviati. The second, *La Spina*, was published posthumously in 1592 by Giovanni Battista Laderchi, Alfonso II's secretary and a friend of Salviati in his last years.[5] As is to be expected, the two comedies adhere very closely to the standards then prevailing with regard both to the nature and purpose of comedy in general and to the imitation of the classical comedy as the ideal. If it is at first sight surprising that one whose programme from an early age was the rejection of the classical model should adhere to the form and content of the Roman comedy we must remember that Salviati was still immature and that his friend Grazzini, who both in the prologues to his own plays and in numerous poems thundered against the imitation of Antiquity in the sixteenth century as unhistorical, nevertheless did not himself stray far from Plautus and Terence.

Both plays follow, by and large, the lines laid down with a certain measure of agreement by the theorists of preceding decades. The action of both is in a formal sense complete and a unity, and progress is from a state of 'agitation' or unhappiness to one of tranquillity, brought about in the space of five acts by a sudden reversal (or series of reversals) of fortune, and by a 're-cognition': the action takes place in a fixed setting within a single revolution of the sun: it concerns people of medium or low status (both socially and in human terms). Both plays could, no doubt, have been defended as helping to improve behaviour by ridicule had the need arisen, but no moral lesson is deliberately pointed in either. Both plays adopt the formal conventions and techniques of the classical comedy.

The merits and defects of the plays need not occupy us in detail. Once the typically Plautine plot of *Il Granchio* for example—trickery conceived and put into practice by the servant on behalf of the master, a tissue of misapprehension, deliberate and accidental, in many forms and guises—gets under way, the defects

---

[4] See supplementary note 5, p. 247.
[5] *La Spina* (Ferrara, Benedetto Mammarelli, 1592).

of Salviati as a playwright are quickly revealed and the play is an irritating combination of complexity and triviality. Both plays are uninspired creations, poor in humour, poor in character, and especially poor in plot. One only needs to read a comedy by Aretino or the Intronati after reading *Il Granchio* or *La Spina* to regain a sense of proportion, and to see how far are Salviati's plays from drawing life from the world in which the author lived. We likewise look in vain for the rollicking good fun of *La Calandra*, *La Cortigiana*, or *Il Marescalco*, or indeed anything which in its absence would give the plays life, such as the two developments which gave interest to other contemporary plays, namely the combination of the classical material with that of the *novellistica* and the creation of new 'types' drawn from the contemporary world of the authors. Salviati drew on the same sources as many of these plays, used the same conventions and situations (with modifications which we shall shortly consider), and lacked nothing 'eccetto una qualità senza la quale, ahimè, tutto il resto serviva a ben poco: e cioè una qualche scintilla di genio.'[6]

Yet despite the aesthetically negative quality of these comedies, they are by no means without significance in the history of Salviati's development, in at least two respects. Of these the first concerns language. In the Prologo to *Il Granchio* Salviati states that he has written his comedy

> non in prosa
> Ma in versi, ed in quella qualità
> Di versi, che al suo facitore
> Sono al parlar sciolto, ed ai domestici
> Ragionamenti parsi più conformi.[7]

The language of the play is in fact modelled as closely as the verse would allow on Florentine speech. Whilst this has not made for

---

[6] M. Praz, 'Rapporti tra la letteratura italiana e la letteratura inglese' in *Letterature comparate*, Vol. iv of *Problemi ed orientamenti critici* (Milan, 1949). (Praz is here speaking more specifically of the tragic authors, but the principle applies.)

[7] I. Sanesi, *La commedia* (Milan, Vallardi, 1954, in the series 'Storia dei generi letterari italiani' examines the comedies of Salviati and their language and states (p. 352) of the hendecasyllables that; 'si conformano [i.e. 'al parlar familiare'], tanto sono brutti'. The theory that the verse of the comedy should resemble speech as closely as possible was by no means exclusive to Salviati, but it plays a particularly important part in his views on the disputed question of whether prose or verse should be used in the comedy in Italian (see pp. 115–18).

beauty of verse, the result is certainly an illusion of colloquial speech which taken all round has a naturalness and a living quality. It is not only the movement and the syntax which have this natural character. Being idiomatic Florentine it is full to overflowing with Florentine expressions, turns of phrase, and figures of speech. Whilst passages such as those which record witty exchanges between two such thoroughly *Mercato Vecchio* characters as Fanticchio and Granchio (e.g. Act II, Sc. iv) are packed not only with idiomatic expressions but with downright slang, the language is nevertheless 'correct' according to Salviati's own later definition of the term. Phonologically and morphologically, that is to say, it is distinctively Florentine, but it is purged of the *scorrezioni di favella* which Salviati in the *Avvertimenti* finds not only in his own times, but in the popular Florentine of the age of Boccaccio. Though there are any amount of *pure e nostrali* Florentine words and expressions, however unliterary, the language does not have any plebeian morphology and syntax.

Yet in the other play, *La Spina*, all this is changed. The aim, in its prose, is the reproduction of the cadence of Boccaccio, principally by the imitation of his syntax. In place of the richness of idiomatic flavour with which the characters expressed themselves in *Il Granchio*, their language now seems almost a parody of the literary language. Despite a few colloquial words and expressions Salviati has given his prose an overwhelmingly literary character, stilted, ponderous, and artificial. One could almost be reading a page of the *Prose della volgar lingua*.[8]

This radical change of technique demands some investigation. It could possibly merely represent two moments in Salviati's linguistic thought. In the period of his consulship the dominant

---

[8] e.g. Trappola, whose status is summed up as 'cagnotto di Guelfo finto' (the whole comedy revolves on a double mistaken identity, elaborating on the *Menaechmi*), thus addresses Guelfo's servant Rocchio on his arrival: 'E in ogni tale accidente, pensando, che per mille buon rispetti egli era bene che io sopravvenissi qua, nuovo affatto, e ci fossi sconosciuto per tutto, non volli che io m'appalesassi altrimenti, ma mi trattenessi a questo modo due, o tre dì travisato a una certa bettola fuor di strada un mezzo miglio presso alla terra: dove essendo io stato fino a ora, e non sentendo nulla di voi, temendo, come fa chi ama, di qualche caso, non mi sono potuto tenere di non venirmene in qua: avendo massimamente considerato, che non essendo qui persona, che mi conosca, non ci sarà anche niuno che per una volta solo, massimamente così per passo e in questo abito comunale, mi sia per mente' (III. ix).

influence on Salviati, linguistically speaking at least, was Varchi's 'linguistic naturalism' (the phrase in this context is Vitale's), which placed the virtue of the language in its natural 'Florentineness'. It was the period of the *Orazione in lode della fiorentina favella*, in which the colloquial, idiomatic, living, and intensely Florentine but 'correct' language of *Il Granchio* would meet all his requirements. In the succeeding years Salviati works out the archaist theories to be expounded in the *Avvertimenti*. Perhaps it is as a result of the application of the theory that the 'art' and 'example' of the greatest writers of the 'best' period of the language should be brought to bear on its 'natural' qualities that we have the Boccaccesque prose of *La Spina*, which, whatever its date, is almost certainly a later composition than *Il Granchio*.

But an explanation at first sight more plausible is to be found in Salviati's increasing friendship with Antonfrancesco Grazzini. As has already been seen, Grazzini had been prominent amongst the defenders of Lionardo against Corbinelli in 1563, and in 1564 he had voiced approval of the *Fiorentina favella* oration which echoed his own sentiments on the quality and potential of the *volgare*. On the question of the rejection of the authority of Antiquity (after the oration Grazzini told Frosino Lapini, the classicist grammarian, to throw away his ferule, the symbol of his authority) and on the superiority of the Italian tradition, there was a complete identity of opinion between the two, with a strong suggestion that even as early as 1564 the older man is not without some influence on the younger, an influence which was to increase steadily throughout the following decades and to make itself felt even after Grazzini's death in 1584.

It was in his stanze, *Contro le commedie in versi*, that Grazzini expressed certain ideas on comedy deriving from this vision of contemporary culture which they both shared. The reason he gave for insisting on prose, as against verse, was that it was 'natural' to comedy in Italian, and therefore the much-quoted example of the classical use of verse counted for nothing. On this subject he had written: 'Ma questi, che le regole hanno in pronto | allegando Aristofane e Terenzio, | non fanno delle commedie in prosa conto, | parendo loro amare più che assenzio. | Io col parer di costor non m'affronto, | ma seguo volentieri Arno e Bisenzio.'[9] It is clear, moreover,

---

[9] 'Contro le commedie in versi' (*inc.* 'Apollo vuole che sempre un calzaiuolo') in Verzone, op. cit., pp. 424–6, *Ottave*, No. XCV. For Lasca's views on the

that what determines Grazzini's stand on this question of the medium for comedy, his obsessive insistence on the use of prose rather than verse, is precisely this conception of an Italian tradition which must be free to develop in accordance with its own nature rather than be distorted by classical models and classical standards. Praising Lotto del Mazzo, who uses prose in his comedies, he attacks those *letterati* who adopt the classical models as the norm, who 'allegando Aristofane e Terenzio / non fan delle commedie in prosa conto', and he cries 'Or questi dotti e letterati stiensi / a passeggiar Parnaso ed Elicona; / e lascin compor lui . . .' (37–9). In the same poem he insists that what matters in Italian literature is invention, whilst verse in the comedy is simply a relic of that classical tradition whose imitation he condemns. All the best comedies, all the comedies which his contemporaries really find entertaining and enjoyable, he insists in this poem, are in prose (and this includes the first versions of *I Suppositi* and *La Cassaria*): all others are second-rate affairs.

Grazzini's own plays were, of course, in prose but despite his noisy condemnation of classical models he never got as far away from them in other respects as perhaps he imagined. As for Salviati, since internal evidence shows that he was already composing *Il Granchio* by 1564 it was no doubt too early for him to have absorbed the older man's theories on the use of prose or verse.[10] That *Il Granchio* in its plot and over-all conception was still dependent on the pseudo-Roman tradition, despite its author's insistence even by then on freedom from the classics, is hardly surprising, not only because of Salviati's extreme youth (he was 25 in 1564) but because he was no Machiavelli, and was no more capable of striking out on untrodden ways than was Grazzini himself.

relationship between classical and Italian comedy, see particularly the sonnet *inc.* 'Ben dovresti Cristo e tutti i santi' in Verzone, op. cit., p. 112, and the prologues to *La strega* and *La spiritata*. For discussion of the subject see G. Gentile, *Delle commedie di A. F. Grazzini* (Pisa, 1886), esp. pp. 30 ff. See also, for a critical analysis of Grazzini's production, including the comedies, R. J. Rodini, *Antonfrancesco Grazzini, Poet, Dramatist and Novelliere* (Madison, Milwaukee, and London, Univ. of Wisconsin Press, 1970), to whose very full bibliographies both of the works of Grazzini and of works on him the reader is referred for further study of Lasca.

[10] Internal evidence suggests that *Il Granchio* may have been written as early as 1564. In Act IV, Sc. iii Vanni says that he lost his son, then aged four, in the 'anno quarantacinque': and Duti, (v. iii) states that he took the boy, still aged four, from a Turk 'farà diciannove anni', bringing us to 1564.

The question is whether the prose of *La Spina* represents an attempt to conform to the theories and the practice of Grazzini. Perhaps the situation is illuminated by an examination of more fundamental differences between the two works. For despite the influence of the all-powerful conventions, characters, and plots of the Roman comedy on both works, a close examination of *La Spina* leads us to the inescapable conclusion that in this play, however falteringly, Salviati has made a conscious attempt to 'Italianize' the comedy in vogue, and that this attempt has been carried out under the influence of the *Decameron* of which the echoes are everywhere. There are echoes of Frate Cipolla for example, whose very words 'India Pastinaca' are repeated by the character Ciappelletto, and whose description of Guccio Imbratta obviously inspires Ciappelletto's reference to Trappola as 'Il maggior mentitore, il più sfacciato adulatore' to be found between East and West (Act i, Sc. iv).

A glance at the dramatis personae of *La Spina* suggests that with 'Ser Ciappelletto notaio', the 'Bargello', the 'Quattro birri del civile', and the 'Cinque birri del criminale' Salviati seems to be trying at least to break out of the narrower, disembodied, classical convention and move towards the freer use of characters more deeply rooted in Italian society, and particularly characters from the *novellistica*. We are plunged into the world of the *Decameron*, the 'great merchant epic' as Branca calls it, the age of the commune, of the expansion of trade, of the Italian merchant whose domain was all Europe and the East, an age in which fortunes were made and as quickly lost, and in which Italian bankers dictated their terms to kings. No longer merely Venice and Padua, but London, Milan, and Lisbon figure here. Guelfo and Ghibellino have roamed the world with rich merchants. The background to the young men's adventures is the Guelf–Ghibelline struggle which stamps the Italian Middle Ages with their particular character, and is such a vital element in the world of the *Decameron*. As in the case of Madama Beritola and her two sons (*Decam.* ii. 6), historically authentic civil strife necessitates the concealment of the identity of the two boys which, as in the *novella*, can only be revealed after a further political development. Like the pirate from Monaco who stole the wife of Riccardo di Chinzica, Ghibellino's father was called Paganino: Spina herself, of course, never appears on the stage, but we can find her in *Decameron* ii. 6, imprisoned by her broken-hearted father, Currado. Ciappelletto comes to us ready-made (though with some important modifications in practice) from the first story of the first day. Bernabò da Genova, also in the play, is to be found in *Decameron* ii. 9. Guelfo's father was Belcurrado, his wife Ginevra de' Brancadori—all names which could have come from the pages of the *Decameron* and all of them redolent of this splendid moment of Italian history.

True, in practice all this turns out to be but a noble veneer, laid on the classical base already analysed. In practice, Guelfo and Ghibellino are fairly typical *adulescentuli*, Bernabò a typical *senex*, Gozzo and Rocchio servi, Rosa and Agata *nutrix* and *ancilla* respectively. Ciappelletto and Trappola both play the traditional part of the *servus* in helping the young men in their plans, which are inspired by the typical action of the Roman comedy. For the most part the medieval Italian background and the historical allusions remain a veil covering but thinly the Roman body below.

But even though the practical effect of this attempted transformation of the comedy is very limited (and after all, Grazzini scarcely achieved anything more fundamental) the fact that it was attempted at all has a certain importance. What Salviati has tried to do here is something fully in line with the rest of his activity. He has attempted the *Italianization* of the comedy. He has constructed it out of something which appeared to him to be the most *national* of all material, namely Italian history, the Italy of the commune, of civil strife, of commercial enterprise and adventure, as it emerged from the *Decameron*—an ideal substitute, it seems to him, for the classical material.

All this is in keeping not only with the main trends of his thought as we have seen it, but even more in certain respects, and particularly in the matter of the use of prose, with the ideas of Antonfrancesco Grazzini. Tempting though it may be, however, to see here the natural result of views held in common with Grazzini, evidence on the whole is against the two plays representing two stages in the maturing of Salviati's ideas on the comedy, at least as far as the use of prose or verse was concerned. The preference for prose may have been a passing phase, but it was not a permanent development.

If we look at Salviati's published references to the comedy we

find they throw little light on the problem. Commenting in the
Avvertimenti on certain verses by Berni he writes: 'Né vale il
dire, che in quei versi s'imita il parlar basso: perciocché si fa nella
commedia altresí, e pure in tutti i linguaggi, e appo tutti i buoni
è regolata la sua favella. Ma se si debba, nello scrivere essa commedia, nelle parole, e ne' modi seguir l'uso moderno, ò l'antico,
delle nostre cose della Poetica sarà ragionamento' (*Avv.* Vol. i,
Bk. ii, p. 126). This tells us little. If, following Salviati's own
directions, we look at the extant fragment of the unpublished
Poetics we find a good deal more on the subject. Commenting on
the fourteenth of his own divisions of Chapter I of the *Poetics*
he writes: 'Assegna il verso alla commedia Aristotile in questo
luogo, onde vano è lo sforzo di quegli espositori, i quali con le
parole del terzo testo o del nono studiano di dar luogo in questa
guisa di poesia alla prosa.'[11] In other words Salviati is convinced
at this point that Aristotle states categorically that an essential
feature of that genre of 'poetry' known as comedy is verse.

It is Salviati's Aristotelianism, so important in later controversies
over the *Gerusalemme Liberata,* which determines his attitude to
the whole question. Unlike Grazzini, who appears to have rejected
Aristotle on the grounds that he represented solely Antiquity,
Salviati, as we shall see in discussing these controversies, considers
him to be virtually a timeless authority whose precepts are universally valid in modern times as in Antiquity. There is thus no
conflict in his mind between the independence of the Italian
tradition and the precepts of Aristotle. Since he is convinced
that Aristotle calls for verse in comedy Salviati therefore takes
pains in his commentary to defend comedy in verse. Moreover,
that defence, when examined in detail, has every appearance of
being a closely reasoned rebuttal of the views contained in his
friend Grazzini's *stanze, Contro le commedie in versi.*

Having made the case for verse, he uses a later section of the
Poetics to prove that Aristotle insists on a type of verse in comedy
which creates as nearly as possible the illusion of speech and
thereby facilitates the *verosimile.* This corresponds, as he points
out, to his own practice in *Il Granchio.* He first contradicts

<hr>

[11] This commentary is to be found in Florence, B.N.C., Cod. Magl. VII, 87,
and the quotation is from fol. 184ʳ. The section of the work dealing with the
comedy runs from fols. 184ʳ to fol. 189ᵛ. Page-references to this manuscript will
follow quotations, in brackets.

Piccolomini, who had declared the Italians to be in a very different position from the Greeks because the nature of the Italian language and Italian prosody precluded the possibility of a type of verse which was not too far removed from natural speech. He declares that on the contrary Italian verse is more like speech than classical verse was, and that just as Greek speech naturally produced iambics (according to Aristotle) so the hendecasillable frequently occurs in speech, or when one is attempting to write prose 'senza che quasi punto l'orecchio se n'accorga' (185ᵛ). In support of this he quotes the prose of Boccaccio, Villani, and Della Casa, all of it sprinkled with what he believes to be 'spontaneous' hendeca-syllables.¹² (The *sdrucciolo*, on the other hand, he considers to be not natural, which explains in his view the unpopularity of Ariosto's plays in verse.) In all this Salviati's purpose is to defend the Italian language as the equal of the classical languages by asserting that it, too, has the qualities, and potential, required by Aristotle of a vehicle for comedy.

There are, he says, those who consider that verse is classical and prose 'Italian'; that verse inhibits pleasure and also, by removing conviction (the *verosimile*), robs a work of any utility; that it is absurd deliberately to create verse of such a kind that it appears not to be verse. It is impossible not to recognize the pattern and expression of Grazzini's arguments here in the very pattern and expression of their rebuttal. In dismissing them Salviati takes us right to the heart of his own convictions. To those who adduce the above arguments against verse, he says,

dobbiamo rispondere la differenza delle lingue non deve variare quelle cose, che a tutte le lingue comuni sono ugualmente. Comuni ad ogni lingua è lo scrivere in versi, od in prosa, ma più in questo, che in quel verso è spezial proprietà di questo idioma o di quello. La commedia è poema, la qual verso di sé a tutte le favelle è comune. La legge che in

---

¹² Commentary, fol. 185ʳ⁻ᵛ. Salviati is unaware of Boccaccio's rhetorical use of the *prosa versificata* as analysed by V. Branca, *Boccaccio medievale* (Firenze, Sansoni, 1956), who on p. 62 mentions the other reference by Salviati to the 'natural' occurrence of the hendecasyllable, namely in his *Avvertimenti* (I, II, III). There Salviati writes of Boccaccio: 'Verso, ch'avesse verso nel verso non fece mai, ò così radi, che nella moltitudine de' lor contradj restano, come affogati. Di che leggendo il Filostrato, e l'Amorosa Visione, agevolmente possiamo certificarci. Ma nelle prose, dove non bisognava, ne fece, non accorgendosene, molti de' molto belli: La luce il cui splendor la notte fugge. Era già l'oriente tutto bianco, e altri simili assai.' In the commentary Salviati quotes these examples, and many more, including some of those quoted by Branca.

legata locuzione debba farsi è data alla commedia non alla greca lingua
o ad altra: e la ragione sopra la quale la predetta legge è fondata a tutte
le lingue è comune: ciò si è l'artifizio, il quale, come che utile, o gio-
vamento all'uditore non recasse, solo, che noia, o disutile non arrechi,
per non ispogliare l'autore della lode, e del privilegio del suo titolo non
dovrebbe trascurarsj. E chi farà il verso nella guisa, che s'è detto,
niun fastidio, e niun danno all'orecchie et all'animo dello spettatore
porterà. E vedesi, che altrettanto dagli antichi poeti s'adoperava, cioè
che si sforzavano nelle commedie di nascondere il verso in maniera, che
della prosa difficilmente si potesse conoscere. (188^v–189^r)

All this is built on the firm rock of what we shall see to be
Salviati's brand of Aristotelianism, namely the universal applica-
tion of Aristotelian precept, but in a manner suited to the special
exigencies of the individual language-medium, culture, and epoch.
That his argumentation here is tailor-made to rebut the thesis of
Grazzini seems clear on close scrutiny.

This commentary, though composed over a long period, was
subjected to unceasing modification, and must be considered, in
its final form, to represent Salviati's mature views on the subject.
It is to it, after all, that he refers the reader in the *Avvertimenti* of
1584 for enlightenment on his conception of the comedy. So whilst
we may concede that *La Spina* may represent some form of
experiment on the lines proposed by Grazzini, it does not represent a mature conception of the *volgare* comedy invalidating the
conception represented by *Il Granchio*. *La Spina* was not published
in Salviati's lifetime. Nowhere does he refer to it, whereas he
makes several references to *Il Granchio*—and as a linguistic
model what is more—in the commentary. This, of course, may be
an argument in favour of *La Spina* being a late work. If one
might hazard a conjecture, *La Spina* does seem more likely, on
the evidence available, to have been an experiment which was
then suppressed. Olgiati, who published it posthumously, says
merely that it 'came into his hands' in the 'manner known' to
Laderchi (to whom it is dedicated), and never suggests that
death prevented Salviati from publishing it, evidence *e silentio*
perhaps that Salviati himself never intended to do so. In this case
he no doubt had his good reasons, probably the ones we have seen
expressed in the commentary.

The second point of interest in *Il Granchio* concerns content.
In the period following the Council of Trent, in a prevailing mood

very different from the one which saw the birth of the *Mandragola*, the *Clizia*, the *Lena*, and others, there was the problem of modifying the material of the Roman comedy in such a way that it satisfied the moral exigencies of the times. The attitude shown by Salviati in this period towards the question of morality in art, a question on which his contemporaries assumed widely differing standpoints, is illuminated by an examination of *Il Granchio*.

An unmistakable pointer here is found very early when Duti, the *senex* and supposed father of the *adulescens* Fortunio, finds that people believe he, Duti, has fallen in love with a young girl. The following conversation then takes place:

Duti   Innamorat'io? Dio me ne guardi!
        O siam noi pazzi . . .
        L'amore mio non è di questa fatta.

Granchio E quando e' fosse, se ne veggon tutto
        Giorno degli altri: se non altro nelle
        Commedie d'oggidì.

Duti   Ed anco nelle
        Commedie, die 'l sa, come e' vi stanno.

Granchio Non so poi tanto in là. S'e' se ne trovano
        De' veri, se ne doverà ben anche
        Poter trovar de' finti.

Duti   Si ritruovano
        Anche delle cornacchie bianche: e pure
        Per questo i buoni artefici . . . Ma basta (Act. I, Sc. i).

The meaning is clear enough. Comedy is not an excuse for the portrayal of what is morally offensive, however consecrated by tradition. Accordingly the unsuitable characters, the *leno*, the *lena*, prostitutes, old men as rivals in love, have disappeared as characters in their own right, though they inevitably colour to some extent those who take their place. The young women, who (like Roman maidens of good family) never appear on the stage, are both of them ladies of impeccable upbringing and virtue. Contemporary theorists on the question of the 'example' disputed at length over the legitimacy of portraying 'bad' characters who paid the price of their wickedness and therefore became 'exemplary'. Salviati himself begins by removing, as Duti's words would lead us to expect, all characters who would be morally offensive because of their profession or because they were tied essentially to a specific undesirable state or condition. As for those left, Salviati's reluctance to relinquish the comic potential of bad characters, combined with a parallel reluctance to portray them as such, leads to many of his characters being endowed with a strange double life. This consists in a discrepancy between their reputation, or their conception of themselves as they advertise it, on the one hand, and their character as presented in action on the other, Salviati having apparently decided that what matters is not what they are *said* to be, but what they actually *do* in the course of the plays. Though they build up pictures of themselves and their companions as hypocritical, deceitful, bawdy, antisocial, good-for-nothing moral delinquents, these aspects of their character are completely cast aside for the duration of the plays, during which they behave with faultless moral rectitude.

With the characters on their best behaviour the action undergoes a similar moralization. Though like the Roman *adulescens* Fortunio is ready to deceive his guardian Duti he nevertheless cherishes the highest moral standards in his relations with the opposite sex. He himself does not allow us to forget it, and the other characters, though commenting with surprise on the fact and on his consequent behaviour, make little or no attempt to change him. Throughout the play the conception of love which dominates is a courtly-romantic one, uncontaminated by reprehensible carnal passion, and after an action completely free from unlawful or immoral elements it is not a temporary illicit union which results, but a regular, permanent marriage. Nor is there any of the full-blooded coarseness of many of the earlier works. Its place is taken by furtive, frustrated, oblique references to immorality or obscenity. In this way the Roman comedy is adapted to the demands of a counter-reformation society, and the result, in a mediocre craftsman such as Salviati, can only be insipid. A comparison between Fanticchio's account, in *Il Granchio*, of what he saw when Fortunio was closeted with his love, i.e. 'paroline senza / Pro' and 'sospiri gittati al vento' (Act. III, Sc. iv) and the parallel uproariously funny scene of the *Ingannati* when Cittina describes what *she* hears, as she is hearing it, more than suffices to convince one of the futility of this cleaning-up of the *commedia erudita* and the loss of comic potential which results.

In at least one significant aspect, therefore, *Il Granchio* is a milestone in Salviati's development, being a manifestation, in this early period, of the current moral conformism. Over the next decade and a half his ideas on the matter, in keeping with the developments in his times, were to be modified considerably, until the *Liberata* polemics reveal a quite different conception of the problem. In the meantime, however, *Il Granchio* and other contemporary works indicate that Salviati was ready to take up the cause as his own, either from conviction or from expediency. The early orations, for example, confirm this. When, in the oration *In lode della pittura*, he embarks on what is virtually an aesthetic tract, he embraces as has already been seen the moralizing current, and puts the stress with monotonous repetitiveness on the moral function of art, and on its usefulness 'per emendare i costumi . . . potendone proporre esempi di persone rivestite di qualunque qualità, ed i premi delle laudevoli e delle biasimevoli operazioni più evidentemente potendo farne apparire' (V). It is on these grounds that the painters are pronounced superior to poets, and poets in their turn superior to philosophers, and though the immediate purposes of the oration determined this particular configuration of the hierarchy, the important fact still remains that the valuations are made entirely on moral grounds.

It is of great significance in the history of Salviati and his times that two parallel connections are made. First, moral conformism is always linked to religious conformism, the latter a constant element in his work from now on. It culminates in his violent denunciation of heresy in his *Orazione intorno all'incoronazione del Granduca Cosimo I* (1570), a denunciation coupled with a call to destroy the Protestant heretics 'sì che di loro non resti pur nome o memoria, non che semenza o radice' (X). In all those whom he extols, in orations or in dedications, the quality most strongly stressed is their religiousness, be it Cosimo or the small boy Garzia.

The second, and by far the more important connection which became a commonplace of Salviati's writing was the link between morality, religion, and the Italian tradition (and more specifically language and literature) on the one hand, as against immorality, paganism, and the classical languages on the other. Varchi as usual had pointed the way, singling out *onestà* and *gravità* as the two qualities in which the *volgare* was superior to the classical languages, praising the chasteness of Petrarch and condemning the immorality of the classics. Once again, as so often in this period of the sixteenth century (cf. the discussions on history, defence of the national tradition, etc.), we find statements which would not have come amiss in the Romantic disputes almost three centuries later.[13]

Echoing Varchi, and uniting as always the religious and moral content of Italian literature with the language itself, he had written of Petrarch's verse in the *Fiorentina favella* oration: 'La qual guisa di poetare, dico quella del Petrarca, parmi che agli antichi fusse ascosa del tutto, e credo che sia uno degli speziali privilegi della nostra favella, prodotto massimamente dalla naturale onestà, e gravità, e grandezza che essa, siccome io stimo, ha prese dalla religione' (IV). As we have seen, the *Orazione seconda* on Don Garzia had also contained hints of a similar nature.

In exactly the same way as we were given, in the *Fiorentina favella* oration, an implicit condemnation of the effects on the *volgare* of linguistic classicism, later to become a cornerstone of Salviati's linguistic theory—so we have now a condemnation of the effects of classicism in general on the pure stream of Italian national culture, whose Christian moral values are represented in Petrarch, a poet, as Salviati sees it, who antedated the classical revival. Imitation of Antiquity is likewise blamed in the *Orazione in lode della pittura* for the immorality characterizing Italian literature and painting until the very recent past. Here again we are struck by Salviati's affinities with the early anti-humanists.

Salviati's many pronouncements on the subject compositely constitute an attack on fifteenth-century classicism which in its manifold aspects he sees as a subservience to Antiquity alien to the Italian tradition, resulting in paganism, immorality, and linguistic deterioration. The interesting thing about this attitude is not how far it is accurate (if this could have any meaning) or what had in

---

[13] e.g. Varchi's references (*Ercolano*, p. 451) to the immoral behaviour of the Gods: 'forse in quei tempi, quella religione, e quelle usanze lo comportavano: il che i tempi nostri, la religione nostra, e le nostre usanze non fanno'. As an example of Varchi's attitude to the 'immoral' classics, p. 451: '*V.* Considerate quel che fa Omero, non dico dire, ma fare a Giove, Padre e Re di tutti i loro Dii, con Giunone, per impazienza di libidine. *C.* Plutarco, Porfirio, e alcuni altri non pure lo scusano, ma il lodano ancora eziandio in coteste stesse sporcizie, dicendo che elle sono favole, sotto i velamenti delle quali con maraviglioso ingegno trovati si ricuoprono di grandissimi e bellissimi e utilissimi misteri. *V.* Tutto credo: ma con tutto questo credere non mi può entrare nell'animo, ciò essere ben fatto, e che meglio non fosse stato ritrovare con più degne favole meno disonesti velamenti.'

fact been the relationship of the classicist to the native current in the humanistic fourteenth century. It is interesting rather because it stresses the twofold nature of the development which it documents. That development is not merely the expected maturing of a long-established movement towards the vindication of the national tradition. It is also an alienation from a state of mind which gave the classics their significance for the fifteenth century.

So in this respect even *Il Granchio*, with its use of idiomatic Florentine and its insistence on morality, takes its place in that pattern of Salviati's thought which will eventually lead him to a theory of language which justifies archaism even for the Florentines. In that theory Salviati integrates archaism completely into his over-all view of the relationship of the Italian national tradition to classical culture.

The former must be revived in all its (fourteenth-century) purity and the damaging effects of the latter must be removed. A number of references in the play to the law and order prevailing in Florence, guaranteeing the rights of its citizens under the guidance of a paternal and benevolent ruler, complete the picture of Salviati as Consul of the Florentine Academy, Rector of the Studio, faithful servant of Cosimo, and convinced apostle of the essential oneness of the Florentine state and Italian culture.

But on the whole the years 1566–7 were lean ones for Salviati. An academical lecture entitled *Della poetica, lettura terza*, copied out in his own hand and dispatched to the rich and influential cavalier Gaddi, seems to be little more than an extract from the *Lezzion prima*.[14] During the consulship of Jacopo Pitti, to whom Salviati handed on his office, he delivered one lecture (subject unknown) to the Accademia, and the three orations on taking up and leaving his consulship were published with a dedication to 'il cardinal De' Monti', whose favour and patronage he had recently enjoyed.[15] In the year 1566 there appeared, anonymously, his translation of Vettori's oration in praise of Francesco's bride,

[14] This is the *Della poetica lettura terza* (see also Ch. vii n. 14), published with many errors by Manzoni, *Prose*, in 1873 and taken from Cod. aut. Magl. VII, 715, B.N.C., Florence (the ded. lett. is 1566). It is merely the third quarter of the *Lezzion prima* doctored to look like an independent composition, see Brown, 'L'edizione del 1873'.

[15] Published in the *Primo libro delle orazioni di Lionardo Salviati* of 1567. For the cardinal see K. Eubel, *Hierarchia Catholica* (Monasterii, 1898), for May 1550. 'Innocentius de Monte, nepos (adoptivus) S.S. in C.R. 1577 nov. 3.'

later published with the title *Orazione delle lodi della Serenissima Giovanna d'Austria* in the *Primo libro delle orazioni* of 1575. The earliest documented contact between Salviati and Vettori, however, relates almost certainly to another kind of literary co-operation, and one moreover which suggests that Vettori was satisfied with the translation of his oration. On 8 March 1566 Salviati wrote to Vettori informing him of the progress which he was making with 'l'opera di Vostra Signoria', and expressing concern that through no fault of his own news of what he was doing, which was supposed to be confidential to the two men, seemed to have got around in Florence. Though Salviati never mentions the title of the work in question his references to it, for example 'io haveva cominciato a *toccar* [italics mine] qualche cosa per conto del numero' and 'il mio studio sarà tutto su l'osservare della lingua, su le parole, e su le locuzioni. Io non credo mancare di renderla al tempo promesso', indicate that what he has undertaken is some kind of linguistic revision of a work of Vettori. Inevitably this must be a *volgare* and not a Latin work. Since the translation of the oration was published in 1566 and this particular work is said in March of that year to be proceeding slowly, and since the references suggest a revision and not a translation, it seems that the subject of this revision, done clearly as a preparation for publication, can only be Vettori's *Trattato . . . delle lodi e della coltivazione de gl'ulivi*, eventually published in Florence in 1569. For centuries Vettori was as well known for this, his only substantial *volgare* work published and a composition of which the linguistic physiognomy was considered an important pointer to Vettori's attitude to the *volgare*, as he was for his philological erudition. The fact that if Salviati is indeed revising this composition the style of the work consequently reflects not so much the principles of Vettori as of Lionardo Salviati is thus a point of some significance in the assessment of Vettori's relationship to the vernacular. The letter reveals both the care Lionardo took over the language of the work and his great respect for his master. At the same time it is a testimony both to the esteem which Vettori had for Salviati and to the reputation which the latter enjoyed already in matters of language.[16]

[16] Salviati writes: 'Perciò che dove io mi reputo il favore fattomi da V. S. per uno de' maggiori, che mi potesse essere fatto, se ella facesse del fatto mio qualche sinistro concetto, mi parrebbe che la mia fosse stata sventura.' U. lett. Salviati to Vettori, Florence, 8.3.1566, London, British Museum, Additional MS. 10278, fol. 45ʳ.

Finally, in 1567, in the dedication of the farewell speech on leaving his consulship, we find the first mention since Canigiani's letter of 1563 of a person destined to be the most important influence on Salviati after Varchi and Grazzini, namely Don Vincenzo Borghini to whom the oration is offered, and with whom Salviati must have been establishing in this period ever closer contacts.

With the end of his consulship in 1567 Salviati comes to the end of a well-defined period in his life, characterized by a multilateral philosophical, oratorical, poetic, and philological activity. In no branch of this activity has he produced work worthy of a place in Italian literature: yet in every branch he has already manifested the orientation which makes him even in this early period a figure of no small historical significance, and which will lead in later years to works of a calibre to leave a lasting mark on the development of Italian culture. As a member of a closely knit literary society he has concentrated on academic activities, supported by subsidies from his own family, from the Medici court, and from numerous other patrons. After his period of office as Consul the aspiring courtier in Salviati claims more and more of his time and attention.

X

FURTHER ORATIONS: THE ORDER OF
ST. STEPHEN

As a Florentine who identified his literary activities with the service of the state, Salviati on relinquishing his consulship in 1567 could look around him with pride and satisfaction. Far from being a tool in the hands of the Hispano-Imperialists Cosimo had by 1557 succeeded in making his little state so important in Italy that even Philip II had been unwillingly obliged to acquiesce in the seizure of Siena, achieved against powerful military opposition from the *fuorusciti* and France, and had saved his face only by insisting on military garrisons in the coastal towns. Cosimo was the first prince of Italy in fact if not in title. That the former should appear vain and hollow without the latter is a revealing comment on his times. For though in his own state his word was law and his voice was heard in the councils of the nations, he lacked what mattered most to a ruler in his times and country—a title. He lacked a title which would be the outward manifestation of the hidden power of one who in the Italian feudal hierarchy was but Duke of Florence, one over whom even the petty Duke of Ferrara had a substantial claim to precedence.

As early as 1560, on his protracted visit to Rome, Cosimo was negotiating for titular elevation with Pius IV, a pope extremely well disposed towards Cosimo and thus a welcome change from his predecessors. In a flurry of reciprocal favours Cosimo accepted back *fuorusciti* recommended by Pius, helped to straighten out the Pope's relations with Italian rulers, and aided negotiations for the reopening of the Council of Trent. Pius for his part had given a cardinal's hat first to Giovanni, and then on the latter's death to Ferdinand, and declared himself willing to give Cosimo the desired promotion. The title of Grand Duke was the only one which did not present insuperable technical difficulties. There were long negotiations, whose reverberations were felt through the courts of Europe. Pius IV died in 1569 but collusion between

Cosimo and Pius V resulted in a papal bull proclaiming Cosimo Grand Duke arriving in Florence in December 1569, where there were great festivities.[1]

When Cosimo left Florence in February 1570 for his spectacular coronation in Rome, Isabella de' Medici was with him, and so was her husband, Salviati's patron Paolo Giordano Orsini. Indeed he was amongst the most prominent figures in the retinue, for at the coronation ceremony in the Sistine Chapel on 5 March it was he who handed the sceptre to Cosimo. Isabella and Paolo were far from pleased, however, when on 29 March, a few days after his return to Florence, the Grand Duke married his mistress Camilla Martelli as part of his agreement with Pius.

In Cosimo's absence Lionardo had not been idle. By 1 April, a little over a week after the Grand Duke's return, he was able to sign the dedication of a new and typical composition, to wit, an *Orazione intorno all'incoronazione del Serenissimo Cosimo de' Medici Gran Duca di Toscana*.[2] It was dedicated to Jacopo Sesto d'Aragona d'Appiano, Signor di Piombino. This unfortunate ruler, virtually obliged by popular sentiment to abdicate in 1562 from his state of Piombino shortly after its restitution to him after the Sienese war, had recently gained a new dignity as commander of the Tuscan fleet. His wife had recently had a sonnet dedicated to her by Salviati ('Donna vie più che bella, honesta e bella' (23), 'Alla signora di Piombino', later modified to become a sonnet in praise of Bianca Cappello), and now Lionardo refers to himself as Jacopo's 'spezialissimo servidore'. As we shall shortly see, there is a special reason for this.

Though a welter of rhetorical verbiage devoid of artistic merit, the oration has its interest. For although form does not match up to content as in the *Fiorentina favella* oration, it does have the same character of enthusiasm. However exasperatingly artificial, stylistically speaking, this composition is, there does emerge from it a sense of national pride, joy, and exultation. Exult, he cries to Florence, exult 'o mia generosa e nobilissima patria, che ben hai

[1] See Lapini, *Diario*, also C. Firmano, *Della solenne incoronazione del Duca Cosimo de' Medici in Granduca di Toscana* (Florence, 1819). For details of the negotiations see particularly L. Carcerieri, *Cosimo I Granduca* (Verona, 1926), and V. Maffei, *Dal titolo di Duca di Firenze e Siena al titolo di Gran Duca di Toscana: contributo alla storia della politica di Cosimo I de' Medici* (Florence, 1905).
[2] Florence, Sermartelli, 1570.

tu in questo tempo, più che in altro ancor mai, di rallegrarti, e di far festa degnissima cagione'. The oration is shot through with the thrill of success, of recognition, without reserves or hesitation, that the trials and dangers of the immediate past are over; that Florence has successfully negotiated the dangerous reef on which she might have foundered; that the past is vindicated and that from being a broken relic as in 1530 Florence, by the skill, courage, and tenacity of one man, has achieved her rightful place in Italy. All this, Lionardo declares, is the doing of Cosimo de' Medici:

Imperocchè qual altro si sentì, che in ispazio di poco più di trent'anni di privato, Principe divenisse: nuovo Principe l'intera libertà, e l'antiche giuridizioni al suo principato ricuperasse: de' potenti nemici l'orgogliose armi abbattesse: di grandi, e minaccevoli eserciti trionfasse, così di territorio, come ancora di potenza lo stato raddoppiasse: ordini militari, e religioni innovasse, dotasse, accrescesse: del fior delle provincie, non solamente il dominio, ma la corona e lo scettro finalmente ottenesse? (X)

Nothing succeeds like success. Salviati was here expressing the feelings of those Florentines whose hearts had been won over by their share of the national prestige. 'Godi, eccelsa repubblica', writes Salviati, 'del tuo venerando nome rinvigorito'—for had not the crowd of diplomats and ecclesiastical dignitaries gathered in the Sala Reale of the Vatican burst out spontaneously, as Cosimo walked past them holding the Pope's train, into loud cries of 'Palle, palle', of which Agostino Lapini wrote that it 'fu tenuta cosa di grandissimo amore per il nostro serenissimo Gran Duca, che uno popolo alieno mostrassi tanta allegrezza fuori della sua città'? Mingled with this new-found national pride and self-respect is the truly Salviatesque nationalistic note, for it is in this very oration that Lionardo reminds the world how Rome in religious and other spheres was the pupil of Etruria, making this resurrection of Tuscan supremacy part of the natural order of things.

Meanwhile externally and also internally (where a merchant aristocracy, weakened by political and administrative changes and consisting in part of repentant rebels anxious only to prove their loyalty to the new regime, no longer presented a challenge to absolutism) the coronation of Cosimo de' Medici as Grand Duke did indeed mark the triumph of the policies which the Duke had been pursuing for thirty years. That so much importance should be attached to the title rather than the substance of power almost eludes our comprehension. The attitude is often attributed, with doubtful justification, to Spanish influence. Yet it is only one aspect of a more widespread and fundamental development discernible in Italian thought, culture, and behaviour.

For it is a fact that a further aspect of the times emerging clearly from Salviati's orations, and from this one in particular, is precisely that strange separation of word and thing, of form from content, which took place in this period. This phenomenon already manifests itself in the overwhelming importance, in the orations, of the externals of language and style as opposed to content, and in the poems the dominant importance of musicality and rhythmic effects. Concomitant with this phenomenon is the rhetorical exaltation of the word, and the consequent power of appearance over fact, of which the oration on Cosimo's coronation is a truly remarkable document since it turns entirely on a change of title— *par excellence* a verbal matter and a matter of appearance only. Duke Cosimo has become Grand Duke Cosimo and at one stroke the state is transformed 'almost into a kingdom', the 'Republic' becomes a 'Grand Republic', and 'quelli che i suoi senatori erano avanti, gran senatori sono testè: e come egli d'illustrissimo, serenissimo è fatto, così de' suoi nobili di nobili chiarissimi, i chiarissimi di chiarissimi illustri, i magistrati di magistrati eccelsi: il popolo d'onorato gloriosissimo, la plebe di non sordida orrevole è diventata.'

Presumably Salviati sees himself as one who benefited from the metamorphosis. In a passage which seems deliberately composed to illustrate this power of form, of externals, of appearances, and consequently of rhetoric, he asks in the same oration if anyone will deny that this is 'non pur reale, ma realissima esaltazione', or that the Grand Ducal dignity 'non che reale, realissima sia?', when no necessary regal element is lacking. For in what does the essence of kingship lie, he asks, if not in a crown, a sceptre, and a title? See the crown, he invites the world: is there to be found a better crown? Look at the sceptre: does there exist a more regal sceptre? Consider the titles: is not Cosimo *Altezza* and *Serenissimo*? What then does Cosimo lack, to be the greatest Prince, not only of Italy but of the world? These are but the grosser manifestations of an outlook which subtly permeates the *Orazioni* and colours Salviati's treatment of any subject. It merely happens that this particular oration presents a unique opportunity in the form of a political event which embodies to perfection this distinctive feature of the times.

Naturally almost as much praise is showered on Pius as on Cosimo. This reflects certainly the new and very satisfactory relations between Florence and the Vatican, for which Cosimo had striven hard and patiently, but it also reflects the lot of the professional men of letters in the late sixteenth century. Once religious persecution had flared up again in the pontificate of Paul V, the Italian literary scene came to be characterized by the almost complete absence of even the mildest questioning or dissent. Protestations of orthodoxy and condemnation of any sign of deviationism in others (we have already had the example of the 'Corbi') intensified that atmosphere of artificial religious conformism which being largely based on hypocrisy is one of the most unattractive features of the letters of the times.

In this context it is important to remember that in 1564 Salviati had dedicated his oration *In lode della pittura* to Pietro Carnesecchi, subsequently handed over by Cosimo to Pius V who had him executed for heresy. Whatever the motives behind this action on the part of the Duke,[3] once Carnesecchi was tried, hanged, and burned, Salviati was left with an oration dedicated to a condemned heretic, with its dedicatory letter in the form of an important policy-document. Fortunately for him he had said nothing in the letter of any close attachment between Carnesecchi and Cosimo, though he had made the unfortunate and unconsciously ironical statement that never in his life had he met anyone who had 'nella faccia, nelle maniere e ne' ragionamenti una cotale maravigliosa forza di guadagnarsi gli animi, e farsegli perpetuamente soggetti'. It was the oration on Cosimo's coronation which gave him the opportunity to clear himself and to erase from his contemporaries' memories his misplaced praise of a heretic by whose persuasive powers he had declared himself enchanted. This he did, not so much by his exaltation of the principle which gave the Vicar of God a divine right to create princes, though in the end the emperor had in fact been presented with a *fait accompli* with regard to the Grand Ducal crown, but by the outwardly impassioned attack on heresy with which he ends the

---

[3] For discussion of Cosimo's motives see particularly Booth, *Cosimo I*, especially pp. 201–13, and Winspeare, *Isabella Orsini* pp. 111–14.

oration. Though the rest of the oration prepares the ground for it, it is still staggering for the intensity of its violence. He follows a description of the present sad state of the Holy Land with the following outburst:

Ma la colpa è pur d'altri, cioè della diabolica perversità di coloro che fra i cristiani falsamente s'annoverano: i quali quando tempo sarebbe di rivoltarsi contra la barbarica persecuzione e tirannide, il cristianesimo col loro pestifero veleno attendono ad ammorbare, del tosco riempiendolo, e della rabbia delle maledette eresie. Contra 'l furor de' quali rivoltiamoci una volta tutti, non dico solamente religiosi di qualunque maniera, ma tutti i popoli e tutti gli uomini e tutte le nazioni, e senz'aspettar più, o dieta di Principi, o governo di generale o ordine di Capitano, tumultuosamente, e a furia di popolo corriamo unitamente tutti senza mai arrestarci, finchè siamo loro addosso, e confondiamgli, e disperdiamgli, e sprofondiamgli tutti subitamente, sì che di loro non resti pur nome o memoria, non che semenza o radice.

By this explosion of fury two aims were achieved. Salviati's own record was cleared, but so was Cosimo's. The Grand Duke is quite understandably said to have liked the oration, for with its defence not only of the purifying zeal of Pius V but also of any action against heresy it no doubt made the Grand Ducal crown sit a little more easily on his head. For on the crown, according to Lapini, were engraved the words 'Pius V Pontifex Maximus, ob eximiam dilectionem ac catholicae religionis zelum precipuumque justitiae studium donavit.'

Though aesthetically negative, the oration as a contemporary and biographical document is full of interesting hints and veiled information throwing light on Salviati himself and on his relations with the Florentine authorities. In particular, woven into the dominant theme of the restoration of Florence to her ancient and rightful glory, are two closely associated references requiring special attention. At one point Salviati highlights all Cosimo has done for the city of Pisa, including all that went with the founding of the Order of St. Stephen; and towards the end of the oration he takes it upon himself to preach a crusade. As most informed readers of the composition well knew, the stress laid on these two matters was no sudden fancy, nor was it, in the case of the second of them, the mere routine repetition of a rhetorical commonplace. Rather, their inclusion here was due to recent developments which closely concerned the Grand Duke of Tuscany and Pius V himself, a man single-mindedly dedicated to the extirpation of heresy (it was he who excommunicated Elizabeth I) and to the improvement of public morality. It was common knowledge that during Cosimo's recent visit to Rome the two had discussed at length the Turkish menace and were agreed on the desirability of action.

It was in the context of this menace that Cosimo, early in the 1540s, had begun slowly but steadily to build up a fleet, partly to secure his shores against predatory raids, partly as a bulwark against the inevitable French opposition to his designs on Siena, and partly as an element in his policy of gaining independence from Spain.

In the meantime the world saw his fleet (the first galleys *La Saetta* and *La Pisana* were ready in 1547, and with the *San Giovanni* went into action against the Turks at Mehedia) as a contribution to the task of checking the advance of the infidel. Despite some setbacks, notably at Jerbah, and at Famagusta, where *La Lupa* was confiscated by the Venetians for piracy, the fleet was a valuable addition to Tuscan strength and prestige, for the Tuscan galleys were fine ships, well equipped and well manned. As his naval strength grew and his reputation with it, Cosimo founded in 1561–2 the Military Order of the Knights of Saint Stephen. With their statutes based in the first place on those of the Knights of Malta, their base was Pisa where the old Palazzo della Carovana, transformed for the purpose by Vasari, became their headquarters. Ancillary industries and a supply organization sprang up to support the Order; and all this new activity made no small contribution to the revitalization of Pisa. How great was Cosimo's achievement, cries Salviati in the present oration— '. . . lo sa la nobile città di Pisa, lo mostra quel real palagio, lo testifica quel magnifico tempio, ne fanno fede quegli opportuni edifici, ce ne chiarisce la dote di tante e sì ampie commende, ce lo 'nsegnano le sontuose fabbriche degli strumenti, de' navigli, e de' legni' (X)—all of which seemed to be turning Pisa into a bustling, thriving city.

Thus the oration also acquires the character of a manifesto. Salviati proclaims abroad the policy of Cosimo and Pius V, directed towards concerted action against the Turks, and at the same time vaunts Tuscan sea power. In view of the fact that on other occasions Salviati has openly declared himself to be saying 'what he has been expressly commanded to say', the possibility that he was to some extent officially prompted in all this cannot be excluded. Whatever the facts, this aspect of the oration illuminates the dedication to the commander of the Tuscan fleet, for it pinpoints the special importance attached to the material. But there was another reason why Salviati should take pride in Cosimo's fleet and refer to his 'special attachment' to Jacopo Sesto D'Appiano. He, Lionardo, had just been made a Knight of the Order of Saint Stephen.

Proceedings had begun for his admission as a *cavalier sacerdotale* on 29 June 1569, when investigations, first into his claim to nobility and then into his personal life and record, were set in motion. After a short delay resulting from the need to obtain from the Town Council of Iesi confirmation of the noble status of Lionardo's paternal great-grandfather who was an Ambrogini of that city, the *provanza* proper could begin, and witnesses gave evidence that Salviati conformed to the seventeen traditional 'claims' which he put forward about himself. The evidence of these witnesses, who included Pier Vettori, is a valuable source of biographical information on Salviati. Once it was completed, and a certificate from Iesi was received, all was ready for the investiture, which took place a little over a month later in Pisa on 12 August 1569, at the hands of Piero dal Monte, in an impressive and lengthy ceremony aimed at reminding the new knight that, as the statutes of the Order said, 'gli bisogna divenire un'altr huomo da quello che egli era'.[4]

These words must have been felt by Salviati to have had more than a merely formal significance in his case, as there is proof that in March 1569 he suffered a temporary fall from grace at court.[5] But in view of the fact that as early as four months after this incident he was admitted into the Order of St. Stephen,

---

[4] *Statuti, capitoli et constitutioni del Ordine de' Cavalieri di Santo Stephano* (Florence, Appresso Lorenzo Torrentino, Impressor Ducale, MDLXII), p. 5. This publication gives much information on the workings of the Order, illuminating Salviati's letters which are concerned with his activities on behalf of the Order. Information on Salviati's entrance into the Order is taken from (*a*) Pisa, A.S., A.S.St., Indice del repertorio delle filze di Provanze di nobiltà dalla Istituzione dell'Ordine di Santo Stefano fino alla sua soppressione, Numero d'ordine 302, Lionardo Salviati, filza settima, parte prima; and (*b*) Giornale 'A', 1561–1624, d'Apprension d'Abito di Lettera in the same archive.

[5] Documented by an unpublished letter Salviati to Vettori, 23.3.68 (i.e. 1569 st. com.), B.M., Additional MS. 10281, fols. 86^r–87^r. On the subject of the handwriting of this and other documents see P. M. Brown, 'Nota sui manoscritti di Lionardo Salviati', *Studi di filologia italiana*, xx (1962), 137–46.

he must have been rehabilitated fairly swiftly, with or without the assistance of Vettori (for which he made a pathic request), who once again enters Lionardo's life as a witness in the latter's *provanza di nobiltà* for the Order. His consistently high opinion of his pupil is vouched for by his evidence, which in addition to confirming the warmth of their mutual respect and affection indicates the esteem in which Vettori and his literary friends held Lionardo's poetry as well as his other works. The investigators record of Vettori that he 'Disse che ha conosciuto il detto M. Lionardo da pueritia di esso M. Lionardo et ha visto che è vissuto sempre honoratamente et da gentilhuomo et ha implicato tutto il tempo alle buone lettere et è stato et è di gran dottrina et elegantia et ingegni sublimi sì nelli studi come nella poesia et è in grande aspettatione di tutti i litterati.'[6]

Coming from Pier Vettori this is indeed praise, and we may suppose that Vettori had helped him in his difficulties of a few months earlier, which evidence suggests may have concerned his relations with Francesco rather than with Cosimo. If this is so, and he had in some way offended Francesco, then certain aspects of the future development of his relations with the court are more satisfactorily explained.[7]

However, for the moment a renewed sign of favour is found in the fact that on 22 April 1571 he delivered an oration, dedicated to Francesco, to the assembled Knights of St. Stephen at their Annual General Meeting, at which the statutes decreed that a distinguished orator should give an address 'trattando dell'utilità pubblica della Religione' and exhorting the Knights to devote themselves in every way to its glory and service. It was not the first time he had been called upon to perform this duty, for in January 1570 he had already been asked to do so. To the respectful, flattering, and complimentary letter of invitation from the Council of St. Stephen Salviati replied with eagerness and gratitude, despite the bigger business afoot, namely Cosimo's coronation. Of this 1570 oration there is no trace.[8]

[6] See supplementary note 6, p. 247.

[7] See Lett. Salviati to Francesco de' Medici, 24.4.71, Florence, A.S., F.M., Carteggio Universale, Filza 559, p. 312, pub. Contin, *Lettere*, No. 11, which consists largely of apologies for unspecified shortcomings in the past. The sestina *inc.* 'D'Arno gentil su la fiorita sponda' (16) also seems to make reference to the episode.

[8] See U. letts. Cons. S.St. to Salviati, 21.1.69 (i.e. 70) Pisa, A.S., A.S.St.,

The Order itself, however, soon began to occupy a good deal of Salviati's time. Exactly what office he first held is not clear, but his *patente d'anzianità*—his certificate of seniority which allowed him to join the queue for a *commenda*—issued 21 October 1575, states that he has qualified for this 'parte con lo stare al convento in offizio di consigliere'.[9] This must have been during the years 1571 or 1572, the only years not documented to the contrary after his entry into the Order, though the absence of documents for the previous year, 1568, may mean that Salviati was then fulfilling the requirements of the statutes, which declared that no *Cavalier cappellano* (or *sacerdotale*), such as Salviati was, could be created 'infino à tanto che egli non hara servito in detto convento un'anno intero'—so that a check could be made on his behaviour. During this period the novice lived at the expense of the Order. In this connection it is of interest that Vincenzo Borghini, in a letter to Grand Duke Cosimo dating from 1571, states that Salviati 'hoggi sta a Pisa', indicating that his permanent residence was there.[10]

Much of the business (though not all) to which he attended during the year 1571 was concerned with the printing of the statutes and rules of the Order in preparation for the General Assembly to be held on 22 April. After long negotiations with astute printers, in which Salviati showed great zeal despite being severely hampered by the obsessive meanness of the Council, the printing was finished in time and Salviati was praised for his diligence. It was at this meeting that he delivered his oration.[11]

R.L.M., to the Cons., Filza 1320, fols. 82ᵛ to 83ʳ and ibid., F.L.O. to the Cons., 23.1.69 (i.e. 70), Filza 1365, fol. 417. The oration referred to in these letters is *not* the one published in 1571 and delivered, as stated on its title page, on 22 April of that year. No letter is extant calling on Salviati to deliver the 1571 oration, but there is no possibility of mistaking the date of the invitation and acceptance here under consideration, as they both have an *ab inc.* dating of 1569, placing them in January 1570. (Salviati writes from Florence and so is unquestionably using Florentine dating, and this is normally used by the Council in Pisa.)

⁹ 'Patente del Cav.re Lionardo Salviati fior.no', Pisa, A.S., A.S.St., R.L.M., No. 1323, fols. 94ᵛ–95ʳ. The regulations of the Order made some residence at the headquarters in Pisa obligatory.

¹⁰ *Prose fiorentine*, Vol. iv, pt. 4, p. 326.

¹¹ *Orazione recitata in Pisa al Capitolo Generale della Religione di Santo Stefano* (Florence, Giunti, 1571). Ded. lett. 24.4.71 to Francesco. In the period from 21.1.70 to 3.12.72 there are extant 10 letters from Salviati to the Consiglio and 8 from the Consiglio to Salviati.

No one could say that he did not hold to the letter of the statutes, for he calls eloquently on the Knights to keep their vows of obedience, chastity, and charity. Unfortunately in doing so, and in praising the Order and its founder (who was in his audience for the first and last time in the speaker's career) Salviati reveals some of the worst features of his own personality, and some of the undesirable effects which a generation of absolutism had had on the mentality of the man of letters in his relations with the state. For the oration, like the others, is characterized by a fundamental dishonesty stemming not so much from opportunist unscrupulousness in the author himself as from a spontaneous inclination to distort the truth in the service of political expediency. The author's irresponsible willingness to perpetrate any verbal injustice if it serves his political-conformist requirements appears to us as distastefully immoral, particularly when its victims are persons or institutions to whom the reader may have a bond of respect, admiration, or affection. For example, in order to carry out his task of praising the Order, Salviati unashamedly belittles other venerable Orders, deriding their claim to distinction through antiquity, numbers, or achievements, seeking out and magnifying out of context any blemish on their reputation. These Orders are judged by absurdly external criteria, their genuine glory is deliberately dimmed, and facts are distorted with a lack of respect which alienates our sympathies.

Nevertheless, one cannot but admire his prophetic qualities, for in the midst of exhortations to action against the infidels, of references to the fall of Rhodes and Cyprus, of graphic descriptions of heroism in the siege of Malta, he calls on the Order to distinguish itself and strike a once-for-all crippling blow 'Il che tosto, la Dio mercè, siccome io spero, avverrà'. And in October of that year there took place the battle of Lepanto in which Cosimo's fleet, amongst whose commanders was Salviati's patron Paolo Giordano Orsini, played a significant part fighting under the papal colours. By it the sea power of the Turks was permanently shattered.

It is the archives of the Order of Saint Stephen which bear testimony to the fact that in the year 1572 Lionardo was in Rome, though they do not enlighten us on the purpose of his residence there, where the long arm of the Order reached him in July in the form of an appointment as *Ricevitore* [i.e. virtually debt-

collector] della Religione della città di Roma et sua provincia'.[12]
With this appointment (ill paid, though Salviati thanks the
Council for the honour done to him) began the tedious and frus-
trating task of exacting from reluctant *cavalieri* the various dues,
taxes, and other charges imposed by the Order on its members,
none of which moneys they were ever prepared to hand over
(despite the fearful penalties laid down in the regulations of the
Order), unless they were threatened with legal proceedings—
and proceedings moreover which they were convinced in advance
they would lose. For their part the *Riscuotitori* (the office is
referred to by a variety of names) were equally bound by rigid
instructions and threats of severe disciplinary action for any
breach of them.

Interesting though they are, Salviati's activities as revealed in
great detail by his correspondence with the Council cannot be
studied minutely here. In any case, scarcely had he got into the
rhythm of his work when he was obliged to ask the Council to
relieve him of the post, the sudden death of his brother Giuliano
in October 1572 obliging him to resume residence in his native
Florence. As his successor he suggested Ottaviano de' Medici,
firmly established in Rome with wife and children in the service
of the Cardinal Ferdinando de' Medici.

In the Florence to which he returned the moral decline was
gaining impetus, thanks in no small degree to Salviati's esteemed
and much-praised patron Isabella de' Medici, now a bosom
companion of Bianca Cappello. The murder of Bianca's husband,
probably connived at by Isabella and Francesco, the acquittal of
his murderers by the Grand Duke, the farce of Bianca's simulated
pregnancy with its sordid accompaniment of murder and deceit,
symbolized the growing moral depravity. Cosimo had had a severe
attack of apoplexy whilst dining with Isabella in the old palace
in the Via Larga as early as 1568 and now his health was declining
in a climate of callous selfishness and cynicism on the part of
Francesco and the courtiers.

During these relatively thinly documented years 1570–5 the
health of Salviati, too, seems to have been deteriorating. As early
as March 1568 he was in bed with a fever and again in August 1571

---

[12] See Lett. Cons. S. St. to Sal. 23.7.72, Pisa, A.S., A.S.St., R.L.M., Filza
1321, fol. 159ʳ.

evidence shows that he was far from well. Having travelled from
Pisa to Florence on the occasion of the illness of his brother
Giuliano, he himself fell ill with severe stomach pains, nausea,
dizziness, and fever which forced him, despite an initial determination to do without medical assistance, to call in the aid of
a doctor who subjected him to a purgation lasting several days.
Then once again, as he was preparing to leave Prato for Pisa in
March 1575 to attend the Annual General Meeting of his Order
(at which non-attendance, in the case of Knights in Tuscany at
the time, was a punishable offence) he was taken ill suddenly
with a fever. The journey had to be abandoned, and the official
letter of apology had to be drawn up by a notary in the house of
Bastiano Rocchi, where his illness was confining him. Finally,
when informing the Council on 6 May that year of an offer by the
Giunti to print the statutes, he indicates that his continued
absence from Florence, where he had returned only about 4 May,
was due to this prolonged bout of illness from which he was not
yet fully recovered.[13]

   In general, however, his personal affairs did not seem to be
going too badly, though whether the fact that he was his brother
Giuliano's heir was his gain or loss is not clear. What is known
is that he was left to settle all the affairs of the deceased Giuliano,
a businessman in Florence. Certainly he inherited some property
from him, as he had done from his father, to which he added
further land bought in 1572. Towards the end of 1574 he was
negotiating with one Ruberto Pini to exchange a piece of land
'posta nella villa di Figline di Prato, luogo detto Carbonaglia' for
'altri beni posti nella villa di Coiano'. In that same month of
October 1574 he took a new house at Prato.[14]

   The years of this 'Pisan period' were less fruitful for his literary

---

[13] See Pisa, A.S., A.S.St., Letts. Salviati to the Consiglio, 27.8.71, 29.3.75,
and 6.5.75, F.L.O., Nos. 1366, fol. 121, 1367, fol. 731, and 1367, fol. 818
respectively: see also Florence, A.S. Notarile Moderno, 4533 (Ser Raffaello
Godenzi, Atti dal 1574 al 1575), fol. 34ᵛ, *Procura*, dated 7 April, lett. of Salviati,
'infirmus et egrotus febre in terra Prati in domo habitationis Bastiani Leonardi
de Rocchio' to the cav. Buonamico Buonamici, to excuse himself for his forced
absence from the forthcoming meeting.
[14] For the negotiations concerning the acquisition and sale of land and
property see Florence, A.S. Decima granducale, 2309 (Arroti dell'anno 1574,
Quartiere di S. Croce), fol. 259ʳ; also No. 53 (formerly 3594), fol. 534; also
Notarile Moderno, Ser Raffaello Godenzi, Atti dal 1573 al 1574, fols. 104ᵛ–105ʳ,
Permutatio bonorum, etc.

and intellectual pursuits. Three orations, in praise of Justice, Religion, and Religious Military Orders, delivered to a circle of Salviati's friends in his villa, belong to the years 1570–1 as far as can be judged by the Razzi edition of the Orations (with comments by the editor) and by their general subject-matter, which as far as it conforms to the titles of the orations links them with this moment in which Grand-Ducal support for the papacy in its anti-heretical measures is stressed and the Order of St. Stephen (which enjoined its Knights to 'servare i precetti della Santa Sede Apostolica') was playing such a big part in his life and thought. Already the courtier and ambitious petty noble has succeeded to the eager youthful intellectual. Yet there are pointers to the continuance of his manifold interests. Amongst these pointers we may or may not include Salviati's contemporaries' suspicions that he was the author of the *Discorso contro Dante* bearing the name of Ridolfo Castravilla, when began to circulate in manuscript in Florence in 1571 and was directed against a judgement in favour of Dante as against Homer contained in Varchi's *Ercolano*, in whose posthumous publication in 1570 Salviati had had a hand. Despite investigations and studies it cannot be said that indisputable evidence has come to light concerning the authorship, and if Salviati—one of Florence's most fervent admirers of Dante—wrote it, he certainly did so with his tongue in his cheek.[15]

Of more immediate interest are two letters, dated 7 and 8 May 1570, to the Dukes of Ferrara and of Parma and Piacenza respectively. These letters, apart from a minimum of necessary variation (e.g. change of titles), are identical, and in them Salviati requests each Duke to employ him on the work on which (as he says) he is most keen, namely the writing of history—the history either of the families concerned or of their states. In the first, to the Duke of Ferrara, he writes of 'la servitù che con V.a Ecc.a Ill.ma e coi suoi hanno sempre tenuto i capi della mia famiglia, e la

[15] Two documents give some weight to the suspicions: (*a*) a copy of the *Discorso* in the hand of Salviati's intimate friend Baccio Valori on the back on which the latter has written: 'C.r. Salviati sotto nome finto del Castr. — se Dante — per scoprire gli animi ne dubitò' (Florence, B.N.C., Filze Rinucciniane, Autografi Borghiniani); (*b*) a letter from Belisario Bulgarini, who in 1583 sent Lionardo a copy of his *Considerazioni* asking him if, as rumour would have it he is the author of the *Discorso*. See also in this connection M. Rossi, 'Il discorso', who believes that the author is Salviati.

spezial devozione che ho sempre avuta io alla persona di V.a Ecc.za'.[16]

As the first recorded contact with and first expression of esteem for, the house of Este and the city of Ferrara, this letter is of great interest in view of the future history of Lionardo's association with both. It might have been even more so had not these very words (with a preceding 'Casa d'Este' changed to 'Casa Farnese') been repeated in the letter to the Duke of Parma and Piacenza of the following day. However, it is worth noting that to Salviati's literary aspirations is to be added a desire to shine as a historian, in which he presumably saw himself as filling a void left by Varchi. One remembers that in his letter to Cosimo of 12 October 1564 he had modified his request to be employed on the translation work he considered so important by adding 'mentreché il Varchi è occupato nello scrivere la storia'. Now Varchi was dead.

In the meantime we know that Lionardo did not neglect his linguistic studies, and that his reputation as a specialist in the *volgare* was growing in Florence. Between 1571 and 1573 one of the principal events of interest in the Florentine literary world was the 'correction' of the *Decameron* undertaken, under the supervision of the Inquisition, by a group of Florentine men of letters with Vincenzo Borghini at their head. Borghini had already noted him a person well versed in matters of language. Listing for the benefit of Cosimo in 1571 those people who in his opinion could make a valuable contribution to the formulation of the rules of the language, he had written: 'sono dunque, de' quali posso parlare: . . . Lionardo Salviati, Cavaliere: hoggi sta a Pisa, e la lingua si vede, che la possiede bene.' Although we do not know just how important a role Salviati played in this first correction, both in his correspondence with Francesco de' Medici over his own revision of the work between 1580 and 1582 and in the annotations which accompany this revision, as well as in the 1584 and 1586 *Avvertimenti*, he shows a much more detailed knowledge of the work of the earlier correctors than could have been gained through familiarity with their published *Annotationi*. Moreover, in his reports to the Maestro del Sacro Palazzo, Borghini includes Salviati in his list of the Florentine men of letters who have helped him in the expurgation of the *Decameron*. This was in fact the

---

[16] U. lett. Salviati to the Duke of Ferrara, 18.5.70, Modena, A.S., Archivio per letterati, Salviati (autograph).

period when his contacts with Borghini must have been at their closest. For there is no doubt that Borghini supplied the basis of Salviati's philological method in the *volgare*; and when, after a long absence of several years in Rome, Salviati returned to Florence in the 1580s, Borghini was already dead. Yet those contacts are not documented except by scanty notes and one letter, albeit dealing exclusively with linguistic and philological matters.[17]

As for Salviati's triumph in having in his audience the Grand Duke, the Gran Maestro dell'Ordine di Santo Stefano as he was, this was not to be repeated; for on 21 April 1574, when Salviati had just been informed of his election to the post of *commissario* of the Order in Florence (a change of title but not of duties, to any extent) Cosimo died, and the Council invited Lionardo to compose an oration to be delivered in the Chiesa dei Cavalieri in Pisa. Buontalenti, his fellow commissioner, thus took over the work whilst Salviati wrote the funeral oration which he delivered on 30 April. It immediately ran into two editions in Florence.[18] Other official funeral orations were given in the city by Pier Vettori, in the Church of San Lorenzo, and by Giovanni Battista Adriani in the courtyard of the Palazzo Vecchio, with the Knights of St. Stephen, including no doubt Salviati, in his audience. On the same day as they spoke Pier Angelio da Barga gave a similar oration in the Duomo of Pisa, and practically every other man of letters in Florence wrote one and had it printed.

For Florence it was the end of an epoch. For twenty-seven years the personality and strength of character of Cosimo had held together his own creation, and as long as he remained, there lived on in Florence something of the old spirit. For his presence was a link with recent Florentine history—of independence gained, of territories conquered, of threats foiled, of self-respect renewed, of battles won, peace established, and prestige renewed; and his person was also a reminder of what might have been. It has been

[17] To be precise (i) a note by Salviati to Borghini of uncertain date concerning the exact interpretation of words in a passage of a translation of Crescentius, published in the *Prose fiorentine*, Vol. iv. pt. 4, and by Manzoni, *Prose*; (ii) Lett. Salviati to Borghini, Florence, 7.8.76, published by Zambrini, Manzoni, etc. The document in which Borghini refers to Salviati's participation is in Florence, Bib. Laurenziana, Cod. Plut. LXXXX, Cod. CXI Sup., fol. 85b.

[18] *Orazione funerale per Cosimo I de' Medici*, 1st edn. (Florence, Giunti, 1574), 2nd edn. (Florence, Sermartelli, 1574). Ded. lett. to Francesco de' Medici, Granduca di Toscana.

well written by the historian Caggese that the first day on which
Francesco de' Medici assumed full power—22 April 1574—was
the first day in the decline of the Medici. The whole political
situation, in which the merchant aristocracy had been reduced to
a parasitic court nobility and the upper classes stripped of real
political power, lost both its glamour and its temporary justification. The ambivalent attitude of the Florentines towards the
regime, composed of pride in their ruler's achievements despite
resentment at his absolute power, which had assured support for
Cosimo the Redeemer, now collapsed.

Artists and men of letters felt stifled by the reduction of artistic
life to a round of petty intrigue in the uninspiring setting of the
court. Cellini had painted a damning picture of a Medici court without a sign of greatness or genius in itself or appreciation of these
qualities in others, seething with malicious gossip, where the
honours went to pedestrian inferiors such as Bandinelli and
Ammannati. He is undoubtedly biased, but the picture is nevertheless a broadly valid one. It was part of the inevitable price of
Cosimo's construction, out of the ruins of the Republic, of a
unified, centralized, Florentine power. The new spirit was one of
restless yet ineffectual dissatisfaction. The working of this spirit
in Salviati, a member of the class most affected at this stage, is the
story of the next few years of his life.

XI

FIRST CONTACTS WITH FERRARA: THE 'ROMAN' PERIOD

IT was on 2 March 1574 that the assembled Consiglio di Santo Stefano considered the request made by the Cavaliere Argentino Nofi that he should be relieved of his post as Commissioner for the Order in Florence, as he was obliged to return to his home in Arezzo. At the foot of his letter the President of the Council added the ominous words: 'Letta in Consiglio il dì 2 di Marzo 1573 [i.e. 1574] e ne fu fatto partito di licentia et in suo luogo fu eletto il C.re Lionardo Salviati.' The same day a dispatch was sent off informing Salviati of this decision, and telling him that he would be working with the cav. Andrea Buontalenti. Salviati having been for some time resident at his villa in Prato, this letter did not reach him until the 15th, whereupon he began preparations to transfer himself to Florence, informing the Council of his imminent arrival there and thanking them for the new honour.[1] For his own part he seems to have been genuinely pleased to have this post, which despite its irksome features enabled him to show by his efficiency in carrying out the Council's business that he was not merely a philologist and a dreamer, but also a person of not inconsiderable ability in practical affairs.

Nevertheless, the work of Commissioner was arduous and totally unglamorous. Naturally, as in Rome, it consisted of collecting, or attempting to collect, the endless variety of debts which the Knights, and others, had contracted with the Order. For the most part the extraction of rents for land and houses of the Order (which owned much property in Tuscany, a good deal of it formerly belonging to Florentine rebels and presented to it by Cosimo) was like squeezing blood from a stone. In addition the Commissioners had to keep account of the Order's credits with the

[1] U. letters documenting this correspondence are in Pisa, A.S., A.S.St., (i) F.L.O., No. 1367, Nofi to the Council, 28.2.74, fol. 20, and Salviati to the Council (from Prato), 15.3.74, fol. 59ʳ, (ii) Council to Salviati, R.L.M., No. 1322, fol. 117ʳ.

Monte di Pietà, collect interest, make payments to the Salviati bank, and in short attend to all financial transactions (frequently accompanied by legal action) which took place in Florence.

If land was bought or sold it was Salviati who attended to the drawing-up of contracts by the official notary Ser Frosino Ruffoli. Frequent visits had to be made to the Decima Granducale, to the customs and other tax offices, all of which work Salviati seems to have carried out swiftly, efficiently, and to the Council's entire satisfaction. The main obstacle to the smooth execution of the Commissioners' duties was the chronic meanness of the Council, its unremittingly suspicious attitude towards it officers, and its refusal to trust them without minute supervision. From March 1574 Salviati slaved for the Order, having its statutes printed, supervising the manufacture of a new seal of the Order, purchasing their pens, paper, and ink for them at favourable prices, and performing innumerable chores for them until they abruptly terminated his services by a letter of 12 July 1575 which informed him in the crudest terms that it was the Grand Duke's wish that the post which he occupied should cease to exist.[2]

It may or may not be a coincidence that it is almost immediately after this bombshell that Salviati's name appears for the first time in the diplomatic correspondence of Ferrara. It was almost five years since he had written his letter to Alfonso II asking to be employed in writing a history of Casa d'Este, but his interest in Ferrara had by no means lapsed completely. Its persistence finds testimony in two sonnets, first 'Quest'onda Apollo in sé pietosa accolse' (57), which heaps praises on Ferrara, the Este, and Pigna, and which (since Alberto Lollio, to whom it is dedicated, seems to have been alive at the time of its composition) must have been written before 1568; and secondly 'Potrai tu, chiaro sol, l'altero nido' (48), written in an equally complimentary vein on the occasion of the earthquake at Ferrara in 1570.

The person through whom he now re-established contact with Ferrara was Ercole Cortile, *ambasciatore ordinario* of the Duke of Ferrara at the Medici court since December 1574. Within a

---

[2] U. lett. Consiglio to Salviati, 12.7.75, Pisa, A.S., A.S.St., R.L.M., No. 1323, fol. 44ᵛ. Between 2.3.74 and 5.8.75 there are in the A.S.St. 7 letters from the Council to Salviati, 30 to Salviati and Buontalenti together, and 2 to Buontalenti alone. From Buontalenti and Salviati to the Council there are 14, from Salviati alone 14, and from Buontalenti alone 10. Internal evidence in the letters shows that this list is by no means complete.

few months of his arrival, and with his encouragement, Salviati approached Alfonso d'Este's secretary, Laderchi (whom he knew to have literary aspirations), and sent him 'alcune lezioni', whereupon there ensued an exchange of compliments and expressions of esteem. For the months which follow these first contacts the correspondence between Cortile and Ferrara is a fertile source of information on Salviati's activities in a period in which he is trying hard to establish himself in the Medici court. His success was obviously minimal for by 15 September he had accepted an invitation from his relation, the Vescovo Anton Maria Salviati (courted by Lionardo in the past, as we have seen), to join him, as paid man of letters, at the court of France. Anton Maria was papal nuncio there and seems to have had the privilege of foreknowledge of the Massacre of St. Bartholomew, in which as representative of His Holiness he rejoiced though few would pretend it was perpetrated for religious reasons. Preparations for this move were well under way by September, by which time Lionardo had let all his property and was ready to set off in a few days' time, determined to make a new start in France under the protection of his powerful relations and 'molto mal satisfatto di questo Sig.re [i.e. Francesco] et di queste parti per non haver mai potuto spuntare qui in alcuna cosa, non havendo mai questo Sig.re voluto conoscere la virtù sua et il suo valore.'[3]

For an understanding of Salviati's present position and conception of himself this correspondence, and these words in particular, are invaluable, for the picture is one of thorough dissatisfaction, disgruntlement, disappointment, and ill-suppressed resentment against Francesco. He was sharing the feelings common to his fellow Florentines since the death of Cosimo and the accession of Francesco who, with none of the powerful compelling personality of Cosimo, succeeded in a remarkably short space of time in making himself thoroughly unpopular with all but his chosen favourites. Vicious and brooding, morose and unprepossessing, despicable in his private life and manifesting human feeling only in his infatuation for Bianca Cappello, he nursed grudges over long periods, and was the very incarnation of the *puntiglio* and false sense of honour which had come to him through his mother, his Spanish education, and his contacts with Spain.

---

[3] Modena, A.S., C.A.F., 1575, U. letters Cortile to Laderchi of 20.8.75 and 3.9.75, and to Alfonso of 15.9.75.

But whilst Lionardo obviously shared this vague general malaise, it is quite clear that personal factors also were concerned. At court the winds blew decidedly chill for him. Whether or not this attitude was linked with his previous misdemeanours we do not know, but Salviati was so out of favour, and so resentful of the fact, that he had made up his mind to shake the dust of Florence from his feet once and for all. Yet so strong in him was the aspiring courtier that the slightest gesture from above would bring him back, grovelling. This undignified pattern of resentment and subservience, hatred and ambition, was to characterize his behaviour virtually for the rest of his life.

His approach to Cortile was natural, since admiration and affection for Ferrara seem to have been an early, sincere, and lasting passion with him; moreover with his enthusiasm for Ferrara, its history, and its poetic traditions, he could always capture the sympathy and friendship of the Ferrarese themselves. Needless to say he did not get the coveted job of ambassador to Ferrara on the retirement of Canigiani, though Cortile says that he both rejected the Vescovo Salviati's invitation to join him, and withdrew an application for the post of ambassador in Paris (for which post in any case the all-powerful Bianca favoured another) on the strength of his Ferrarese hopes. A similar failure, disastrous in more ways than one for his future both as a courtier and as a man of letters, was the attempt which he now undertook to dedicate his *Poetics*—revealed by this correspondence to be almost completed—to the Duke of Ferrara, presumably as a preliminary to his being taken into the latter's service.

It was on 11 December that Cortile first raised the question. the snag, inevitably, lay in the choice of titles to be used, since that of *Serenissimo*, assumed by Cosimo on being created Grand Duke, was claimed now by Alfonso too and equally firmly denied him by Francesco. Alfonso was adamant: no proper titles, no dedication. If Salviati still insisted, then Salviati must ask Francesco's opinion on the matter 'et quando faccia difficoltà che egli ci dia i miei titoli sarà meglio che desista et pensi ad altro'.

Disconsolate at the apparent impasse, Salviati explored every possible way round the difficulty, requesting from Francesco the ten-year copyright of the work, which he had decided to publish in Venice. Here he was baulked by Francesco who, having guessed what was afoot, refused to consider granting the copyright if the commentary was not printed at Florence in the first place. As a final effort Lionardo composed a dedicatory letter to Alfonso couched in vague terms such as to present a compromise acceptable to both parties. This letter Alfonso returned on 23 January repeating exactly what he had said previously.

Salviati was hopelessly caught up in a political web from which it appeared that there was no escape, for the conflict between Ferrara and Florence over titles engaged all the passions of the two courts, incarnating as it did the formal spirit of the new age. Neither would yield an inch. Yet a ray of light came from the least-expected source, namely from that very dispute over precedence which lent such importance to the titles. Cortile informed Alfonso that a certain Florentine 'frate' was busy preparing a book on the much-contested subject of precedence, in which dispute the Ferrarese historian, Pigna, had not surprisingly given a decision in favour of the Este. The 'frate' concerned was, equally naturally, busy reversing this decision.

Seriously perturbed, Alfonso ordered his ambassador to find out, using due circumspection, all he could about this work, how it was progressing, how soon it would be ready for publication, and all possible details on its author. Possibly apprised by Cortile of Salviati's usefulness as an ally here, he cunningly suggested that Salviati be given hopes of a future compromise on the matter of titles. Salviati fell into the trap. By 11 February Cortile was able to report the operation successfully completed. He had the name of the author and full details about him, and a promise from Salviati personally that he would hand over the manuscript of the work in question—which would not be ready for the printers for another eighteen months at the least—as soon as the author had finished it. And who should the letter reveal the 'frate' to be but the Priore degli Innocenti himself, Don Vincenzo Borghini, Salviati's friend and tutor, from whom he is at this very moment learning a philological method of which the fruits will be his most genuine claim to the esteem of future generations. Nor was Borghini the only person he intended to betray in order to win over Alfonso. It was also his plan to deceive his friend Giovanni Rondinelli, who had requested him on Borghini's behalf to correct the work—that same Rondinelli to whom he was later to refer in the *Proemio* to the *Avvertimenti* as 'mio virtuosissimo amico'.

Salviati had chosen to write the *Dialogo dell'amicizia* because, as Canigiani put it, he was 'alla amicizia oltre ogni umana credenza mirabilmente inclinato'. Yet when faced with a choice between personal advantage and loyalty to his friends he chose the former on all occasions known to us. Ironically enough in this case he fell, in doing so, into a trap engineered by Alfonso and set, perhaps unwillingly, by Cortile, with whom Salviati, though courting him for ulterior motives, seems to have been on good terms, even writing a Tuscan grammar for him.[4]

As the matter dragged on, Salviati became desperate and in March 1576, in a fury of anger against Francesco and perhaps confident of being accepted into the service of Alfonso, he made a dangerous move. The Grand Duke having refused a copyright for the *Poetics* unless it was printed in Florence, Salviati set out to forestall him by appealing to a higher authority. On 10 March he asked the Duke of Ferrara (now, as he thought, tied to him by a bond of obligation) to intercede on his behalf with the Pope and obtain a universal copyright for the work. Cortile transmitted the request, carefully worded by Salviati himself. Certainly Salviati was throwing all caution to the winds.

Nevertheless it was in vain that he sold his soul for spite against Francesco and for love of Ferrara and the Este. For from this moment the *Poetics*—to which we are told in the correspondence he was giving the finishing touches—are never so much as mentioned. For Salviati this was a personal disaster. If the *Poetics* (as we know them now from the extant manuscript fragment) had been published in 1576 they would have gone down in history, for they would have been the first full-scale Italian translation, paraphrase, and commentary on Aristotle. In this same decade 1570–80 there appeared the works of the more fortunate Piccolomini and Castelvetro, whose publication no doubt delayed further, because of the adjustments they necessitated, the publication of Salviati's own work in which frequent reference is made to them. Nor was he one whit nearer to getting away from Florence to Ferrara. Baulked in his plans, and having demonstrated his own

---

[4] No autograph copy of this *regoletta*, as Cortile refers to it, exists. Nevertheless the *Regole della toscana favella* found in Florence, B.N.C., Cods. (*a*) Magl. Cl. IV, 65 and (*b*) Pal. 727, would seem by their style and composition to be this same grammar written in 1575 for Cortile. The grammar is unpublished, see P. M. Brown, 'Una grammatichetta inedita del cav. Lionardo Salviati', *G.S.L.I.* cxxxiii (1957), 544–72.

ingenuous ineptitude in intrigue, he was left to smoulder in impotent rage against the morose, deceitful, obstructive, ungrateful Grand Duke who had systematically thwarted whatever plans he had made for his own advancement. His own situation— a mixture of hate and ambition—is summed up in a remarkable letter of Cortile, who says of him:

Egli è stimato qui per il primo huomo che sia in Fiorenza nelle cose di lettere et che sia il vero, nessuno fa cosa che non si cerchi il suo parere et i cortigiani di questa corte come ignoranti però ne fanno poco conto, dicendo che è filosofo, et lui si è risoluto di non andare mai nelle camere del Sig.r Duca, et che sia il vero, mi ha accompagnato due o tre volte sino al Palazzo, et poi se n'è subito tornato addietro, facendo scusa con me che mi terrà compagnia in tutti i luoghi eccetto che in Palazzo, et ha speranza una volta di havere acquistato V. Alt.a conoscendola per Principe che fa molta stima di virtuosi e tanto più de' nobili come egli è.[5]

This letter brings out the features of his state which so irked Salviati, the paradoxical situation of being highly rated in the literary sphere (and this sketch of Salviati's standing in Florence is precious) yet derided by the courtiers whom he secretly despised, whose superior he considered himself, yet to whose status he aspired. Hence the bitterness which now creeps into his life. Salviati's position is, in short, one of which examples are never lacking in a court-dominated society such as Cosimo had created, that of the unsuccessful courtier, dissatisfied, consumed with hatred of the sovereign, yet ready to serve him slavishly in the hope of advancement, and doomed therefore to perpetual hypocrisy. Evidence is not lacking to show that Francesco despised him, and events were to prove that he utilized Salviati for his own ends with the most callous ingratitude.

In the meantime one further contact with Ferrara could be established, on the literary plane. Parts of Torquato Tasso's epic were already circulating in manuscript amongst Tasso's friends, among them Orazio Capponi, a Florentine and a friend also of Salviati, to whom he showed two cantos which had come into his possession in 1576. On 6 January of this same year Tasso came to Florence. He stayed with Giovambattista Deti, a friend of Salviati and future first Arciconsolo of the Crusca, and carried with him letters of introduction from another of Lionardo's friends, Bernardo Canigiani (brother of Alessandro, Lionardo's closest intimate, and Orazio Urbani's predecessor as Florentine ambassador in Ferrara) to Salviati's 'friend' Vincenzo Borghini. Yet Lionardo and Torquato do not seem to have met. At the end of June 1576, however, Capponi sent Tasso 'due scritture' in defence of the *Gerusalemme Liberata* written by Salviati, who had particularly asked Capponi to express his admiration for Tasso and his goodwill towards him.

Tasso was delighted, for he already had a high opinion of Salviati, having read a number of his works including the oration on the coronation of Cosimo. This had appeared to him 'piena di tutti quelli ornamenti, e di quelle amplificazioni che son proprie di quel genere, ed in somma perfetta'. At the beginning of July he wrote to thank Capponi for his good offices on his behalf with Salviati, whose defence of the *Liberata* he considered worthy of the 'dottrina e giudizio' of its author.[6]

In the defence in question Salviati had accorded the work the highest praise, including in it a confutation of Castelvetro's theory on the use of history in the epic, and the assertion that ornamentation far in excess of that needed in the case of Latin or Greek was essential in Tuscan. This was obviously calculated to make a profound appeal to the young poet. (Since it is a blatant contradiction of Salviati's true sentiments on the matter it can hardly have had any other purpose.) Indeed Tasso was so enthusiastic that he wanted Salviati's opinion on the poem as a whole. But as it was not possible to let him have the whole work immediately he sent him an ample résumé of the plot, requesting him to give an opinion on this without fear or favour, to expand points already made, and also to mark all words and expressions of which he did not approve in a third canto dealing with 'feats of arms'. This canto he had sent him so that he might judge the style of the work. It was his intention to write a letter of thanks to

---

[6] All information on Tasso's visit to Florence and the exchanges between Tasso and Salviati in 1576 comes from C. Guasti (ed.), *Lettere di Torquato Tasso*, 5 vols. (Florence, Le Monnier, 1854), especially Tasso to Capponi, 1.7.76, 10.10.76, and Tasso to Gonzaga, 27.7.76. In his letter dating to the beginning of July, to Orazio Capponi, Tasso refers to 'due scritture' sent to him by Salviati; writing to Scipione Gonzaga 27.7.76 he refers to 'una scrittura'. It is in the *Avvertimenti* (I. iii. 138) that Salviati refers to Capponi as one of the highest hopes for Tuscan prose.

Salviati himself in the near future, but for the time being he relied on the continued good offices of Capponi.

At some point in the early part of July, Salviati replied to Tasso. By then he had read all three cantos which, along with the complete plot of the work, he praised unreservedly. As far as the plot and the *verosimile* were concerned, he considered that nothing needed altering or adding. Encouraging Tasso to develop the 'ornamentation' of the work, he offered to make favourable mention of the poem in his *Poetics*, which he was about to send to print. Jubilant over this newly established friendship—'abbiamo per lettera non solo cominciata, ma stabilita in guisa l'amicizia, ch'io ho conferito seco alcune mie opinioni'—Tasso rejoiced in Salviati's extreme kindness towards him, and it was apparently with genuine disappointment that he learnt, presumably from Orazio Capponi, that Salviati was still planning to go to Paris, since this, as he states in a letter to Capponi of 10 October, would delay for some years any meeting between the two. None of the letters forming the direct correspondence between Salviati and Tasso is extant. We do not know how long it continued after 1576. Years later, in the heat of the polemic over the *Gerusalemme Liberata*, Salviati and De' Rossi made no attempt to conceal this correspondence, or to falsify its contents and tenor. They rather brought these facts to the fore, and even used the correspondence as evidence of their own impartiality.

Nor is Salviati's favourable reaction to the *Gerusalemme Liberata* at this point (though obviously influenced by his own designs on Ferrara) any proof of opportunist unscrupulousness later in the debates over the epic, in which he condemned it. At this point the *Gerusalemme Liberata* had acquired none of the status, which it was later to be given by Pellegrino, of a challenge to those principles on which Salviati had based his life's work. Here, in 1576, it was simply a poem competent and pleasing in many respects, and as such he gave it its due.

One interesting point in the correspondence is this further mention of the imminent publication of the *Poetics*, one of many such mentions, another one being perhaps the principal feature of interest in Razzi's 1575 edition of the *Primo libro delle orazioni*. Despite the editor's statement that the orations (consisting of all those previously published except *Garzia III*, with the addition of the orations *In lode della Giustizia*, *In lode della Religione*, and

In lode della Religione militare, and the translation of Vettori's oration in praise of Joan of Austria) had been 'riveduti, racconci, ed emendati da lui', the variations from their original form are largely restricted to linguistic and stylistic detail. More important was the promise, in the letter of the printer Jacopo Giunti, to print in the very near future 'la traduzione della Poetica d'Aristotile fatta dal medesimo Cavaliere: che per quello, che intendo da chi l'ha veduta, e chi più di me ne sa, l'ha tanto fedelmente tradotta in fiorentina favella, e con di molte annotazioni, in guisa d'un compendioso, e gentil comento, che piacerà a chiunque la vedrà.' This is an interesting piece of information. It tells us that the *Poetics* were now more or less completed in their full form, a translation, paraphrase, and commentary. It proves that Salviati's own references to the work in this period, unlike the reference in the letter to Isabella Orsini, concern not odd essays on the subject but a full-scale work of considerable proportions representing a tremendous amount of study on the part of Salviati. If we take this fact into account we can well understand why the previous years had been so meagre from the point of view of literary production. His talents had been exercised only in the funeral oration for Cosimo and in the *Cinque lezioni sopra un sonetto del Petrarca*.[7] Though these *lezioni* had not been printed they seem by their style and the wording of the dedicatory letter to Antonmaria Vescovo de' Salviati (dated 15.6.75) to have been written some time previously.

The explanation of the dedication of this work and of Razzi's edition of the orations to the bishop in question at this point is, of course, found in the Cortile–Ferrara correspondence. To accept the previously mentioned invitation to join him in Paris of so influential a relative as Anton Maria Salviati, formerly Bishop of Saint-Papoul in France and papal nuncio at the French court since 1571, must have been a lingering temptation. For Anton Maria was quite a prominent figure. He had introduced the Capuchins into France, treated for a league against the Turks, and worked tirelessly for the extermination of heresy in France. In this respect at least Lionardo would have found a kindred

---

[7] *Cinque lezioni nell'occasione del sonetto 'Poi che voi, ed io, più volte abbiam provato'* . . . *lette nella Accademia Fiorentina* (Florence, Giunti, 1575). There is no indication, or record, of *when* these were delivered unless it was during the Consulship of Jacopo Pitti (see p. 123).

spirit. But at the same time it is amusing to speculate on what his reactions would have been to finding his old enemy Jacopo Corbinelli firmly established as a minor favourite at the court of France, where there was a sizeable colony of Florentine exiles. Corbinelli himself was still considered very much a politically implicated figure, harbouring exiles hostile to the Medici. Moreover, he still took an interest in matters linguistic, for in 1572, in a letter mainly concerned with the Massacre of St. Bartholomew, he had referred to 'il Varchi, il quale è mal concio dal Castelvetro'.[8] It may well be that a sober look at the difficulties facing a pro-Medici in Paris contributed to his final decision against the move. At all events, plans for transferring to Paris were eventually abandoned, though they still seem to have been under consideration late in 1576.

Now, disgusted with Francesco, frustrated at Ferrara, he expressed his dissatisfaction in a sonnet addressed to Alberto Bolognetti, 'Da questo al surger mio terreno avverso'—and presumably continued his work on the *Poetics*.[9] For the whole of 1577 and the beginning of 1578 there exists hardly a shred of evidence as to his activities. But on 20 May 1577 Joan of Austria gave birth to a boy—the first boy after six girls and thus the heir to the throne. Coins of all denominations were thrown in great abundance from the windows of the Palazzo Vecchio, and wine flowed free on the *ringhiera* below. Guns were fired, there were the usual firework displays, and for days there was jousting, merry-making, and processions in the streets. For the official baptism on 29 September the representatives of the princes of Europe converged on Florence. The 'Signor di Piombino' carried the baby to church and amongst the guests was Giacomo Buoncompagni, Duca di Sora, Generale di Santa Chiesa, Castellano di Sant'Angelo, son of Pope Gregory XIII. Salviati met him there, and arranged to enter his service. Thus Lionardo Salviati the arch-Florentine achieved his aim of escaping from Florence, the 'terreno avverso' where his growth was stunted. Yet his departure

---

[8] Lett. Corbinelli to Pinelli, 8.10.72, quoted P. Rajna, 'Jacopo Corbinelli e la strage di San Bartolommeo', *Archivio storico italiano*, Serie V, xxi (1898), 80.

[9] Alberto Bolognetti was in Florence from 1576 to 1578 on an important mission, from Pope Gregory XIII and as the content of the sonnet—a plea to be given the opportunity to leave Florence—expresses to perfection Salviati's sentiments at this period, the poem may well have been composed during Bolognetti's Florentine residence.

for Rome is not entirely without its puzzling features. Its most probable explanation, in view of future developments and hints strewn throughout Salviati's own correspondence, is that he had become potentially useful to Francesco, whereupon the latter's coldness had given way, as usual, to blandishments. Whether the initiative for joining Buoncompagni's household came from Salviati himself or from Francesco it is morally certain that the idea was fostered by the Grand Duke with an eye to Lionardo being useful to him in Rome.

This would seem to be substantiated by the wording of a letter sent by Lionardo to the Council of St. Stephen when he was once again—rather to his annoyance it appears this time—created 'Ricevitore della religione a Roma'. He accepts, but points out that he is a very busy man in Rome, and makes the proviso: '. . . solo che elle sappiano, che io sto con altri, et obbligato al servizio dell'Ecc.mo Sig.r Marchese Buoncompagni, dico obbligato, perchè ci sono stato messo dal Ser.mo Gran Maestro, e ci sto assai occupato.' Other equally persuasive statements suggest that, if not forced against his will to enter the service of Buoncompagni, he was at least influenced towards it. Despite the contempt he expressed for the Medici court, it was obvious that one sign from Francesco would awaken the ambitious courtier in him, and all the more so when it began to be obvious that negotiations with Ferrara were making no headway. In a future letter he was to refer to this post with the Duke of Sora (addressing Francesco) as 'questa servitù dove io mi trovo per sua [i.e. the Grand Duke's] bontà'.

Whatever the ultimate intentions of Francesco, the dismal round of duties as *Ricevitore* took up much of Salviati's time between 1578 and 1581, when he was again inexplicably relieved of the post. By this time, however, he had already been active in the service of the Grand Duke. His services can be followed in minute detail through the years 1578–82 in the files of the Medicean Archives in Florence and add up inescapably to one thing: Salviati was acting as a spy for the Grand Duke of Tuscany. Though nominally in the service of the Duke of Sora he was more than willing to put the interests of Francesco—fondly hoping that they were also his own—before loyalty to his immediate master. He tells us so himself, for he writes to Francesco: 'Basta, che io so qual è l'ufizio di buon suddito e qual è quello di buon servidore e per quanto io saprò e potrò farò sempre l'uno e l'altro ingenuamente. E dove nascesse l'incompatibile conosco quel che mi s'appartiene.'[10] As a diligent informer stationed permanently in Vatican circles Salviati was invaluable to Francesco, who soon began to employ him on a variety of missions which brought him into contact with some thoroughly disreputable characters—the notorious Geremia da Udine for example, and Vittorio Cappello, ne'er-do-well brother of the Grand Duchess as Bianca now was. For on 9 April 1578 Joan of Austria had died in childbirth. On the 12th she was buried in San Lorenzo. The following year Francesco married his mistress, who was declared a 'daughter of the Republic of Venice'—by that same Republic, be it noted, which on behalf of its outraged 'son' Bianca's father Bartolommeo had fifteen years previously carried its persecution of her, her husband, and the latter's family, into the heart of the world of Florentine commerce. Thus do circumstances alter cases. At all events, whatever the intrigue of the moment, Salviati was called upon to play his part, which seems to have consisted principally of collecting information and passing it on, sometimes to Francesco himself and sometimes to Geremia da Udine, the more important agent.

Florentine archives abound with proof of his spying activities in connection with the most diverse matters, from negotiations over the fate of the Landi feud of Borgotaro (which had recently rebelled against its lords and had become the centre of plots and intrigues involving Medici, Farnese, and Pope known collectively as the 'Valditaro affair') to a campaign to persuade influential cardinals to support the election of Geremia as General of his Order, the Franciscans. Naturally he was most conveniently placed to be of the greatest assistance in all this, for he could not

---

[10] Lett. Salviati to Francesco, pub. Contin, op. cit., No. 21. The earlier quotation comes from a lett. Salviati to Francesco from Rome, 15.4.79, pub. Contin, No. 13. A further letter, from Salviati to Cortile, dated 27.12.86, quoted by Campori, runs as follows: 'io, che nella stessa mia patria ho voluto sempre vivere sciolto, e a me medesimo e a i miei studi, e che alla servitù del preterito pontificato nel passar che fece di qua lo stesso figliuol del Papa, *m'indussi* [italics mine] nel modo che ella medesima si ricorda per lo contrario di servir la serenissima casa d'Este . . . arsi sempre di desiderio'—again suggesting outside pressure. In Pisa, A.S., A.S.St., are to be found the Council's letter of appointment to the Ricevitorato dated 15.7.78 (R.L.M., No. 1325, p. 2, followed by a list of debtors) and Salviati's letter of acceptance, dated 29.8.78 (F.L.O., No. 1369, fol. 119).

only keep a close eye on the movements of Buoncompagni, on his meetings, negotiations, and relations with other Roman and ecclesiastical notables, but could usefully act as the 'snapper-up of unconsidered trifles' which were then referred back to Florence. On top of all this he was constantly employed as ambassador of goodwill between Medici and Buoncompagni father and son. He was even asked by Bianca Cappello to intercede on her behalf with the Pope, and was made use of in a multitude of minor diplomatic and political matters. Naturally he became involved in the kaleidoscope of changing relationships between Pope, cardinals, Medici, Farnese, and even came close again to his old patron Paolo Giordano Orsini, now in conflict with the future Pope Sixtus V (Felice Peretti, Cardinal Montalto) over the sordid affair of Paolo's relationship with Vittoria Accorambona. Paolo's wife Isabella, who in Lionardo's early days had lent him her best litter, had in 1576 been strangled for infidelity on the orders of Francesco and Paolo.

Writers who have investigated the squalid career of Geremia da Udine have been amazed that he was able to send back to Francesco such detailed and accurate information, for even when Geremia was in Florence in 1580 he kept himself up to date with news from Rome. The answer is that Salviati regularly sent off to Geremia all the information he could gather. Even as early as 24 August 1580 he tells Francesco that he will communicate directly with the friar—'e de' particolari darò conto al detto Padre per manco fastidio di V. A. S.' On 17 October of that year, shortly before Geremia went to Florence, Salviati wrote to Francesco: 'Della cosa di M.o Geremia le darò conto, quando sarà spedita, assicurandola in questo mezzo, che ci fo tutto quello, che dal canto mio si possa desiderare, *et a lui ne scrivo giornalmente* per manco fastidio di V. A. S.' Salviati's activities are here summed up in his own words. To follow them in all their ramifications is tempting but would be sterile for present purposes. Nevertheless this not very edifying period in Salviati's life does tell us certain things about the man—that he is ever ready to crawl to Francesco's feet, and that he does not eschew treachery and disloyalty if they appear to serve his ends. Despite his previous complaints to Cortile that he was ill treated, and would have no more truck with the Medici court, a minimum of princely encouragement had amply sufficed to reawaken his hopes.

Yet his deceit availed him nothing. First he was openly made a fool of by Geremia da Udine himself. This caused Salviati to urge others to punish Geremia, an action which can only have angered Francesco, since Geremia was still his favourite, for whom he interceded when he fell from power and was imprisoned. Moreover, the hoped-for reward for his slavish devotion, Grand Ducal recognition and gratitude, never came. The plain fact was that such favour varied in Salviati's case in direct proportion to his immediate utility. The correspondence of Francesco and the Grand Duchess with Salviati himself, their letters to Buoncompagni, and Lionardo's replies to them, all illustrate the way he was systematically deceived by concentrated blandishment. Salviati's later disillusionment was thus exacerbated by his having been tricked into thinking that this long-overdue recognition, now at last appearing, was due to a genuine high regard for his person. Francesco, in particular, wrote numerous letters of encouragement, in which he praised him for his efficiency in carrying out his tasks, affirmed his own esteem for him, and generally ended with a promise of future favours: 'Et se andate continuando sempre che havete occasione di qualcosa degna delle nostre orecchie', the Grand Duke writes, encouraging him to spy with even greater dedication, 'potete esser certo, che oltre all'aggradirci la buona volontà vostra, procureremo sempre di farvi ogni beneficio et honore'.[11]

No wonder Salviati had firmly believed that his star was at last in the ascendant. Yet it was not so. For despite the assiduity with which he fed information to Geremia, and despite his numerous closely documented journeys between Florence and Rome and other cities to perform more delicate missions requiring personal contacts, the decline in his political activity on behalf of the Grand Duke during the year 1582 brought a perceptible cooling-off in Francesco's attitude toward him. At best he was only a second to Geremia da Udine, and with the latter's disappearance Salviati did not step into his shoes. His correspondence gradually assumes a more domestic character, until in the following year 1583 there is no trace of his having undertaken any political mission, and though he is apparently still in the service of the Duke of Sora there is no record of his being in Rome later than May 1582. Looking back in later years on this Roman period,

[11] See supplementary note 8, p. 248.

filled with bitterness, he complained to Cortile of the manner in which false hopes had been fostered in him and of 'le grandi speranze nelle quali io fui tenuto di continuo in quella servitù'.[12]

In these years in fact his energies had been largely dissipated in political intrigue, for almost all available documentation—and it is more voluminous, ironically, than for any other period—relates to this aspect of his activities. But even whilst in Rome Lionardo maintained contact with some of his older friends, including Giovambattista Strozzi, to whom he wrote from Rome in October 1578 praising his *Orazione in lode della Granduchessa Giovanna*, and more particularly with his old friend and master Pier Vettori, for whom the genuine warmth of his affection suggests that Vettori did come to his assistance in that moment of need in 1569.[13]

Such was Salviati's brief hour of glory as Francesco's agent in Rome. In view of the many tasks of a political nature on which he was employed it is an exaggeration to say, as Salviati did in his dedication to Buoncompagni of his corrected *Decameron*, that his Roman master kept him in 'ozio tranquilissimo ed honorato'. The two works he produced, the *Discorso intorno alla ribellione di Fiandra* and the *Discorso sulle prime parole di Cornelio Tacito*, both of them probably composed under the influence of the political writer Scipione di Castro, who was at Buoncompagni's court at the same time, and whose acquaintance with Salviati is well documented, are of a strictly political character. Yet they are not without interest, especially the latter, which gives Salviati a modest place in the early history of *tacitismo* in Italy.[14]

But rather than productive of new literary works, this was a

---

[12] Lett. cit. Salviati to Cortile, pub. Campori.

[13] U. letts. Salviati to Vettori, from Rome, 6.12.78 and 17.12.80, in B.M. Additional MSS. 10272, fols. 130^{r-v}, and 10278, fol. 46^r respectively. The letter from Salviati to Strozzi (from B.N.C., Florence, MS. Magl. VIII, 1399), dated by Manzoni and Contin to 1588 dates in fact to 1578 (cf. A. S. Barbi, *Un accademico mecenate e poeta*, G. B. Strozzi il giovane (Florence, Sansoni, 1900), p. 25.

[14] Since this *Discorso* was discussed by the present author in 'Lionardo Salviati and the "Discorso sopra le prime parole di Cornelio Tacito" ', *Italian Studies*, xv (1960), 50–64, further examination of the relevant manuscripts has revealed close connections with Scipione di Castro, some of whose manuscripts in the A.Bu., A.V., Rome, seem to be in the same hand as an early version of the *Discorso*, which was first published under the initials C.L.S. with Giorgio Dati's translation of Tacitus' *Annali* (Florence, 1582). It was published by Manzoni, *Prose*, from a corrupt manuscript, with many errors. For details of the manuscripts of this work see Bibliography, A. (i), also P. M. Brown, 'L'edizione del 1873 delle prose inedite del cav. Lionardo Salviati', pp. 111–29.

period of intense investigation of the documents of the fourteenth century, on the results of which Salviati was to base the future exposition of his linguistic theory, a gigantic undertaking which required great determination and strength of purpose. In these years of scant literary output he was laying, by means of pains-taking methodical research and first-hand examination of old manuscripts, the sound foundations which were to allow him to speak with such supreme authority, and with abundant documen-tary evidence, in the *Avvertimenti* and in his introduction to his own edition of the *Decameron.* Though his ideas did not coincide on all points with those of the Priore degli Innocenti, it was never-theless Borghini, with his historical research of a new type into the old language for the purpose of defending Dante, who was the inspiration of the philological activity of Salviati. Manuscripts testify to the vast fields which Salviati covered, and correspon-dence between him and Borghini, though scant, shows their mutual historical sense and their inauguration of a synchronic study of the language of the Trecento. By the time he returned from Rome Salviati not only had the convictions on *volgare* culture which we have seen him to possess since his earliest literary works. He also had to hand all the tools and materials to create works which enshrine these convictions and give him a place in the history of the Italian language and of Italian culture.

XII

THE *RASSETTATURA* OF THE *DECAMERON*

D URING 1580, still in the service of Giacomo Buoncompagni, Salviati played an active part in the exchanges
between the Grand Duke and Bianca on the one hand,
and the Duke of Sora on the other, exchanges characterized by
a mutual desire to please, both sides at that point having need of
the other's goodwill. In many letters to Buoncompagni the Medici
couple say that Lionardo will report verbally on their behalf. It
was a favourable atmosphere for polite concessions by Rome to
Tuscany, and when on 30 July 1580 Grand Duke Francesco received a letter from Buoncompagni (via Lionardo Salviati himself)
informing him that he had been conceded 'libera facultà di deputar
a piacer . . . una persona idonea alla correzione' of the *Decameron*,
the circumstances of the delivery of the letter indicate that Buoncompagni's object was that the task should go to his Florentine
protégé. On 9 August Francesco responded to the request by
writing to Lionardo and officially appointing him to the task
of 'correggere et purgare detto libro'.[1]

For Lionardo it was a triumph. The outstanding importance
attached to the *Decameron* not only as a work of art but as the
golden key which unlocked the treasure-house of the Tuscan
language had made the establishment of a satisfactory text, as
Guasti says, 'per quei tempi una grave faccenda di stato': one
might add also 'di Chiesa'. Though the *Decameron* had found
an early place on the Index (1559) its importance both linguistically and as literature in an age which was turning to the great
masters and models in its own tradition made its complete suppression practically impossible.

[1] Both extracts are from a lett. Gr. Duke Francesco to Salviati, 9.8.80,
Florence, A.S., F.Med., R.L.M., No. 254, fol. 93ʳ, publ. P. M. Brown, 'I veri
promotori della "rassettatura" del *Decameron* nel 1582', *G.S.L.I.* cxxxiv (1957),
314–32. The mandate eventually published with the 1582 *Decameron* is a later
letter (16.8.81) antedated to the date of the letter here quoted.

Early documentation of the consternation caused in Florence by the Tridentine ban is provided by the *Atti* of the Accademia Fiorentina, which relate how on 10 October 1562 the Academicians wrote to Cosimo informing him how 'li Deputati al Concilio di Trento sopra il censurar le opere stampate si erono lasciati intendere voler al tutto levar via la opera di M. G.i Boccacci detta il Decamerone' and asking him to intervene in its favour 'con detti S.ri Deputati perché l'opera non perisse'. The Duke assured them by a letter read in the Academy on 17 October that he would do all he could, and instructed that in the meantime the Academy should elect a commission to correct the work. This they got down to on the twentieth of that month, and under the guidance of Lelio Torelli they finally chose for the purpose Francesco Cattani da Diacceto, Lionardo Tanci, and Francesco Guidetti. For some time after this the records are silent on the matter, until 27 March 1566 to be precise, when as we have seen (p. 106) one of Salviati's first acts as Consul was to send Mario Colonna and Domenico Mellini to Cosimo requesting his intercession on precisely this question of the correction and printing of the *Decameron*. The letter which the Consul sent with these Academicians tells how it has come to the Academy's ears that the *Decameron* 'corretto secondo l'ordine del Sacrosanto Concilio da' Reverendissimi Monsignori Nuntio, & Arcivescovo di Raugia, & dal Reverendo Inquisitore, & confermato per commissione della Santissima Memoria del proximo Pontefice da dua Illustrissimi Cardinali Deputati' has been handed over to Paolo Manuzio in Venice for printing. That anyone but the Academy should be responsible for bringing the *Decameron* out again for the first time since the ban seems to the Consul and his colleagues to be an affront against the Academy, against Tuscany, and against the Prince himself.

Just what the connection is between this work now ready for printing and the 'correction' set in motion by Cosimo's letter of 17 October 1562 is not clear. Beccadelli, the 'Arcivescovo di Raugia', who seems to have had a hand in it, was resident in Florence at the time, and the letter states that Domenico Mellini had been chosen as adjutant to Colonna in this mission because he was well informed on the background to the affair and had indeed already been busy trying to 'recover' the work. Though nothing seems to have come of this particular initiative on the part of the Academy, no 'corrected' *Decameron* being allowed back into circulation at this point, the concern of the Academicians represents a not unimportant piece of the proto-history of the 'correction of the *Decameron* normally overlooked when the expurgation of that work is studied, yet revealing of the impact in Florence of the ecclesiastical ban.[2]

When five years later in 1571 the more fortunate 'Deputati' of the Florentine Academy, chief amongst them Vincenzo Borghini, set out on the authority of Pius V to produce a suitably revised version of the *Decameron* the book had been granted a conditional reprieve in the Tridentine Index of 1564 as being one of the books which, once expurgated, might be considered suitable reading-matter for the faithful. Carried out by the Florentine Academicians appointed by the Grand Duke, and under the supervision of the Congregation of the Index headed by the Master of the Sacred Palace, who scrupulously checked in person the revised version of every part which he had singled out for attention, the work was completed by 1573, in the pontificate of Gregory XIII.

An examination of the nature of this revision is revealing of the demands which at this stage the Inquisition made on literature. The main purpose of the work is the one outlined in the 'nota santa': 'Nota hauta da Roma dal R.mo Mons.r del Sacro Palazzo. Avvertimento per rassettar il Boccaccio . . . terzo: che per niun modo si parli in male o scandalo de' preti, frati, Abbati, Abbadesse, monaci, monache, piovani, provosti, vescovi, o altre cose sacre, ma si mutino lj nomi, o si faccia per altro modo che parrà meglio.' The attention of the Inquisition, as is here plainly seen, remained focused on those aspects of the *Decameron* which might bring the Church into disrepute.

Having an artistic conscience, Borghini and his team regretted this forced mutilation of one of Florence's most revered authors and did their best to reduce to a minimum the proportions of the inevitable damage. Cuts, and the substitution of lay characters for ecclesiastical ones, were the limits of the interference which the

---

[2] MS. *Atti dell' Accademia Fiorentina*, Florence, Bib. Marucelliana, Cod. B. III, 54, recorded under the relative dates (most folios are unnumbered). Salvini, *Fasti*, p. 162, partly paraphrases, partly transcribes, the entries for 10, 17, and 22 October 1562, and transcribes (pp. 185–6) the whole of the text of the letter sent by Salviati to Cosimo on 27 March 1566.

Deputati allowed themselves. Only occasionally was a morally offensive expression replaced by another and less offensive one.

Yet this 1573 correction left both the Inquisition and the Florentines profoundly unsatisfied—though for widely differing reasons. Shortly after the completion of the revision the Roman Curia produced a list of 157 'censure' against the *Decameron*, attacking not only its irreligiousness but its immorality, against which accusations it was defended, principally by Borghini and the Deputati, but also by such persons as Cardinal Ferdinando de' Medici and Pier Vettori.[3] This exchange certainly indicates that in the period immediately following the first revision dissatisfaction with it was very strong in Roman circles. Some have gone so far as to say that only Borghini's staunch defence of Boccaccio restrained the Curia from ordering a new and more drastic revision on the spot. As to the dissatisfaction of the Florentines, evidence of this is abundant. But in their case the objection was to excessive, not insufficient, interference with the text, despite the fact that linguistically speaking the latter had to some extent benefited from the attentions of a philologist of the calibre of Borghini.

Among these fellow citizens of Salviati none was more effectively vociferous in his disgust and exasperation than Lionardo's close friend Grazzini. It was bad enough that ignorant but presumptuous non-Florentines should make bold to bring out unsatisfactory, and to the Florentines deeply offensive, editions of Florentine classics, and Grazzini had attacked the arch-offender Ruscelli for his *Decameron* in a sonnet remarkable for its eloquence and ferocity. But that the Florentines should themselves set to and mutilate the same text was too much—a veritable nightmare—which is precisely how it is described in his two sonnets on the 1573 correction, where he tells how the ghost of Boccaccio appears to him nightly full of bitter complaints over the great wrong done him, and begging Grazzini to do something about it. 'Storpiato sono, e fuor d'ogni ragione', says the disconsolate spectre: 'E tu stai cheto, come fussi morto: / dammi co i versi tuoi qualche conforto, / Biasimando, ohimè! sì poca discrezione.' But Grazzini realizes that he would be up against forces too strong for him, and that for a person in his shaky political position further to antagonize authority could mean disaster. So he sadly

[3] See supplementary note 9, p. 248.

replies: 'Io nè versi, nè prosa / non vo' per te compor: ch'io non vorrei / Far nell'ultimo male i fatti miei.'[4] In this way he effectively expressed his feelings by means of a poetic refusal to do so.

In view of Grazzini's sharp reaction to this revision the continuing harmony between him and Salviati throughout, and after, the second correction may seem surprising. Grazzini's general hostility to older Academicians may have partly influenced his earlier attitude, and the consideration of his later behaviour will be more opportune when the aims and methods of Salviati's own edition are considered in detail. In the meantime it is obvious that the existing play of forces—the demands of the Curia on the one hand, the resentment of the Florentines on the other—could well lead to a re-examination of the whole position, especially as it appears likely that permission to print the book was no longer forthcoming. Certainly Borghini's edition was never reprinted.

So when a second revision was eventually ordered, and the task assigned to Lionardo Salviati, it appeared to many, and particularly those later historians who saw their vocation in the exaltation of the Grand Dukes of Tuscany, that on the death of Borghini in 1580 Grand Duke Francesco had taken the initiative on the matter and promoted negotiations leading to a second revision of the *Cento novelle*. This belief was strengthened by the wording of the mandate from Francesco to Lionardo (printed with the 'corrected' *Decameron*) beginning: 'Disiderando noi, per beneficio, e splendore, della nostra lingua Toscana, che si ristampi il DECAMERON del Boccaccio . . .' etc.

The truth, however, is almost certainly very different. In the first place negotiations for a new revision were not only under way, but completed, some time before Borghini's death. Moreover one of the constant, outstanding features of the extant documentation is that it points to a good deal of behind-the-scenes intrigue on the part of the eventual corrector, a person who had the greatest possible interest in a new revised edition of the *Decameron*. In this his chief ally was his Roman master, Giacomo Buoncompagni.

---

[4] The quotations are from the sonnets (i) *inc.* 'Ogni notte m'appare in visione' and (ii) *inc.* 'Ond'io mi sveglio poi subitamente', pub. Verzone, *Poesie burlesche*, pp. 102–3, *Sonetti*, No. CXXVII, primo & secondo. The attack on Ruscelli is in the sonnet *inc.* 'Com'hai tu tanto ardir, brutta bestiaccia', ibid., pp. 87–8. (*Sonetti*, No. CVII, secondo). In the 'sonetto primo' he had attacked Ruscelli's Dante.

Indeed the Duke of Sora looked on himself as personally responsible for the fact that it was Salviati who undertook the revision, as he reveals in a letter of 5 August to the Duke of Mantua, in which he states: 'Io procurai con ogni istanza, e ottennilo finalmente, che al cav. Salviati, mio amatissimo gentil-huomo, fosse dato il carico del purgare il Decameron del Boccaccio' —giving the reason why he asks Gonzaga for the copyright as being in order that 'oltre all'honore ne succeda quel profitto che da principio mi mosse a procurargli questo assonto.'[5]

Clearly to undertake a revision of the *Decameron* at this stage would be an attractive proposition for Salviati for a multiplicity of reasons. He had had a hand in the 1573 correction. Given both the extreme importance which he attached, linguistically, to the *Decameron*, and the fact that at this point he had just completed a profound study of the language of the fourteenth century, a study which had given final form both to his attitude to language in general and to the technique of correction, a new revision by himself could from the philological point of view be the fulfilment of many cherished aspirations. To a person chronically impecunious as was Salviati the financial possibilities of the undertaking must also have been a powerful attraction. Indeed, this seems to have been the aspect of the situation which most influenced the Duke of Sora. But foremost was his consuming desire to promote the interests of the national tongue of which the *Decameron* was by common consent the finest prose model.

Exactly who made the first move is uncertain. What is quite clear, however, is that Lionardo Salviati was strongly and successfully supported by Giacomo Buoncompagni (and possibly also the Cardinal d'Este) in his campaign to persuade both the Inquisition and the Grand Duke to nominate him for the work. Once in possession of the Grand Duke's mandate Lionardo fell to work with a will. He was in Florence for most of the second half of the year 1580, so found no difficulty in accumulating the necessary equipment, particularly the *Decameron* manuscripts which the previous correctors had utilized. Some of these were already in the Laurenziana, and as early as 14 August Lionardo asked Francesco to arrange for Baccio Baldini to hand them over to him. Others had remained in the hands of Borghini. When he died in

[5] Lett. Giac. Buoncompagni to the Duke of Mantua, 5.8.81, pub. A. Bertolotti, *Bibliofilo*, vi (1885), No. 3.

1580 Salviati requested the Grand Duke to authorize Baccio Valori to open a locked case of the Priore in which were the books in question (bequeathed by Borghini to the Laurenziana) and consign them to the corrector, who had told Francesco only a few days after the issue of the mandate that 'm'ingegnerò d'eseguirlo conforme all'obbligo e desiderio mio, e di cavarne prestamente le mani.'[6] Thanks to the extremely detailed background work done on the thirteenth- and fourteenth-century texts in the preceding few years, he was able to complete the work in a surprisingly short time. The correction appears in fact to have been finished early in 1581, by the end of May if not earlier, whereupon Salviati enlisted the help of his Roman master to obtain copyrights for all the states of Italy. Buoncompagni wrote personally to his fellow princes, and his request to Ottavio Farnese for the Parma copyright was delivered to the Duke personally by Lionardo on a visit to Parma in February 1582.

When the book (dedicated to Buoncompagni with Francesco's permission) eventually came out in Venice at the end of July 1582 the proud editor sent copies at once to the Duke of Mantua and the Grand Duke of Tuscany. Almost immediately the Venetians, in their customary manner, began to pirate it, and Francesco was obliged to take swift action in response to Salviati's request that Mons. Abbioso, the Florentine minister in Venice, should take steps to see that the printers be punished 'con esempio degl'altri insolenti'. Something must have been done, for when the Florentine edition was ready in November Salviati was able to accompany the copy he sent to the Grand Duke with a letter of thanks for the prompt protection afforded to his privileges.[7]

But if Salviati's corrected *Decameron* met with the approval of the Inquisition it had less success with contemporary men of letters, though little criticism was open because of the protection

---

[6] Lett. Salviati to Gr. Duke Francesco, 14.8.80, pub. Contin, op. cit., No. 20, which also deals with the Borghini Boccaccio manuscripts. The letter of 14 August was published Contin, op. cit., No. 19.

[7] Lett. Salviati to Gr. Duke Francesco, 18.11.82, pub. Contin, op. cit., No. 44. The original request for protection is dated 29.10.82 (pub. ibid., No. 42), and Francesco's reply is to be found in Florence, A.S., F.Med., R.L.M., No. 259, fol. 58ᵛ. It is dated 20.11.82 and runs as follows: 'Con la vostra de 18 habbiamo ricevuto il nuovo Boccaccio stampato costì il quale anderemo vedendo con nostro comodo come fatica vostra et come opera da esser letta da ciascuno havendo havuto molta cura che in Venetia si sieno quietati per il desiderio che teniamo d'ogni vostro benefitio.'

of the Pope and the Grand Duke. According to Salviati it was occasionally necessary for the Grand Duke (who had mysteriously forbidden him to engage in polemics on the subject) to intervene on his behalf. For his own part he attributed the criticism to the envy of those who would have liked the commission for themselves, 'tanta è stata l'invidia che per quel solenne favore m'è piovuto addosso per ogni parte . . . le mia fatica è stata lacera da chi mai non la vide; e molti n'hanno renduta testimonianza che non ne lessero pur mai il titolo.'[8]

The criticisms in question were levelled above all at the seemingly ruthless mutilation of the stories with apparent small regard for aesthetic considerations. And in truth the second revision must have been something of a puzzle to contemporaries. For this new expurgated *Decameron* is quite different in scope and character from the previous one of 1573. It emerges as a totally new book such as neither the 1573 correctors nor the Inquisition of that time, and least of all Boccaccio, had ever remotely visualized, namely a 'moral' *Decameron*. It is a *Decameron* uncompromisingly remodelled to conform to the exigencies of the extremist moralistic critical current of the times: that is to say, it is a textbook of morality, serving the purpose attributed to literature by such contemporaries as Varchi.

To this formidable task of transformation Salviati had applied himself with vigour and determination, his 'correction' involving sixty of the stories to a greater or lesser degree. The number of stories which suffer only from severe cuts remains at four, but the number of those drastically transformed by secularization or other manipulation of characters is increased to twenty-four.

To accomplish this task of 'moralization' Salviati employs a combination of three principal devices. First of all, as in the 1573 edition, all unfavourable references to Church or clergy are eliminated. The 'Inquisitore dell'eretica pravità' (i. 6) becomes the 'capitano di giustizia', and the story changes from one in which 'un valent'huomo confonde con un bel detto la malvagia ipocrisia

---

[8] Lett. Salviati to Gr. Duke Francesco, 2.3.84, pub. Contin, op. cit., No. 52. It contains also the following passage: 'V. A. Ser.ma come diritto e supremo giudice m'ha difeso più d'una volta per conto della correzione del Boccaccio — ora siccome ella, secondo la sua discretissima, e santa mente ha difesa la ragion mia, così avrei io da principio, se mi fosse stato permesso il metterlo in iscrittura, apertamente (se non fosse presunzion il dirlo) difeso il giudicio suo nell'elezion fatta per quella impresa nella persona mia.'

de' religiosi' to one in which 'un valent'huomo confonde con un bel detto la malvagia *avarizia* de' *giudici*'. The total exclusion of the story under Borghini was perhaps a kinder fate. Respect for the Church leads to such changes of character as this in twenty-two *novelle*. The 'monaco caduto in peccato' (i. 4) becomes 'un giovane', whilst his 'abate' is named his 'superiore'. The story is, moreover, an example of a phenomenon frequent in Salviati's *Decameron*, namely the migration of the characters, and the setting, to other times and climes; that is to say to an age or country which frames the whole in a pagan civilization. In the story in point the setting, the Lunigiana, is retained: but the time is the age of the 'dei falsi e bugiardi' and 'nei primi tempi della falsa religione'. Likewise the abbess, her nuns, and their monastery in the story of Masetto da Lamporecchio (iii. 1) are transmuted into a secular 'madonna' and 'donzelle' in a 'grandissima e bella torre' in pagan Alexandria.

Seven stories are rendered respectable in this manner. Salviati here kills two birds with one stone, for not only does this removal of the setting to pagan times or countries protect the name of the Church, but it also plays a part in the uphill job of converting the *Decameron* into a moral guide. For by means of it Salviati solves, with a certain ingenuity, the problem of the 'moral example', otherwise insuperable by any process short of suppressing the whole story. For pagans must, by definition, set a *bad* example, to be recognized as such by the reader.

But though this device was a practical expedient enabling Salviati to some extent to reconcile the Inquisition's aims with his own, it is at the same time interesting in that it provides an example of the workings of a tendency prevalent in Salviati's times, namely the divorce of literature from life. The change of setting and epoch neutralizes immorality by transferring it to a setting which divorces it from real life. Thus Boccaccio's characters go to join the ever-swelling crowd of shepherds, shepherdesses, and rustic high priests who peopled the harmless never-never land of the late sixteenth-century pastoral, their spiritual brothers if not their immediate compatriots.

Salviati's second device is the use of copious glosses, which set up an entirely new relationship between the reader and the text, a relationship in which the stern figure of the editor directs the reader's attitude towards each episode of each *novella*, stressing that its function was to give an 'example' and to provide moral instruction—*ammaestrare dilettando*: amuse it might or might not, but instruct it must. It was a brave man who could approach the *Decameron* with this purpose in mind, for not all episodes could be treated in the same manner. Whilst some acts and statements are pointed out as examples of the abhorrent ways and thoughts of pagans and reprobates, which thus act as a salutary warning, others must be stressed as the example to follow. The process required a certain nimbleness of mind on the part of the reader, too.

But a third and more drastic device was also used. There were, Salviati realized, stories which did not respond to such gentle treatment, and for these he had in mind measures so radical that they amounted to the transformation of the entire structure in which their interest lay. The comparatively simple expedient which he adopted was to alter the end in such a manner that the whole became a 'moral tale' with a medieval flavour. Sometimes he introduced repentance and voluntary reformation by 'bad' characters themselves, sometimes they were overtaken by just retribution as the wages of their sin: and occasionally some outside element was introduced to redress the balance and restore the 'good' example. Thus Ricciardo Minutolo (iii. 6) finishes his days in penitence on a desert island and his love Catella, having 'pretended' to be reconciled with him, falls ill and dies on realizing the extent of her own folly. Such modifications, however, inevitably lead to a chain-reaction necessitating further modifications in character, situation, and plot. The facilitation of eventual marriages (bringing respectability) necessitates, for example, initial changes in the characters' relationships and status. Married women here involved obviously have to be reduced to spinsterhood. The general meddling with characters and situations, whether called for by religion or lay morality, has a snowball effect, leading to yet further meddling and many absurdities.

As a result of the moralizing aspect of the 'correction', the *Decameron* remains, artistically, a pathetic mutilated remnant, far inferior to the 1573 edition, which was subjected to less profound modification, was treated with more artistic insight and understanding, and was of course based on different critical principles. Even should one ignore the glosses, the fact remains that the many modifications in plot, structure, situation, character, and character-relationships are such as to destroy the inner harmony of the stories. Beyond doubt the rearrangement of many of the stories was carried out hastily, without due regard for continuity and verisimilitude. With a little more care and a modicum of ingenuity the same or a similar effect could have been achieved at less cost to the harmony and coherence of some of the *novelle*. As we have seen, Lionardo's correspondence bears witness to the extreme haste with which he carried out the revision, for having on 14 August 1580 informed Francesco that he hopes to 'cavarne prestamente le mani' he has the edition ready by early 1581.

Yet the traditional picture of Salviati as an insensitive pedant enthusiastically mutilating his favourite author in an excess of misplaced zeal is far from being an accurate one. New documents have shed new light on the question, and suggest that our ideas on the expurgation itself—as distinct from the linguistic correction —must be radically altered. First of all, there is clear, abundant, and incontrovertible evidence recently brought to light that the radical 'moral' transformation was imposed on Salviati as the price of that aspect of the work which was really close to his heart, namely the linguistic correction.[9] In the later polemics over the *Gerusalemme Liberata* he was able (despite his moral conformism) to elaborate an aesthetic which, by making 'pleasure' the aim of literature and the criterion of morality, was able to reconcile moral exigencies with complete freedom of content. It is by this means in fact that he justifies the all-too-obvious lack of a conscious exemplary or didactic moral element in the *Orlando Furioso*. The work 'pleased': it gave a certain 'experience', it was thus 'moral'. And there is no reason whatever to suppose that left to his own devices he would have lacked the ingenuity to do the same for the *Decameron*, since the same basic principles largely determined his attitude to both works. If his passion for the national tradition could lead him (notwithstanding his basic moralist–conformist orientation) to a moral defence and justification of the Ferrarese *Furioso*, with how much more enthusiasm would he have fought for the preservation intact of the Florentine *Decameron*. Unquestionably the Inquisition was of the opinion that the moral leniency of the earlier correction had been a

⁹ For discussion of this documentation see P. M. Brown, 'I veri promotori' and 'Aims and Methods of the Second "Rassettatura" of the *Decameron*', *Studi secenteschi*, viii (1967), especially pp. 4–7.

blunder which Salviati, as the price of the linguistic revision and the return of the book into circulation, was now to remedy.

In the second place, the traditional view of Salviati must also be modified if we analyse carefully the devices which he used in the expurgation. For the inescapable conclusion is that this method was devised with the aim of minimizing interference with the text. Glosses may distort interpretation, but at least they leave the text intact. Alterations to beginnings and endings, modifications in character-structure and settings, change the over-all spirit of the story but interfere little with the telling, and wording, of it. Worse, much worse, could have happened if the *Decameron* had been moralized by less external means than those employed by Lionardo Salviati.

Heavy though the price was, to Salviati it was unquestionably worth it in the context of his vision of the *volgare* and of Florentine and Italian culture. The one fact alone of making available again this most important of all texts no doubt outweighed the harm which might be caused by the forced manipulation of content. If one then adds the supreme gain of the production of a more accurate text—a gain in his eyes no less aesthetic than linguistic— then one realizes that he may well have seen the linguistic correction of the text as making a positive contribution to the artistic value of the *Decameron*, a contribution in fact such as would go some distance towards compensating for the deterioration resulting from his other, externally imposed, modifications. Indeed, he himself tells us that his position *vis-à-vis* the moral correction was precisely such as we have analysed it, when he writes afterwards to Francesco, saying of his edition: 'quell'acquisto che s'è recuperato, si dee riconoscere dall'opera mia: e quel che ci ha di spiacevole è fuor d'ogni mia colpa, e s'è tollerato per minor male.'[10]

It was to the linguistic correction that his energies were thus principally directed. As already seen he quickly acquired from the Laurenziana the basic tools of his trade with which, it must not be forgotten, he was already thoroughly familiar. In fact all the experience of the 1573 correction is to be understood as contributing to Lionardo's own revision in 1582. As far as the texts go he concurs wholly in the 1573 correctors' evaluation of the available manuscripts and printed books, stating in his Preface to the

10 Lett. Salviati to Gr. Duke Francesco, 2.3.84, pub. Contin, op. cit., No. 52.

Decameron, 'Lionardo Salviati ai lettori', that he has maintained the same graduation. Naturally he confines his comments to the linguistic aspect of the oration.

For this work he was eminently suited by training, by industry, and by cast of mind. Vast research had been undertaken into the old texts by Salviati during the years preceding the 1582 revision, and as the study of the development of Tuscan, with the aim of acquiring a precise knowledge of its state in the middle of the fourteenth century, was the basis of the correction of his master Borghini, so it was the basis of Salviati's philological method. Indeed the notes which precede the 1582 edition and those pertaining to the correction which are published as Vol. I, Bk. 2 of the *Avvertimenti* reveal him to be Italy's greatest contemporary vernacular philologist. At the same time they bring out no less forcefully how the school of historical philology initiated by Borghini and developed by his pupil placed Italy in the vanguard of European vernacular philology.

In these notes, in which Salviati explains and justifies his method, we see the true richness of his erudition, the penetrating quality of his interpretation, and the soundness of his analysis. Fortified by his historical research and his intimate knowledge of all facets and levels of the contemporary language, he is aware of the perpetual process of change in the spoken language which has misled editors familiar only with contemporary linguistic manifestations into erroneous interpretations. He concludes that all places which rouse doubts must be closely scrutinized in the light of information which other texts of the same period, giving a deeper understanding of the 'language' of the times, can provide. Thus one must proceed cautiously, not suspecting that everything which appears unfamiliar is an error to be rectified by reference to modern usage. His over-all procedure reveals him to have the prime essential qualifications for the work of textual criticism—thorough acquaintance with the language of the period and intimate knowledge of the habits of his author. His study of the development of the language allowed him for example to recognize in Boccaccio 'l'uso di due età, e tal volta di tre'.

Yet even here he avoided excessive rigidity, examining closely each individual case, not only referring to the usage of Boccaccio and his contemporaries but taking into account the context, and hence stylistic, and even grammatical, licence and variation on the part of the author. Therefore with regard to this aspect of Salviati's correction, namely his attitude to the text as a personal artistic use and elaboration by the author of the language of his times, it can be said that he proceeded with due caution and regard, and with great skill and insight.

Unfortunately the same cannot be said of his textual method in so far as it concerns the critical use of texts. Here and there we find some suggestion of methodical collation—he even foreshadowed modern conclusions in his view, derived directly from limited collation, of the 'due originali'. But the overriding authority of the Mannelli text, and the inconsistent, capricious concession of authority to the others, means that his over-all method is that of the *textus optimus* with minor modifications and remains utterly unscientific.

But the task which Salviati had set himself did not end with this aspect of the reconstruction of the original text. More important, in his eyes, was the orthographical revision. And it is this orthographical revision which gives the *rassettatura* not only a place in the orthographical disputes, but its polemical significance, its importance in the context of Salviati's vision of the *volgare*, and its place in the history of the linguistic quarrels in the sixteenth century in Italy. In brief, the correction anticipates certain theories eventually elaborated in the *Avvertimenti*.

In this work Salviati was to argue the identity of the literary language of the fourteenth century with the language of Florence, indicating as proof of this the equal force, in the old language as in the modern, of the distinctive Florentine feature of *dolcezza* produced by the phonetic genius of Florentine. Examination of the old texts, he believes, demonstrates to the practised eye the extent to which these forces were operative in the fourteenth century, yet at the same time reveals how the clumsy, contradictory orthography of the time, lacking adequate consistent correspondence between sound and symbol, was incapable of conveying this fully. In other words the faulty orthography of the manuscripts fails to reveal the full extent of the intended *Florentine* character of the original, and his task, as he conceived it, was therefore to restore to the *Decameron* this *dolcezza* which Boccaccio meant it to have.

For Salviati this inevitably meant making orthography reflect Florentine pronunciation. The big problem was—Florentine

pronunciation of what period? The logical answer in the context
would be Florentine pronunciation of the time of Boccaccio,
but the inadequate fourteenth-century orthography, the confused
and contradictory orthographical practices, bringing the danger
of misinterpreting the value which the *antichi* placed on their
symbols, made this impossible to ascertain. But one of Salviati's
basic beliefs was that the language of the Trecento shared with
modern Florentine speech a characteristic of supreme importance
—its phonetic genius impelling it towards *dolcezza*. The nearest
one could get, therefore, to restoring the original character of the
text of the *Decameron*, was to apply the criterion of 'good' modern
Florentine pronunciation in areas of doubt. He considered that
in practice the need for the application of this criterion would be
very limited.

But it is in further justifying this procedure that Salviati reveals
an attitude which gives his correction its significance as a document
of contemporary cultural developments reflected in attitude to
language. What he does is to insist repeatedly that there is good
reason to believe that in the fourteenth century, despite the
lexical 'purity' of the language, pronunciation was in many respects
inferior to that of modern Florentines, if by 'pronunciation' we
mean the working of certain phonetic tendencies.[11] To apply the
criterion of modern Florentine pronunciation is therefore to give
Boccaccio, as far as the *dolcezza* is concerned, the benefit of
a higher and more perfect stage of development. In short, there
emerges quite clearly, from Salviati's own comments on his
orthographical revision of the text of the *Decameron*, a fact of the
utmost importance. In one respect at least the speech of his own
age represents the greatest perfection of the *volgare*, and that is
in degree of *dolcezza*, that unique characteristic of Florentine
on which he had laid so much stress twenty years earlier in the
Orazione in lode della fiorentina favella.

So here again, as in his vision of a developing Italian tradition
with an unlimited future, already forcibly expressed in his
references in the orations to modern achievement, in his prog-
nostications for the future triumphs of the *volgare* in the *Fiorentina favella* oration, and in his vision, to be expressed in the
Avvertimenti as a whole, of a *volgare* continually developing and
improving in the future, Salviati reveals how the notion of 'pro-

[11] See particularly *Avvertimenti* (I. i. 8 and I. iii. 174–5).

gress', like the modernist anti-classicism with which it is indissolubly connected, is basic to his thought, governing his approach to any question, whether it be the restricted one of orthography or the wider one of the whole relationship of the Italian tradition to the classical.

As far as the text of the *Decameron* is concerned, the result of the application of his principles is a thorough 'Florentinization' of the language, which was a triumph for the Florentine faction in the linguistic disputes, but which has been justly criticized. It was condemned, in particular, by an indignant Foscolo, principally if not exclusively for the fact that, as he said, it overlooked the literary quality of the language and its consequent inevitable artificiality with respect to the spoken. All of which may be true: and the exaggerated spoken Florentine quality given to the text may amount to a minor falsification of the elaborate artistic prose of Boccaccio. Yet the corrected *Decameron* remains another solid monument to the editor's sound scholarship, his historical vision of the *volgare* as a Florentine phenomenon, to his vigour, and to his single-minded pursuit of his goal.

For whatever shortcomings we may find in this Florentine Boccaccio, we must integrate the undertaking into the fabric of Florentine philology and linguistics as represented also by contemporaries of Salviati such as Borghini and Varchi, particularly the former. Like them Salviati was reacting, albeit somewhat violently, to the ravages of the non-Tuscan critics and commentators, headed by Ruscelli, whose general tendency was to remove the great Trecentisti from their Florentine context entirely, misinterpreting, misunderstanding, and in general misleading. If they even went so far as to propose on occasion an etymology-based orthography which severed all contact with Florentine pronunciation of any period, increasing disproportionately the margin of artificiality, Salviati's errors may be regarded as a corrective, in self-defence, to theirs. As far as Salviati's own development is concerned moreover, the correction of the *Decameron* must be regarded as an important bridge between the early Varchi-influenced 'linguistic naturalism' and the *Avvertimenti*, which achieve the final reconciliation between this and the authority of the great authors of the Trecento.

In general, as we have seen, the new correction was badly received, in Florence as elsewhere. In this connection it is not without significance that no hostile word seems to have been uttered by the man who was most outspoken against the earlier correction, namely Anton Francesco Grazzini. He was, of course, already ill at the time of publication, and was associated with Lionardo, as we shall shortly have occasion to see, in another academic enterprise. Yet his silence here, and his support for Lionardo in this other enterprise, are more likely to be due to his acquaintance with the inside story of the correction and to a fundamental sympathy with Lionardo than to his ill health. For the two were to the end linked by a basic unity of views and principles which was too solid to be shaken by divergencies on detail.

Subsequent generations have with one voice condemned the correction as a piece of unscrupulous butchery, most contemporaries and immediate successors seeing Salviati's motives as purely mercenary. Boccalini, insinuating moral depravity, accuses him of having undertaken the revision 'ad istanza de' Giunti stampatori di Firenze per avarizia di venticinque scudi, che gli hanno donati per premio di sì grande scelleratezza', whilst Celso Cittadini, writing to Giulio Cini in 1615, asserts that 'Il Cav.r Salviati ebbe da' Giunti dua mila piastre, e in poco tempo ve ne guadagnarono altrettante.'[12] Certainly Giacomo Buoncompagni himself seems to have hoped that financial benefits would accrue to Salviati from his nomination as corrector. He appears, however, to have been a bad prophet, for Salviati's own correspondence at this time reveals that in these years, when he was under fire from all sides yet forbidden to reply to his critics, he was also burdened by financial troubles partially caused by, and certainly linked with, the fortunes and misfortunes of his branch of the family. He seems to have gone to great trouble on behalf of the offspring of his brothers and sisters. In September 1581 he asked the Grand Duke to pardon, for some unspecified offence, his nephew Cosimo Mannelli, for the sake of the 'onorata memoria della madre di questo giovane, e mia carnal sorella', and a month later had to ask for his protection for a niece of his whose husband, Neri Pepi, was ill-treating her. This involvement was a notable contributory

---

[12] C. Guasti, *Opere di T. Tasso* (Florence, Le Monnier, 1814), Vol. i, p. xxviii. For the Boccalini quotation see T. Boccalini, *Ragguagli di Parnaso*, ed. Luigi Firpo, 3 vols. (Bari, Laterza, 1948), iii. 52. Firpo's notes to the text perpetuate a tissue of traditional errors.

factor in the worsening of Lionardo's already desperate financial situation, and it is a tribute to his highly developed sense of family responsibility that he was ever willing to sacrifice himself and his own interests for their welfare.

The first indication of his renewed straitened circumstances and their causes is found in a letter to Sperone Speroni of 25 June 1583, in which he promises to pay his debt to Speroni as soon as certain legal formalities 'dopo la quale sarò signore del mio' are completed. November of the same year, however, finds him still putting Speroni off with promises only, and when we hear of the matter for the last time on 24 August 1585 the debt of 120 scudi to the Paduan is still outstanding. This time the delay in payment is attributed to further family burdens and duties which have devolved on Salviati. The death of another brother has plunged him into debt, and to make matters worse he is having to struggle to provide a dowry for the daughter of one of his dead brothers.[13]

Despite these practical irritations, there are indications that Salviati was settling down again into the intellectual and cultural life of the city. One such indication commands our attention as being of maximum significance for the future. It concerns Salviati's friend Giovanni de' Bardi dei Conti di Vernio, a neighbour of his who with his 'camerata dei Bardi' played such a vital part in the development of Italian opera. At some point during the year 1582 De' Bardi had undertaken to lecture to that other renowned Academy in Florence, the Alterati, his lecture being intended as a reply to Francesco, Bonciani, the 'Accademico Aspro'. This learned gentleman had made his personal contribution to the current disputes over the merits of the *Orlando Furioso* of Ariosto by comparing that work unfavourably with the Homeric and Virgilian epics, using Aristotle as his criterion of judgement in the manner of the day. Precisely how he had gone about doing this is not certain, since his lecture is no longer extant. The form of the attack on Ariosto may have been determined by the formal Aristotelian categories, with individual episodes being used in illustration, or the starting-point may have been certain more or less parallel episodes in the Italian and classical poems which were thereafter analysed in the light of

---

[13] Letts. Salviati to Speroni dated 26.11.83 and 24.8.85, in *Opere di Sperone Speroni*, 5 vols. (Venice, Occhi, 1740), iv; also Contin and Manzoni, *Prose inedite*.

Aristotle. At all events the accusations fell into a by now familiar pattern of attack against Ariosto of un-Aristotelianism and of inferiority to the classical models. The structure of the plot was certainly specifically condemned, as was Ariosto's handling of the *costume*, whilst several more or less parallel episodes in Ariosto and the classics were compared, with the palm going to the latter. Over all, Ariosto seems to have emerged as a decidedly mediocre poet.

To all this De' Bardi had taken strong objection. The whole subject was, of course, by this time a commonplace of the Academies of Florence, in which the relationship of the *Orlando Furioso* to Aristotelian theory had been hotly debated for some time. Was the *Furioso* (and/or the romance in general) an 'epic'? If so, did it correspond to the Aristotelian rules for such compositions? Did a 'modern' epic have to conform to the exemplification of these rules as represented by the classical epics? Indeed, did a modern epic have to conform to rules formulated in Classical Antiquity at all? These and many other related questions occupied the minds of the Alterati in particular, divided roughly as they were into the 'ancients', who considered that the epic of Antiquity provided an immutable blueprint for any such work (with corresponding disparagement of Ariosto or anyone else who departed from it) and the 'moderns' who maintained a more historical perspective, believing that the rules could be implemented differently 'secondo i tempi' as De' Bardi, a militant modern, was himself eventually to state.[14]

Determined to refute Bonciani, De' Bardi—the 'Accademico Puro'—set to work on the text of Ariosto. His original aim, it seems, was to collect a sufficient number of examples to prove, by the same comparative method used by Bonciani, that Ariosto was a greater poet than either Homer or Virgil. Purely theoretical matters were probably secondary. What is most significant for

---

[14] In his *Difesa dell'Ariosto*, unpublished in MS., B.N.C., Florence, Cod. Magl. Cl. VI, 168, fols. 50ʳ–75ᵛ, sixteenth-century. See also my article, 'In Defence of Ariosto: Giovanni de' Bardi and Lionardo Salviati', *Studi secenteschi*, xii (1971), 3–27. For information on the 'ancients and moderns', see B. Weinberg, *A History*, esp. pp. 808–9, but see also his Index under 'Quarrel of the Ancients and Moderns'. By the same author, 'Argomenti di discussione letteraria nell'Accademia degli Alterati (1570–1600)', *G.S.L.I.* cxxxi (1954), 175–94, gives information on the whereabouts of the de' Bardi manuscript as does the *History*, p. 1116, in which (ii. 985–7) there is also a critical summary of the contents of the *Difesa*.

us is that in this task he called on the help of Lionardo Salviati. Lionardo set to work with a will, and by late September he had assembled from the text of the *Furioso* a good forty examples which would serve De' Bardi's purpose. At that point, having heard of the project and full of good intentions, Salviati's protégé Bastiano de' Rossi turned up with copies of the editions of the *Furioso* edited by Lodovico Dolce and Girolamo Ruscelli which, he thought, might be of some use. Perusing these volumes Lionardo was dismayed to find that every single one of the examples which he had extracted with such an outlay of time and labour had been noted in their appendices '. . . che mi fece presso che bestemmiare,' he writes to De' Bardi, 'parendomi haver pisciato nel vaglio'.[15] Annoying as it was for him personally, he was more concerned about De' Bardi, who was now in a most difficult position, faced with either not fulfilling his commitment to the Academy—since to start the work all over again would have entailed an expenditure of time which just was not possible—or using second-hand material. For a few days he turned it over in his mind, and finally set down his conclusions in a letter to De' Bardi dated 28 September 1582. De' Bardi must reorientate his lecture. Salviati advises that he 'lasciasse stare le cose particulari poiché elle sono in istampa, e parlasse de' fondamenti dell'arte che non sono stati tratti da questi ciurmadori.' He then proceeds to tell him what he himself would say 'quando io mi risolvessi a questo'. This information it is which is so important for the development of Salviati's thought.

He plunges directly into an Aristotelian condemnation of the *Aeneid* from the point of view of the *favola*—plot or construction. Arguments adduced by others to prove that the construction of the *Furioso* was defective when judged by the same Aristotelian yardstick are demolished. Virgil's offence against the *costume* and his deviation from Aristotle's prescriptions for the use of history are illustrated in some detail, and the *Furioso* again examined to prove wrong those who would find it unsatisfactory in either of these senses. Having completed these comparative demonstrations Salviati proceeds to pure praise of Ariosto,

---

[15] This letter(non-Aut. but undoubtedly authentic) from Salviati to De' Bardi, dated 28 September 1582, is to be found in Milan, in the Bib. Ambr., Cod. Q, 113 sup., fols. numbered 89–91 (and also 1–3), recto only. As a manuscript item within the Cod., the whole letter is numbered 26.

adducing extracts from his poem in illustration of his unsur-
passed ability as a verbal artist. Finally he declares that Ariosto
'pleases' more than any other poet (though he by no means pleases
only the unlettered crowd) and since 'pleasure', according to the
interpretation of Aristotle which Salviati here puts forward, is
the criterion of excellence, then verifiable fact proves the *Furioso*
to be the greatest poem of all.

What this letter to De' Bardi reveals is a whole pattern of thought,
concerning both the relationship of the *Furioso* to Aristotelian
precept and the position of the work in this respect *vis-à-vis* the
epic of Classical Antiquity, which can only have been the product
of long reflection. It indicates, in other words, that by 1582
Salviati has studied the *Furioso* within the context of those very
issues which we have seen to be his main concern, namely the
relationship of the modern Italian tradition to the classical.
It is quite obvious that already Salviati not only has unbounded
admiration for the *Furioso* itself, but that it has already established
itself in his vision of things as the most perfect creation of the
Italian tradition and also the 'perfect Aristotelian epic'. As long
as this letter remained unknown there were some grounds—
however slender—for believing that Salviati's later participation
in the Ariosto–Tasso polemic (in favour of the former, as we shall
see) was motivated by a many-sided animosity against Tasso,
for the expression of which 1585 was a favourable moment. No
such grounds can any longer be considered to exist. The first
contribution by Salviati to the discussions over Ariosto was
written in 1582, and this is it.

If, then, we see this as the first time that Salviati participates in
the current debates, what matters is first that this letter springs
entirely from a desire to *defend* Ariosto, and along with him those
principles of which we have seen Salviati to be the spokesman,
and secondly that his defence is based on precisely those notions
which characterized Salviati's later contributions to the polemics
over the *Gerusalemme Liberata*. The *Furioso*, for example, is
firmly classed as a 'heroic' poem, of which it is also considered
to be the perfect example, and Salviati's procedure is to interpret
Aristotle in such a way as to justify at all costs the practice of
Ariosto. Both the classical epics and the *Furioso* stand equal
before Aristotle, with a firm 'modernist' repudiation of any
suggestion that Aristotelian precept was to be identified with its

exemplification in the epic of Antiquity. In the comparison between classical and Italian, therefore, whether within or without the sphere of Aristotelian precept, the former emerges triumphant. It is this 'Italian versus classical' aspect of the letter in particular which gives it its significance and provides such an illuminating gloss on later developments. It reveals that the chief enemy of Salviati's theories and principles in his defence of Ariosto is the lingering authority of Classical Antiquity, manifested in this case in the enshrinement of the classical epic as the model for all time. It reveals that by 1582, against this view, Salviati had already worked out his notion of the relationship of Ariosto and the classical epic both to each other and to Aristotle, and possessed a theory, and a vision, which made him a seasoned thinker, if not yet a public campaigner, in the context of the polemics over Ariosto and Aristotle as they had been going on in Italy for decades. De' Bardi, in a strongly 'modernist' lecture, used much of the material supplied by Salviati, material which, as we shall eventually see, was re-used in large part by its original author.[16]

This episode is one of several which illustrate how, as he established himself more permanently in Florence once again, Salviati's activities were being orientated steadily back towards language and literature—witness the edition of the *Decameron*—and away from the life of the courtier. That life had been an inglorious failure. His attempt to identify himself with the state it its latest developments had been rebuffed, but the experience had been sufficient to do for him what it was doing for many of his compatriots. It had revealed to him the aridity of that state, its rottenness, and made him detest its symbol and figurehead, Francesco. From now on he ceased to identify the Florence he loved with the Medici regime, characterized as it was by partiality, abuse of power, disorder, by violence unpunished and often condoned, even promoted or abbetted, by the highest authority.

---

[16] De' Bardi, after at least one postponement, it appears, read his lecture in the Accademia degli Alterati, on 24 February, 1583, just five months after Salviati's letter. For an analysis of the use he made of the letter, see my article 'In Defence of Ariosto'. Weinberg, in his 'Argomenti', p. 186, transcribes the entry for that date from the *Diario* of the Alterati (Florence, Bib. Medicea Laurenziana, MS. Ashburnhamiano 558), entry in Vol. ii, fol. 36^v, 'Lesse il Puro difendendo l'Ariosto da certe accuse dategli dall'Aspro in una lezione da lui recitata nell'Accademia Fiorentina. Contradisse l'Aspro, In favore del quale sentenziò il Reggente.'

There were further exchanges between him and the Grand Duke, but his connections with the courts of Florence and Rome grew more tenuous, and he does not seem to have found further employment on missions of a political nature. His next important undertaking, even more than the correction of the *Decameron*, places him firmly back in the cultural and literary world of Florence and, though he can scarcely have foreseen or suspected quite how, chiefly determined the image which he was to have for the next four centuries.

XIII

THE CRUSCA AND THE *AVVERTIMENTI*

SOME years before Lionardo Salviati fully resumed his connections with the academic life of Florence a group of Florentine Academicians had begun to meet for the purpose of holding *lezioni in burla* in the Florentine tradition as a relief from their more serious academic occupations. These lectures they called *cruscate*.

It is not certain how long they had been holding their meetings when they asked Lionardo to join them, nor is the date of his entry certain, though it is undoubtedly 1582 or 1583. The Diary of the Crusca indicates 1582 as the date of the first organized meetings, the founders of the company including friends of Salviati—Bernardo Zanchini, Giovambattista Deti, Bernardo Canigiani, Bastiano de' Rossi, and particularly Antonfrancesco Grazzini. Evidence is generally in favour of 1582 being the year in which Salviati accepted the invitation of the Crusconi as they called themselves, who hoped that his prestige would help their society to survive—'istimando, mediante sì fatto appoggio, dover la lor compagnia più resistere a' fortunevoli colpi.'[1]

Whatever the date of the famous *stravizzo*, a kind of inaugural banquet which coincides with Lionardo's first participation in the activities of the Crusca, his influence on the latter was inestimable. In considering the motives which induced Salviati to join this Brigata dei Crusconi it must not be overlooked that Lionardo was by no means renowned for his serious and scholarly works only. He valued the *letteratura in burla*, and so must have been attracted to the Crusconi, especially as they numbered so many of his friends.[2] The Accademico Trito (conte Piero de' Bardi)

---

[1] The origins of the Accademia della Crusca, the significance to be attached to the word *cruscata*, and the climate in which this activity took place, have been amply treated in Marconcini, *L'Accademia della Crusca*, Chs. i and ii. Some information on the early years of the Crusca is found in the first of the two so-called *Frammenti del Trito*, in manuscript in the Archivio della Crusca, from which comes the extract quoted.

[2] See *Avvertimenti* (I. ii. 125) devoted to the *basse poesie* which he regards

says that on being invited Salviati declared that this was all he needed to give him pleasant relief from his many cares. Others, however, believed that he already saw the company as a potential instrument for attacking rival *letterati* who had irritated him by their pompousness, in so much as it would give him the opportunity to present his case in a mock-frivolous garb contrasting favourably with their pedantry.

There may be some truth in this. The revised *Decameron* had raised a storm of abuse and protest against which Lionardo had not been allowed to defend himself. At all events, scarcely had he become one of their number than he suggested to the company that they should adopt this policy of making known 'il lor valore sotto la piacevolezza'. He began to urge them to organize themselves on the lines of an Academy, and one day he harangued them with 'exceptional eloquence' on the subject, adding that should they follow his advice he would give them every possible support. The suggestion was not accepted without opposition. Bernardo Zanchini declared himself flatly against. The ever-loyal Grazzini, however (though it cannot have been without regret that he saw slipping away for the second time his ideal of a company made for Florentine wit and *piacevolezza*), spoke warmly in favour, and succeeded in swaying the other Crusconi over to Salviati's proposals. Deti was elected Arciconsolo of Salviati's new Academy and it was decided that his solemn investiture, a ceremony which would mark and symbolize the rebirth of the *brigata* as an *accademia*, should take place in a month's time.

Whilst the Crusconi awaited the day of the investiture, fixed for February 1584, Salviati, who had by now assumed the academic name of the Infarinato, persuaded the Academicians that if their Academy was to have a solid foundation it must publish something which would be typical of its 'double nature'—'cioè della dottrina e della piacevolezza'.

Lionardo himself undertook the composition of the work at once. The outcome was the *Paradosso* or *Dialogo* entitled *Il Lasca*[3]

as a 'genre' in their own right. His manuscript commentary on the *Poetics* (Florence, B.N.C., Magl. VII, 87) also indicates the importance he attached to this kind of poetry and literature (see especially fols. 298 ff. and 251ᵛ).

[3] *Il Lasca, Dialogo, Cruscata ovver Paradosso, d'ORMANNOZZO RIGO-GOLI; rivisto ed ampliato da PANICO GRANACCI, Cittadini di Firenze, e Accademici della Crusca* (In Firenze, per Domenico Manzani, 1584). Both Gamba and Poggiali state that there are copies of this work which bear the

in which, according to the title-page, it was proved that 'non importa, che la storia sia vera'. This has all the external trappings of a typical *cruscata*: the names of the speakers were Gatta Bidello, Ormannozzo Rigogoli (Deti), and Panico Granacci (Lasca). The dialogue ends on a would-be comic note—that the historian should relate the truth because otherwise he is beaten by his master. The 'paradox' in the arguments is treated in such a way as to appear frivolous. All these are features of the *cruscata*, though the work does deal with problems taken all too seriously by the critics of the sixteenth century. It was written and published between 25 January and 18 February, on which day Grazzini died. The externals of the *cruscata* are in truth thin. As the sole genuine attempt to unite the elements of *dottrina* and *piacevolezza* it is a failure. Its contents and the method of their exposition both came under fire, especially on moral grounds, from contemporary critics. From the publication of this work onwards, Salviati's career and reputation were linked with the Accademia della Crusca, virtually his own creation, even if after his death a heated debate did take place amongst the Academicians as to whether or not he was to be considered the founder of the Academy and in consequence whether his portrait (still to be seen there) should be given the place of honour.

In the meantime, however, there was a natural sequel to the revision of the *Decameron*. This revision had furnished Salviati with a mass of co-ordinated material, analysed and classified, with which to illustrate his by now fully mature linguistic theories. The first volume of the work in which he was to give a full exposition of these, the *Avvertimenti della lingua sopra 'l Decameron*, was ready for printing by the second half of 1583. After a prolonged residence in Padua (July to September) with visits to Venice made to supervise the printing, Salviati returned to his villa at Vernio to await the finished work which he wanted to take to his master Giacomo Buoncompagni in Rome as soon as it was available. Following the rough handling that the *Decameron* had received and the many enemies that the correction had made him, it was not without some trepidation that Salviati awaited the publication of the *Avvertimenti*, though he did pluck up

impresa of the Crusca, but this is unlikely. The introductory letter refers to critical voices raised against the *Dialogo*, which must have been in the Academy itself, if they preceded publication.

the courage to tell Sperone Speroni in November that he considered himself more than a match for potential adversaries.

In February 1584 the long-awaited edition of volume one was ready.[4] Embittered by the attacks on the *Decameron* and by the news of attacks on the *Avvertimenti* being prepared even before their publication, Lionardo left for Rome on 2 March 1584 to present the new work to Buoncompagni, to whom each of its three books was dedicated. Although Salviati was still nominally attached to the Duke of Sora he was highly discontented with his master. He now looked upon his Roman years, and probably rightly, as so much time wasted, and on the very day on which he left Florence to present the *Avvertimenti* to Buoncompagni he wrote to Francesco begging him to find him more profitable employment for his talents. This is his last recorded visit to Rome, marking the end of his service with Buoncompagni.

That hostile critics were waiting to pounce on the *Avvertimenti* was no idle figment of a suspicious mind. Salviati had just spent a prolonged period in Padua, where resided Gian Vincenzo Pinelli, whose most prolific correspondent was none other than the old adversary Jacopo Corbinelli. From beyond the Alps Corbinelli bombarded Pinelli with a succession of letters of which a constant feature was abuse of Salviati, both of his personal abilities and his linguistic notions and practices. As Crescini says, 'Si può dire che sia costui [i.e. Salviati] come un fantasma, il quale perseguiti il Corbinelli, tanto spesso gli offre argomento in queste lettere di lungo ed acre discorso.' And truly Corbinelli seems to be obsessed. Throughout the latter half of 1584 he worked himself up into a frenzy of excitement waiting for the *Avvertimenti* to reach him. 'Quanto desidero io veder le cose del cavalier Salviati, et conoscere che huomo riesca', he tells Pinelli, 'poi che mette le mani a cose tali.' Not that he expected much, or so he pretended, 'per essere [il Salviati] sofisticuzzo nelle sue cose, nè haver tanto fondo al mio giudizio che possa nobilitar in certo modo quelle cose ch'egli intraprende'. Almost at the end of his patience by December he reveals his malicious intentions to Pinelli, urging him to send the *Avvertimenti*, 'il quale scotennerò subito'.[5] No doubt some inkling of all this had reached Salviati's ears in Padua.

---

[4] *Degli avvertimenti della lingua sopra 'l Decamerone, volume primo* (In Venezia, 1584, presso Domenico e Gio. Battista Guerra, Fratelli).

[5] For details of this correspondence, and especially Corbinelli's criticisms of Salviati, see Crescini, 'Jacopo Corbinelli', especially pp. 189–96.

In the dedication of volume one Salviati describes how the more careful and detailed study of the text necessitated by his revision of the *Decameron* had opened his eyes to many things, 'le quali da me, in forse venti volte, ch'io l'aveva trascorse, erano appena leggerissimamente state considerate', which he now felt he must reveal to others. His treatise is thus divided into two parts, the first and shorter of which is devoted to the details of the linguistic correction of the *Decameron* whilst the second is to deal with certain disputes over the language, with grammar, and with rhetoric. This plan was never completed. The three books of volume one were devoted respectively to the details of the correction, to linguistic theory, and to orthography. Volume two, published two years later, has two books which cover the use of the noun, the article, and the preposition.

Of these volumes by far the more important is the first: and of its three books the one which gives the *Avvertimenti* their greatest significance in the context of sixteenth-century culture is the second. Had only the rest of the *Avvertimenti* survived, his immense erudition and his philological method would still have aroused our admiration. But it is in Volume I Book ii that Salviati presents to us in a powerful, compelling form that vision of the *volgare*, of its history, its use, its intimate nature, and its future, which we have seen to lie behind all his works. In this 'meraviglioso secondo libro degli *Avvertimenti*' as Chiappelli has called it, Salviati gives us in mature form, and supported by the fruits of many years of painstaking research, that conception of the *volgare* as the symbol of Italian achievement which had been the distinctive feature of the *Orazione in lode della fiorentina favella*. The details of his theory, though frequently misunderstood and misinterpreted, are well enough known.[6] The theory itself is in its main lines simple, and presents through the mass of supporting material a clear picture to whoever approaches it without prejudice.

Dominating the exposition, colouring Salviati's thought on every point, his attitude to every controversial question, and dictating the solution to every problem, is that same Florentine modernism which inspired the *Orazione*. Salviati no longer states this in the

---

[6] For an analysis of Salviati's conception of the literary *volgare* see P. M. Brown, 'The Conception of the Literary *Volgare*'. The quoted remark by F. Chiappelli is made in his *Studi sul linguaggio del Machiavelli* (Florence, Le Monnier, 1952), p. 16.

rhetorical terms of the earlier composition, nor do we have emphatic but inconclusive comparisons between classical and Italian languages and literatures. The superiority of the *volgare* and of its literature is largely presupposed. There is no longer any need for accusations of hypocrisy, or abuse of the classics. It is taken for granted that the subject of Salviati's treatise—the *volgare*—represents the highest manifestation of the human mind within a civilization which itself has surpassed that of Classical Antiquity which for so long it took as its model. Only when all the experience of the *Orazioni* is borne in mind are the *Avvertimenti* fully comprehensible, and only when they are related to this central idea of the *volgare* as the symbol of the modern world developing in its own terms do their various aspects dovetail and interlock completely.

It is in fact Salviati's references in the *Avvertimenti* to the position of the *volgare vis-à-vis* Latin (references which appear modest and subdued in comparison to the youthful excesses of the *Orazione*) which provide the key to his vision of the *volgare*. Italian, he insists, is first of all an *independent* organism, and to drive home this notion of independence—absolutely fundamental to his vision—he constructs the theory of a clear-cut distinction between Latin and Italian, which latter was formed 'non dal Latino, ma dalla corruzion del Latino, e non dal Latino solamente, ma d'altro linguaggio insieme'.[7] Of particular importance for Salviati's conception of the vernacular is this use of the word 'corruzione'. Though itself harking back to a long-established controversy over the origins of the *volgare*, and particularly to the *Ercolano* in which Varchi expounds the same theory in an attack on the *anti-volgarista* Bonamico and his associates, it is here not merely a polemical commonplace but the clue to the whole orientation of Salviati's linguistic thought as seen in the context of his over-all anti-classicism, manifested first in the *Fiorentina favella* oration and then to dominate his work.

For in the preceding 150 years he sees the Italian language—a 'new' language for him and not merely an inferior form of Latin—as having been forced into a line of development wholly alien to

---

[7] *Avvertimenti* (I. ii. 79). The statement on the origins of the *volgare* from 'corruption' must, of course, be seen also in the context of the long-standing polemic on the subject, see R. G. Faithfull, 'The Concept of "Living" Language in Cinquecento Vernacular Philology', p. 290.

its nature, resulting in what he labels the 'peggioramento della favella'. This deterioration he considers to have taken place since the end of the fourteenth century in the spoken language and consequently in the written language, the latter having hitherto inevitably reflected the former's 'improvement' or 'decline'. Salviati's untiring stress on this fact is no accident, for he is aware that this assessment is widely echoed by his contemporaries. His repeated assertion that the bulk of Florentines considered that the language had declined since the fourteenth century is amply substantiated by contemporary testimony—Borghini comes to one's mind at once—and by the obvious fact, of which Salviati takes full advantage in his orations, that to write in the language of the fourteenth century, the period before this 'deterioration' took place, was to be sure of giving pleasure regardless of content.

Of supreme importance is the *cause* to which Salviati attributes this 'peggioramento della favella', for this attribution of responsibility illuminates all the rest. The cause, he says, of the decline which he and his contemporaries are at one in feeling to have taken place, is the spread of Latin which began to take place soon after the death of Boccaccio: 'L'allargamento della lingua latina', he says, 'la quale, avendo alquanto prima, quasi da lungo sonno, dato principio a svegliarsi, finalmente in quel tempo, cioè, non guari dopo la morte del Boccaccio, per entro il Popolo cominciò a diffondersi' (1. ii. 77). Since the principal change has been the influx of new words, then these have been the chief cause of deterioration, for they were 'tutte di quella guisa, cioè tratte dal Latino, e delle scuole uscite, e delle cattedre della lingua latina' (1. ii. 77). Here then lies the whole cause of the ruination of Italian—the failure to realize that Italian is an organism completely independent of Latin, with the result that during the humanistic period its true nature was submerged in a flood of Latinisms, many of them, he states, introduced by 'uomini di poca autorità', all of them conflicting with the real character of Italian.

From this it follows automatically that if the *volgare* is to regain its character; if it is to develop freely, independently, in terms of its own nature, then the effects of this violence done to the language must somehow be eliminated. In the *Fiorentina favella* oration Salviati had called on his fellow Florentines to nurture and revitalize, within their Academy, the Italian tradition. The false classical standard must be replaced by an Italian national one. Inevitably in the *Avvertimenti*, which represent the maturing of a vision only hinted at in the oration, that standard is found for language in the fourteenth century, the period which Salviati's contemporaries, for a variety of reasons, generally recognized as the high-water mark of the Italian literary and linguistic tradition.

Hence Salviati's call for a return to the fourteenth century. To the language of Boccaccio and Villani he looks back nostalgically across the repugnant Latinized language of the fifteenth century, and makes a calculated appeal to the emotions of his readers by quoting selections from the *Libro degli ammaestramenti degli antichi*, certain that they will feel as he does about the superiority of the language of the works which he quotes over the language of succeeding periods. It is in this appeal to the emotional effect on his contemporaries that Salviati illustrates how in tune is his whole basic vision of the *volgare* with those forces which were working occultly in those contemporaries and compatriots. For the general anti-classical movement representing the spearhead of thought in the times, with which Lionardo had from the first identified himself and which demanded in general independence for the national tradition, has produced, as a linguistic fact of the first importance, that widely attested sense of the 'peggioramento della favella', which sense, as a linguistic reality, is at the basis of Salviati's theory of language.

The extent to which this sense of 'decline' in the recent past— of a 'golden age' of the national language—is part of a wider movement concomitant with the triumph of the nationalist spirit inspiring Salviati's thought in all branches of his activity, is obvious. As the spirit of classicism died away the externals of the movement ceased to have any significance for the new age, eager to exalt the national tradition as the medium of self-fulfilment and self-perfection. The greater hold this tradition took on the mind of the late sixteenth century, the greater the reaction against those externals which increasingly presented themselves as 'corruption' and 'contamination'. In attacking the Latinization of the language Salviati integrates his linguistic theory into the nationalist campaign waged on the widest possible front in his works. He well knew that now that the spirit and atmosphere which had made them a living manifestation of thought had passed for ever, the results of the humanistic Latinization were beginning to affect adversely the sensibilities of his contemporaries, who were seeking a language which would be the perfect expression of their strongly felt national identity.

So Salviati's anti-Latinism, interpreting the emotions of his contemporaries, is the linguistic reflection of a basic shift in sixteenth-century thought recorded throughout his production. His linguistic theory, of which it is the mainstay, is thus deeply embedded in the currents of thought of his times. For he bases his return to the fourteenth century on the need to eliminate the effects of violence which now, on the demise of the classicist spirit, is felt to have been done to the language during the humanistic Latinization of it.

Independence and freedom to develop in its own way—these are the claims which Salviati makes for the *volgare* in his *Avvertimenti*. From this attitude all the rest develops naturally. The main problem which he has to solve is how to eliminate the effects of the humanistic Latinization, restoring the original 'purity' of the language in order that it might then grow organically, undistorted. His answer is to return, as a first step, to the fourteenth century, adopting its 'pure' language and moving forward from there, allowing the language to develop in keeping with its own nature, governed by the linguistic consciousness of users sensitive to that nature—which was what 'purity' in the last analysis really meant to Salviati.

But it is at this point that the Italian nationalist Salviati joins hands with the Florentine. The model in language must be the great writers of the fourteenth century who present in 'regular' form the living language of the time: as a starting-point, at least, their language must be analysed to provide the 'rules' which, he insists, are not 'imposed' by them but 'collected' from them. They must be the door to the 'language' of the fourteenth century which has so sadly deteriorated to become the spoken and literary language of the sixteenth. And here lies the snag. Salviati must resolve a mighty paradox which he himself has, if not created, at least confirmed.

The traditional Florentine claim to superiority and authority in matters linguistic had been based on their, and others', conception of the literary language as a specialized form of the everyday spoken language of Florence, hence their original hostility to Bembo who seemed 'to reduce all Italy, including Florence, to the same bilingualism of speech and literary expression, in which the Florentines had no more privilege than anyone else, and possibly even less.'[8] Cultural factors, of which Salviati himself was the spokesman, had caused the Florentines themselves to see a 'Golden Age' in the fourteenth century, since when their own language had declined. How then were they to maintain their position as arbiters of the language if they themselves admitted the need to 'learn' the 'correct' language from works equally available to all? Salviati himself describes how the privileged position of the Florentines is under fire on this score from non-Tuscans: 'I quali pur troppo essendo, senza questo, orgogliosi, si vantino, che noi medesimi finalmente siam costretti dalla ragione, e dal vero, a ceder quella prerogativa, che della volgar lingua, e del suo nome, e del suo uso, e del suo padronaggio, non giustamente, ci siamo appropriati' (I. ii. 127).

To answering this accusation (and there is a specific reference here to a passage by Tasso) much space in the *Avvertimenti* is devoted. Salviati's archaism—an archaism undertaken in the name of modernism since its essential purpose is to free Italian for natural development unshackled by Latin, and in general classical, influence—does not mean that he yields an inch from his staunchly Florentine position, in which as always the identification of 'Florentine' and 'Italian' in matters linguistic is virtually complete. Rather he brings all his skill and erudition to bear in an attempt to prove that though in certain externals the language has 'declined', something far more important, amounting to the 'spirit' of the language, has been preserved intact. A Florentine linguistic consciousness, he insists, gives a sense of the language applying equally to the new and the old, thus enabling the modern Florentine to manipulate the old language as his natural tongue with a minimum of effort. It is not only a question of phonology, morphology, or even idiomatic expression, though even here the Florentine has an inestimable natural advantage over the non-Tuscans who 'con parole, e con modi, e con terminazioni e con regole, e con pronunzia nascono, e vivono, quasi tutta diversa' (I. ii. 127). It is something deeper, though the nearest Salviati gets to defining it is in phonological terms, when he demonstrates that the same phonetic tendencies are operative in the new

---

[8] C. Grayson, *A Renaissance Controversy*, pp. 16–17.

as in the old. If Florentines study the old authors it is merely as
a means to the regulated use of their native tongue.[9]

In this way archaism is reconciled with traditional privileges,
and in the second part of Book ii Salviati the Florentine triumphs
over his non-Tuscan opponents, mocking and ridiculing them.
But the forward-looking character of Salviati's archaism means
that the language, as he states, can grow and blossom provided
modifications introduced are in keeping with 'purity' as defined
above. It also, of course, means that the rest of Italy must mould
its language to the pattern evolving in Florence. But his is emphatically not a static conception of the literary language, and
the *Avvertimenti*, with their natural corollary the *Vocabolario della
Crusca*, provided a blueprint according to which the Italian
language could—and largely did—develop in the years to come.

For both in his archaist exposition and in the indications which
he gives for the practical use of the language Salviati reveals how
his conception of the literary language, contrary to what is often
supposed, is one of a living, vital organism, alive in the mind of
its users, and constantly given new life, and even a new character,
by the modifications of those who write in it, capable of growth
and development, with unlimited possibilities. His linguistic
anti-Latinism, necessitating the archaism, was linked to a theory
of the 'natural' development of the language, a theory summed up
in the notion of *autorità*.

He considers it 'natural' that the literary language should absorb
new elements which will then, by this process of transformation,
themselves become 'pure' and 'Florentine'. But new words must
be introduced with tact and judgement. In the letter to Borghini
of 1576 Lionardo says that on those occasions when the literary
language of the fourteenth century did not have a satisfactory
word 'ne accatterei dall'usanza, o da altri linguaggi, ma tuttavia

<hr>

[9] Long before, Salviati's late friend Grazzini had vigorously stated the
need for the Florentines to study their own native classical Florentine authors:
amongst other places he does so in the *stanze A' riformatori della lingua toscana*
(especially lines 89–96 and to a lesser extent lines 97–120) and in the *canto
carnascialesco De' poeti* (especially lines 12–27), in both of which he bemoans the
fact that the neglect by the Florentines of their own language, and particularly
of the norm set by the great writers (including, however, Ariosto), is resulting
in the non-Florentines writing better than the Florentines themselves. He, too,
had stressed the 'potential' of the language in the hands of the Florentines
themselves when supported by a normative grammar based on the great
Italian classics.

con giudicio, e col farne la prima volta scusa sempre.' When he
comes now to the *Avvertimenti* he states: 'E ciò che diciamo del-
l'arricchire il linguaggio, si vuole intendere sempre, come addietro
s'è detto, cioè, che legittimo sia l'acquisto, e da legittimo giudice
confermato: ciò senza fallo sono gli approvati autori: e oltr'a
ciò in convenevole spazio di tempo, bisogna, che sia fatto, altramente d'illecito guadagno si dà sospetto, e dalla 'nvidia è non
poche volte superchiata l'autorità' (I. ii. 105). What matters is that
the process of transformation should take place. The origin of
the word is of little significance. The essential is that the writer,
already having a sense of the language resulting from familiarity
with its living, spoken manifestations, should have a similar familiarity with the 'good' authors of the fourteenth century, which
will confer on him the ability to choose such elements as can
appropriately be used to supplement their language.

In general, Salviati did not encourage innovation and experi-
mentation for their own sakes, but only where circumstances
made them necessary. In the letter to Borghini he had written:
'voci non usate dagli antichi non userei, sempre che io avessi delle
loro d'egual valore, e d'egual bellezza, ed anco fossero manco due
carati: mancandone ne accatterei all'usanza. . . . E l'antiche non
solo con la mano, come disse colei, ma seminerei col sacco.'
But at the same time, equally concerned that the language must be
a living reality in the mind of its users, and must not contain
elements which it is impossible for them to feel as part of their
natural means of expression, Salviati advises against the use of
certain archaisms, saying in the same letter: 'tra le antiche voci,
ne sono alcune, che dalle moderne orecchie par che sentir non si
possono, così appaiono elleno dure loro, e spiacevoli.'

Extremely significant, within the context of Salviati's thought,
is his constant stress on development and improvement of language, which 'ogni giorno nuova facoltà acquistando, di tempo in
tempo più ricco si conviene fare' (I. ii. 105). The natural outcome
of all this theorizing on the use of vocabulary would have been the
much-promised *vocabolario*—'nel qual volume si son raccolti
e dichiarati tutti i vocaboli, e modi del favellare, i quali abbiam
trovati nelle buone scritture, che fatte furono innanzi all'anno
1400', which vocabulary is frequently referred to in his works,
and must have been at a fairly advanced stage at his death. Through
his last years it increasingly occupied his time and energies, and

must be considered his principal, long-term project, continuing behind the scenes during the period of the *Avvertimenti* and the Tasso polemics. Had it ever been completed and published it would undoubtedly have been his major work. It never in fact appeared in Salviati's lifetime, but its principles were inherited by the *Vocabolario della Crusca*.

In the meantime the *Avvertimenti* enhanced immeasurably Salviati's reputation both in his native Florence and throughout Italy, where the *Avvertimenti* established themselves as the most significant work on language in the late sixteenth century, though when volume two, dedicated to Francesco Panicarola, appeared in June 1586, not all reaction was favourable. As expected, Jacopo Corbinelli, released from his almost unbearable agony of waiting by the arrival of the *Avvertimenti* in January 1585, had thrown himself upon volume one with all the fury he could muster. Not for several months, during which he poured out a stream of frenzied abuse against Salviati, did his passion subside. By that time he had declared his intention of compiling a dictionary on principles directly opposed to those followed by Salviati, whose Boccaccio, received at about the same time, visibly shocked him. 'Ho avuto il Boccaccino di Salviati', he writes, 'che è una sciocca cosa a vedere il modo fratino di disertare i libri', thus adding his distant voice to the general clamour of protest.

The editor of the 'Boccaccino' in the meantime was much occupied with the Crusca, though he did not neglect the Accademia Grande either. Lionardo was there as Censor when his friend and Arciconsolo of the Crusca, Giovambattista Deti, was installed in 1585 as its fifty-eighth Consul. Nor was he idle in other respects. A third edition of his revised *Decameron* was published in Venice and in 1585 he published an edition of Passavanti's *Specchio di vera penitenza* already promised in the *Avvertimenti* (I. ii. 113). It was the Accademia Fiorentina, however, which chose Salviati to deliver the funeral oration for Pier Vettori, who died in December 1585. He delivered the oration in the church of Santo Spirito on 23 January 1586. As had been the case on the death of Varchi, the choice of Lionardo was certainly not uninfluenced by the close personal relationship between the orator and his present subject, a relationship which is documented over twenty years of their lives. Yet there is no greater contrast in Salviati's production than the contrast between these two orations. Whereas the Varchi

oration is a monument of insincerity, hollow and rhetorical, the
keynote of the oration for Vettori is conviction, and the author is
inspired throughout by genuine affection, esteem, and admiration.
Vettori himself as a Florentine, a humanist, a teacher, and a
friend, completely dominates the work, which contains a great
deal of anecdote and personal reminiscence. Much of Salviati's
material, particularly the anecdotal material, was supplied by a
'Life' of Piero which the latter's grandson Francesco wrote to
assist Salviati on this occasion, but much was derived from
memories of the many years of friendship between the two.
However much the path of Salviati the *volgare* nationalist di-
verged from that of Vettori the classical philologist the two clearly
felt a strong affinity of aim and principle. Vettori's humanism was
not circumscribed by any narrow classicism. His aim in his
philological studies was first and foremost educational, with the
classics as his chosen means. The most important aspect of his
conception of the relationship between the classics and the *volgare* was his conviction that a familiarity with, and the discipline
of, the former could not but be beneficial to the latter, of which
he was a strong supporter and in whose potential he firmly
believed. When Salviati himself stated in the *Avvertimenti* of
1584 that no one who did not have a background of training in
the classics could ever really handle the *volgare* perfectly, and
that to be steeped in the classics was no impediment to good
composition in Florentine, he was echoing the sentiments of his
master. The oration reveals both a genuine belief on Salviati's
part that Vettori was the greatest Florentine of his day, and an
earnest desire to convince his audience of this.[10]

Despite the fact that amongst the illustrious audience the Grand

----

[10] Florence, B.N.C., Cod. Magl. IX, 64, fols. 12–55ʳ ('provenienza Biscioni'),
described as 'ANON. Vita di Pier Vettori', is in fact a life of his grandfather
Piero by Francesco Vettori, and appears to have been composed immediately
after Piero's death for the express purpose of supplying information on Piero
to Salviati, who in his oration made liberal use of it to supplement his personal
knowledge of Vettori. Fol. 1ʳ bears the heading 'Instruttione al S.r Cav.re Salviati'. The Vettori oration was published as *Oratione funerale del cavalier
Lionardo Salviati, delle lodi di Pier Vettori, Senatore e Accademico Fiorentino* (In
Firenze, per Filippo e Jacopo Giunti, 1585) (Ded. lett. to Panicarola dated
27.1.1586, i.e. 1587 st. com.) and the Passavanti as *Lo specchio di vera penitenza
del reverendo maestro Jacopo Passavanti dell'Ordine de' Predicatori* (In Firenze,
appresso Bartolomeo Sermartelli, 1585). A further edition of this latter work,
based fundamentally on Salviati's text but extremely inaccurate, was published
the following year in Venice.

Duke was not present in person, this oration marked the zenith of Salviati's career as a fashionable orator. But the signs are that even before this Salviati was once again beginning to grow restive in Florence, where he seems to have been ever more irked by not receiving in court circles the respect and attention to which his eminence in cultural circles entitled him. Indeed the very dedication of the Passavanti to Panicarola in 1586 was not the spontaneous expression of esteem which it might at first sight appear, for on 30 April of that same year, when the volume was ready for publication, Salviati had approached the Grand Duke in the following terms, referring to the *Avvertimenti*: 'avendo io qualche sentore che il signor duca di Ferrara, se io glielo dedicasse, lo gradirebbe volentieri: ma essendomi accertato, che non lo accetterebbe senza il titolo che egli vuole, e sappiendo che io non posso, nè debbo farlo, senza sapere se questo conviene a me: supplico umilmente V. A. Serenissima, che si degni farmi grazia che io abbia intorno a ciò qualche consiglio.'

It was the old question of the titles all over again, and though no reply is recorded it cannot but have been negative. Alfonso, in the meantime, was informed of this attempt by Salviati's old friend the ambassador Cortile.[11] Panicarola, too (of whom Francesco was the implacable enemy), fitted into the scheme in so much as he was now suffragan bishop of Ferrara. Acquaintance between the two seems to have been already well established when Panicarola asked Lionardo's opinion of criticisms of his (Panicarola's) oration on Cardinal Borromeo in December 1584. Salviati was complimentary. It is quite clear that his intensified contacts with Panicarola, including the dedication of the *Avvertimenti* and of the oration on Vettori (with the request that he present the latter to the Pope), were part of a strategic plan for the conquest of Ferrara. He also gives the *Avvertimenti* a decidedly Ferrarese orientation when after his ludicrously exaggerated praises of Panicarola he includes, amongst the people named as having encouraged him by their praise of the first volume to publish the second, two who have close associations with Ferrara, Francesco Patrizi

---

[11] It is morally certain that a dispatch from Cortile to Alfonso (Modena, A.S., C.A.F.), undated but seeming to belong to this precise period, which describes Salviati's attempts to dedicate 'questo suo ultimo libro che ha messo fuori' to Alfonso, giving him all his titles, refers to this second volume of the *Avvertimenti*. The quoted passage comes from a letter Salviati to Grand Duke Francesco, 30.4.86, Contin, op. cit., No. 61.

and Giovambattista Guarini. The third person mentioned is Jacopo Mazzoni.

Of the two, Patrizi had long been associated with the Crusca in the dispute with Tasso, by this time well under way, and since 1578 had been teaching philosophy at the University of Ferrara, whence he corresponded with Lionardo. Guarini's opinion on the first volume of the *Avvertimenti*, on the other hand, must have been referred to him by a third party, since there was never any direct contact between the two before 26 April 1586, a month, that is, before the publication of volume two. Since their correspondence even during this month bears no mention of volume one, one can only conclude that Salviati was looking for an excuse to strike up an acquaintance with Guarini.

It was nevertheless Guarini himself who took steps to establish the first direct contact by expressing to Lorenzo Giacomini, in a letter of 4 April 1586, his wish to be remembered to the Accademici della Crusca and in particular to Salviati, for whom he declares he has a great admiration. Salviati in his turn lost no time in seizing the opportunity to make contact, and a correspondence full of compliments, gratitude, and promises was initiated. From this correspondence we learn that Cortile has been Lionardo's main informant, and that Guarini's praise of the *Avvertimenti* has consisted entirely in his asking Cortile for a copy of them.

It is nevertheless quite clear that Guarini, too, was keen to develop a relationship with the Florentine man of letters. Through a screen of compliments his purpose gradually emerged. He wanted Salviati to 'correct' his *Pastor Fido*. Perhaps he had not heard of the 1575 correspondence between Salviati and Tasso. Even if he had, Salviati's reputation now sufficed to impel Guarini, the non-Tuscan, to seek his advice on the language and structure of the work. The question is, whether it was Salviati's enhanced prestige as a linguistic and literary critic resulting from events now taking place in the polemic over the *Gerusalemme Liberata* which chiefly influenced Guarini, or whether it was not rather the fear which the names Infarinato and Crusca now inspired in literary contemporaries, especially those who were about to publish works of their own, as was the case here.

Whatever the truth, Guarini, warmly encouraged by Salviati, sent the manuscript of the *Pastor Fido* off to Florence accompanied by a letter begging Salviati to criticize it from all points of view 'ma molto più negli avvertimenti della lingua', and indicating the method which he would like him to follow. Though inconvenienced in the following months by a long and troublesome illness, by the beginning of October Lionardo had read the pastoral and following the author's instructions had shown it also to various members of the Accademia degli Alterati. Personally, he tells Guarini, he had found the work excellent in every respect. Nevertheless, he had complied with the author's request for criticism by compiling a list of suggested corrections. For comment on the poem as a whole a place was to be reserved in the commentary on Aristotle, still of course unpublished and still able to be modified.

When Guarini replies he expresses his great appreciation of the tact and delicacy shown by Salviati in the 'correction', and indeed a tone of friendship, esteem, and admiration characterizes all Guarini's future references to Salviati. Not that he accepted without question all the observations which Salviati had made on his poem, especially on its form. With typical love of polemic, to which he now invited Guarini, Salviati appended to his linguistic *correzioni* a series of *opposizioni*, mainly regarding the form of the work, and when Guarini replied to each point he eventually countered with a 'replica'. Thus the first polemic over the *Pastor Fido* really took place in an atmosphere of friendliness and cordiality between the author and Salviati. In the same year Guarini became a member of Salviati's Accademia della Crusca with the pseudonym Vagliato.

In the meantime he had adopted most of the linguistic corrections in the printed editions of the *Pastor Fido*.[12] This personal triumph, which can be said also to set the seal on Lionardo's reputation as a linguistic authority, must have been all the more satisfying as Guarini had been Alfonso's personal secretary since the previous year, an item of no mean importance when viewed in the context of Salviati's approach to Ferrara. His renewed attempt to dedicate the *Poetics* to Alfonso having failed, Lionardo turned once again to his friend the ambassador Cortile, who only a few days before Guarini sent his manuscript off to Florence had written to his master:

Havendo inteso il Cav.re Lionardo Salviati gentilh.o letteratissimo come V. A. deve essere informato da molti, che il Panigarola suo

[12] See supplementary note 10, p. 248.

intrinsechissimo et carissimo amico s'è accomodato al servizio di V. A. è venuto ancora a lui il medesimo desiderio di venire a servire l'A. V. et ha confidato questo suo desiderio con me mostrando di non desiderare luoco nessuno ma solo di entrare nel numero de' suoi servitori et esser trattenuto dall'A. V. di quella maniera che parera a lei.

The letter reveals all. It even suggests that Salviati has others working in his favour at the court of Ferrara. But no reply is recorded, which is perhaps why Salviati resorted to his old expedient of gaining favour by informing on friends. This time the victim was the Florentine ambassador, Albizzi, who had been indiscreet enough to confide to Salviati his grievances against the Generale delle Poste of Ferrara, whom he considered to have tampered with his mail. Lionardo informed Cortile, who at once informed his master, stressing the part which Salviati had played.

When the Albizzi affair produced thanks but no tangible fruits the Ferrarese ambassador resorted to a lengthy panegyric of the *cavaliere*, mentioning also the latter's delight on receiving word from Panicarola that a post for him at Ferrara was a distinct possibility. In lauding Salviati he makes an acute, revealing, and for us interesting observation. 'È uomo', says the ambassador, 'per quello che posso conietturare dalla sua parola, che desidera più la riputatione che altra cosa, e però gli sarebbe caro quando fosse in Ferrara a essere honorato di qualche nobile titolo dall'A. V.'[13] This is a penetrating assessment of Salviati's character. Above all he wanted to be recognized—and to be seen to be recognized. This being so, it is not difficult to believe that he was overjoyed at the prospect of a job in Ferrara, quite apart from his long-standing affection for that city and its poetic traditions. For in addition to the smart of Grand Ducal indifference his own private affairs were not going well. Above all his illness seems to have been troubling him more often, being partly responsible (along with the appearance of Ottonelli's *Discorso*) for the delay in publishing the reply he was preparing to Pellegrino's *Replica* in the polemic over the *Gerusalemme Liberata*.[14]

[13] U. lett. Cortile to Alfonso, 18.10.86, Modena, A.S., C.A.F., 1586. Other relevant U. letters (mostly with corresponding replies) are dated 13.9.86, 6.10.86, 15.10.86, 18.10.86, 22.11.86, 26.12.86, from which these and other quoted passages are extracted.

[14] Though he informed Attendolo in the last letter of their correspondence, that is to say on 8 November, that the reply was already at the printers (Lett. Salviati to Attendolo, 8.11.86, Florence, B.N.C., Cod. Magl. II, IV, 557, Copie di lettere di Belisario Bulgarini ed altri).

On top of the troubles of ill health came a rapid deterioration in Salviati's financial position. In despair he begged the Grand Duke in this same November to take him into his service either as historian or as lecturer in the Studio or as translator and commentator of Greek classics. All his income, he tells Francesco, has been given over to his nieces and nephews to pay debts, leaving him destitute. So great is his need that should the Grand Duke find no profitable employment for his talents, then as an alternative he would like permission to try his fortunes once again at the court of Rome, where his past relations with the present Pope had been such as to give him some hope of a favourable reception. The Grand Duke did not reply. Salviati had not been too discreet of late, and perhaps Francesco already knew of the negotiations with Ferrara.

If Salviati on 12 November had written in this vein to Francesco despite these negotiations, it may have been because they had taken a dramatic and unexpected change for the worse. Panicarola, the mainstay of his onslaught on Ferrara, had been driven with ignominy from Alfonso's court, and all Florence was clamouring to know the reason. Yet in this very moment of the apparent downfall of all Lionardo's hopes, the day after he had written his pathetic letter to Francesco, like a bolt from the blue came the opportunity to turn disaster into triumph—a *rivolgimento di fortuna* worthy of the author of the *Granchio*. Panicarola wrote to him, and in the letter were indiscreet references to the court of Ferrara. Letter in hand Lionardo made a bee-line for Cortile, who equally promptly communicated its contents to Alfonso.

Ironically enough this characteristic betrayal of yet another 'friend' was unnecessary, for Cortile's dispatch crossed with one from Alfonso instructing his ambassador to find out with due circumspection how little Salviati would be willing to come to Ferrara for. The mission was not easy, Salviati hedging continually over the question of pay, refusing to commit himself, yet insisting that financial considerations were not in themselves a factor of any great importance. As usual, he wished to be treated with the honour and respect which he considered his due. 'Solamente vorrebbe haver tanto che potesse vivere al servizio di V. A. honoratamente et da gentilhuomo', Cortile tells his master, stressing the while Lionardo's linguistic eminence and his devotion to the court of Ferrara, and pointing out that whilst Lionardo would be perfectly

willing to lecture in the university, his anxiety to preserve his
dignity and reputation demands that he enter Alfonso's service
'sotto pretesto di condotta', and not as a mere teacher, which
presumably would never do for one who had in his time been
Rector of the Studio di Firenze.

Between 16 November and 26 December Salviati was unin-
terruptedly the subject of dispatches passing between Ferrara and
Florence. Believing he had good reasons for suspecting that
Salviati's salary with Buoncompagni had been only 15 *scudi* a
month, Alfonso suggested Cortile should offer 200 *scudi* a year,
and to put an end to negotiations which showed signs of dragging
on interminably he also thought it a good idea that Lionardo be
told that princes made all final arrangements for their households
at New Year (it was then 22 December). Salviati (who in the meantime had had the temerity to request from Francesco the post of
ambassador to Ferrara in place of the retiring Albizzi) was not
altogether pleased with this development, 'havendo inteso dal
Patritio', as Cortile says, 'che lui ha più di dugento scudi l'anno'—
further proof of contacts at this period between Lionardo and
Patrizi. Unavailingly he struggled to convince the wily Alfonso
that he judged a stipend solely on its adequacy to maintain his
dignity and reputation: 'desidererebbe bene particolarmente',
writes Cortile, 'per la riputatione sua d'esser trattato in maniera che
si potesse trattenere da gentilhuomo et che il Mondo conoscesse
che l'A. V. facesse conto della persona sua.' He was temporarily
outmanœuvred, and the ultimatum had its effect. On 27 December he left a letter of acceptance at Cortile's home as he passed it
on his way to his villa at Prato.

This is a most revealing document. It sums up his present
condition and is also a résumé of his past life as a courtier. In his
lifelong devotion to the Estense he sees himself as continuing a
family tradition from which he has been unwillingly diverted by
his unprofitable service with Buoncompagni. Of this service the
sole fruit has been a pile of debts (so much for the Roman salary
as a criterion). Though treated so delicately as to appear of
secondary importance, the question of remuneration is the main
theme. Keeping up one's dignity is difficult enough at any time,
but he has a niece who is such a financial burden that it is impossible for him to use his private income for his own purposes.
In short, he will come to Ferrara, but hopes that Alfonso's mag-

nanimity will in the end allow him to solve all his problems honourably.

This devotion to his family, this affection for the children of deceased sisters and brothers is probably the only endearing aspect of Salviati's otherwise generally unlovable character. It seems to have helped to move Alfonso, who on having Salviati's letter forwarded to him (the writer had asked that it should be burned, knowing well that it would not) considered the case sympathetically, suggesting that if Lionardo would accept to 'leggere una lettione d'humanità' he would have a further 200 *scudi*, at the same time saving his face since in the first place the position was always given to a person of a certain importance such as one of the Duke's secretaries and in the second place no one considered worthy of the job had lately been available.

Salviati accepted, pleased with the salary but without enthusiasm for the post. He had returned to his old idea of writing a history of Casa d'Este, and lecturing was not greatly to his taste. At this point, however, 1 January, news of the death of the Cardinal d'Este reached Florence. By 24 January, with the help of biographical material supplied by the Duke's secretary, Laderchi, Lionardo had completed a funeral oration which he was determined should at all costs be superior to the one he wrote for Cosimo de' Medici. Printing was completed on 7 February and the author sent off a copy to Alfonso at once. The oration was addressed to the King of France because of the relations between the Cardinal and the Most Christian King, and it was dedicated to Sixtus V. Whilst still in Florence Salviati did not wish to raise again the tiresome question of titles by attempting a dedication to Alfonso, but he sent a copy to Laderchi requesting him to draw the Duke's attention to the first four pages which consisted of a eulogy of the House of Este.

All was now ready for the move to Ferrara. The Grand Duke granted permission with good grace. When after long delays due to bad weather Salviati finally did set off in the middle of March 1587 (having had time to supervise the Florentine fourth edition of the *Decameron*) he took with him a glowing letter of recommendation from Cortile extolling amongst other things his 'bontà e sincerità'—which inexplicably was the way in which his really intimate 'friends' spoke of him. To be an acquaintance of Lionardo Salviati seems to have been fraught with dangers, but to those with whom he had a real emotional bond he seems to have been lavish with affection, and to have given of himself unstintingly.

In the waiting period before his departure he passed an anxious moment, wondering if Alfonso's silence was due to any dislike of the oration. The silence turned out to be due, in fact, to both the Duke and his secretary thinking that Lionardo was already on his way. The oration, Laderchi eventually assured him, pleased Alfonso greatly and everyone, including himself, was looking forward to seeing Salviati in Ferrara.

XIV

FERRARA: THE DISPUTES OVER THE
GERUSALEMME LIBERATA

IT was one of Lionardo Salviati's perennial illusions that by
changing his surroundings he could change his existence for the
better. As he left for Ferrara he, no doubt, thought once more
that he was leaving his cares behind him. If so the simultaneous
arrival of the new Florentine ambassador must have broken the
spell, for he was none other than the Balì Raffaello de' Medici,
a man who malicious and cynical nature had made him hated
and feared in Florence. He was a friend curiously enough of
Grazzini but an enemy in particular of Cortile and probably
responsible for his removal from office shortly afterwards.

Some degree of disillusionment with the university post, too,
was swift to follow. The title 'lettore d'umanità' he now considered
an affront to his dignity. His wish that it should be changed to
'lettore delle morali d'Aristotile' was granted and as such he went
down in the annals of the university.[1] But his myopia was growing
rapidly worse. During the course of a conversation with Cortile,
Francesco de' Medici observed in his cynical manner that he
could not imagine how Lionardo Salviati could possibly lecture
on anything, given the rapid deterioration of his eyesight. Others
in Florence thought and spoke of him with more respect. The
Accademia Grande offered him a second term of office as Consul,
which he had to refuse because of his imminent departure, and
Baccio Valori, in whose first Consulship Salviati had entered the
Academy twenty-three years previously, took his place.

He had scarcely had time to settle in Ferrara, however, when
domestic family affairs claimed his urgent attention. Like Lionardo,
other members of the Salviati family were in debt, including
Lionardo's distant relation Giannozzo (his great-grandfather and

---

[1] See F. B. Borsetti, *Historia almi Ferrariae Gymnasii* (Ferrara, Bernardinus
Pomatelli, 1735), part 1, p. 227 (referring to 1588), and part 2 (Index lectorum),
p. 213.

Giannozzo's grandfather were cousins). The fact that he and his son Diamante, a Knight of St. Stephen like Lionardo himself, resisted arrest and were imprisoned in Florence, would be of no great interest to us if it did not reveal something of Alfonso d'Este's attitude to Salviati. The Duke of Ferrara did, in fact, intervene untiringly with the Grand Duke through his ambassador in Florence in order to secure the release of his new servant's kinsmen. His anxiety to relieve Salviati of all worry on their score is a striking example of the high regard in which Salviati was held in Ferrara from the moment of his arrival and which was to be frequently manifested in the Duke's constant support and concern for his welfare, until the very end of his life. The outcome of the Giannozzo affair is uncertain, but until well into July Alfonso was instructing his ambassador to renew his offices with the Grand Duke on behalf of Lionardo, 'il quale ha caro S. A. che riceva quella consolatione che si possa con sua dignità'.[2]

As the paid servant of the Duke Salviati occasionally followed the court in its meanderings from Ferrara to Belriguardo, from Belriguardo to La Mesola. The latter was a favourite with the Duke and his secretaries, especially Laderchi, whom Salviati was able to advise on literary matters and to whom he on one occasion forwarded two madrigals sent him by Bastiano de' Rossi, one of his protégés in Florence. As for his own literary activities they were dominated by what has been called by Vivaldi 'the greatest polemic of the sixteenth century', which linked Salviati's name for ever with his creation, the Accademia della Crusca.

Even whilst the latter was celebrating its emergence as an Academy, there had appeared in 1584 the work which was to spark off the whole controversy, namely *Il Carrafa ovvero dialogo dell'epica poesia* of Camillo Pellegrino, in which the author favourably compared the *Gerusalemme Liberata* of Tasso with the *Orlando Furioso* of Ariosto. Though this was the first work dealing with the respective merits of the two works to see print, the subject was already a commonplace of the academies including

² U. Lett. Alfonso (via Imola) to Cortile, 15.7.87, Modena, A.S., C.A.F., Minute di lettere, 1587, fol. 30. For the case of Diamante and Giannozzo Salviati, the Filze degli Otto di Guardia in the A.S., Florence, especially No. 166 fols. 108ᵛ and 109ʳ, give a detailed account of the offence. The correspondence between Cortile and Ferrara for the period April–July provides coverage of subsequent developments.

that Accademia degli Alterati to whose members Salviati had shown Guarini's *Pastor Fido*, and in whose activities he seems to have shared. The Cavalier Ricasoli had read a paper there entitled 'Che l'Ariosto merita più lode del Tasso' in 1582—in December, moreover, when Salviati was himself in Florence and in the process of resuming the rhythm of his academic life, and only three months after his own first, though private, contribution to this dispute in the form of the letter to De' Bardi. Since the subject had been cropping up amongst the Alterati in one form or another since 1575, Pellegrino's book cannot have come as such a very great surprise.[3]

It was, nevertheless, a surprise to Pellegrino when the counterattack was opened by a reply from the Accademici della Crusca. This was the so-called *Stacciata prima. Difesa dell' Orlando Furioso dell' Ariosto contra 'l dialogo dell'epica poesia di Camillo Pellegrino*, the first publication to bear the Cruscan symbol of the *buratto*, though not, of course, the motto 'Il più bel fior ne coglie' which was only added much later. The nature of this work shook and offended him, and he was only to be calmed by assurances from Scipione Ammirato that the Crusconi meant no ill will but expected a reply couched in a similar style. Had the correspondence between the parties directly and indirectly interested continued in this vein the character of the whole business as a *cruscata* might have been maintained, the reputation which the Florentine contingent gained for itself in the debate might have been very different indeed, and Salviati would have been better thought of by succeeding generations. As it was, the polemic took an unpleasant turn. In May 1585 there appeared Bastiano de' Rossi's 'Letter' to Flaminio Mannelli. Here the Crusca's attacks on the *Liberata* are justified as reprisals for Tasso's slighting references to the Medici in the *Dialogo del piacere onesto* published in 1583 in the third part of Tasso's *Rime e prose* in which dialogue Vincenzo Martelli, the Florentine exile, is made to repeat anti-Medicean sentiments already expressed in Martelli's letters published exactly twenty years before.

By this act De' Rossi gave the polemic the petty, local patriotic

---

[3] For an up-to-date bibliography on the polemics over the *Gerusalemme liberata* see B. Weinberg, *A History of Literary Criticism in the Italian Renaissance*, which also gives a definitive bibliography of all relevant works both in print and in manuscript, and B. Hathaway, *The Age of Criticism* (Cornell University Press, Ithaca, 1962).

character for which it is renowned, and which has tended to swamp its other and much more important features. The argument was never convincing, and at best it was utterly inappropriate. Then and throughout it was clear that behind this interpretation of the dispute as the work of a number of Florentines rallying to the defence of the ill-used Medici was a despicable attempt to curry Grand-Ducal favour and to secure shelter from a mounting tide of hostility on the part of an Italian literary public which, to do the Florentines justice, did not quite understand either the undertones of humour in the *Stacciata* or the real issues which it treated. Although De' Rossi seems to have been the actively aggressive force here it is unlikely that the pretext of the *Piacere onesto* did not have the approval of Salviati, who was notoriously unable to resist the temptation to lick the boots of the Grand Duke whom he so detested, even on occasions such as this when he was again turning his attention towards Ferrara.

At all events Salviati did not hesitate to associate himself with De' Rossi, which was a stupid mistake, all the more regrettable because so unnecessary, and one which was to cost him dear in that it obscured to his detriment his real aims in participating in the dispute. When he heard that Scipione Gonzaga on his way through Florence had condemned the Academicians' abuse of Tasso in their *Stacciata* he hastened to send him (about the beginning of August) a copy of De' Rossi's letter, 'dicendo che sperava', says Gonzaga, 'veduta quella, io fossi per mutar opinione circa l'inurbanità de' suoi Fiorentini'.[4] Salviati's letter may well have been a considered tactical move here, since Tasso's *Apologia* had appeared precisely at this point, and the Infarinato had in mind to administer some very rough treatment. He had little success, however, with Gonzaga, who delivered a sharp rebuke which may well have been a contributory factor in the violence of Salviati's reaction in the work which followed.

In the meantime, nervous epistolary exchanges took place between Pellegrino and Attendolo on the one side and Salviati, the Crusca, and adherents such as Scipione Ammirato on the other, in which the former were the victims of a cat-and-mouse game with a touch of hide-and-seek about it. The tone was superficially friendly, but through the letters of Pellegrino there runs

---

[4] Lett. Scipione Gonzaga to Luca Scalabrino, 13.8.85, in Guasti (ed.), *Lettere*, ii. 342.

a note of apprehension which the Florentines, enjoying the situation immensely, did little to alleviate. Whether or not Pellegrino was absolutely certain at this point that Salviati was his chief opponent, he must have suspected it. Though the *Stacciata prima* appeared under the name of the Crusca, the reply to Tasso's *Apologia*— the so-called *Infarinato primo*—was openly attributed to the 'Infarinato Accademico della Crusca', whom it would have required no great effort to identify as Lionardo Salviati. Certainly some of Pellegrino's friends were not sure that he had ever known until the disputes were ended.

The *Infarinato primo* was composed by Salviati, possibly with the collaboration of De' Rossi, in two months during which he was again beset by financial difficulties.[5] It was dedicated to Francesco de' Medici and published in September 1585. By this time the personal interchanges between the contestants had acquired a curious 'sporting' character originally proposed in a letter from De' Rossi to Pellegrino in November 1585 and eagerly accepted by the latter, of whom it can truly be said that he was never really at ease during any phase of the disputes. The idea was that the participants in the polemic should be as severe, as harsh, as rude even as they wished—in their printed works—and the harsher the merrier. But it was all to be a 'sport between gentlemen': one must play to win, and play with all one's might, but there was to be no element of personal animosity intended. The only one to suffer in this attempt to steer the dispute back to the character of the *cruscata* which it was originally meant to have was apparently to be Tasso, who not unnaturally complained bitterly. Sonnets were exchanged, membership of the Crusca was offered to a Pellegrino delirious with delight and relief. Letters from Pellegrino and Attendolo were read, discussed, and lavishly praised in gatherings held at the house of Jacopo Salviati. Lionardo himself sent off to Capua, the headquarters of the opponents of the Crusca, a complimentary copy for Pellegrino of his newly composed funeral oration on Pier Vettori. By common consent they dubbed their exchange of letters a 'battaglia di cortesia'.

[5] In Firenze, per Carlo Meccoli and Salvestro Magliani, 1585. For certain curious bibliographical features of this edition, see D. Decia, 'La prima edizione della Risposta all'Apologia del Tasso dell'Infarinato primo e i suoi veri stampatori', *Bibliofilia*, xiv, No. 9.

Within this 'battaglia di cortesia' Salviati gave himself endless amusement penning missives stuffed with what appear at first sight to be nothing more than a succession of harmonious compliments devoid of any reference to the disputes then raging. On close inspection, however, these courteous phrases reveal themselves to be masterpieces of ambiguity based on the supposed ignorance on the part of his correspondents that the Academician Salviati whom they so praised was also their implacable enemy the Accademico Infarinato. Of a flattering sonnet sent him by Pellegrino, Lionardo writes to its author: 'forza d'occulto amore ha nascosa la verità a V. S. dove ella mi pregia e mi loda', adding 'dovendo la sua bella composizione passare a secolo, nel quale potrà nascondersi, che troppa affezione abbia il giudizio offuscato.'[6] All of which is in the typical Salviatesque vein of humour, that delight in ambiguity which was responsible for the succession of false names under which he rejoiced in working whenever the opportunity occurred. Whether Pellegrino did or did not know the identity of his adversary mattered little. In Florence, at least, a good time was had by all, and the picture with which we are left is one of a group of *letterati* holding gay reunions to discuss the most recent letters, to concoct replies, and to work out tactics, enjoying themselves thoroughly in the process.

At one such high-spirited party lasting from eight in the evening until three in the morning, Pellegrino's *Replica* was read and discussed, and the Infarinato was detailed to reply to it. The Infarinato, we are told, unsuccessfully tried to excuse himself from this duty, alleging pressure of work. In this story, on the face of it an unlikely one, there may have been a grain of truth, since Lionardo was at that time probably engaged in putting the finishing touches to the second volume of his *Avvertimenti*, due to appear in June. De' Rossi's further amusing picture of a Salviati—or rather an Infarinato—torn between friendship and duty is likely to be much further from the truth. In view of the sporting character with which the disputes had been invested such an apologia was in any case superfluous.

This exchange of *lettere di cortesia*, in which the Florentines occasionally succumbed to the understandable temptation to

---

[6] Lett. Salviati to Pellegrino, Firenze, 2.1.86—one of the so-called *lettere di cortesia* published in Appendix to the *Infarinato secondo* (Florence, Padovani, 1588).

make Pellegrino experience a little of his old terror, continued for some time, and though at first sight it may appear to consist of little more than expressions of friendship, goodwill, and esteem it does contain certain useful indications of the motives and standpoints of the various individuals caught up in the polemics. But by May 1586 it is at least clear that there is no longer any secret about the identity of the Infarinato, though the fiction of the separate identities is maintained for the sake of the established convention. From this correspondence we also learn that by the beginning of June Salviati's reply to the *Replica* was completed. Printing was delayed, however, owing to the appearance of Giulio Ottonelli's *Discorso* attacking the Crusca. At first the attitude of the Crusca was that this work did not merit a reply, since it contained nothing new and in any case the author was socially beneath their notice. They must have had second thoughts on the matter for at the beginning of September there appeared a work by Carlo Fioretti da Vernio confuting the arguments of Ottonelli. These *Considerazioni di Carlo Fioretti intorno ad un discorso di M. Giulio Ottonelli* (Firenze, A. Padovani, 1586) bore the unmistakable stamp of Salviati's authorship. If the content and style were not enough to establish its paternity, contemporary correspondence contains virtually conclusive evidence of it. How Salviati managed to use Fioretti's name for his purpose here has given exercise to the imagination, if not the intellect, of successive generations of hostile critics.

Delayed by this minor consideration, the reply to Pellegrino's *Replica* was already printed in November 1586, having presumably been modified since its completion in the middle of the year. A further hold-up was caused, however, by the loss of the second half of the book (from p. 192 in its final printed form), which then had to be rewritten.[7] But by this time Salviati's possible transfer to Ferrara was already a steady subject of ambassadorial correspondence, and his final contribution to the polemic, the *Infarinato secondo*, was not to be published until after the move.

This transfer to the court of Ferrara, coming as it did at the height of the disputes over the *Gerusalemme Liberata*, has been

---

[7] Weight of evidence (Salviati's references in the *Infarinato secondo* itself and in letters of various periods, and the fact that the book was printed part in Florence and part in Ferrara) seems to support Salviati's statement that 'uno strano accidente' took place during the printing of the work.

naïvely interpreted as marking the triumphal success of Salviati's whole aim in attacking Tasso, namely to gain by foul means the favour of a prince with whom he had been unable to make any headway by fair. This myth, based on the already doubtful assumption that to belittle Tasso would be to please Alfonso d'Este, receives a severe blow from close scrutiny of the Florence–Ferrara diplomatic correspondence. It also leaves out of account Salviati's life's work, his interpretation of the culture and history of his times, and the targets which he had set himself since that day in 1564 when he exhorted the somnolent Accademici Fiorentini to wake up to their duties towards their native language and their national culture. For if any element of Salviati's activity sums up his vision of his own times it is his participation in the polemics over the *Gerusalemme Liberata*, as will be revealed by an analysis of his contribution.

Adding as it did an important new Italian element of comparison, the publication of Tasso's epic gave a new dimension to the discussions of the merits and defects of Ariosto's *Orlando Furioso* which for decades had been taking place within the general framework of sixteenth-century critical activity, occupying the time and energy of such men as Pigna, Giraldi, and Minturno. In the course of sporadic debates, as already mentioned in connection with the Accademia degli Alterati, certain positions with regard to the epic and romance in general, and to the *Furioso* in particular, had been taken up and clarified. There now appears, in 1584, a book—Pellegrino's *Discorso*—which examines the *Orlando Furioso* and the *Gerusalemme Liberata* in the light of Aristotelian theory. Its conclusion is that Tasso's work, obeying the rules of the epic as analysed by Aristotle and, more importantly, as exemplified in the classical epics, is splendidly 'regular', appealing therefore to the highest intellects. Ariosto's *Furioso*, being utterly un-Aristotelian because unclassical in conception, belongs to a lower order of creation and can appeal only to the untutored crowd. To put oneself in Salviati's position on the appearance of this treatise is infinitely more profitable than seeking hidden, disreputable motives for his championing of Ariosto against Tasso. Contact with the *Carrafa ovvero dialogo* seems to have proved an illuminating experience. For he realized at once that the principles behind this exaltation of Tasso are the very negation of virtually all those principles which he himself held dear and to which he had devoted his life. Yet in 1576 he had praised the plot at least of the *Gerusalemme Liberata* and certain of the literary principles of its author. The discrepancy between his reaction to the *Gerusalemme Liberata* in 1576 and his reaction now is quite simply accounted for by the *status* to which this poem has now been elevated, and it is in enabling us to understand this that the letter to De' Bardi of 1582—three years, be it remembered, before the *Stacciata*—is so inestimably important. This letter reveals to us that long before Tasso was raised in the *Carrafa* to what Salviati justifiably saw as the symbol of subservience to Classical Antiquity, Salviati had conceived the defence of Ariosto essentially in terms of emancipation from that Classical Antiquity. One could be entirely 'epic' and 'Aristotelian-epic' yet go about it in a completely different manner from that of the epic writers of Antiquity. To his own satisfaction he had proved that this was precisely what Ariosto had done, producing in the process an Aristotelian epic superior to anything which had gone before. In the letter Salviati defended Ariosto against the classics and with his criticisms of the latter moved towards the counter-attack. The person who associated Tasso with those classics and arrayed them both against Ariosto, giving Salviati no choice but to react against them as one unit, was Camillo Pellegrino in his *Carrafa*. Thus, whereas the *Gerusalemme Liberata* was previously a work with fine poetic qualities but virtually devoid of emotive significance for Salviati, the *Carrafa* has presented it as the perfect specimen of the epic poem, as the model to be followed in conception and execution by all ambitious writers in that genre, with implicit and explicit condemnation of those who do not. The crux of the matter lies in the *reason* for its assumption to exemplary status. This is its achievement in squeezing the native material of the romance, which for Salviati demanded a 'modern' treatment, into the mould of the classical epic.

The *Carrafa* was thus the incarnation of the principle of the identification of the rules of Aristotle with their exemplification in the ancient epics. To imitate the practice of Homer and Virgil was the only way to comply with Aristotle: to diverge from them was to diverge from Aristotle. The conflict with Salviati's principles of the validity of the national tradition, its superiority to the classical, its necessary *independence*, and the need for the modern Italian to express himself in terms of his own tradition, is obviously utter and complete. His outlook and the task he sets himself are virtually identical with the outlook expressed and the task undertaken in the letter to De' Bardi of three years earlier, conceived and written before ever Tasso had been brought on to the scene at all. No wonder then that in this *Stacciata prima* Salviati was able to draw widely on that letter as he did (despite its use in the meantime by De' Bardi), paraphrasing passages of it in the later work and occasionally lifting sections bodily out of it.

Salviati had always been devoted to Ariosto. His comedies borrow from him; his earliest poems have lines which echo the *Furioso*. Any mentions which he makes of him are uniformly favourable. In language he could not but share with the Florentines the feeling that Ariosto possessed 'un maggior sapor vernacolo, un'urbanità più schietta, una più ricca vena di linguaggio'.[8] Already in the letter to De' Bardi the *Orlando Furioso* was seen by him to be the symbol of Italian achievement, a poem which, whilst new and typically and unmistakably Italian in all its aspects, was not inferior to the classical epics. The *Gerusalemme Liberata*, on the other hand, as exalted by Pellegrino represents that subservience to Antiquity which he had condemned solidly and indefatigably since the *Orazione in lode della fiorentina favella*.

This being Salviati's view of the two works, and given his obsessive vision of the relationship of the ancient to the modern, his task was to 'defend' the *Furioso*, that is to say to prove its superior legitimacy and validity as an expression of contemporary culture. For Pellegrino had after all produced a violent attack on Ariosto in the *Carrafa* and continued a tradition which disparaged the *Furioso* from two principal points of view. He and his like-minded predecessors, if they considered it to belong to the epic genre at all, found that it transgressed the eternal immutable rules for the epic as exemplified in the classical epics and was thus a bad poem. If they came to the conclusion that it was a new genre not subject to these laws of the epic as they conceived them, it was only to label it *ipso facto* an inferior type of composition suitable only for an inferior, that is to say uninformed and unin-

[8] F. D'Ovidio, *Un'antica testimonianza circa la controversia della Crusca col Tasso* (Naples, 1894), p. 5, quoted by A. Solerti, *Vita di Torquato Tasso* (Turin, Loescher, 1895), p. 420.

structed audience. Salviati aims to destroy both these arguments, thus rehabilitating both the *Furioso* itself and establishing the independence of the modern literature which it represents.

In the execution of this task two preliminaries have first to be dealt with. The first is the status of Aristotle, that is to say whether or not the method of Pellegrino, who had taken the *Poetics* as his yardstick, was valid. The second, which follows naturally from the first and presupposes a positive answer to it, is whether or not the *Orlando Furioso* belonged to an established Aristotelian genre, or whether it was a new genre unknown to Aristotle.

With regard to the first point, Salviati agrees with Pellegrino on the 'absolute' authority of the *Poetics*; but not because Aristotle was an 'ancient'—rather in spite of it. His authority derives, not from the fact of his being the classical theorist *par excellence*— that was purely coincidental—but because his rules were the embodiment of Reason, timeless Reason valid in all times and places, in the modern world as in the classical. Of supreme importance as a policy-statement here is the following passage from the *Stacciata*:[9]

Le regole dell'arte sono veramente nella poesia, come le massime nelle scienze: ma non per ciò, che dice l'Attendolo, cioè per avere avuti più chiari scrittori [he refers to Pellegrino's assertion that the rules of the epic were to be found in the great classical epics because the classical languages were the greatest, and they had the finest writers] ma per l'essere fondate su la ragione: senza la quale non basterebbe ne l'esemplo d'Omero, ne l'autorità d'Aristotile, il quale non ne lasciò ammaestramento nella Poetica, che non fosse fondato sulla stessa ragione.

Here we have a succinct summary of Salviati's view of the issues in the controversy: there is first the separation of the *authority* of Aristotle from the *example* of Homer; and secondly there is the separation of both the above from Reason, which alone is judged a sufficient basis for the validity of 'rules'. Aristotle's rules are valid only because they represent 'Reason'. Likewise Homer's poem is great because it does not contradict Reason, not because it represents some absolute standard conferred on it by

---

[9] References for quotations will be given henceforward as bracketed page-numbers relating to the 'cumulative text' of the *Infarinato secondo* of 1588, in which were embodied the texts of the previous works in the controversy. The present quotation is to be found on p. 144.

the Classical Antiquity which it represents. If Salviati had achieved no more than establishing this distinction and making it the basis of his dialectic he would have deserved notice from the historians of thought and culture in the sixteenth century. For its interest as a foreshadowing of imminent developments in European thought need hardly be stressed. This importance given throughout the polemics by Salviati to this conception of the *Poetics* as the incarnation of 'Reason', independent of specific example, is indeed one of the most important features of the controversies. As a result we once again see Salviati in a forward-looking movement.

On the grounds, therefore, that Aristotle represents disembodied Reason, there is no question of Salviati's defence of Ariosto being based on anything but Aristotle. A corollary to this belief in the supreme rationality of the *Poetics* is, of course, that it precludes a defence—which one might otherwise possibly have expected from Salviati—based on the 'independence' of the *volgare* from the classics and hence from classical theorists. To defend Ariosto's practice, as did Giraldi, on the grounds that composition in the *volgare* did not have to obey rules laid down in a classical work whose authority applied only to the classical languages, appeared to him at once to be dangerous ground. Rules based on Reason must be applicable to all works in all times and places, and the application of Aristotelian rules to contemporary literature was entirely compatible with that independence of the *volgare* which he everywhere vigorously asserted.

The second preliminary concerns the all-important question of 'genre'. Here he steadfastly refuses to accept that the romance was a 'less perfect' kind of poem, even if within the romance the *Furioso* is to be considered perfect 'in its own way', for to do so would be tacitly to admit a distinction between a poem which corresponds to 'Reason' and one which does not. If the rules of the epic are valid, he maintains, then Ariosto, no less than Tasso, is worthy to be judged by them. Examining, as a necessary preliminary, the two types of poem from the triple viewpoint of object, manner, and means, he concludes that they are basically identical and thus liable to be judged by the same criteria.

Here the real point at issue—and it is fundamental—is that any distinction of genre between epic and romance would seem not so much to exempt, as to disqualify, the latter from being judged according to the Aristotelian rules. Such a situation, if those rules were considered to be the embodiment of Reason and thus omnivalent, would establish a hierarchy of merit to the detriment of the Ariostesque romance and hence of that modern Italian literary independence which Salviati wishes to establish. Thus he refuses to budge. He and his antagonists remain at loggerheads with Salviati firmly asserting, here as elsewhere, that the practice of Ariosto is perfectly in accordance with the precepts laid down in the *Poetics* if the latter is accurately interpreted.

Other issues in the polemic fall into place as they are related to this main issue and to Salviati's over-all aim and technique. The manner in which he counters another attempt by Pellegrino to grade poems according to their aim is typical. Pellegrino in the *Carrafa* asserts that Ariosto did not follow that precept of Aristotle (i.e. of Aristotle as Pellegrino interpreted him) which said that a poem should please and instruct, but satisfied himself with a lower aim, namely that of pleasing only. Thereby he again assigns him to a lower grade, and restricts his appeal to an ignorant, unlearned audience. True to his procedure of taking Ariosto's practice as his starting-point, which we shall see to be his method, Salviati declares that 'Aristotile, (chi sa ben ripescare nel libro suo) dice, che quando il poema è piaciuto, il poeta ha ottenuto il suo fine' (p. 131). Pleasure, which is alike for all, is Salviati's criterion (and, according to him, Aristotle's) for judging the excellence of a poem, and a poet is 'better' or 'worse' according to his capacity to give pleasure. Once having established the right of the *Furioso* to be judged according to the timeless and absolute principles of Aristotle, Salviati sets out to prove that Ariosto was no less an observer of the rules than Tasso, and perhaps even more so.

Thus Salviati's defence of the *Furioso*, no less than his opponents' attack, is carried out on the authority of Aristotle: but on the strength of a totally different interpretation of the *Poetics*. Since he genuinely finds the *Orlando Furioso* a near-perfect realization of the potential of the modern *volgare* it is legitimate for him to assume that it exemplifies any rules based on Reason. So his task, as he conceives it, is not to examine the *Furioso* by the standard of 'Aristotle plus Homer', which was the method of his adversaries, but rather to examine and analyse the *Poetics* with a view to an interpretation of the 'rules' which would sanction every detail of Ariosto's practice, and this he is convinced that any rules based on Reason must inevitably do. Lionardo's polemical works undoubtedly assume the character of an attack, but the general tenor of his argumentation is that of a justification, on to which is then grafted, inevitably, criticism of the *Liberata* in so much as the latter epitomizes the negation of the principles which he expounds and defends.

In all this it is worth noting, in connection particularly with the motivation of the *Stacciata*, the complete agreement with what he had written to De' Bardi in 1582. In his letter one finds the insistence on the authority of Aristotle; the interpretation of him designed to justify the practice of Ariosto; the equality of 'classical' and 'modern' before Aristotle, denying that the second need model itself on the first; the insistence on 'pleasure' as the criterion of literary excellence; the unreserved praise of Ariosto as the supreme poet. The sole difference of substance is that Tasso played no part in the letter (with one possible exception as we shall see), whereas having been allotted the principal role in the *Carrafa* he was inevitably called upon to play in the sequel.

Inevitably the discussion of detail centres principally round the four 'qualitative' parts—plot, character, thought, and diction. To follow Salviati's argumentation in detail on these individual issues, though interesting, would require much space, and the detail (with its many lengthy digressions and irrelevances) has only marginal significance in an examination of the principles underlying his strategy in the polemic. Salviati himself was aware that his method of procedure in proving at all costs that in all matters Aristotle sanctions the practice of Ariosto led to excesses and critical falsification. In a well-known letter to Pellegrino he admits as much. 'Resteranno appo molti sempre diverse l'opinioni,' he says, 'essendo queste cose probabili e dialettiche e senza certa definizione. E vedrallo V. S. in esso medesimo Infarinato, il quale in altre sue scritture, dove da senno favellerà di cose di poesia, sarà in molte cose contrario a quelle, che avrà detto, per ragion di disputa.'[10] The 'altre sue scritture' are, of course, the translation, paraphrase, and commentary on Aristotle's *Poetics* which he had twice tried to dedicate to Alfonso d'Este and in which he promised practically all his 'friends', including Tasso, that they would receive honourable mention. There is every

---

[10] Lett. Salviati to Pellegrino, 19.4.86, published with *Infarinato secondo*.

reason to believe that Salviati makes this statement in complete sincerity, since it accords with all we have seen of his practice in the disputes over the *Liberata*. In these it is the broad principle of 'modern' versus 'classical' which dictates his attitude to the detail of the practice of the two poets, who have become for him symbols of the one and the other principle. Thus the interpretation of Aristotle which emerges, and the views expressed on the individual questions of Truth, Verisimilitude, History, Plot, etc., have an exclusively *ad hoc* basis, and most decidedly do not derive from an over-all consistent and coherent vision of art, poetry, or the creative process. If here and there Salviati has flashes of critical insight into such matters as the relationship of historical truth to poetic truth, the 'vero' to the 'verosimile', ideal unity, art, and the experience of pleasure—all matters which sixteenth-century theorists discussed passionately and indefatigably in this first great critical awakening—we are not to imagine that such flashes are the fruits of deep and prolonged meditation on the mysteries of art. Necessity is the mother of invention, and when Salviati declares that pleasure is the criterion of moral art we are to see behind this principally the plain fact that Ariosto made no pretence of making the moral instruction of his readers a primary aim, whereas Tasso did. No doubt when reading Ariosto, conditioned as he was by his vision of contemporary culture, he enjoyed what might be described by a discredited phrase as an 'aesthetic experience' which convinced him that a deliberate attempt at instruction was superfluous. No doubt this implies a certain triumph of the critical and intellectual faculties. But to attribute to him a consciously elaborated, universally applicable (if not original) aesthetic theory identifying Pleasure, Truth, and Morality is perhaps to give credit where none is due.[11]

The coherent expression of any critical theory should have been embodied in Salviati's work on the *Poetics*. But the surviving fragment of this work contains little which is relevant to the disputes over the *Liberata*, since it covers only the first part of

---

[11] B. Hathaway, *The Age of Criticism*, analyses the stand taken by Salviati on the many issues basic to the critical disputes of the sixteenth century. Salviati is treated throughout as a serious theorist, but from this very analysis the fragmentary and *ad hoc* nature of his stands and pronouncements emerges quite clearly.

Aristotle's text, namely not quite the whole of Chapters i–v.[12]
Even had it covered the ground of plot, character, thought,
language, etc. in the epic, it is doubtful whether the commentary
completed and published would have had, in the eyes of posterity,
the critical importance of the polemic over the *Gerusalemme
Liberata*. Whereas in the latter what Salviati says acquires
historical significance precisely because he has a strong bias and
moulds his authorities in his support, revealing himself as he does
so to be the representative of an important current of thought,
in the commentary his attempted dispassionate analysis is not distinguished by any significantly new direction. His hesitation over
publication of the commentary may have been caused not only by
the fact that there were, as he himself admits, discrepancies
between what he said when speaking 'da senno' and his statements
in the disputes, or by difficulties over dedication, but also by a
realization that the prejudices and passions which animated him in
these disputes were in their way the more valid expression of his
mind. Nevertheless, it is interesting to see that in the commentary,
as in the disputes, he still insists on 'invention' as the distinguishing
feature of poetry, and though he now considers that poetry should
both please and benefit he still puts the accent on pleasure, as in
the *Stacciata*.

In this and Salviati's other polemical works discussion of the
locuzione, and also of the *sentenza* in so much as the adequate
linguistic expression of this is important, is a quite different matter
from discussion of such matters as plot, character, invention,
truth, the *verosimile*, etc. For in matters of language Salviati
is judging the two poems according to criteria which he has
worked out elsewhere, albeit impelled by the same motives and
principles which governed him in the polemics. And although the
preoccupation with the interpretation of Aristotle in such a way
as to support these criteria still remains, Tasso and Ariosto are
in linguistic matters judged according to formulae owing their
existence to neither.

This being so, and in view of its importance in the context of
Salviati's other works, this aspect of the polemic deserves separate

[12] Florence, B.N.C., Cod. Magl. VII, 87. This work was the subject of an
article by V. Follini, 'Sopra la traduzione e comento della Poetica d'Aristotile
del Cavalier Lionardo Salviati', *Atti dell'Accademia Italiana*, Vol. i, part 2
(Leghorn, 1810), and has been examined in detail by Weinberg, *A History*, i.
609–20.

consideration, whereupon we find that the consistency between Salviati's statements in his theoretical works on language and his contributions to the polemics is quite impressive. In the former he had identified the literary language as a distillation of Florentine with all its idiosyncracies, its idioms and usages, its phonetic genius—something which could be mastered only as a result of intimacy with the spoken language. The literary language, he believed, could therefore only be handled by those who felt its spirit as a living language and thus would not misuse and abuse its component parts by employing them in a manner not consonant with its genius. From this sense of the language properly used— the *proprietà*—derived, as Salviati saw it, the attraction and efficacy of the language. Though the language was not meant to be static, innovation must be slow, achieved almost imperceptibly, and through 'authority' in such a way that the language retained its Florentine character and there was no sense of violence being done to it, as had happened in the fifteenth century.

Tasso's poetic language could hardly have been in more violent conflict with this ideal. In essence it denied completely Salviati's 'Florentine-linguistic' conception of poetic style, attributing almost exclusive importance to the notion of literary-stylistic moulding. The extensive linguistic side of the polemic had three main aspects in which were incorporated most of the issues raised by conflicting conceptions of language and style. In substance they are the time-honoured themes of the *questione della lingua*. The first was the relationship of the language of Petrarch and Boccaccio to the *volgare fiorentino* of the authors' times: the second was the identity or otherwise of this language with that of modern Florence (with the dependent question of the importance of contact with modern Florentine): the third, and the one which naturally loomed largest in these controversies, concerned the practical use of language in poetic composition. These issues are, of course, not independent, and were frequently crossed and intertwined in the course of the polemics. But together they form an issue over which the basis of the quarrel is narrowed from a national to a Florentine one. It is on the question of language that the disputes become a vehicle for that identification of 'Italian' and 'Florentine' basic to Salviati's thought since 1564. Behind the conflict over language lies the violent clash between Florentine linguistic imperialism intensified by the local patriotism which the Medici state fostered, and the anti-colonial movement which characterized the non-Tuscans, who rightly considered that regardless of its origins the literary language (and hence their use of it) was independent of Florence. It had been adopted by the whole of Italy and was the property of the whole of Italy. All Italians had their say in its use and development, and Florentine, as Cesarotti later put it, was but a 'principal dialect'.

This was the principle which Tasso and his defenders largely represented in the linguistic clashes. Tasso had suggested in his *Apologia* that the more attention the great writers of the fourteenth century paid to the rhetorical ornamentation of their linguistic material, and thus drew away from the spoken, idiomatic language of their times, that is to say the more they relied on the literary modification of the language, the better writers they were. We have already seen the opinion, attributed to his father in the *Piacere onesto*, on the Florentines' own use of what they insolently chose to call *their* language (see Ch. xiii, p. 192). Against this Salviati throws his full weight. The dispute degenerates into petty squabbling over detail. But implicit in the many inconclusive exchanges is the fundamental clash of differing conceptions of the literary language. First, as a disembodied entity, to be given, arbitrarily, the stamp of the author, which was the view of the anti-Florentine supporters of Tasso. Secondly, as something which for its very life and efficacy depended on contact with, and nourishment from, the spoken living language, and therefore largely subject to the latter, which was Salviati's view. The one was, partially at least, Bembist in a sense unacceptable to the Florentines, the other exclusively Florentine and thus unacceptable in the present state of cultural development as a universal solution to the linguistic impasse in Italy.

On the second point, namely the connection if any between literary and spoken languages and the identity of old and modern, we find the same dialogue of the deaf so typical of the literature of the *questione della lingua*. In the course of lengthy wrangling all Salviati says is fully consistent with his statements in the *Avvertimenti*. Pellegrino naturally insists that the literary language can be acquired exclusively from literary sources: Salviati insists as in the *Avvertimenti* that the "proprietà del linguaggio" are what give the literary language its efficacy and beauty, not the rhetorical ornaments arbitrarily applied to it or any personal manipulation.

Although a purification is necessary, once one has acquired the feel of the language by steeping oneself in its living manifestations, it is the sense of *proprietà* which really counts. Tasso rejects this notion in its entirety and Pellegrino reaffirms the principle that the fact of Italian, as it is now known, having had its origins in Tuscany, and more precisely in Florence, by no means implies that it remains exclusively Florentine property.

In general then, the linguistic polemics follow familiar lines in which the Florentine world clashes with that of the non-Florentines and the main issue is the old one of the dependence or otherwise of the literary language on the spoken language of Florence. Here the position of Salviati remains in all respects his position in the *Avvertimenti*. Even the much-discussed references to Latinisms—one of the elements which Salviati believes rob Tasso's language in the *Liberata* of any fundamentally Florentine character—are seen to correspond to his pronouncements on the subject in the theoretical treatise, once one penetrates the screen of detail. Throughout he contests the legitimacy of unorthodox manipulation of the language and a poetic style so far removed from natural Florentine usage as to constitute a new and independent language.

Such a language cannot, for him, be the vehicle of true poetry. The 'pleasure' which he names as the aim of literature is the result of the use of *modi propri*. Pleasure thus cannot be produced by a work written in a language such as that of the *Liberata*, which denied the authority of living Florentine and substituted for these *modi propri* the whimsical constructions, arbitrary combinations, fanciful figures, and extravagant images of the author.

Such is the pith of Salviati's linguistic views expressed in the polemics.[13] As was the case in the discussion of the Aristotelian categories, so here in the linguistic aspect of the controversies Salviati's position in the thought of his times as revealed in his attitude to the classics emerges clearly. Italian language and literature are superior to their Greek and Latin counterparts. Italian has already had the 'più perfetto poeta lirico che fosse mai'. Supreme excellence in any genre was the result of the perfect combination of the perfect language-medium with a poetic mind suited to it, and if so far Italian had not had an epic poet superior

---

[13] See supplementary note 11, p. 249

in *every* respect to the classical ones it was merely because these conditions had not been found in ideal combination; 'Nell'eroico quest'attitudine dello 'ngegno non s'è trovato in niuno: che se trovata si fosse, così in questa, com'in quell'altra poesia, avremmo forse avuto la palma' (pp. 348–9). But even this view amounted to modesty, for it only applied if one excluded Dante from the roll of epic poets. If on the other hand one included him, 'non solamente pari, ma al di sopra resta la nostra lingua alla Greca e alla Latina, nell'epica poesia' (p. 349). Ariosto himself surpasses the classical epic poets in some respects. We find we are hearing the theme of the *Orazione in lode della fiorentina favella* as well as of other orations and the *Avvertimenti*, and like these works the polemics over the *Liberata* put Salviati firmly amongst the 'moderns' who consider that Antiquity has nothing to offer that cannot be better exemplified in the national tradition, which it is the duty of Italians to develop according to its own genius and potentialities, and of which the future possibilities moreover are unlimited.

From this brief review of the polemics, the real significance of the stand taken up by Salviati will be obvious. The character which his defence of Ariosto assumed is a result both of his conviction of the excellence of the *Furioso* and of his determination to prove that the new *volgare* epic poem, whilst having its own characteristic form and features, nevertheless conforms to timeless reason as represented by Aristotle. If Salviati progresses from this stand to an attack on Tasso this is inevitable, for his whole outlook makes him violently opposed to Tasso's practice, which he interprets as the imitation of Antiquity in a manner quite indefensible in the author's times. To Salviati the *Poetics*, being the embodiment of timeless Reason, does not, as we have seen, represent merely Antiquity. Homer and Virgil, on the other hand, do. Whilst the works of Homer and Virgil are useful in giving perspective to the rules of the *Poetics*, to which in their own individual fashion they conform, the 'modern' Salviati rejects them as models for contemporary literary composition. So Salviati is basically opposed to the *method* of Tasso who, as he sees it, has confused the *specific example*—Homer and Virgil—with the *rule*, giving the former the absolute authority of the latter. What he considers the author of the *Liberata* to have done is misguidedly to reproduce, as indispensable to an epic anywhere at any time, details of ancient works which were nothing more than one particular implementation, suited to Antiquity, of the rules later formulated by Aristotle. But Tasso—and this is Salviati's main point—was not writing in Antiquity: he was writing in the sixteenth century. The result of his procedure could only be an anachronism. This Salviati clearly and directly states in so many words, saying of the *Liberata* that it is 'oltr'a ciò murata in sul vecchio, o più tosto rabberciata, non altramente che quei granari, i quali in Roma, sopra le reliquie delle superbissime Terme di Diocleziano si veggiono a questi giorni' (p. 138). In the sixteenth century the rules must be implemented in a sixteenth-century manner. As Grazzini had said in the prologue to the *Strega* long before: 'Abbiamo altri costumi, altra religione, e altro modo di vivere, e perciò bisogna fare le commedie in altro modo: in Firenze non si vive come si viveva già in Atene e in Roma.' Salviati's historical sense, and his 'modern' orientation as expressed in the quoted passage make him the champion of Ariosto, who, whilst adhering as closely as ever Homer or Virgil did to the rules of Reason, has yet produced an epic quite unlike Homer in detail, and a legitimate expression of a new language, a new civilization, and a new culture. They make him the enemy of Tasso who, by writing what Salviati sees as a Homeric epic in the late sixteenth century, has given birth to a monster. From Salviati's point of view it would not be going too far to say that he sees in the *Liberata* something akin to the fifteenth-century Latinization of the languages a symbol of that subservience to Antiquity which he combats at every point and against which he hurled his first thunderbolts in the *Fiorentina favella* oration. Within the sphere of the epic itself he identified Tasso with the attitude summed up by Trissino, who boasted that in writing his *Italia liberata dai Goti* he had chosen Aristotle 'per Maestro' and Homer 'per Duce, e per Idea', thus making precisely the identification of 'rules' and 'specific classical example' which Salviati abhors.

Seen in this light the disputes over the *Liberata* fall into place in the general pattern of Salviati's thought as manifested in all his works. Tasso is seen as perpetuating subservience to Antiquity whilst Ariosto sets out to develop and exploit the national tradition in which he, Salviati, takes such pride. So Salviati transcends purely Florentine considerations in the debate, making himself

once again the spokesman of contemporary culture. One person
who would have rejoiced in the polemics was Salviati's old comrade
in arms Grazzini, for he, as usual, had said it all before. But as
usual the task of making the principle effectively felt at the highest
cultural level fell to Lionardo.[14]

The disputes themselves contain a huge mass of varied material
ranging from wide statement of principle to cavilling over petty
detail, a good deal of which is only tenuously linked to the main
questions. Much is dictated by purely polemical spirit. But when
the clutter of detail is removed it is obvious that the main issues
were of the very greatest consequence to Salviati, partly as a
Florentine and partly as an Italian. The bad name which he
gained with his contemporaries and succeeding ages is due in part
to their failure to appreciate that he was sincerely and passionately
defending principles very dear to him and not taking a malicious
delight in abusing a supposedly defenceless Tasso. Tasso had
defenders with teeth, who were basically aggressive detractors
of Ariosto and consequently opponents of Salviati's principles.

Nor is Salviati to blame for the apparently nasty tone of certain
of the exchanges or for the effect of the vulgar abuse to which he
occasionally descended. This aggressive character derived on the
Florentine side directly from the original conception of the nature
of the brigata dei Crusconi, of which one of the characteristics
was precisely this good-humoured but nevertheless lively abuse.
Insults, coarseness, and mock anger were part and parcel of its
personality. The author of the work they were examining was
seen as a cringing victim—but all in the cause of entertainment.
The opening pages of the *Stacciata*, in which Pellegrino's work is
described as a sack of corn left on the Academy's doorstep for
winnowing, are an attempt to confer this character on the dispute.
If the abuse continued without the good humour we are, nevertheless, bound to see in the violence of language the last echoes of

---

[14] Works of Grazzini particularly relevant to the romance are: (i) *A' riformatori della lingua toscana*, especially lines 82–4; (ii) *Contro le commedie in versi*,
where he stresses that 'invention' is the essential element in Tuscan poetry; and
particularly (iii) *Al sig. Balì Medici di Firenze* (*inc.* 'D'armi e d'amor chi vuol
cantando fare'), Verzone, op. cit., pp. 266–367 *Ottave* No. XVI, which
contains praise of Ariosto and the 'native' material of the romance and a
denunciation of Tasso's choice of material, his characters, his inventive weakness, etc., as a result of which 'n'andrà in corto in perdizione / coll'Avarchide
insieme e col Girone' (lines 15–16).

this prose *in burla*, and must consequently take it less seriously than we otherwise might.

Certainly the Florentines continued throughout the debate to view it in this light, and evidence suggests that they derived from it a great deal of harmless entertainment. It was a foolish mistake on the part of De' Rossi to suggest that the opposition to Tasso was undertaken on patriotic grounds, and even more foolish of Salviati to subscribe to this in what seems to have been a moment of misgiving. But, in any case, he did not really have the personality, as his unsuccessful attempts at humorous poetry show, to carry off a good-humoured pretence of aggression. It is doubly unfortunate that a polemic for the most part sincerely argued, but which so unfavourably affected public opinion, should have been indissolubly associated with the Accademia della Crusca almost from its birth, for this nursling Academy acquired thereby a reputation which it perhaps did not entirely deserve but which was to dog it for several generations.

XV

LAST ILLNESS AND DEATH

RESUMPTION of work on the *Infarinato secondo* had been delayed because of the imminent publication of the *Dialogo* of Niccolò degli Oddi. Now on 17 July Giovambattista Deti, Arciconsolo of the Crusca (and solidly behind Salviati as were the other members of that body) informed Salviati that this work had arrived in Florence, and not only the *Dialogo* but a reply to it in manuscript. Salviati now went ahead with his own composition. Very soon after this, however, he fell ill again, which he was now doing with ominous regularity, and after a long and troublesome period of indisposition he was granted leave by Alfonso to retire for convalescence to his villa at Vernio.

When on the point of leaving there to return to Ferrara he learnt that Zoppini and Farra, printers in Venice, were publishing a mutilated version of his revised *Decameron* under the pretence that it was the work of another corrector, and as soon as he managed to lay his hands on a few pages of it he sent them to Francesco, begging him to instruct his ambassador in Rome to protest to the Pope under whose supervision and protection (when Cardinal Montalto) the work had originally been undertaken and published.[1] But the moment was unfortunate, and Francesco may never have had the letter, for four days later on 10 October the Grand Duke died. The following day Bianca Cappello too died, both of them victims of a malarial fever. Immediately Cardinal Ferdinando de' Medici hastened to Florence, where he was proclaimed Francesco's successor. Once the hue and cry had settled down Salviati, now back in Ferrara, wrote him an elegant and

---

[1] The edition of which Salviati complained was the so-called 'correction' by Luigi Groto, published with the addition of Ruscelli's *Vocabolario*. It is generally admitted to be as bad an edition of the *Decameron* as is recorded, and Salviati is justified in saying that the printers 'l'hanno ripiena tutta d'errori di stampa, e diminuitala stranamente' (U. Lett. Salviati to Francesco, Vernio, 6.10.87, Florence, A.S., F.Med., F.L.O., No. 790, fol. 89). See also B. Gamba, *Serie de' testi di lingua*, who describes it as 'un pessimo guazzabuglio, in cui si trovano porzioni di novella, e novelle intere sostituite al testo originale'.

flattering letter of condolence. But Ferdinando appears to have associated Salviati, whom he had known in his days at the court of Rome, with such things as the intrigues of Geremia da Udine, whom along with others concerned in the affair, such as Abbioso, Ferdinando hated as favourites of Bianca Cappello, and no reply is recorded. A few days later Salviati was again confined to his home, ill and taking purgatives.

For him the death of Francesco cannot have been a matter of great concern, since the Grand Duke had shown him singularly little consideration. Nevertheless he kept closely in touch with his friends in Florence. They discussed the flood of literary compositions which the death of the Grand Duke had stimulated. Bastiano de' Rossi kept him fully informed of Florentine affairs, of the sweeping purges effected by Ferdinando, of which some of Salviati's friends were the victims. He told him of recently published literary works, of Giacomini's oration in praise of Francesco delivered in San Lorenzo despite the protestations of the author who wanted the Sala de' Cinquecento, of the imminent publication of Strozzi's description of the funeral. Both these authors themselves sent him copies of their works, which he commended enthusiastically, welcoming them as being to a certain extent the fruits of his own campaign to persuade the Florentines to state their case for the vernacular by producing works of literary merit rather than by arguing. There is a note of nostalgia as he encourages the younger writers such as Giacomini to exercise their talents, and he eagerly and proudly shows their works to the Ferrarese.

For despite the constant kindness which he found in Ferrara, life there had its minor drawbacks. Being a friend of Cortile he was inevitably drawn into the hostility between Cortile and the Balì Medici, who whilst at Ferrara was constantly operating to influence Alfonso against his ambassador in Florence, as the Balì's dispatches to Florence clearly reveal. Salviati, to his credit, tried his best to help his friend. He kept constantly on the alert, sending Cortile detailed accounts of the Balì's machinations aimed at destroying the ambassador's reputation. Unfortunately, there is good cause to believe that the Balì was aware of this, and that he was cleverly using Salviati as a pawn in his own game.

Nor were Lionardo's troubles all diplomatic ones. In July his relatives were still in prison in Florence, and renewed intercession by Alfonso via Cortile eventually produced only a conditional pardon (the condition being that Giannozzo should undertake a six months' voluntary exile in Volterra), much to the disgust of Cortile, who in his exasperation could only remark that 'il Sig.r Cav.re Salviati che deve intendere l'humor dell'huomo bene potrà forse dar qualche lume'.[2] Moreover, what seemed a splendid opportunity for Salviati to show his paces as an orator once again, namely the death on 1 November 1587 of Donno Alfonso d'Este, brought unforeseen complications in its train. The funeral oration being ready for delivery on 13 December, Salviati requested the Duke to favour him with his presence. The ceremony, however, had to be postponed, for Alfonso, who had asked to read the oration in advance, went off to Comacchio with it in his possession. After a week Salviati, too, betook himself to Comacchio (though whether on his own initiative, to retrieve the manuscript, or because he was summoned is uncertain), and it was the general opinion in court circles that the Duke had effected a censorship operation of major proportions. General opinion was right. On being questioned by Cicognini, the Florentine resident in Ferrara, Salviati's amanuensis admitted that Alfonso had removed a substantial section. The offending passages referred to the services rendered by Donno Alfonso to the French crown, which had led Salviati to refer to the fact that Piero Strozzi, by then a Marshal of France but still the son of Cosimo's most hated adversary, had died in his arms. Once again Salviati was the victim of inter-state politics. Now, that relations with Florence were improving Alfonso saw no reason to offend the Medici by recalling his own family connections with their enemies. Although the Duke himself was not present as Salviati had hoped, the oration, given in the Sala dell'Accademia, was attended by Don Cesare d'Este, by the Bishop of Ferrara, and by a large part of the Ferrarese nobility.

But there was a brighter side to Salviati's experience in Ferrara. The cynical contempt characterizing the attitude of the Florentine courtiers (and, one imagines, their Grand Duke) towards Salviati is more than offset by the generosity and sincere respect shown by the Ferrarese from the Duke and his secretaries downwards. If the Balì Medici could sneer at the Duke of Ferrara taking with him 'tutti gli arrolati della sua corte (sino al C. Salviati)' on his journey

2 U. Lett. Cortile to Laderchi, 6.8.88, Modena, A.S., C.A.F., Lettere originali, 1588.

to Modena to meet the Duke of Mantua, the Duke of Ferrara himself was happy to have his representatives in Florence recommend that Lionardo be given a seat in the Senate traditionally given to the Salviati family, '. . . desiderando S. A. per le molte buone qualità sue che sia favorito dove buonamente si possa, et essendone per sentire molto piacere'.[3]

Indeed this seems to have been the happiest time of Salviati's life. Reasonably comfortable, respected, treated with dignity and honour, he felt that he was at last receiving the recognition he deserved. Every effort seems to have been made to facilitate his literary activities, though 1587 saw only the orations on Cardinal Luigi d'Este and Donno Alfonso d'Este and a fourth edition of his *Decameron*. In addition to lecturing in the university he was working on the *Infarinato secondo*, and was occupied with the duties of the minor courtier. Apart from scattered letters to Laderchi and other members of the court, however, there is little information available as to his activities. Eventually the *Infarinato secondo* was finished. The printing, though begun in Ferrara, was probably completed by the Padovani in Florence, and it was certainly published by them.[4] It was dedicated to Alfonso II of Este, a notable feature of the dedication being the use of the title 'Serenissimo Principe', which was more than half-way to the title 'altezza Serenissima' reserved by Florentines for the Grand Duke—at least as far as Italian princes were concerned. Indeed the reference to Alfonso as the 'Serenissima persona di V. A.' really amounted to the full title. Inability to use these terms had on two occasions prevented Salviati from publishing his *Poetics*.

Serenely settled as a happy and honoured 'exile' in Ferrara, Lionardo looked forward to a long and productive association with Alfonso and his friends of the court. But in the summer of 1588 he fell seriously ill. Given leave once again to retire to his villa at Vernio he moved at the beginning of September to Florence,

[3] U. Lett. Alfonso to Ercole Tassoni, February 1588, Modena, A.S., C.A.F., Lettere originali, 1588. The quotation from the Balì Medici is from an U. Lett. Balì Medici to Belisario Vinta, 15.6.88, Florence, A.S., F.Med., 2901. The Balì was angry because he himself had been excluded.

[4] According to Gamba, *Serie de' testi*, 'vi sono esemplari che hanno il Buratto sul frontispizio; altri che hanno invece un'Aquila, impresa dello stampatore'. The unlikely interpretation put by Guasti (ed.) *Lettere*, iv, p. xix, on this phenomenon, is that the other Accademici della Crusca, disapproving of Salviati's actions, obliged him to remove the device of the Crusca.

suffering from a 'febbre doppia terzana continua', but was then advised by his doctors to return north of the Apennines, preferably to Reggio or Modena, where the air was healthier than at Florence. From this point onwards, with only brief intervals of relief, and despite every care and attention on the part of his doctors in Florence, which he did no leave, his illness grew steadily worse.

On 10 September, though still too weak to leave his bed, he appeared much better, but a month later his condition was more serious than ever. 'Il Cav.re Salviati', writes Cortile to his master, 'sta con la febbre doppia quartana continua, et l'ho visitato spesso, et lo trovo molto afflitto, et stracco, et i medici, per quello che m'hanno riferito, non ne credono molto bene.'[5] Cortile is our main informant on developments at this stage, for throughout Salviati's illness in Florence he was a constant visitor to him, both as a personal friend and in his capacity as representative of Alfonso, who had issued orders via his secretaries that the Cavaliere should not be neglected. Bulletins on Lionardo's condition formed a regular feature of his dispatches, and one gratifying fact which emerges from these diplomatic exchanges is again the esteem and respect in which the court of Ferrara held Salviati. Nothing is too much trouble if it will help the Cavaliere on his way to re-covery. For his part, his only concern was to improve sufficiently to be able to return to Ferrara and to tell of Alfonso's magnanimity. The devotion which this new-found dignity inspires in him is at times almost pathetic. Cortile, and Alfonso's secretary Imola, urged on by the Duke himself, made generous grants of money during the last months of 1588 and the first months of 1589.

In this latter period, however, Salviati's condition worsened even more rapidly. Two sores having developed on his thighs, the doctors despaired of his life. Cortile's own personal doctor, Lorenzini, then had him transferred to his own house, the better to keep an eye on him, and spared no effort or personal expense in treating him. Eventually the patient was apprised of the true gravity of his case, whereupon he made a will, with Cardinal Aldobrandini and Cortile as his executors. It was his wish to leave all his possessions to Alfonso, and when it was pointed out that this was impossible he decided to leave him all his own written works, along with all his books both in print and in manuscript,

---

[5] U. Lett. Cortile to Laderchi, 8.10.88, Mod., A.S., C.A.F., Lettere originali, 1588.

his dedication to the House of Este being as firm as ever, so firm in fact that he had refused, or so he alleged, an invitation from the new Grand Duke to remain in Florence in his service. He even told his friends that his now inevitable death saddened him only because it robbed him of the opportunity to render further service to the house of Este.

Yet incredible though it may seem, even when Salviati was reduced to this pitiful state and awaiting death, the proof of his devotion to the House of Este took the all-too-familiar form of the betrayal of a friend. This time the victim was Guarini, now a member of the Accademia Grande and the Crusca, who was never known to say a word about Salviati that was not one of praise, friendship, and gratitude, but who was unwise enough to make certain indiscreet references to the Duke of Ferrara in a letter to 'certain Academicians' (whether of the Fiorentina or the Crusca is not clear) written in February 1589. This letter Salviati contrived to procure and hand over to Cortile, informing him at the same time that Guarini had sent a similar letter, complaining that Alfonso had not treated him according to what he considered were his merits, to none other than the Grand Duke of Tuscany. As duty demanded, Cortile hastened to send the letter and information, albeit with apologies for injuring Guarini, to his master in Ferrara. It was a further manifestation of this strange conception of loyalty, in direct conflict with Salviati's lifelong stress on the all-importance of friendship.

Meanwhile, it seemed at first that Lorenzini was going to be successful, for by devoting all his attention night and day to the Cavaliere he had brought about a perceptible improvement in his condition. At the end of March he was even considered out of danger. Giovanni de' Bardi da Vernio, Accademico della Crusca, who was in charge of the production of the inevitable comedy in the celebrations for the wedding of Ferdinando, was even delaying preparation of the show in the hope that Salviati would be able to supervise the proceedings, since the Grand Duke, surprisingly, considered his assistance essential if a good job were to be done. Ironically Salviati's 'friend' Guarini begged Bastiano de' Rossi, who had given him a more pessimistic account of Salviati's condition, to persuade the Cavaliere to take better care of himself.

In April, for no known reason, Cortile was removed from his post in Florence and his place taken by a certain Giglioli. Salviati in the meantime was moved to the Monastero degli Angeli in Florence, of the Order of Camaldoli, with which he had always had strong connections. Continuing the regular visits and gifts of money begun by his predecessor, Giglioli gained the confidence of Salviati, who spoke much to him of his private affairs and of his desire to show his gratitude to Alfonso by dedicating to him the commentary on Aristotle. At this point he might well have had greater success. The *rapprochement* between Florence and Ferrara was proceeding apace since the accession of Ferdinando, whose relations with the Cardinal d'Este in Rome had paved the way for it. But the question did not arise. On 15 July Giglioli, who had not been in the habit of sending routine bulletins on Salviati's health, told his master: 'andai una mattina, e trovai che la notte era morto.'[6]

Salviati's illness had been long and his suffering great. Cambi's realism in his funeral oration brings vividly before us the image of Salviati in his last year of agony, as he speaks of 'quella ostinatissima infermità, che lo spogliò a membro a membro di vita, perchè con pazienza esemplare soffrì un anno di febbre, un anno il non poter levarsi di letto, un anno una disformità, e magrezza di viso spaventosa a chi la mirava, una penetrante, e insanabil piaga, e in ultimo una corpulentissima idropisia.'[7] In giving this description Cambi was speaking from first-hand experience, for on 1 March of that year, along with Bernardo da Castiglione (the Accademico Rinvenuto), he had been sent by the Accademici della Crusca to visit Salviati in their name. Now, the morning after their founder's death, the Crusconi gathered to discuss his funeral oration which was entrusted to Il Fresco—Ottaviano de' Medici—who had been a 'friend' of Salviati since the latter's days as *Ricevitore* in Rome and had apparently emerged unscathed from the perils inherent in such a relationship.

Amongst the Italian men of letters there was a great show of lamentation, especially amongst the Florentines. Certainly there had long been general respect and admiration for his linguistic knowledge, unrivalled in his day, but it is obvious that in reality little love was lost between him and his contemporaries generally. A good deal of relief must have been experienced by some of them,

---

[6] U. Lett. Giglioli to Alfonso, 15.7.89, ibid. 1589.
[7] Cambi, *Orazione*. He also states that Salviati spent only a short time in the Monastero degli Angeli.

and especially his antagonists in the *Liberata* disputes, Pellegrino in particular. The mixture of humility, terror, and servility which characterizes Pellegrino's letters at certain stages in the controversy illustrates the powers of intimidation which the Infarinato had acquired—and obviously enjoyed.

On his death, and remembering what Salviati had confided to him about the dedication of the commentary on Aristotle, Giglioli took prompt action to ensure that the Cavaliere's books and manuscripts were not dispersed, repudiating with a certain abruptness Bastiano de' Rossi's claim that he was heir to the commentary provided it was dedicated to Alfonso d'Este. In fact, De' Rossi was right. Salviati's will left all his books, printed and in manuscript, both in Florence and Ferrara (where they were in the custody of Giovan Filippo Magnanini, his close friend, and a co-Academician of the Crusca since February 1589), to Alfonso, but a special clause made an exception for the commentary, exactly as De' Rossi had claimed. Other heirs were the Opera del Duomo, Spadini, and De' Rossi (who were to share what was due to Salviati in royalties for the revised *Decameron*), Lodovico Capponi, Fabrizio Caramelli Salviati's secretary, Lorenzini the doctor, and Angela Salviati, a nun in the Convent of St. John of Jerusalem. 'Eredi universali' were his cousin Diamante di Giannozzo, now presumably a free man again after his brush with the law, and his nephew Cosimo Mannelli.

Lengthy squabbles arose over the will. When Olgiati returned in August to collect the cases which he had sealed immediately on Salviati's death, the latter's creditors were already harrassing the Abbot. Upon Olgiati's suggestion that the heirs should pay the debts out of the inheritance, leaving the books aside, the Abbot informed him that Salviati's relatives had refused to accept this as yet, since the debts outweighed the assets. Diamante, on whose behalf Lionardo had enlisted the help of Alfonso, and Cosimo Mannelli, whom he had defended before the Grand Duke so many years earlier, were obviously not hampered by Lionardo's self-respect and family pride. A further complication arose from the fact that the Giunti of Florence claimed rights over the commentary because of advance payments made. This undignified three-cornered tussle over the *Poetics* was concluded by the manuscript being allowed to go to Ferrara on condition that it eventually be handed over (for printing in Florence and dedication to

Alfonso) to the winner of the lawsuit between De' Rossi and the Giunti. Even then the monks of the Convento degli Angeli refused to release the books until the sum of 150 scudi was handed over to them in payment of Salviati's debt to them. Not until July 1590 was permission finally granted, and only in January 1591 were the papers transported to Ferrara. By April of that same year the manuscript of the commentary had already been returned to Florence, since we find De' Rossi reporting at that time that his work on the editing of it was proceeding well. Nevertheless it was never printed, and only part of the manuscript is now extant.[8]

In the church of St. Stephen in Pisa, where Salviati had triumphed in 1571 with his oration to the assembled Knights, a funeral service was held for him on 24 July. His place of burial is uncertain, but though the family vault in Santa Croce does not bear his name there is no reason to suppose that the wish to be buried there, expressed in his will, was ignored. Not until 22 February of the following year, however, was Pierfrancesco Cambi ready to deliver to the Accademia Fiorentina the funeral oration for its youngest Consul. Of the oration which Ottaviano de' Medici was chosen to deliver to the Accademia della Crusca there is no trace.

---

[8] For details of events subsequent to the death of Salviati, see V. Santi, 'Lionardo Salviati e il suo testamento', *G.S.L.I.* xix (1898), 22 ff. The article is based on information in the diplomatic correspondence between Giglioli and Olgiati and Ferrara, 1589–91, and on documents in the Archivio per letterati, A.S., Modena. The will is in Florence, A.S., Notarile Moderno, 1186 (also marked 1149), 'Protocolli di Ser Francesco Parenti'.

CONCLUSION

THE life which ended in July 1589 presents itself as one of failures, frustrations, and disappointments. Lionardo's career is littered with uncompleted projects. Only a fraction of the *Avvertimenti* as planned was ever written: the *Vocabolario*, which was to have represented the practical application of his linguistic theories, and to whose compilation he had devoted so much of his time, seemed to have died with him; and the work on which he had lavished sixteen years of his life, the paraphrase and commentary to accompany his translation of Aristotle's *Poetics*, not published in his lifetime because of rivalry between petty courts, was not published after his death either, despite initial keen interest on the part of publishers, and most of it was eventually lost. In the literary field the first impression is one of the dissipation of his forces.

As a person he had achieved notoriety rather than popularity. The 'Infarinato Accademico della Crusca' was a person to be feared, not loved. Respect for his obvious personal talents seems to have been accompanied by a minimum of affection on the part of his contemporaries, who found in his personality and behaviour little which might endear him to them. Both his attack on Tasso in the *Gerusalemme Liberata* polemics and his treatment of the *Decameron* were interpreted as evidence of personal unscrupulousness and other undesirable traits of character.

Nor did he fare better in the social and political field. Born an insignificant member of a large and powerful family, he became resentful, once that first youthful enthusiasm for literature which had given a glow to his early life had faded, of his inferior status. Yet all his attempts to remedy this accident of birth met with disaster. Financial difficulties bedevilled him all his life; as an aspiring courtier he was unscrupulously utilized, and left callously unrecognized, by Francesco who despised him, ill-treated him, and made a fool of him into the bargain. A product of the stifling atmosphere of late Medicean Florence in decline, he suffered from its general complex malaise. Only in Ferrara did he receive the recognition for which he craved, and his new-found contentment there was cut short by an early death.

Yet, despite all this, such works as Lionardo has left present him as a person of outstanding intellect and penetrating insight, a person characterized in all his activities by a firm sense of direction and a clear, well-defined purpose. Of his intellect we are left in no doubt by the numerous testimonies to his pre-eminence in his times as a vernacular philologist, and by his brilliantly perceptive linguistic works. It is not merely the erudition, remarkable enough in itself, which impresses us in the *Avvertimenti*, the astounding historical knowledge of the vernacular which they reveal. It is the fact that this immense knowledge is illuminated and co-ordinated by a synthetic vision of the history and development of the language, and in his mind is all ordered into a comprehensive pattern to which every smallest detail makes its contribution, and which adds up to a vast vision of Italian culture from the commune to the high Renaissance. Within this pattern the detail can still arouse admiration—Salviati's brilliant examination, assessment, and grading, for example, in Chapter xii of Book two of the first volume of the *Avvertimenti*, of the hundreds of texts, printed and manuscript, which he has used in his linguistic studies. The more profound one's investigation of the *Avvertimenti* the greater one's admiration for his intellect and his achievements as a philologist.

No less impressive is the coherence, the fundamental unity underlying all his activities, despite their superficially disparate character, ranging as they do from the oration to the moral dialogue, from the linguistic treatise to the pseudo-classical comedy. We have seen, in brief examinations of these works whilst following Lionardo's career, how they were dominated at all stages by an advanced, unifying vision of contemporary culture, especially with regard to the *volgare*, which was for him a symbol, and at the same time the most central, most absolute manifestation, of that culture. Throughout his life he worked untiringly for the cause which coloured his view of any literary or linguistic phenomena of his time.

In the practical field his most obvious achievement, the one of which his contemporaries were most conscious and for which they gave him a good deal of credit in his lifetime, was as a co-ordinator of Florentine linguistic activity in the late sixteenth century. He it was who after the shock of Bembo, the onslaughts of Trissino, Castiglione, Castelvetro, Muzio, and in the face of the inadequacy of the solutions of the preceding generation of Florentines, ill-adapted to changing moods and contemporary shifts of thought, took up the frayed ends of Florentine linguistic thought, and with the inspiration and support of Florentines of generally less embracing vision and lesser articulacy knitted them up again into a powerful system which expressed, and catered for, the confused feelings of his fellow citizens. This is what is unique in Salviati. It is not the individual ideas on language or culture, traceable virtually all of them in such men as Grazzini, Varchi, even Machiavelli, but the ability to combine them into a system which not only provided a solution of the Florentine dilemma but which presented itself, to Florentines and non-Florentines alike, as an expression of their unvoiced feelings on their native culture, especially in its relationship to Antiquity. Hence the wide success of the *Avvertimenti*, with their particular logical combination of modernism and archaism, amongst non-Florentines as well as Florentines.

It is to be noted, moreover, that subsequent events very largely confirmed his prophecies in the realm of language. Controversies raged, theory and practice varied, but by and large, until the late eighteenth century at least, developments were what Salviati had predicted they would be. It is indeed difficult to imagine, all things considered, any other solution or development in Italy as a whole. In the centuries after Salviati it was generally recognized that despite the dominance of the archaizing principle the native Tuscan had considerable advantages, as Salviati had said would be the case. Writers, as Salviati had said they would, came to Florence to steep themselves in the spoken language in order better to use the literary language based on the great authors. The *Vocabolario della Crusca* allowed the cautious absorption of new words into the language on the 'authority' of great writers as Salviati predicted, whilst the change in morphology and syntax, even to modern times, was negligible, as Salviati said it would be.

It is when we look back on the over-all vision of which his linguistic theory is but one facet that Salviati acquires his full stature, gaining a significant position not only in Italian, but in European thought. The vision found its expression in that reasoned reorientation of contemporary man's relationship to

Antiquity which characterized Salviati's lifelong campaign, a reorientation which constitutes a significant landmark in the history of humanism and of European culture. It foreshadows developments which assume front-rank importance in succeeding centuries. There is the constant opposition of Reason (as in the dedicatory letter of his Michelangelo oration and in the disputes over the *Gerusalemme Liberata*) to the authority of Antiquity, which later is accepted only to the extent that it represents that Reason. On these grounds the 'rules' of Aristotle are accepted as valid in Salviati's times, but not the 'example' of Homer. There is the concept of unlimited progress within the national tradition once the restricting influence of Antiquity has been removed. Such a concept of progress informs his notions on the development of language, of literature, and indeed of Italian civilization in general. In fact that very idea of the necessary independence of the national tradition, so fundamental in Salviati and implying principally, as it did, the repudiation of all classical influence, may itself be said to derive from the desire to shake off the last restrictions of a cramping cyclic conception of history.

Yet the importance of the *Avvertimenti*, and of Salviati the creative writer, pales into significance beside the importance of what was in reality the greatest product of Salviati's vision, albeit a posthumous product, namely the *Vocabolario della Crusca*. On several occasions in his works he refers to a 'vocabolario' intended to be the chief instrument whereby his linguistic theories would be put into practice. The *peggioramento della favella*, it will be remembered, was overwhelmingly a question of vocabulary, the result of words 'tratte dal Latino, e delle scuole uscite, o dalle cattedre della lingua Latina', which had been 'per capriccio introdotti, o nigligenza d'huomini di poca autorità'.[1] Therefore, although syntactical and other Latinisms were deprecated and must be corrected, if possible on the model of the simple language of the pre-Boccaccian Trecento as represented chiefly by Villani, what was principally needed was a 'vocabulary'. On such a vocabulary he had been working for many years in close association with his protégé Bastiano de' Rossi, Secretary of the Accademia della Crusca.[2] When this latter body finally gave

---

[1] *Avvertimenti*, Vol. I, Bk. ii, pp. 77 and 79 respectively.
[2] He mentions his *vocabolario* and his work on it in many places, e.g. *Avvertimenti*, pp. 58, 113, and 178.

birth to the *Vocabolario della Crusca* in 1612 it openly acknowledged its debt, in creating such a work, to its founder Lionardo
Salviati. But the greatest acknowledgement was in the fact that in
its Florentine purist inspiration, in its use of the 'good' authors
for the development and enrichment of the language, in its whole
conception and execution in short, it was a monument to Salviati's
principles. It is almost more than probable, though there is no
proof, that his own work over the preceding years provided its
material nucleus.

This *Vocabolario della Crusca*, to which it would be difficult to
deny the status of the incarnation of the greatest single principle
in Italian linguistic history from 1612 until 1827, was thus a
product of Lionardo Salviati's vision of the *volgare* within the
context of his conception of the national tradition. This being so,
the influence of Salviati on Italian culture could hardly be over-
estimated. It is still with us today, as is also, after a period of
suppression, his creation the Accademia della Crusca, where his
portrait still hangs along with his emblem as the Infarinato.

Such were the solid achievements of Lionardo Salviati as we
look back on them after four centuries. Some of his Florentine
contemporaries, Grazzini for instance, were aware that he was the
mouthpiece of their own conscious ideals and aspirations. Others,
on reading or hearing his prose orations for example, merely
confirmed, by their response to his archaic style animated by a
sense of the living language, his own belief in the attraction which
the uncontaminated national tradition held for his times and in the
need first to restore it to its original purity and then to develop its
potential. To most he was, of course, known as a versatile man of
letters and academician, the author of plays, orations, dialogues,
of which the appeal has vanished for ever along with the ephemeral
fashion from which it largely derived.

After considerable fame and prominence in his lifetime, as
a personality he very quickly faded after his death. His image
naturally varied according to the linguistic views of the individual
or the side taken in the disputes over the *Gerusalemme Liberata*—
still a burning issue well into the seventeenth century. Paolo
Beni attacked him in the *Anticrusca* as did Traiano Boccalini
in his *Ragguali di Parnaso*, in the latter case as a person, a de-
praved character who had mutilated the *Decameron* for personal
gain. But in general the *Avvertimenti* gained in prestige and

authority. Their influence, as the most weighty contribution to the linguistic disputes in the late sixteenth century, as the most powerful expression of one of the main principles round which linguistic ideas were crystallized, and as a guide to the use of the language, was enormous. They rapidly became authoritative. The first half of the eighteenth century saw the peak of the prestige both of the *Avvertimenti* and of Salviati himself, who now emerged again as a personality, and whose stature as an all-round author, one of the glories of Florentine letters, tended to be greatly exaggerated, for example by the industrious compilers of lists of illustrious academicians. Even well into the nineteenth century Salviati remained prominent amongst established grammarians as the supreme respected spokesman of the principle of linguistic purism. It will be remembered that De Sanctis records in his autobiography that whilst in the school of Basilio Puoti 'M'era venuta la frenesia degli studi grammaticali. Avevo spesso tra mano il Corticelli, il Buommattei, il Cinonio, il Salviati . . .'.

But this very fact of the identification of Salviati with a principle whose twin expressions were the *Avvertimenti* and the *Vocabolario della Crusca* made inevitable a change of fortune when Romanticism came to overthrow existing linguistic notions and practices. With the purist school, as we have just seen, Salviati enjoyed a brief resurgence of authority, and polemics continued in which the principles he represented were still a living issue, but as the nineteenth century progressed the linguistic vision which his works represented inevitably became a mere historical phenomenon. Salviati was branded more and more, in an unhistorical manner, as a shortsighted purist pedant. The reverence shown towards him as a *letterato* by Luigi Manzoni, who edited his *Rime* and then a collection of his letters and unpublished prose works in the 1870s, was the last failing, anachronistic spark of his eighteenth-century reputation.

Yet at precisely the same time as this dramatic decline was taking place in Salviati's reputation as a grammarian and theorist of language there was a renewed interest in him on a more personal plane. Historical criticism, beginning with Foscolo, had already examined and condemned his role in the history of the text of the *Decameron*, but it was as the antagonist of Tasso in the disputes over the *Gerusalemme Liberata* that he principally acquired new fame with several generations of literary and critical historians—and new notoriety. The Romantic Tasso legend naturally worked in his disfavour, for on him devolved the role of the villain, Guasti in particular making great efforts to assign to him alone the blame for what was considered to be a wanton, malicious, and unprovoked attack, and the image which Guasti created is the one which has largely clung to him ever since, reaching its lowest ebb at the close of the century with Vivaldi, whose conclusions that Salviati's contributions were gratuitous and inconsistent likewise became a commonplace. More recent students of literary criticism in the sixteenth century have in general modified this thesis only to the extent of conceding the possibility that somewhere behind Salviati's participation there probably lurked genuine critical interests without, however, understanding the real significance of the disputes in the complex of Salviati's thought.[3] Even historical critics paid him a minimum of serious attention. Particularly revealing of Salviati's reputation at its nadir is the comment which L. G. Tenconi, writing in 1942, makes on the above-quoted passage from De Sanctis's *La giovinezza*. The note on Salviati in his edition runs 'LEONARDO SALVIATI (1540–1589), fiorentino, celebre accademico della Crusca, oggi quasi non per altro ricordato che per essere stato l'anima delle polemiche intorno al Tasso, scrisse, oltre il resto, anche due volumi di *Avvertimenti della lingua sopra 'l Decameron*, per i quali è qui sopra ricordato.'[4]

Very recent decades have shown some sign of revived interest and some of rehabilitation. Critics such as Vitale have shown an appreciation of the real guiding motives of his linguistic works, and Chiappelli might be said to have set the seal on the process of rehabilitation by referring, as we have seen, to 'quel meraviglioso secondo libro degli *Avvertimenti*'. Even so he has never been dealt with more than incidentally in the context of the *questione della lingua* in the sixteenth century, of the Tasso disputes, or the history of Italian grammar. Little attention has been paid to him in his own right or even as a landmark in Italian humanism. Most remarkable of all, the one work whose subject is precisely that late sixteenth-century concern with the relationship of

---

[3] On this subject see P. M. Brown, 'The Historical Significance of the Disputes over the *Gerusalemme Liberata*', *Studi secenteschi*, xi (1970), 3–23.

[4] F. De Sanctis, *La giovinezza*, ed. L. G. Tenconi (Milan, Casa per edizioni popolari, 1942), p. 88.

contemporary culture to Antiquity from which Salviati's work derives its importance, namely Margiotta's *Le origini italiane de 'la querelle des anciens et des modernes'*, whilst seeing the comparatively ineffectual and certainly ambiguous Grazzini as a vital figure, does not so much as mention Salviati. Likewise Weinberg, analysing in great detail Lionardo's contributions to the polemics over the *Liberata*, does not associate him in so many words with the 'moderns', though in fact Salviati is plainly the chief spokesman of the principles which Weinberg attributes to them.

Virtually complete neglect of the man over four centuries, with practically no serious work done on manuscripts or biographical sources, means that even purely factual knowledge about Salviati is still strictly limited. None of his works has even been seriously and thoroughly examined. The *Avvertimenti* await analysis and interpretation in their every aspect, from Salviati's method as a grammarian down to the identification of the manuscripts and printed texts to which he refers. We still lack almost completely the infrastructure necessary for an authoritative assessment of the man and his works, though as long ago as 1899 that discerning critic J. E. Spingarn was wise enough to perceive that in claiming the superiority of Florentine over classical languages and literatures in his first great manifesto the *Orazione in lode della fiorentina favella*, '. . . the mere fact that Salviati made such a claim at all is enough to give him a place worthy of serious consideration in the history of Italian literature.'

SUPPLEMENTARY NOTES

1. This autograph letter is bound to the Ferrara copy of Lionardo's *Orazione seconda* (see Ch. iv n. 5) and consists of eleven folios, numbered recto only 27–34 and 71–3. It is a rough draft, with many alterations and corrections. The Cod. Ambr. D. 191 inf., fols. 94–7, has a transcription of this letter, too. Authors such as Crescini, in 'Jacopo Corbinelli', and in his review of the book by R. Calderini De Marchi (see Ch. iv n. 4), and also A. Lorenzoni, *Un coro di male lingue*, Frammenti inediti di vita fiorentina (I (Florence) 1905, iv) believed that the anger of Salviati and his group was due entirely to criticism by Corbinelli of Lionardo's *poems* in praise of Don Garzia. The reason why they took no account of the letter of Salviati to Corbinelli, and the annotations to which it referred, was that the letter was believed to be addressed, not to Corbinelli, but to Alessandro Canigiani. The initiator of a tradition of erroneous attribution was Giuseppe Antonelli, librarian of the Bib. Ariostea, who wrote to B. Gamba saying that the letter was provoked by annotations made by Canigiani, an error caused by the fact that Vol. Misc. Est. 343, 1 (a copy of Lionardo's *first* oration, to which the second oration and the manuscript letter are attached) bears a handwritten dedication to Canigiani. Antonelli's letter was published by Gamba, *Serie de' testi di lingua* (Venice, 1839), p. 261, and the error was perpetuated by L. Manzoni, *Prose inedite del cav. Leonardo Salviati* (Bologna, Romagnoli, 1873, Vol. cxxix of the series 'Scelta di curiosità letterarie inedite o rare') who published an extremely inaccurate (and also expurgated!) version of the letter, in which he was followed by E. Contin, *Lettere edite e inedite di Lionardo Salviati* (Padua, 1875). The error was rectified by P. Soldati, 'Jacopo Corbinelli e Lionardo Salviati', *Archivum Romanicum*, xix (July–Dec. 1935), 415–23. The letter has one feature of more than Salviatesque importance: in it Salviati refers to '. . . messer Pietro da Barga, Umanista dello Studio di Pisa'—one of the very few recorded uses of the word umanista during the humanistic and Renaissance periods. For this use see my article: 'Pietro degli Angeli da Barga — "Humanista dello studio di Pisa" ', *Italica*, xlvii (1970), 285–95.

2. The poems are mostly to be found in three manuscripts, namely Florence, B.N.C., Cod. Magl. VII, 306; Florence, Bib. Ricc., Cod. 2849; Naples, Bib. Vittorio Emanuale II, Cod. XIII, D. 52. The poems contained in these manuscripts (which also contain a large number of poems to Salviati) were published by Luigi Manzoni, *Rime inedite del cav. Leonardo Salviati* (Bologna, Romagnoli, 1871, Vol. cxvii of the series 'Scelta di curiosità letterarie inedite o rare'). His edition is full of inaccuracies, and his editorial criteria are extremely defective. A manuscript in Parma, the Cod. Pal. 557, Vol. iii, 'Raccolta di poeti italiani, rime

volgari del '500', contains three unpublished sonnets by Salviati. Numerous selections of his poems have been published over the centuries. For details of the manuscripts and the published editions see Bibliography of this volume and also my article 'Manoscritti e stampe delle poesie edite e inedite di Lionardo Salviati', *G.S.L.I.* cxlvi (1969), 530–52.

3. The point is excellently made by P. O. Kristeller, *The Classics and Renaissance Thought* (Cambridge, Mass., Harvard University Press, 1955, Martin Classical Lectures, Vol. xv), p. 10. After defining the *studia humanitatis*, the studies which perfected the whole man, as 'grammar, rhetoric, poetry, history, and moral philosophy', he goes on: '. . . and the study of each of these subjects was understood to include the reading and interpretation of its standard ancient writers in Latin, and, to a lesser extent, in Greek. This meaning of the *studia humanitatis* remained in general use throughout the sixteenth century and later, and we may still find an echo of it in our use of the term "humanities". Thus Renaissance humanism was not as such a philosophical tendency or system, but rather a cultural and educational program which emphasised and developed an important but limited area of studies. This area had for its center a group of subjects that was concerned essentially neither with the classics nor philosophy, but might be roughly described as literature. It was to this peculiar literary preoccupation that the very intensive and extensive study which the humanists devoted to the Greek, and especially the Latin classics owed its peculiar character.'

4. Varchi had said much of this before him, and at considerably greater length, as the nature of his treatise (in dialogue form) the *Ercolano* permitted. The subject of inherent qualities in a language and their relationship to the potential of a language for development through a literary tradition is dealt with especially on pp. 210, 220–2 of the *Ercolano* (Padua, Comino, 1744). Similarities of subject-matter, attitude, phraseology, and example between Salviati's oration and this work (by this time completed) are too numerous, fundamental, and precise for the possibility of coincidence to be worth considering: e.g. to quote but one minor textual example, on the subject of the *lingue barbare* which Varchi describes as 'Inarticolate, . . . e come nell'Italia la pura Genovese' (op. cit., p. 209), Salviati refers to 'i Genovesi, la favella dei quali, non ch'altro, non è articolata' (F. 67). This general overwhelming interdependence between the *Ercolano* and Salviati's *Orazione* must be borne in mind when occasional reference is made to similarity on specific points. A useful study of the development of Varchi's ideas on language, which provides a background of the history in the Academy of attitudes to *fiorentinità* and to the relationship between the spoken and written languages, thus illuminating the *Orazione in lode della fiorentina favella*, is to be found in F. Bruni, *Sistemi critici e strutture narrative (ricerche sulla cultura fiorentina del Rinascimento* (Naples, Liguori, 1969), Chs. i–iv.

5. The 1858 edition of *Il Granchio* in *Teatro classico* (Trieste, Lloyd Austriaco) has in an Appendix another long prologue, which the editor claims is the 'prologo del *Granchio*, come fu recitato in Mantova nel 1578 . . . ora per la prima volta tratto da una "Memoria" del P. Ireneo Affò intorno a' fatti di Guglielmo Vespasiano Gonzaga', in manuscript in the Archivio di Guastalla. This incorporates much of Salviati's prologue, with the addition of *c.* 40 lines by the producer who recounts the difficulty he has had in persuading the author to authorize the production which in fact, remains unauthorized. Since line 6 refers to Salviati as the Infarinato this prologue must inevitably be later than 1583, and could not have been written for a performance in 1578.

Two *stanze* of Grazzini, however, are of considerable interest in indicating the play's popularity. Criticizing the lack of taste of those Florentines who have favoured a bad poet, he says, ironically: 'E Lionardo Salviati muor di duolo / per che il suo Granchio fu tanto schernito' (ll. 9–11)—thus indicating by implication that the work is well established in general esteem, since it can be quoted as absurd that Salviati should fear for its reputation (Verzone, op. cit., *Ottave*, No. XCII, p. 422).

6. Pisa, 'Provanza di nobiltà'. But not all information contained in the 'Provanza' seems to be entirely reliable. In particular, one cannot overlook several references to a benefice held by Salviati. In the letter written by Alfonso Cambi Importuni in the name of the investigating commissioners, Cambi states 'l'istesso M. Lionardo particularmente esser Piovano di Montevettulini'. This must be an error of detail on the part of one of Cambi's informants. The archives of the parish seem to give positive proof to the contrary. Don Elio Mazzoncini, vicar of the parish in 1955, writes: 'Ho consultato i registri di questo archivio parrocchiale, ma alle date da Lei indicate trovo che pievano di questa chiesa era un certo Galeotti. Non trovo traccia di Lionardo Salviati.' But another witness, Acciaiuoli, states quite clearly that 'per la casta sua, et per sue qualità gli fu comprato un benefizio'. Apparent absence in the Decima Granducale of clerical fiscal exemptions is not proof that Lionardo had not taken orders, and in view of his request for the canonicate in 1564 (see p. 92) and the fact that he enters the Order as a *Cavalier sacerdotale* this would seem probable, though it is surprising that there is no trace of it in the 'Regio Diritto: Suppliche' in the Florentine Archives. For further details of the information on Salviati contained in this 'Provanza' and a consideration of some apparent contradictions, see P. M. Brown, 'Lionardo Salviati and the Ordine di Santo Stefano', *Italica*, xxxiv, No. 2 (June 1957), 69–74.

7. Lett. Cortile to Alfonso, 4.2.76, Modena, A.S., C.A.F., 1576, published G. Campori, 'Il cavalier'. Other letters in the same archive in Modena to which reference is here made in connection with the troubles over the titles are: (a) (Cancelleria) Cortile to Alfonso, 11.12.75, 14.1.76, 2.2.76, 11.2.76, 10.3.76, 20.5.76, and (b) (Archivio per letterati: Salviati) Alfonso to Cortile, 18.12.75. The story of this attempt to dedicate the

commentary to Alfonso has been told, though without precise indications of the sources of many details, by G. Campori, 'Il cavalier Lionardo Salviati e Alfonso II duca di Ferrara', in *Atti e memorie dei R. R. Deputati di Storia Patria per le Prov. Mod. e Parm.*, vii (Modena, 1874), 143 ff. Borghini's work is in manuscript in the Borghini papers in the Filze Rinucciniane, B.N.C., Florence. See also the *Prose fiorentine*, Vol. iv, Bk. 4, ed. Carlo Dati (Florence, 1611–1723), for a connected letter from Borghini to Razzi. For the negotiations over the appointment of ambassadors to Ferrara and Paris, see U. letters in the C.A.F., Cortile to Laderchi, 16.9.75, and Cortile to Alfonso, 7.12.75.

8. U. lett. Francesco to Salviati, 22.11.79, Florence, A.S., F.Med., R.L.M, No. 252, fol. 81ʳ. Also in the same archive are (i) Salviati's letters to Francesco of 17.10.79 (F.L.O., No. 728, fol. 101) (the quoted letter of 21.8.80 is given in Contin); (ii) other letters (all unpublished) from Francesco to Salviati, carrying the thanks, praise, and encouragement of the Grand Duke, are in the R.L.M. and dated 7.11.79, 22.11.79, 29.12.79, 22.4.80 (Reg. No. 252, fols. 68ᵛ, 81ʳ, 106ᵛ, 184ʳ), 14.12.80, 28.1.81, (No. 254, fols. 191ᵛ and 242ʳ). The letter from Bianca Cappello, addressed to Giacomo Buoncompagni from Sarzana, is dated 2.4.80, and is in the A.V., A.Bu., Filza D. 36, fol. 48ʳ. For Bianca Cappello in this period see L. Grottanelli, 'Fra Geremia da Udine e le sue relazioni con la corte del Granduca Francesco de' Medici', *Rassegna nazionale*, lxxii, fasc. 280–3 (1893), 3–43, 185–228, 577–622. See also A. Centelli, 'Fra Geremia da Udine e Bianca Cappello', *Nuovo archivio veneto*, vii (1897), 171 ff. In connection with certain information on conditions in Rome, supplied by Geremia whilst in Florence, Grottanelli exclaims: 'E davvero non si stenta a crederlo, ma come poté Fra Geremia saperlo?'

9. In the Bib. Laurenziana, Florence, Plut. LXXX. Cod. CXI, 'Miscellanea Boccaccio', the process of revision can be followed step by step by means of a record of the correspondence between the correctors and the Master of the Sacred Palace. A similar collection of documents, with instructions from the Master, is in Florence, B.N.C., Cod. Magl. Cl. VIII 1393, from which is extracted the above quotation. For details of this correction see A. Sorrentino, *La letteratura italiana e il Sant'Uffizio* (Naples, Perrella, 1935). Both Sorrentino and D. M. Manni, *Illustrazione storica del Boccaccio* (Florence, 1742), as well as G. Lesca, 'V. Borghini e il *Decameron*' in *Studi su G. Boccaccio* (Castelfiorentino, 1913), all quote parts of a letter dated 16.7.73 from Ferdinando de' Medici to Mons. Cirillo in Rome, asking him to be more lenient with the *Decameron*. With regard to Vettori, there is a letter from him to Cardinal Seripando (*Prose fior.* iv, Part 4, quoted in part by Sorrentino, op. cit., pp. 186–7, and by Lesca, op. cit., p. 258), in which Vettori protests violently against a proposed further revision of the work, defending the 'novelle' as 'favole'.

10. Edition of 1589, then the definitive edition of 1602. There is no work which studies the extent to which these corrections were adopted, and in

which editions, though an analysis of the 'corrections' from a linguistic point of view is to be found in D. Battaglin, 'Leonardo Salviati e le "Osservazioni al Pastor fido" del Guarini', *Atti e memorie dell'Accademia Patavina di Scienze, Lettere ed Arti*, lxxvii, 3 (Memorie della Classe di Sc. mor., lett. ed arti) (Padua, 1967), 249–85. A study of the corrections to the manuscript of the *Pastor fido* in the Marciana would also be useful. For some discussion of these questions see V. Rossi, *Guarini e il Pastor fido* (Turin, Loescher, 1886). All the notes, corrections, *repliche*, etc. are found in the Biblioteca Ariostea, Ferrara, Cod. Cl. H. 276, and the text of Salviati's 'Annotazioni' alone has been published by S. Pasquazi in *Rinascimento ferrarese* (Caltanisetta–Rome, Sciascia, 1957), pp. 251–83: see also idem, 'G. B. Guarini' in *I minori*, Vol. ii of the series Orientamenti Culturali (Milan, Marzorati, 1961), pp. 1339–64.

11. Amongst the qualities of the language of Tasso of which Salviati was to express a dislike in the polemics were what he called its 'asprezza', 'oscurità', and 'durezza', which he contrasted with the 'chiarezza', 'efficacia', and 'agevolezza' of Ariosto. This being so it is interesting to find in the letter to De' Bardi a reference to 'another', different kind of poetry from Ariosto's, to what he calls the 'poesie dure, difficili, sforzate, e che non si possono pronunziar con agevolezza, né imparare a mente'. Anyone who prefers this kind of poetry, he says, goes against 'l'openioni de' migliori'. It is difficult, in view of what followed, not to see an allusion here to the poetry of the *Gerusalemme Liberata*. Yet the very nature of the allusion, if such it is, adds weight to the letter as proof that Ariosto, rather than Tasso, was Salviati's starting-point even in the post-*Carrafa* disputes. Despite the immediate interest in the *Gerusalemme Liberata* in the academies at this point before Pellegrino had given it a new status, that poem is of very marginal interest to Salviati, and then in connection with what is in the letter only a very minor issue—beauty of verse and its effect on pleasure.

APPENDIX A

EDITIONS OF SALVIATI'S WORKS
(EXCLUDING ORATIONS)

FOR further details of editions of Salviati's works (including his letters) readers are referred to S. Parodi, 'Una lettera inedita del Salviati', in *Studi di filologia italiana*, xxvii (1969), 147–74, which includes a critical review of printed editions of Salviati's letters (pp. 150–62) and a 'Bibliografia delle opere salviatesche' (pp. 162–74). The latter (on which I have drawn to supplement my own material) is very comprehensive and is more useful than the former which, whilst clearing up a number of errors, also perpetuates others of long standing.

A. COLLECTED WORKS

(For reference numbers of orations see Appendix B)

Opere complete del cav. Lionardo Salviati, 5 vols. Milan, Classici Italiani, 1810.

Contents:

Vol. i *Elogio del Salviati* by G. Pelli (from the 'Elogi di uomini illustri toscani').
Letter from Alessandro Canigiani to Don Silvano Razzi.
Dialogo dell'amicizia with dedicatory letter.
Cinque lezioni sopra un sonetto del Petrarca.
La Spina: *Il Granchio.*
Vol. ii *Avvertimenti della lingua sopra 'l Decameron*, Vol. i.
Vol. iii *Avvertimenti della lingua sopra 'l Decameron*, Vol. i (cont.).
Vol. iv *Avvertimenti della lingua sopra l' Decameron*, Vol. ii.
Vol. v Letter from Don Silvano Razzi to Antonmaria Salviati.
Avviso degli editori dell'edizione di Firenze del 1575 (i.e. of the *Primo libro delle orazioni* of 1575).
Orations Nos. I, III, IV, V, IX, VI, VII, VIII, X, XIII, XIV, XV, XI, XII.
Salviati's Italian translation of Vettori's oration in praise of Joan of Austria—*Orazione delle lodi della Regina Giovanna d'Austria.*
Discorso sopra le prime parole di Cornelio Tacito.

Rime del cav. Leonardo Salviati, secondo la lezione originale, confrontata con due codici, per cura di Luigi Manzoni, Bologna, 1871 (No. CXVII of the collection 'Scelta di curiosità letterarie inedite o rare').

Contin, E., *Lettere edite e inedite del cav. Lionardo Salviati*, Padua, 1875.

Prose inedite a cura di Luigi Manzoni, Bologna, 1873 (No. CXXIX of the collection 'Scelta di curiosità letterarie inedite o rare').

It contains:

Del trattato della poetica lettura terza.
Discorso sulla ginnastica degli antichi (which is not in fact a work of Salviati).
Discorso intorno alla ribellione di Fiandra.
Part of the *Annotazioni* to the *Pastor fido*.
Letters (23 in number).

B. EDITIONS OF SINGLE WORKS

Dialogo dell'amicizia

De' dialoghi dell'amicizia, libro primo, Florence, Eredi di Bernardo Giunti, 1564, in 4to.
Ded. lett. 18.8.61 to Alamanno Salviati.
Repr. (i) With *Il Granchio* and *La Spina*, Florence, Giunti, 1606, q.v.
(ii) with J. Facciolati, *Il giovane cittadino istruito nella scienza civile e nelle leggi dell'amicizia*, Naples, Muziana, 1740 (iii), *Opere*, 1810.

Comedies

Il Granchio, commedia in versi con gl'intermedii di Bernardo de' Nerli, Accademico Fiorentino, Florence, Torrentino, 1566.

La Spina, commedia in prosa, Ferrara, per Benedetto Mammarelli, 1592 (posthumous edition, ed. Giovambatista Olgiati).
Repr. (i) *Due commedie del cav. L. S. Il Granchio e la Spina e un dialogo dell'amicizia del medesimo autore, nuovamente ristampate e corrette*, Florence, Giunti, 1606; (ii) *Il Granchio, La Spina* in Vol. vi of *Teatro comico fiorentino*, Florence, 1750 (6 vols.); (iii) *Opere*, 1810 (both comedies); (iv) *Il Granchio, La Spina* in *Teatro classico*, Trieste: dalla Sezione letterario-artistica del Lloyd Austriaco, Milan, Carlo Barbini, 1858; (v) *La Spina e il Granchio di Lionardo Salviati* in *Il teatro classico del secolo XVI*, Milan, Presso l'Ufficio Generale di Commissioni ed Annunzi (no date, but Parodi says it is after 1880).

Poems

In addition to the *Rime inedite* cited above, ed. Manzoni, the following works contain poems by Salviati:

Orazione II in lode di Don Garzia, Florence, Giunti, 1562.

Orazione III in lode di Don Garzia, Florence, Giunti, 1562.

CRESCIMBENI, G. M., *Istoria della volgar poesia*, Rome, 1698.

POGGIALI, G., *Serie de' testi di lingua*, Vol. i, Leghorn, Tommaso Masi, 1813.

Canzone in lode del Pino, London, 1831 (with false origin Firenze).

Saggio di rime inedite del cavalier Lionardo Salviati, Faenza, Conti, 1843.

TRUCCHI, F., *Poesie italiane di dugento autori*, Vol. iv, Prato, Guasti, 1847.

ZAMBRINI, F., *Madrigali inediti del cavalier Lionardo Salviati da un codice riccardiano* (no date or other indications).

MANZONI, L., *Capitolo di Lionardo Salviati 'In lode del piatire'*, Imola, Galeati, 1871.

For exact details of poems in each work see P. M. Brown, 'Manoscritti e stampe delle poesie edite e inedite del cav. Lionardo Salviati', *G.S.L.I* cxlvi (1969), 530–52.

Lezioni sopra Petrarca

Cinque lezzioni del cavalier L. S., cioè due della speranza, una della felicità, e l'altre due sopra varie materie, e tutte lette nell'Accademia Fiorentina, con l'occasione del sonetto del Petrarca 'Poi che voi, e io più volte habbiam provato', Florence, Giunti, 1571.
Ded. Lett. 15.6.75 to Antonmaria Vescovo de' Salviati.
Repr. (i) 2nd edn., Florence, Giunti, 1575; (ii) *Opere*, 1810.

The *Paradosso*

Il Lasca, Dialogo, Cruscata ovver Paradosso d'Ormannozzo Rigogoli, rivisto e ampliato da Panico Granacci, cittadini di Firenze e accademici della Crusca, nel quale si mostra che non importa che la storia sia vera, e questionasi per incidenza alcuna cosa contro la poesia, Florence, per Domenico Manzani, 1584 (in colophon 'Nella stamperia di Giorgio Marescotti').
Ded. Lett. 'Il dì di carnevale dell'anno 1583 [i.e. 1584]. Ai nobilissimi ed Ingegnosissimi Accademici Intronati, il Censore dell'Accademia della Crusca.'

The revised *Decameron*

Il Decamerone di messer Giovanni Boccacci, cittadino fiorentino, di nuovo ristampato e riscontrato in Firenze con testi antichi, e alla sua vera lezione ridotto dal cav. Lionardo Salviati, *deputato dal Sereniss.* Gran Duca di Toscana, con permessione de' Superiori, Venice, Filippo, Jacopo e Fratelli Giunti, 1582.
Ded. lett. 26.4.1582 to Iacopo Buoncompagni, Duca di Sora, etc.
Repr. (i) 2nd edn. Florence, Giunti, 1582; (ii) 3rd edn. Venice, Giunti, 1585; (iii) 4th edn. Florence, Giunti, 1588 (in colophon 'Del mese di febbraio, MDLXXXVII' (i.e. 1588 common style). Marconcini, *L'Accademia della Crusca*, without giving details, says that there were at least fourteen editions of this work. Others are: Venice, Angelieri, 1594; Venice, Vecchi, 1597; Florence, Giunti, 1602; Venice, Vecchi, 1602; Venice, Vecchi, 1614; Venice, Antonio Giuliani, 1626; Venice, Bertano, 1638.

Discorso on Tacitus

Discorso sopra le prime parole di Cornelio Tacito 'Urbem Romam a principio reges habuere, libertatem et consulatum L. Brutus instituit'. *Onde avvenne che Roma, non havendo mai provato a viver libera, poté mettersi in libertà e havendola perduta, non poté mai racquistarla.* Discorso primo, *printed with* Gli Annali di Cornelio Tacito Cavalier romano *... da Giorgio Dati fiorentino nuovamente tradotti in lingua toscana, con un discorso del C. L. S. sopra le prime parole dell'autore,* Venice, Bernardo Giunti, 1582.
Repr. (i) Venice, Giunti, 1589, with the 2nd edn. of Dati's translation of the *Annali*; (ii–vii) with Ottavio Sammarco, *Delle mutazioni de' regni*, Venice, Scaglia, 1629; Turin 1629; Milan 1630; Milan 1805; Milan (Silvestri) 1825; Milan (Bettoni) 1830 (in *Scrittori politici*); (viii) in the volume *Trattato del reggimento degli stati, di F. Girolamo Savonarola, con gli avvertimenti civili, di Francesco Guicciardini, e l'Apologia di Lorenzo de' Medici. Con giunta delle mutazioni de' regni di Ottavio Sammarco, ed un discorso di Lionardo Salviati*, Milan, Silvestri, 1848.

Avvertimenti

Degli avvertimenti della lingua sopra 'l Decamerone. Volume primo, Venice, presso Domenico e Gio. Batt. Guerra, Fratelli, 1584.
Ded. lett. (undated) to Jacopo Buoncompagni, Duca di Sora, etc.
Del secondo volume degli avvertimenti della lingua sopra 'l Decamerone, Florence, Giunti, 1586.
Ded. lett. 9.5.86 'Al molto Reverendo Padre Francesco Panicarola.'
Repr. (i) as Vols. iv–vi of *Raccolta degli autori del ben parlare per secolari e religiosi. Opere diverse*, Venice, In Salicata, 1643 (19 vols.),

part 1. This also contains an *opinione* of Salviati on 'Qual sia la favella nobile d'Italia e quale il nome suo', made up from the contents of Chs. xvii and xxi of the *Avvertimenti*, Vol. 1, Bk. ii; (ii) In *Operum Graecorum, Latinorum, et Italorum Rhetorum Tomi Octo*, Venice, In Salicata, 1644 (possibly also 1645). This is the Venetian edition of 1643 with a new frontispiece; (iii) Naples, Raillard, 1712; (iv) *Opere*, 1810. Extracts are also to be found in the following: (i) (from Vol. 1) C. M. Carlieri, *Regole e osservazioni di varii autori intorno alla lingua toscana*, Florence, Gius. Manni, 1715; (ii–iii) two reprints of the last-mentioned, of which the second is Florence, Nestenus, 1725.

Contributions to the disputes over the *Gerusalemme Liberata*

Degli accademici della Crusca, stacciata prima, cioè difesa dell'Orlando Furioso dell'Ariosto contra 'l Dialogo dell'Epica poesia di Camillo Pellegrino, Florence, Manzani, 1584.
Ded. lett. 16.2.1584 (i.e. '85) 'Al molto Illustre Signore il Signore Orazio Rucellai. . . .'
Repr. in *Opere di Torquato Tasso*, Florence, Tartini & Franchi, 1724, (6 vols.), Vol. v.

Dello Infarinato Accademico della Crusca: Risposta all'Apologia di Torquato Tasso intorno all'Orlando Furioso, e alla Gierusalemme Liberata, Florence, Carlo Meccoli e Silvestro Magliani, 1585.
Ded. lett. 10.9.1585 'Al Serenissimo D. Francesco Medici secondo Gran Duca di Toscana.'
Repr. (i) 2nd edn. 'Di nuovo ristampata e corretta', Mantua, Francesco Osanna, 1585; (ii) in *Opere di Torquato Tasso*, Florence, Tartini & Franchi, 1724; (iii) In *Opere di Torquato Tasso poste in miglior ordine, ricorrette sull'edizione fiorentina*, etc., ed. G. Rosini, Pisa, Capurro, 1821–32, (33 vols.), Vol. xix (1828).

Lo 'Nfarinato secondo, ovvero dello 'Nfarinato Accademico della Crusca, Risposta al libro intitolato Replica di Camillo Pellegrino, Florence, Padovani, 1588.
Ded. lett. 20.4.1588 'Al Serenissimo Principe Donno Alfonso secondo d'Este, Duca di Ferrara. . . .'
Repr. (i) In *Opere di Torquato Tasso*, Florence, Tartini & Franchi, 1724, Vol. v; (ii) in *Opere di Torquato Tasso*, etc. (ed. Rosini), Pisa, Capurro, Vol. xviii (1827).

Considerazioni di Carlo Fioretti da Vernio intorno a un discorso di M. Giulio Ottonelli da Fano sopra alcune dispute dietro alla Gierusalem di Torquato Tasso, Florence, Padovani, 1586.
Ded. lett. 1.8.1586 'Al molto Illustre Sig. Piero de' Bardi de' Conti di Vernio suo Signore. . . .'

Repr. (i) In *Opere di Torquato Tasso*, 1724, Vol. v; (ii) *Opere di Torquato Tasso*, ed. Rosmini, Vol. xviii (1827).

Poetics

Del trattato della poetica, lettura terza, ed. L. Manzoni, Imola, Galeati, 1871.
Ded. lett. 1.7.1566 to 'Il cavalier Gaddi.'
Repr. in *Prose inedite*, (ed. Manzoni), Bologna, 1873.

Letters

In addition to the volume *Lettere edite e inedite*, ed. Contin, and the *Prose inedite* of Manzoni, the following contain one or more letters of Salviati:

SALVIATI, L., *Lo 'Nfarinato Secondo, ovvero dello 'Nfarinato Accademico della Crusca, risposta al libro intitolato Replica di Camillo Pellegrino*, etc., Florence, Padovani, 1588.

GUARINI, G. B., *Lettere del Sig. Guarini*, Venice, Minerva, 1593.

PANIGAROLA, F., *Il Predicatore . . . ovvero Parafrasi, Comento e Discorso intorno al libro dell'Elocutione di Demetrio Falereo*, Venice, Giunti & Ciotti, 1609.

Prose fiorentine raccolte dallo Smarrito Accademico della Crusca, 17 vols., Florence, Tartini & Franchi, Part IV, Vol. iv, 1745.

SPERONI, S., *Opere di Sperone Speroni degli Alvarotti*, 5 vols., Venice, Occhi, 1740 (Vol. v).

MANNI, D. M., *Appendice all'Illustrazione storica di Gio. Boccaccio*, Milan, Pirotta, 1820.

BORGHINI, V., *Discorso a Baccio Valori intorno al modo di fare gli alberi delle famiglie nobili fiorentine*, Florence, Magheri, 1821.

ROSINI, G. (ed.), *Opere di Torquato Tasso poste in migliore ordine, ricorrette sull'edizione fiorentina ed illustrate dal prof. G. Rosini*, Pisa, Capurro, 1821–32, 33 vols., Vol. xx (these are the same letters as are printed in the *Infarinato secondo* above).

RONCHINI, L., *Lettere d'uomini illustri conservate in Parma nel R. Archivio di Stato*, Parma, Reale Tipografia, 1853.

ZAMBRINI, F., *Lettere di Luigi Alamanni, Benedetto Varchi, Vincenzo Borghini, Lionardo Salviati, e d'altri autori citati dagli Accademici della Crusca* (Lettere d'uomini illustri del sec. XVI), Lucca, Franchi e Maionchi, 1853(54) (redated by Parodi to 1883, *Una lettera inedita*, 'in base al volume reperito nel Fondo Piancastelli della Biblioteca Comunale di Forlì'. But the date of the Bodleian copy is 1853).

FANFANI, P., *Lettere precettive di eccellenti scrittori*, Naples, Rondinelli, 1857.

CAMPORI, G., 'Il cavalier Lionardo Salviati e Alfonso II duca di Ferrara' in *Atti e memorie dei RR. Deputati di Storia Patria per le Prov. Mod. e Parm.*, Vol. vii, pp. 143 ff., Modena, Vincenzi, 1874.

VERZONE, C., *Le rime burlesche edite e inedite di Antonfrancesco Grazzini, detto il Lasca*, ed. C. Verzone, Florence, 1882.

BERTOLOTTI, A., 'Giacomo Buoncompagni e Lionardo Salviati riformatore del *Decameron*', *Bibliofilo*, Bologna, Anno IV (1883), No. 11.

—— 'Una lettera del castratore del *Decameron*', *Bibliofilo*, Bologna, Anno VI (1885), No. 3.

Le carte strozziane del R. Archivio di Stato in Firenze. Inventario, Serie prima, 2 vols., Florence, Tip. Galileiana, 1884, Vol. i.

PASQUAZI, S., *Rinascimento ferrarese*, Caltanisetta–Rome, Sciascia, 1957.

—— *Poeti estensi del Rinascimento*, Florence, Le Monnier, 1966.

PARODI, S., 'Una lettera inedita del Salviati', *Studi di filologia italiana*, xxvii (1969), 147–74.

Translations

Delle lodi della Regina Giovanna d'Austria (translation of the Latin of Pier Vettori, said to have appeared anonymously in 1566). Printed in *Primo libro delle orazioni*, 1575, and in *Opere*, 1810.

Texts edited by Salviati

La Gostanza, commedia di Girolamo Razzi, nuovamente data in luce, Florence, Giunti, 1565.
    Ded. lett. 2.2.1564 (i.e. '65) to Isabella Medici Orsini, duchessa di Bracciano.

Lo specchio di vera penitenza del reverendo maestro Jacopo Passavanti Fiorentino dell'Ordine de' Predicatori, Florence, Sermartelli, 1585.

There is another edition of this work, based on Salviati's text but manifestly not edited by him, being very incorrect:

Lo specchio di vera penitenza del R. M. Jacopo Passavanti dell'Ordine de' Predicatori. Seconda edizione revista in Firenze e migliorata con un testo di Giovambatista Reti [sic] e con uno di Bernardo Ravanzati [sic], Venice, Pietro Marinelli, 1586.

APPENDIX B

NUMBERED LIST OF THE ORATIONS OF LIONARDO SALVIATI

WITH DETAILS OF FIRST AND SUCH SUBSEQUENT EDITIONS OF INDIVIDUAL ORATIONS AS HAVE BEEN ENCOUNTERED

I. *Orazione prima confortatoria in morte di Don Garzia de' Medici*, Firenze, Giunti, 1562 (i.e. '63).
Ded. lett. Jan. 1562 (i.e. '63) to Paolo Giordano Orsini.

II. *Orazione seconda confortatoria in morte di Don Garzia de' Medici*, Firenze, Giunti, 1562 (i.e. '63).
Ded. lett. (undated) to 'Giulio de' Medici e i valorosissimi cavalieri di Santo Stefano'. (This is the real *Orazione seconda*: the one published in later editions as such is in reality the *Orazione terza*.)

III. *Orazione terza confortatoria in morte di Don Garzia de' Medici*, Firenze, Giunti, 1562 (i.e. '63).
Ded. lett. 16.2.62 (i.e. '63) to Jacopo Salviati. 2nd edn., Florence, Giunti, 1563.

IV. *Orazione di Lionardo Salviati nella quale si dimostra la fiorentina favella e i fiorentini autori essere a tutte l'altre lingue, così antiche come moderne, e a tutti gli altri scrittori di qual si vuol lingua di gran lunga superiori*, Firenze, Giunti, 1564.
Ded. lett. 30.4.64 to Don Francesco de' Medici. Repr. (i) With *Il Cavalcanti overo la difesa dell'Anticrusca* of Paolo Beni, Padua, Martini, 1611; (ii) with the same, Padua, Bolzetta, 1664.

V. *Orazione in morte di Michelangelo Buonarroti*, Firenze, Figliuoli di Lorenzo Torrentino, 1564.
Ded. lett. to Piero Carnesecchi, 19.9.1564.

VI. *Orazione prima nel prendere il suo consolato.* There was no separate edition of this oration. It was printed in the *Primo libro delle orazioni*, Firenze, Marco Peri e Valente Panizzi, 1567.
Ded. lett. to Molto Mag.co M. Bernardo Vecchietti.

VII. *Orazione seconda nel prendere il suo consolato*, Firenze, Figliuoli di Lorenzo Torrentino, 1566.
Ded. lett. to Don Silvano Razzi.

VIII. *Orazione recitata nel lasciare il suo consolato.* There was no
separate edition of this oration. It was printed in *Primo libro
delle orazioni,* Firenze, Marco Peri e Valente Panizzi, 1567.
Ded. lett. to Don Vincenzo Borghini.

IX.   *Nell'esequie di M. Benedetto Varchi,* Firenze, Giunti, 1566.
Ded. lett. 8.2.65 (i.e. '66) to Mons. Lorenzo Lenzi (Poggiali and
Gamba both say that this edition is 'senza nome di stampatore'
but editions which I have examined clearly state the Giunti as
the printers).

X.   *Orazione intorno all'Incoronazione del Serenissimo Cosimo de'
Medici, Gran Duca di Toscana,* Firenze, Sermartelli, 1570.
Ded. lett. 1.4.70 to Jacopo Sesto d'Aragona d'Appiano, Signore
di Piombino.

XI.   *Orazione del cavalier Lionardo Salviati, recitata da lui in
Pisa il dì 22 di Aprile, 1571 al Capitolo Generale della Religione
dei Cavalieri di Santo Stefano,* Firenze, Giunti, 1571.
Ded. lett. 22.4.71 'al Serenissimo Don Francesco de' Medici'.
2nd edn., Florence, Marescotti, 1572.

XII.   *Orazione funerale del cavalier Lionardo Salviati, da lui pubblica-
mente recitata nell'esequie del Serenissimo Cosimo de' Medici,*
etc. Firenze, Sermartelli, 1574.
Ded. lett. 12.5.74 to 'il Serenissimo Granduca Francesco de'
Medici'. 2nd edn., Florence, Sermartelli, 1574; 3rd edn.,
Florence, Giunti, 1574.

XIII. *Orazione in lode della Giustizia.* There was no separate edition
of this work. It was printed in *Il primo libro delle orazioni del
cavalier Lionardo Salviati,* Firenze, Giunti, 1575.
Ded. lett. to Francesco Albani.

XIV.   *Orazione in lode della religione.* (Publication as No. XIII.)
Ded. lett. to Giulio Salviati.

XV.   *Orazione in lode della religione militare.* (Publication as Nos.
XIII and XIV.)
Ded. lett. to Bartolomeo Concino.

XVI.   *Orazione funerale del cavalier Lionardo Salviati delle lodi di
Pier Vettori senatore e Accademico Fiorentino. Recitata pubbli-
camente in Firenze, per ordine della Fiorentina Accademia, nella
Chiesa di Santo Spirito, il dì 27 di gennaio, 1585,* etc. Firenze,
Filippo e Jacopo Giunti, 1585 (i.e. '86).
Ded. lett. to Francesco Panicarola, 27.1.85 (i.e. '86).

XVII. *Orazione delle lodi di Don Luigi Cardinal d'Este, fatta dal
cavalier Lionardo Salviati nella morte di quel signore,* Firenze,
Padovani, 1587.
Ded. lett. 2.2.86 (i.e. '87) to Henry II of France.

XVIII. *Orazione del cavalier Lionardo Salviati delle lodi di Donno Alfonso d'Este, recitata nell' Accademia di Ferrara per la morte di quel signore,* Ferrara, Vittorio Baldini, 1587. Ded. lett. 22.12.87 to Don Cesare d'Este. 2nd edn., Florence, 1587.

The following, some of which have been mentioned above, contain collections of Salviati's orations:

(1) *Il primo libro delle orazioni,* Firenze, Panizzi, 1567 (Nos. VI, VII, and VIII).
Ded. lett. 3.5.1567 'Allo Ill.mo e Rev.mo Monsignore Il Cardinal de' Monti'.

(2) *Il primo libro delle orazioni del cavalier Lionardo Salviati,* Firenze, Giunti, 1575 (Nos. I, III, IV, V, IX, VI, VII, VIII, X, XIII, XIV, XV, XI, XII—in that order).
Ded. lett. 25.11.1574 from the editor, Don Silvano Razzi, 'Al R.mo et Ill.mo Monsig., il Sig. Antonmaria Vescovo de' Salviati'.

(3) *Opere,* 1810, Vol. v—as in the *Primo libro,* etc., of 1575, in the same order.

(4) *Prose fiorentine raccolte dallo Smarrito Accademico della Crusca,* Firenze, Tartini & Franchi, contains orations as follows:

(i) No. I (in part 1, Vol. vi, 1731); (ii) No. XI (in part 1, Vol. ii, 1716); (iii) No. XVI (in part 1, Vol. iii, 1719).

The *Orazioni di diversi uomini illustri, raccolte da Francesco Sansovino,* Venezia, Altobello Salicata, 1584, is said to contain some orations by Salviati, but the present author has been unable to determine which.

APPENDIX C

ALPHABETICAL REFERENCE LIST OF THE POEMS, PUBLISHED AND UNPUBLISHED, OF SALVIATI

WITH INDICATIONS OF (I) THEIR POSITIONS IN THE MAIN
MANUSCRIPTS, (II) PRINTED EDITIONS

ABBREVIATIONS

A. *Type of composition*: C = Canzone; Ca = Capitolo; M = Madrigal; S = Sonnet; Se = Sestina; St = Stanze; Sc = 'Sonetto caudato'.
B. *Printed editions*: (For full details see Appendix B). C = Crescimbeni; G II = *Oraz. sec. in lode di Don Garzia* (1563); G III = *Orazione terza in lode di Don Garzia* (1563); M(c) = Manzoni, *Capitolo* (1871); M = Manzoni, *Rime* (1871); P = Poggiali; Sa = *Saggio di Rime* (1825); T = Trucchi; Z = Zambrini.
C. *Manuscripts*: (For details see Bibliography) M = Magl.; N = Nap.; R = Ricc.; P = Parm.

No.	First line	Type of comp.	MSS. numbered pages				Pr. edn.
			M	R	N	P	
1	A questa amara pioggia	M	39	38	—	—	T, Z, M
2	A te Tirinto suo, formoso, e saggio	S	8	9	9	—	M
3	Aura, che 'n picciol cerchio asconde, e serra,	S	74	73	—	—	G II, M
4	Buonanni, questo è stato un passerotto	S	211	—	—	—	M
5	Canigian mio, ch'a sì gran corso i passi	S	82	81	—	—	G III, M
6	Chiuse valli, alti monti, ombrosi boschi	S	40	39	—	—	M
7	Colli, onde, Marte, la tua santa gesta (*Nap.* Son questi i sette colli, onde superba)	S	84	2	2*	—	T, M
8	Come all'hor ch'al gran Rio germe novello	S	210	—	—	—	M
9	Come, ferendo il sole onda, o rugiada	S	46	45	—	—	M
10	Come in lucido opposto	M	73	72	—	—	M
11	Come languendo all or, pietade, e zelo	S	79	78	—	—	G III, M
12	Come le vene sugge	M	34	33	—	—	Z, M
13	Come morendo il fral, dritta, e spedita	S	83*	82	—	—	G III, M
14	Cotale ha natura angue	M	35	34	—	—	Z, M

No.	First line	Type of comp.	M	R	N	P	Pr. edn.
15	Da questo al surger mio terreno avverso	S	13	14	—	—	M
16	D'Arno gentil su la fiorita sponda	Se	5	6	6	—	Z, M
17	Deh, qual sovr'al bell'Arno, entr'al bel grembo	M	57	56	44	—	M
18	Deh, sicuro foss'io	M	33	32	—	—	T, Z, M
19	Deh, venite, donne, a vedere	C	229	—	—	—	Lond. 1831
20	Del sommo ben mentr'io	M	41	40	—	—	T, Z, M
21	Donna gentil, che con la greca a paro	S	9	10	10	—	T, M
22	Donna gentil, che 'l tuo fattore e nostro	S	49	48	36	—	M
23	Donna vie più che bella honesta, e bella	S	47	46	34	—	T, M
24	D'ostro tirio fulgente	M	216	—	—	—	T, M
25	Dunque è pur ver, che 'l più gradito, e santo	S	16	17	17	—	M
26	Dunque il mio ricco, antico	M	215	—	—	—	T, M
27	Ecco, che questo mio terrestre velo	S	37	36	—	—	M
28	Ed io piansi, Bernardo, e tal n'ho duolo	S	81	80	—	—	G III, M
29	Era il breve dì mio nell'alba ancora	S	25	25	26	—	M
30	Fabrizio, io 'l pur dirò, mio cor sovente	S	21	21	22	—	M
31	Fiume sovran, ch'a noi veloce porti	S	4	5	5	—	M
32	Già fu ch'io desiai d'argento e d'ostro	S	1	1	1	—	M
33	Già voce desiai dolce, e soave	S	30	29	31	—	M
34	Giovinetto signor, ch'Italia intenta	S	15	16	16	—	M
35	Il cor doglioso, e lagrimosi i rai	S	31	30	32	—	M
36	Indarno oscuri, e veli	M	22	22	23	—	T, M
37	Lappole a i vaghi fiori, a i giorni gai	S	72	71	—	—	M
38	Lasso, qual sento, oimè, che 'n questi rivi	S	3	4	4	—	P, M
39	Le crespe trecce bionde	M	56	55	43	—	Z, M
40	Luce, ch'apposta le mie luci avvivi	M	14	15	15	—	T, P, Z, M
41	Ne pompa, che di fuor luce, e risplende	S	—	—	—	360	(unpub.)
42	Nero, ch'al nome tuo contrario chiudi	S	10	11	11	—	M
43	Non per sottrarmi al dolce peso, ond'io	S	18	19	19	—	M
44	O di terrestri Dii	M	28	28	29	—	Z, M
45	Or ch'io spero, Filippo, di finire	Ca	218	—	—	—	T, P, M(c), M
46	Padre, mentre, ch'io vissi in parte ov'io	S	48	47	35	—	M
47	Pianta gentil, che del vezzoso Aprile	S	32	31	33	—	M
48	Potrai tu chiaro sol l'altero nido	S	2	3	3	—	M
49	Quando e' s'udì, che Maestro Maccario	Sc	217	—	—	—	M
50	Quando il possente, che 'l più grave pondo	S	42	41	—	—	M

No.	First line	Type of comp.	M	R	N	P	Pr. edn.
51	Quando io veggio, signor, di sì diverse	S	29*	75	30	358	(unpub.)
52	Quanto sostien la terra, e quanto asconde	St	69	69	57	—	M
53	Questa, ch'alfin dopo dannoso, e rio	S	11	12	12	—	M
54	Questa il suo figlio Amore	C	67	66	54	—	M
55	Questi all'empio consiglio	C	51	50	38	—	M, Z
56	Questi, ch'hor ferro affrena	C	68	67	55	—	M, Sa
57	Quest'onda Apollo in se pietosa accolse	S	26	26	27	—	M
58	Razzi, che quel di noi che men n'abbella	S	78	77	—	—	G III, M
59	Razzi tu pur ten vai; conforto solo	S	24	24	25	—	M
60	Sacro, saggio signor, che 'l corso avanzi	S	—	—	—	359	(unpub.)
61	Saggio signor, cui ne' primi anni elesse	S	17	18	18	—	M
62	S'a tanti segni, e tante	M	36	35	—	—	T, Z, M
63	Scrolli, pur, se gli aggrada, e sfrondi, e schiante	S	44	43	—	—	M
64	Se di senno, e virtù, Vettorio, quanta	S	23	23	24	—	M
65	S'egual fosse alla mia	M	38	37	—	—	T, M
66	Se questa ardente mia fiamma vorace	S	12	13	13	—	M
67	Se questo invido gielo, e questa ria	S	20	20	21	—	M
68	Sicome all'hor, che'l suo viaggio ha torto	S	45	44	—	—	M
69	Sì del mio buon voler s'appaghi, e goda	S	27	27	28	—	M
70	S'io gusti un dì, Signor, securo il frutto	S (a)	77	76	20	—	M
	(Nap. S'io goda un dì de' miei disiri il frutto)	(b)	19*				
71	Spadin, parte di me, parte cotanta	S	80	79	—	—	G III, M
72	Tal fu lo stral, tal fu l'acerba doglia	S	50	49	37	—	C, M
73	Tal'ha vezzoso, e bello	M	43	42	—	—	T, M
74	Varchi, il cui chiaro dir gradito è quanto	S	75	74	—	—	G, III M
75	Varchi, Margite, e chi con esso giostra	S	—	—	—	—	G III, M
76	Vien pur sinistro, e dall'occaso, e piene	S	—	—	14	—	M

An asterisk indicates poems which were subsequently crossed out.

(a) No. 17 includes all the *Intermedii* for the comedy *Il Granchio*.
(b) The following poems are *mascherate*: 39, 52, 54, 55, 56.
(c) First lines are those of the MS. Magl. except in those few cases in which the composition is not to be found in that manuscript.

BIBLIOGRAPHY

A. MS. MATERIAL

I. MANUSCRIPT WORKS BY SALVIATI (EXCLUDING LETTERS)

Asterisk indicates works still unpublished

a. Poetics

i. Firenze: Bib. Naz. Cent. Cod. Magl. VII, 87

* *Traduzione, parafrasi e commento alla poetica d'Aristotile*

XVI cent. Fols. 393. Fol. 369 has the *privilegio* 'Die xxvi Januarii MDLXXXV' and at the end '28 gennaio 1586'. This MS. is described by the catalogues as autograph, but in fact it is not.

A note on the MS. dated 24.7.1931 and signed 't. l.' runs 'Non è di mano del Salviati: autografe di lui sono le postille (non tutte) correzioni e aggiunte (cfr. per es. le cc. 14, 18, 48, 49 ecc.)'. The hand is A.

'After the main body of the MS, these additions: Fols. 373–79 repeat fols. 1–7, on the title of the work. Fols. 380–85 repeat fols. 8–20ᵛ with some differences. Fols. 386–87 "Lionardo Salviati a' lettori". Fols. 390–92 repetition of same, apparently an earlier draft. Two fols. missing between fols. 381 and 382 of this MS, are found in MS II, II, 10, where they are included as fols. 27 & 28.' (This is a quotation from Weinberg, *A History*, ii. 1147.)

The hand A of this MS. is probably that of Fabrizio Caramelli, Salviati's secretary, and will thus be referred to in future as 'Hand A'.

ii. Firenze: Bib. Naz. Cent. Cod. Magl. VII, 715 Autograph

Della poetica lettura terza

XVI cent. Fols. 26. 14·5 by 20 cm. Mod. num. 1–22 rect. only, plus 1 blank unnum. at beginning and 3 blank at end of which 1st and 3rd num. 24 and 25.

fol. 1 (unnum.) 'G. 204' (mod. hand.) and 'D. 715' (old hand) and in pencil in mod. hand 'VII Leon. Salviati, della Poetica let. 3'.

fol. 29 'Al molto Mag.co e Nobiliss.o Sig.e il S.r Cavaliere Gaddi.' Let. to Niccolò Gaddi follows, beginning 'I cortesi modi e gentili . . .' ending '. . . V.S. da qui avanti tenga per cosa sua e viva felice. Di Firenze il p.o. di L.o MDLXVI. Di V.ra Sig.ria, Aff.mo Lionardo Salviati.'

fols. 3ʳ–23ʳ. The treatise, beginning 'Del Trattato della Poetica di Lionardo Salviati Lettura Terza da esso pubbl. recitata nella Fior. Accademia

nel Cons. di ms. Baccio Valori. La passata Domenica fu da me mos-
tro . . .' ending 'ringraziandovi al solito della gratissima attenzione.
Il fine.'

Source, Gaddi 804.

iii. Firenze: Bib. Naz. Cent. Cod. Magl. VII, 307

*Della poetica lezzion prima

XVI cent. fols. 41, 17 cm by 22 cm. fols. 1–2 and 41 unnumbered, fols.
3–40 mod. num. (recto only) 1–38.

fol. 1 (unnum.) 'D. 307' in mod. hand in pencil 'VII Salviati, della
Poetica. Autogr. 1564.' In fact the MS. is not autogr.

fols. 3–4^v. Lett. to D. Francesco de' Medici beginning 'Allo Ill.mo et
Ecc.mo Sig.re il Sig.r Don Francesco de' Medici, Principe di Firenze e
di Siena suo Sig.re: Invece di ringraziare . . .' ending 'Viva V. E. Ill.ma
eternamente felice. Di Firenze a' xij di Dicembre MDLxiiij. Di V. E.
Ill.ma S.re humilissimo, Lionardo Salviati.'

fol. 5^r 'Del Trattato della poetica di Lionardo Salviati allo Ill.mo e
Ecc.mo Sig.re il Sig.r Don Francesco de' Medici Principe di Firenze
e di Siena suo Signore, Lezzion prima.'

fols. 5^r–40^v the treatise beginning 'La bontà di quel secolo . . .' ending
'. . . i vostri meriti della mia opera sodisfare.'

Hand unknown.

b. Poems

Firenze: Bib. Naz. Cent. Cod. Magl. VII, 306

i. Rime di Lionardo Salviati e di altri a lui

XVI. cent. Fols. 227, fols. 1–2 and 226–7 unnum. Fols. 3–225^r mod.
num., recto and verso, 1–445. Blank are fols. 1, 45^r–74^v (pp. 85–144),
83^r–104^v (pp. 161–204), 106^r–v (pp. 207–8), 121^r–139^v (pp. 237–74),
141^r–v (pp. 277–8), 142^v (p. 280), 151^v (p. 298), 159^r–190^v (pp. 313–76),
193^r–v (pp. 381–2), 214^r–224^v (pp. 423–44), and fols. 226–7.

fol. 2^r Title: 'Poesie del Cav. Lionardo Salviati, originali, di Sua mano
scritte.'

fol. 2^v 'Tavole generali de' componimenti di q.sto libro.'

fols. 3^r–44^v (pp. 1–84) 'Rime' of Salviati.

fols. 75^r–79^r (pp. 145–53) Index to 'Rime'.

fols. 79^v–82^v (pp. 154–60) 'Proposte e risposte di diversi a Lionardo Salviati.'

fols. 105^r–v (pp. 205–6) Index of 'Proposte . . .', etc.

fol. 107^r (p. 209) Title: 'Rime in burla del Cavalier Salviati.'

fols. 107^v–120^v (pp. 210–36) 'Rime in Burla' of Salviati.

fols. 140^r–v (pp. 275–6) Index of 'Rime in burla'.

fol. 142^r (p. 279) Title: 'Rime di diversi a Lionardo Salviati.'

fols. 143^r–151^r (pp. 281–97) 'Rime di diversi.'

fols. 152ʳ–158ᵛ (pp. 299–312) 'Rime di diversi' (continued).

fols. 191ʳ–192ᵛ (pp. 337–80) 'Tavole di rime di diversi a Lionardo Salviati.'

fol. 194ʳ (p. 383) Title: 'I CORBI del Varchi e d'altri a Lionardo Salviati.'

fols. 194ᵛ–195ᵛ (pp. 384–6) Ded. Lett. of the 'Corbi', beginning 'Mandovi m. Annibale queste due nidiate . . .' ending 'Di ciascun vostro desiderio vi contenti chi può. Di Firenze il dì . . . di . . . 1564.'

fols. 196ʳ–211ʳ (pp. 387–417) The 'Corbi'.

fol. 211ᵛ (p. 418) Index of the 'Corbi'.

fol. 212ʳ (p. 419) Title: 'CARMINA ad Leonardum Salviatum vel de Leonardo Salviato.'

fols. 212ᵛ–213ᵛ (pp. 420–2) The 'Carmina'.

fol. 225ᵛ (p. 445) Index of the 'Carmina'.

The MS. is *not* aut. It is in hand A. There are aut. corrections on pp. 53–4.

ii. Firenze: Bib. Riccardiana, Cod. Ricc. 2849

Rime serie del cav. Lionardo Salviati (in a volume of miscellaneous works) XVI cent. Fols. 53; fols. 1 and 53 unnumbered: fols. 2–52 mod. num. (recto and verso) 1–102. Fols. 43ʳ, 48ʳ, 53ʳ⁻ᵛ are blank.

fol. 1 (unnum.) Lett. to Lodovico Capponi, beginning 'Al nobilissimo et virtuoso m. Ludovico Capponi. Io non so dirvi mess. Ludovico mio . . .' ending '. . . amatemi come fate e vivete felice, Di Firenze alli 18 di Agosto 1575. Di V. S. mag.ca Affezionatissimo, Lionardo Salviati.'

fols. 2ʳ–48ᵛ Poems of Lionardo Salviati.

fols. 49ʳ–52ᵛ Index of the poems.

The MS. is in hand A.

iii. Napoli: Bib. Naz. Cent. Vitt. Em. II, Cod. XIII, D. 52

Rime del cav. Lionardo Salviati

XVI cent. Fols. 36: fols. 1 and 33–6 unnum.; fols. 2ʳ–32ʳ num. (recto and verso) 3–63. Fol. 26 mutilated.

fol. 1ʳ⁻ᵛ Lett. to Ludovico Capponi, beginning 'Al nobilissimo et virtuoso m. Ludovico Capponi. Io non so dirvi, mess. Ludovico mio . . .' ending 'amatemi come fate e vivete felice, Di Firenze alli 18 di Agosto 1575. Di V. S. Mag.ca Affezionatissimo, Lionardo Salviati.'

fols. 2ʳ–32ʳ 'Rime' of Salviati.

fols. 33ʳ–36ʳ (unnum.) Index of 'rime'.

iv. Parma: Biblioteca Palatina:

1. Cod. Pal. 557, Vol. iii

Raccolta di poeti italiani: Rime volgari del '500. Raccolta già spettante al Beccadelli

*Sec. XVI fols. 358–9 Poesie di Lionardo Salviati.

(a) fol. 358 'Quando io veggio, signor, di sì diverse'
(b) fol. 359 'Sacro, saggio, Signor, che 'l corso avanzi'

2. *Carteggio di Lucca* (*Autografi Palatini*) Scatola 4

(*c*) fol. 360 'Ne pompa, che di fuor luce, e risplende'
(*a*) unknown hand; (*b*) and (*c*) aut.

v. Firenze: Bib. Naz. Cent. Cod. Pal. 1107, Vol. x, No. 27

Raccolta di poesie volgari (XVIII cent.)

p. 176 sonnet 'Un galantuomo pose sotto il letto' doubtfully attributed
to Salviati.

vi. The following are collections of *Poesie volgari* in which figures the
Canzone in lode del pino:

(*a*) Firenze: Bib. Naz. Cent. Cod. Pal. 1107, Vol. xxvi, (XVIII cent.)
pp. 171–5.
(*b*) Firenze: Bib. Naz. Cent. Cod. Magl. VII, 633 (XVI–XVII cent.)
pp. 52 ff.
(*c*) Firenze: Bib. Naz. Cent. Cod. Magl. VII, 343 (XVI cent.) pp.
323–7.
(*d*) Firenze: Bib. Naz. Cent. Cod. Magl. II, IV, 690 (XVIII cent.).
(*e*) Firenze: Bib. Naz. Cent. Cod. Magl. VII, 877 (XVII cent.).

None of these is aut.

c. The 'grammatichetta'

i. Firenze: Bib. Naz. Cent. Cod. Pal. 727

Regole della toscana favella

XVII cent. Fols. 54: fols. 1–3 and 52–4 unnum.; fols. 4–51 num. (recto
only) 1–48; fols. 1ʳ–2ᵛ, 35ᵛ, and 52ʳ–54ᵛ are blank.

fol. 3 (unnum.) 'Si contiene in questo codice quant'appresso. I. Regole
inedite della toscana favella del Cav. Lionardo Salviati. II Osservazioni
intorno alla Toscana favella di Giambattista Strozzi.'

fol. 1ʳ 'Regole della toscana favella del Sig.r Caval.re Lionardo Salviati,
Accd.co Fiorentino fondatore dell'Accademia della Crusca di Fiorenza,
et nella d.a Accademia l'Infarinato. Copiate da quelle che si trovano in
mano del Caval. Giovanni Guidacci Accad.co fior.no l'anno 1622 da me
Vincenzio Fioravanti dottor di legge et Accademico fiorentino.'

fols. 2ʳ–35ʳ Salviati, 'Regole della Toscana favella', beginning 'Le parti
del favellare. Dieci sono . . .' ending 'delle cui parti senza più oltre
allungarmi, sia qui terminato il ragionamento.'

fol. 35ʳ (Hand of Fioravanti) 'A dì 30 d'Agosto dell'anno 1622 in Firenze,
Vincenzio di Domenico Fioravanti, Dottor di leggie.'

fols. 37ʳ–48ᵛ G. B. Strozzi, 'Osservazioni intorno alla toscana favella.'
The text of the MS. is in the hand of Fioravanti. Some corrections in
an unknown second hand.

ii. Firenze: Bib. Naz. Cent. Cod. Magl. IV, 65

Grammatica italiana

XVII cent. Fols. 67. 21·5 by 15 cm. 64 written; fols. 1, 2, and 67 unnum.; fols. 3–66 num. (recto and verso) 1–128.

fol. 2ʳ (unnum.) 'D. 65 Grammatica toscana del Cav.re Salviati.a 1. Osservazioni intorno alla lingua toscana di Gio. Batt.a Strozzi. a 93. Di Luigi del Senatore Carlo Strozzi, 1677.'

fols. 3ʳ–47ᵛ (num. 1–90) Salviati, 'Regole della toscana favella', beginning 'Le parti del favellare . . .' ending 'sia qui terminato il ragionamento.'

fols. 49ʳ–64ᵛ (num. 93–128) G. B. Strozzi, 'Osservazioni intorno alla nostra lingua.'

Hand unknown.

d. The 'Discorso' on Tacitus

i. Roma: Bib. Apostolica Vatic. Cods. Barb. Lat. 5337 and 5338 (Old Num. LVIII, 16 and 17)

XVI cent. They are two of seven volumes containing mostly MSS. copied by Cesare Conti.

fols. 389–95 First copy of the 'Discorso' (Barb. Lat. 5337).
fols. 154–69 Second copy of 'Discorso' (Barb. Lat. 5338).

MS. 5337 bears the dedication 'Al Duca di N' and 5338 'al duca di Sora'. At the end, in both cases, figure the words 'Monsignor Salviati'.

ii. Roma: Bib. Apost. Vat. Cod. Chigi M. VIII, 165

XVI–XVII cent. A collection of MSS. entitled 'Raccolta di vari sermoni in morte di vari animali.'

fols. 103ʳ–108ᵛ have a very careless transcription of the 'Discorso'.

iii. Roma: Bib. Apost. Vat. Cod. Urb. Lat. 852.

Late XVI or early XVII cent.

fol. 161ʳ in a different hand from the rest: 'Discorso d'un Fiorentino sopra la libertà di Roma nel p.o libro di Cornelio Tacito.'

fol. 161ᵛ, in a second hand, list of chapter-headings of the 'Discorso', numbered 1–10.

fol. 162ʳ 'Discorso d'un Fiorentino della libertà di Roma sopra Cornelio Tacito nel primo libro. . . . Discorso primo.'

fols. 162ʳ–171ʳ the 'Discorso' in a fine calligraphic hand, without abbreviations.

All chapter-headings separate from the text, in slightly smaller writing and numbered. Chapters carefully distinguished.

Hand unknown.

268 BIBLIOGRAPHY

e. The *'Ribellione di Fiandra'*

i. Roma: Bib. Apost. Vat. Arch. Buoncompagni–Ludovisi Cod. F. 27

Discorso sopra la ribellione di Fiandra

XVI cent. In a collection of treatises mostly political. The fols. 32–47 (mod. num). which concern us here are loose, and can be detached from the body of the MS.

(*a*) fols. 32^r–39^r, complete copy of 'Discorso', beginning 'Coloro che niegano . . .' ending '. . . ardentemente combatteranno.'

(*b*) fols. 40^r–47^r, another complete copy of the same work with identical beginning and ending.

Each copy has the title: 'Discorso del Cavalier Salviati all'Ecc.mo S.r Jacopo Buoncompagni.' Apart from small omissions the two copies are complete.

The two copies have a number of minor variants, and are not merely both copies of a single original.

The hand is 'A'.

ii. Roma: Bib. Apost. Vat. Cod. Barb. Lat. 5242

Sec. XVI. the 'Discorso' occupies fols. 16, being fols. 129^v–144^v according to old num. on recto only, and fols. 35^v to 50^v according to mod. num. on recto only.

Apart from slight copying errors this text is identical with that of the first copy of the Cod. Buon.–Lud. F. 27.

Hand unknown.

iii. Roma: Bib. Angelica 2288.

XIX cent. from the MS. collection of Luigi Cardinali. fols. 12. The copyist states at the beginning of the MS. that he is taking the text from the Vatican Codices, noting the variants (i.e. Buon. Lud. F. 27).

iv. Bologna: Bib. Universitaria, Vol. v, No. 6, Cod. 1117

XVI cent., in a 'Raccolta di relazioni e lettere'. Fols. 42: numbered (mod.) recto only, 1–42.

The text derives from copy 1 (pp. 32–9) of the MS. Buon.–Lud. F. 27, but it is a corrupt text especially from the orthographical point of view.

Hand A.

f. **Spoglio di libri*

Firenze: Bib. Riccardiana, Cod. Ricc. 2197

XVI cent. Fols. 133, numbered mod. printed 1–133, recto only: numbered fols. 10–133 in old num. 1–247.

fols. 1–9 (mod. num.) Indices of contents.

fol. 1ʳ 'Tavola de' titoli de' libri della miglior favella, cioè, dall'anno 1300, ò poco addietro, sino all'anno 1400: ordinata secondo l'ordine de' lor gradi: della quale i primi numeri significano i detti lor gradi, e gli ultimi le facce del presente quaderno, nel quale son copiate le cose più notabili dei detti libri.'

fols. 10–133 Extracts from the works listed. Many individual words and phrases are underlined throughout the volume.

Hand A.

g. *Notes and corrections to the '*Pastor fido*'

Ferrara: Bib. Ariostea. Cod. Ferr. Cl. I. H. 276

Osservazioni sul Pastor Fido

XVI cent. Fols. 42 with mod. num. (recto only) 76–117.

fol. 76ʳ 'La tragicommedia di G. B. Guarini: Censure e correzioni del Sig.r Lionardo Salviati.'

fols. 77ʳ–77ᵛ Lett. from Guarini to Salviati. Beginning 'L'honore che V. S. mi ha ultimamente fatto . . .' ending 'et col fin le bacio le mani. Di Ferrara 14 luglio 1586.'

fols. 80ʳ–81ʳ Lett. Sal. to Guarini. Beginning 'Ho letto tre volte la pastorale . . .' ending 'le prego intera felicità. Di Firenze addì 8 di ottobre 1586. Lionardo Salviati.'

fols. 82ʳ–109ᵛ 'Correzioni' of Salviati, ordered Act by Act, Scene by Scene, and line by line.

fols. 110ʳ–117ᵛ 'Opposizioni' of Guarini and 'Repliche' by Salviati. This section also has marginal notes in the hand of Giovan Filippo Magnanini.

Almost entirely in hand A with very few aut. notes by Salviati.

h. Proverbi toscani

Ferrara, Bib. Ariost. Cod. Cl. I, 394

Raccolta di proverbi toscani

XVI cent. Fols. 287. 21 cm by 14 cm. The first 13 fols. and the last 12 are blank, and there are other groups of pages left blank after each section of the written MS. to enable the author to enlarge any section. There is no complete numbering. The original numbering (which goes up to 335) takes into account only the written pages.

The proverbs are grouped alphabetically by the first letter of the phrase, but there is no attempt at further alphabetical order within the letter-groups.

fol. 2ᵛ bears the name 'Tassoni F.' and some 'Aggiunte di Giovanfilippo Magnanini'.

There are some corrections and additions in what is probably the same hand, and each group has additions and marginal notes by Magnanini.

The text (original) is in hand A

The 'Bozza di un discorso accademico sopra la ginnastica degli antichi' contained (along, in fact, with two complete transcriptions of the work) in Cod. Magl. Cl. XXVIII, 6 of the Bib. Naz. Cent., Fir., is almost certainly not by Salviati.

2. OTHER MANUSCRIPTS CONSULTED FROM WHICH INFORMATION WAS EXTRACTED

BOLOGNA

Biblioteca dell'Archiginnasio: Cod. B. 233, 'Poesie di Mons. Lod. Beccadelli', fol. 86, sonnet to Salviati.

FERRARA

Biblioteca Comunale Ariostea: Vol. Misc. Est. 343: 2, copy of Salviati's *Orazione seconda in lode di Don Garzia* with marginal notes by Jac. Corbinelli and attached to the MS. draft of Salviati's letter to Corbinelli.

FLORENCE

Biblioteca Nazionale Centrale: Magl. Cl. XXV, 595, pt. 7, 'I Salviati, notizie di questa casa'; *Magl. II, II 140,* 'Informazione' (information, largely erroneous, on the heirs of Salviati and the whereabouts of his *Poetics*); *Magl. II, II, 109,* list of the works of Salviati; *Magl. VII, 600,* 'Carmi sacri d'occasione: Ad Leonardum Salviatium in Benedicti Varchi obitum.' *Magl. VII, 81,* 'Zibaldone di Girolamo da Sommaia' (esp. for information on the cav. Niccolò Gaddi); *Magl. VIII, 1393,* correspondence of Borghini with the Maestro del Sacro Palazzo for the correction of the *Decameron*; *Magl. VI, 63,* exchange of letters between Salviati and Panicarola; *Magl. VII, 466,* 'Copie lacunose di lettere di Belisario Bulgarini'; *Magl. II, IV, I,* 'Libro di capitoli, leggi e composizioni dell'Accademia degli Umidi di Firenze'; *Magl. IX, 64,* 'Vita di Pier Vettori'; *Magl. VI, 168,* fols. 50ʳ–75ʳ, Giovanni de' Bardi, 'Difese dell'Ariosto.' **Autog. Pal. VII, 83,* Lett. Sal. to Bianca Cappello (aut.); *Pal. 1037* 'Costituzione dell'Accademia Fiorentina'.

Archivio di Stato: Notarile Moderno, 1186, 10 (also marked *1149*), 'Protocolli di Ser Francesco Parenti' (for Salviati's will); *4532* and *4533,* 'Ser Raffaello Godenzi, Atti dal 1573 al 1576' (for transactions in property, lawsuits); *Decima Granducale, 53 (già 3594),* 'Quartiere Santa Croce, Ruote, Secondo 1534', *2309,* 'Arroti anno 1574, Quartiere Santa Croce' (for property inherited and transactions in property); *Archivio Mediceo, Filze medicee 175, 220, 236a, 244, 251 to 261, 268, 269, 270, 271,* 'Registri di lettere dai Granduchi ai loro segretari' (Minutes of letters to Salviati and others); (*F. Med.*), *Ambasciatori*

Ferrara 2901, 2902, 2905 (correspondence concerning Salviati from the Florentine ambassadors in Ferrara); (*Fil Med.*), *Magistrato degli Otto di Guardia, 166, 167* (Police records for the case of Diamante and Giannozzo Salviati), *1973*, 'Sentenze originali, 1566–1595'; *Archivio Diplomatico, Santo Stefano di Prato, Propositura di Prato* (Spogli dell'anno 1568) and *Regio Diritto, Filza* No. 4, 'Suppliche' (for Salviati's application for a benefice); *Carte Strozziane, Prima serie, XIX, Lettere, 4*; *Carte Urbinate, Cl. I, F. 244*; *Filze Medicee 684, 685, 686, 687, 785, 786* (lettere originali ai Granduchi), and *Filze Medicee Generali 6409, 59*—all for letters from Salviati to Grand Dukes and *letterati*.

Accademia della Crusca: 'I frammenti del Trito' and 'Il Diario dell'Accademia.'

Biblioteca Riccardiana: Cod. Ricc. 2483 bis, two letters from Salviati to Lorenzo Giacomini; *Cod. Ricc. 2942/6*, a transcription, in an unknown hand, of the two 'Orazioni nel prendere il suo consolato'.

Biblioteca Laurenziana: Cod. Ashb. 558, the 'Diario' of the Accademia degli Alterati.

Biblioteca Marucelliana: Cod. B. 52–4, the 'Diario' of the Accademia Fiorentina.

LONDON

British Museum: Add. MSS. 10272, 10278, 10281, for letters from Salviati to Pier Vettori.

MILAN

Biblioteca Ambrosiana: Cod. D. 191 inf., for transcription of Salviati's letter to Corbinelli and of Marginal notes by Corbinelli to Salviati's *Orazione seconda in lode di Don Garzia*; *Q. 113. Sup.* fols. 89ʳ–91ᵛ, letter from Salviati to De' Bardi comparing Ariosto's poem with the classical epic.

MODENA

Archivio di Stato: Cancelleria, 'Ambasciatori Firenze', Filze for 1575–89, for references to Salviati in diplomatic correspondence; Archivio per materia, 'Letterati', 'Lionardo Salviati', for letters from Salviati to Alfonso II and others.

PISA

Archivio di Stato: Archivio di Santo Stefano, Filze 1320–6, and 1365–9 (records of the correspondence of the Consiglio) for Salviati's letters to the Consiglio and theirs to him) *Filze di Provanze di Nobiltà, Filza quinta, Parte II* (1565–7), *Filza settima, Parte I* (1567–70), *Filza quindicesima, Parte II; Giornale 'A'*, 'Apprension d'Abito di lettera', for details of Salviati's acceptance into the order.

ROME

Archivio Segreto del Vaticano: Archivio Buoncompagni, Carteggio Buoncompagni (1576–83) Filze D. 32–9, letters to, from, and concerning Salviati;

Registri Lateranensi No. 1865 (Pio IV, anno 4–5), *N. 1866* (Pio IV anno 5), for information concerning Salviati's request for a benefice; and for the same purpose, *Armadio 42, Reg. nos. 20, 21.*

B. PRINTED MATERIAL

Select bibliography of works consulted, including all printed works to which reference is made in the present volume (other than works by Salviati)

ACCOLTI, B., *Dialogus de Praestantia Virorum sui Aevi*, in F. Villani, *Liber de Civitatis Florentiae Famosis Civibus*, Florence, 1847.

ADRIANI, G. B., *Istoria dei suoi tempi*, Florence, 1583.

AGENO, F., 'Le frasi proverbiali di una raccolta manoscritta di Lionardo Salviati', *Studi di filologia italiana*, XVII (1959), 239–74.

ALBERTINI, R. VON, *Firenze dalla repubblica al principato*, Turin, 1970.

AMMIRATO, S., *Delle famiglie nobili fiorentine*, Florence, 1615.

ANZILOTTI, A., *La costituzione interna dello stato fiorentino sotto il duca Cosimo I de' Medici*, Florence, 1910.

BAJA, A., *Eleonora di Toledo, duchessa di Firenze e Siena*, Todi, 1907.

BALDACCI, L., *Il petrarchismo italiano nel '500*, Milan, 1957.

BALDINI, B., *Orazione fatta nell' Accademia Fiorentina in lode del Sereniss. S. Cosimo Medici Gran Duca di Toscana*, Florence, 1578.

—— *Vita di Cosimo I Granduca di Toscana scritta da Baccio Baldini, suo protomedico*, Florence, 1578.

BARBI, A. S., *Un accademico mecenate e poeta, G. B. Strozzi il giovane*, Florence, 1900.

BARBI, M., *La fortuna di Dante nel secolo XVI*, Pisa, 1890.

—— 'Degli studi di Vincenzo Borghini sopra la storia e la lingua di Firenze' *Il Propugnatore*, N.S. ii, pt. 2 (1889), 5–71.

—— 'Sul testo del *Decameron*', *La nuova filologia e l'edizione dei nostri scrittori da Dante al Manzoni*, Florence, 1938.

BAROCCHI, P., *Trattati d'arte del Cinquecento*, Bari, 1960.

BARON, H., *The Crisis of the Early Italian Renaissance*, Princeton, N.J., 1955.

—— 'The Querelle of the Ancients and Moderns as a Problem for Renaissance Scholarship', *Journal of the History of Ideas*, xx (1959), 3–22.

BATTAGLIN, D., 'Leonardo Salviati e le "Osservazioni al Pastor fido" del Guarini', in *Atti e memorie dell' Academia Patavina di Scienze, Lettere ed Arti*, lxxvii, pt. 3 (1967).

BATTISTINI, M., 'Documenti italiani nel Belgio', *G.S.L.I.* xlvii (1931), 304–5.

—— 'La condanna di Jacopo Corbinelli', *Archivio storico italiano*, lxxii, Serie V, i, Dispensa prima (1914), 61–3.

BERTOLOTTI, A., 'Giacomo Buoncompagni e Lionardo Salviati riformatore del *Decameron*', *Bibliofilo*, iv (1883), No. 11.

—— 'Una lettera del castratore del *Decameron*', *Bibliofilo*, vi (1885), No. 3.

BIAGI, E., 'La rassettatura del *Decameron*', in *Aneddoti letterari*, Milan, 1887.

BIANCHINI, G. M., *Ragionamenti istorici dei Granduchi di Toscana*, Venice, 1741.

BISCIONI, A., 'Vita del Lasca', prefaced to A. Grazzini, *Novelle*, London, 1793.

BOCCALINI, T., *Ragguagli di Parnaso*, Bari, 1948, Vol. iii (Scrittori d'Italia).

BOOTH, C., *Cosimo I de' Medici*, Cambridge, 1921.

BORGHINI, V., *Annotationi et discorsi sopra alcuni luoghi del 'Decameron' sopra la correttione di esso Boccaccio stampato l'anno MDLXXIII*, Florence, 1575.

—— *Il ruscelleide*, ed. C. Arlia (Collezione di opuscoli danteschi, 57–60), Città di Castello, 1898.

BORSETTI, F. B., *Historia almi Ferrariae Gymnasii*, Ferrara, 1735, 2 vols.

BROWN, P. M., 'I veri promotori della "rassettatura" del *Decameron* nel 1582', *G.S.L.I.* cxxxiv (1957), 314–32.

—— 'Aims and Methods of the Second "Rassettatura" of the *Decameron*', *Studi secenteschi*, viii (1967), 3–41.

—— 'Lionardo Salviati and the *Discorso sopra le prime parole di Cornelio Tacito*', *Italian Studies*, xv (1960), 50–64.

—— 'L'edizione del 1873 delle *Prose inedite del cav. Lionardo Salviati*', *Rinascimento*, viii, No. 1 (June 1957), 111–29.

—— 'Una grammatichetta inedita del cav. Lionardo Salviati', *G.S.L.I.* cxxxiii (1957), 544–72.

—— 'The Conception of the Literary *Volgare* in the Linguistic Writings of Lionardo Salviati', *Italian Studies*, xxi (1966), 57–90.

—— 'Lionardo Salviati and the *Ordine di Santo Stefano*', *Italica*, xxxiv, No. 2 (June 1957).

—— 'Nota sui manoscritti di Lionardo Salviati', *Studi di filologia italiana*, xx (1962), 137–46.

—— 'Manoscritti e stampe delle poesie edite e inedite del cavalier Lionardo Salviati', *G.S.L.I.* cxlvi (1969), 530–52.

—— 'A Significant Use of the Word 'Umanista' in the Sixteenth Century', *M.L.R.* lxiv, pt. 3 (July 1969), 565–75.

—— 'Jacopo Corbinelli and the Florentine "crows" ', *Italian Studies*, xxvi (1971), 68–89.

BROWN, P. M., 'The Historical Significance of the Disputes over the *Gerusalemme Liberata*', *Studi secenteschi*, xi (1970), 3–23.

—— 'Pietro degli Angeli da Barga: "Humanista dello Studio di Pisa" ', *Italica*, xlvii (1970), 285–95.

—— 'In Defence of Ariosto: Giovanni de' Bardi and Lionardo Salviati', *Studi secenteschi*, xii (1971), 3–27.

BRUCKER, G., *Renaissance Florence*, New York, 1969.

BRUNI, F., *Sistemi critici e strutture narrative (ricerche sulla cultura fiorentina del Rinascimento)*, Naples, 1969.

BURCKHARDT, J., *The Civilization of the Renaissance in Italy*, London, 1878.

CAGGESE, R., *Firenze dalla decadenza di Roma al Risorgimento d'Italia*, Florence, 1912–21, 3 vols.

CALDERINI, A., *A proposito di una gita di J. Corbinelli a Épernay nel 1576*, Milan, 1916.

CALDERINI DE MARCHI, R., *Jacopo Corbinelli et les érudits français*, Milan, 1914.

—— and CALDERINI, A., *Autori greci nelle epistole di J. Corbinelli* (MSS. Ambros. B. 9 inf.; T. 167 sup.), Milan, 1915.

CAMBI, P. F., *Orazione funebre di Pierfrancesco Cambi: delle lodi del cavalier Lionardo Salviati*, Florence, 1590.

CAMPANA, A., 'The Origin of the Word "Humanist" ', *Journal of the Warburg and Courtauld Institute*, lx (1946), 60–73.

CAMPORI, G. (Marchese), 'Il cav. Lionardo Salviati e Alfonso II duca di Ferrara', in *Atti e memorie dei R.R. Deputati di Storia Patria per le Prov. Mod. e Parm.*, Vol. vii, Modena, 1874, pp. 143 ff.

CANTINI, L., *Storia di Cosimo de' Medici primo Granduca di Toscana*, Pisa, 1805.

CAPASSO, C. *Paolo III*, Messina, 1924, 2 vols.

CARCERIERI, L., *Cosimo I Granduca*, Verona, 1926.

CARO, A., *Lettere familiari*, 3 vols., Venice, 1751.

CAROCCI, G., *I dintorni di Firenze*, Florence, 1906.

CELLINI, B., *La vita*, Milan, 1958.

CENTELLI, A., 'Fra Geremia da Udine e Bianca Cappello', *Nuovo archivio veneto*, vii. 171–80 (review of Grottanelli, 'Fra Geremia da Udine').

CHIAPPELLI, F., *Studi sul linguaggio del Machiavelli*, Florence, 1952.

—— *Studi sul linguaggio del Tasso epico*, Florence, 1957.

CINI, G. B., *Vita del Serenissimo Sig. Cosimo de' Medici primo Granduca di Toscana*, Florence, 1611.

CITTADELLA, L. N., *Storia della famiglia Guarini*, Bologna, 1870.

COCHRANE, E. (ed.), *The Late Italian Renaissance, 1525–1630*, London, 1970.

Componimenti latini e toscani da diversi suoi amici composti nella morte di M. Benedetto Varchi, Florence, 1566.

CONGEDO, U., *La vita e le opere di Scipione Ammirato*, Trani, 1901.

CONTI, C., *La prima reggia di Cosimo I de' Medici nel palazzo già della Signoria in Firenze*, Florence, 1898.

CONTIN, E., *Lettere edite e inedite di Lionardo Salviati*, Padua, 1875.

CORRAZZINI, G. O. (ed.), *Diario fiorentino di Agostino Lapini*, Florence, 1900.

COSCI, A. G. D., *L'Italia durante le preponderanze straniere dal 1530 al 1789*, Milan, 1875.

COSMO, U., 'Le polemiche tassesche', *G.S.L.I.* xlii (1903), 112–60.

CRESCINI, V., 'Jacopo Corbinelli nella storia degli studi romanzi', *Per gli studi romanzi* (ed. Crescini), Padua (1892), pp. 181–222 (repr. with minor alterations of 'Lettere di Jacopo Corbinelli', *G.S.L.I.* ii (1883), 303–33).

CROCE, B., *La Spagna nella vita italiana durante la Rinascenza*, Bari, 1949.

DECIA, D., 'La prima edizione della *Risposta all'Apologia del Tasso* dell'Infarinato primo e i suoi veri stampatori', *Bibliofilia*, xiv, No. 9.

DE GAETANO, A., 'The Florentine Academy and the Advancement of Learning through the Vernacular', *Bibliothèque d'Humanisme et Renaissance*, xxv (1968), 19–52.

DEJOB, C., *De l'influence du Concile de Trente sur la littérature et les beaux-arts chez les peuples catholiques*, Paris, 1894.

DEL MIGLIORE, F. L., *Firenze città nobilissima illustrata*, Florence, 1684.

DEVOTO, G., 'Il Tasso nella storia della linguistica italiana', *Torquato Tasso: Comitato per le celebrazioni di Torquato Tasso: Ferrara, 1954*, Milan, 1957.

D'OVIDIO, F., *Un'antica testimonianza circa la controversia della Crusca col Tasso*, Naples, 1894.

DUCKWORTH, G. E., *The Nature of Roman Comedy*, Princeton, N.J., 1952.

EUBEL, K., *Hierarchia catholica*, Monasterii, 1898.

FABBRONI, A., *Historiae Academiae Pisanae*, Pisa, 1791–5.

FAITHFULL, R. G., 'The Concept of "Living" Language in Cinquecento Vernacular Philology', *M.L.R.* xlviii (1953), 278–92.

FANFANI, P., 'Osservazioni sulla traduzione fatta dal Salviati in lingua del Mercato Vecchio della novella del Re di Cipro', *I parlari italiani in Certaldo* (ed. G. Papanti), Leghorn, 1875.

FARLATI, D., *Illyricum Sacrum*, Venice, 1800.

FERRAI, L. A., *Lorenzino de' Medici e la vita cortigiana del '500*, Milan, 1895.

—— *Cosimo de' Medici duca di Firenze*, Bologna, 1882.

FERRETTI, I., 'L'organizzazione militare toscana durante il governo di Alessandro e Cosimo I', *Rivista storica degli archivi toscani*, i (1929), 248 ff; ii (1930), 58 ff.

FIRMANO, C., *Della solenne incoronazione del Duca Cosimo de' Medici in Granduca di Toscana*, Florence, 1819.

FOLLINI, V., 'Sopra la traduzione e comento della Poetica d'Aristotile del Cavalier Lionardo Salviati', *Atti dell'Accademia Italiana*, Vol. i, pt. 2, Leghorn, 1810.

FONTANINI, G., *Biblioteca dell'eloquenza italiana*, Venice, 1753.

FOSCOLO, U., 'Discorso storico sul testo del *Decameron*', *Saggi storici e critici*, vol. x of *Opere*, Florence, 1953.

FUSCO, E. M., *La lirica*, Milan, 1950.

GALLETTI, A., *L'eloquenza italiana*, Milan, 1938.

GALLUZZI, R., *Istoria del Granducato sotto il governo della Casa Medici*, Florence, 1781.

GAMBA, B., *Serie de' testi di lingua*, Venice, 1839.

GAMURRINI, E., *Istoria generale delle famiglie nobili toscane ed umbre*, Florence, 1679, 5 vols.

GAYE, G., *Carteggio inedito degli artisti dei secoli XIV, XV, XVI*, Florence, 1840.

GELLI, G. B., 'Lettera sopra la difficultà di ordinare detta lingua', prefaced to P. Giambullari, *De la lingua che si parla e scrive a Firenze*, Florence, 1551.

GENTILE, G., *Delle commedie di A. F. Grazzini*, Pisa, 1886.

GIAMBULLARI, P. F., *Apparato et feste nelle nozze dello illustrissimo Signor Duca di Firenze, e della Duchessa sua consorte, con le sue stanze, madrigali, comedia, e intermedii in quella recitati*, Florence, 1539.

GRAF, A., *Attraverso il Cinquecento*, Turin, 1888.

GRAYSON, C., 'Lorenzo, Machiavelli and the Italian Language', *Italian Renaissance Studies*, London, 1960.

—— *A Renaissance Controversy, Latin or Italian?*, Oxford, 1960.

GRAZZINI, A. F., *Tutti i trionfi, carri, mascherate o canti carnascialeschi, andati per Firenze dal tempo del Magnifico Lorenzo Vecchio de' Medici, quando egli hebbero prima cominciamento, per infino a questo anno presente 1559*, Florence, 1559.

GRAZZINI, G., *L'Accademia della Crusca*, Florence, 1952.

GRENDLER, P. F., 'The Concept of Humanist in Cinquecento Italy', *Renaissance Studies in Honor of Hans Baron* (Florence, 1971), pp. 447–63.

—— *Critics of the Italian World, 1530–1560: Anton Francesco Doni, Nicolò Franco & Ortensio Lando*, Madison, Milwaukee, and London, 1969.

GROTTANELLI, L., 'Fra Geremia da Udine e le sue relazioni con la corte del granduca Francesco de' Medici', *Rassegna nazionale*, lxxii, fasc. 280–3 (1893), 3–43, 185–228, 577–622.

GUARINI, G. B., *Lettere del Sig. Guarini*, Venice, 1593.

GUASTI, C. (ed.), *Lettere di Torquato Tasso*, Florence, 1854 (see esp. the preface to Vol. iv, 'La Crusca e il Tasso').

—— 'Le poesie di Don Francesco de' Medici a Bianca Cappello', *Rassegna nazionale*, 1895.

HALL, R. A., *The Italian 'Questione della lingua', an Interpretative Essay*, Chapel Hill, N.C., 1942.

HATHAWAY, B., *The Age of Criticism*, Ithaca, N.Y., 1962.

HERRICK, M. T., *Italian Comedy in the Renaissance*, Urbana, 1960.

IMHOF, J. W., *Genealogiae Viginti Illustrium in Italia Familiarum*, Amsterdam, 1710.

KRISTELLER, P. O., *The Classics and Renaissance Thought* (Martin Classical Lectures, Vol. xv), Cambridge, Mass., 1955.

LABANDE-JEANROY, T., *La Question de la langue en Italie*, Strasbourg, 1925.

LANDUCCI, L., *Diario fiorentino*, Florence, 1889.

LESCA, G., 'V. Borghini e il *Decameron*' in *Studi su G. Boccaccio*, Castelfiorentino, 1913.

LITTA, P., *Celebri famiglie italiane*, Milan–Turin, 1819–99; Turin, 1902–1923.

LORENZONI, A., *Un coro di male lingue* (Frammenti inediti di vita fiorentina, Opusc. i), Florence, 1905.

MABELLINI, A., *Delle rime di B. Cellini*, Rome, 1885.

MAFFEI, V., *Dal titolo di Duca di Firenze e Siena al titolo di Gran Duca di Toscana; contributo alla storia della politica di Cosimo I de' Medici*, Florence, 1905.

MANACORDA, G., *Benedetto Varchi, l'uomo, il poeta, il critico*, Pisa, 1903.

MANFRONI, C., *Storia della marina italiana dalla caduta di Costantinopoli alla battaglia di Lepanto*, Rome, 1897.

—— 'La marina di guerra del Granducato mediceo', *Rivista marittima*, 1895.

MANNI, D. M., *Vita del celebre Lelio Torelli*, Florence, 1770.

—— *Illustrazione storica del Boccaccio*, Florence, 1742.

MANUZIO, A., *Vita di Cosimo de' Medici primo Granduca di Toscana*, Pisa, 1823.

MANZONI, L., *Prose inedite del cav. Leonardo Salviati* (Vol. cxxix of the series 'Scelta di curiosità letterarie inedite o rare'), Bologna, 1873.

—— *Rime inedite del cav. Leonardo Salviati* (Vol. cxvii of the series 'Scelta di curiosità letterarie inedite o rare'), Bologna, 1871.

MARCONCINI, C., *L'Accademia della Crusca dalle origini alla prima edizione del Vocabolario*, Pisa, 1910.

MARGIOTTA, G., *Le origini italiane de'la querelle des anciens et des modernes'*, Rome, 1953.

MAYLENDER, M., *Storia delle Accademie d'Italia*, Bologna, 1926–30, Vol. v.

MAZZUCCHELLI, G. M., *Gli scrittori d'Italia, cioè notizie storiche e critiche intorno alle vite, e agli scritti dei letterati italiani*, etc., Brescia, 1753–63, fol.

MECATTI, G. M., *Istoria genealogica della nobiltà e cittadinanza di Firenze divisa in tre parti*, Naples, 1753–4,

MELLINI, D., *Descrizione delle dieci mascherate delle bufale mandate in Firenze il giorno di Carnevale l'anno 1565* [i.e. '66] *con la descrizione di tutta la pompa delle Mascherate, e le loro invenzioni*, Florence, 1566.

——— *Descrizione dell'entrata della Serenissima Reina Giovanna d'Austria et dell'apparato fatto in Fiorenza nella venuta, per le felicissime nozze di S. Altezza et dell'Illustrissimo & Eccell.mo S. Don Francesco de' Medici, principe di Fiorenza e di Siena*, Ristampata e riveduta, Florence, 1566.

——— *Ricordo intorno ai costumi, azioni e governo del sereniss. Gran Duca Cosimo I*, Florence, 1820.

——— *Descrizione dell'apparato della commedia ed intermedii d'essa, recitata in Firenze in giorno di Santo Stefano l'anno 1565, nella gran sala del palazzo di Sua Ecc. Illust. nelle reali nozze dell'Illust. & Eccell. S. il S. Don Francesco Medici Principe di Fiorenza & di Siena & della Regina Giovanna d'Austria sua Consorte*, Florence, 1566.

MIGLIORINI, B., *Storia della lingua italiana*, Florence, 1960.

MILANESI, C., *Trattati . . . di B. Cellini*, Florence, 1857.

MINI, P., *Discorso della nobiltà di Firenze e de' Fiorentini*, Florence, 1593.

MONDAINI, G., *La questione di precedenza fra il duca Cosimo I de' Medici e Alfonso II d'Este*, Florence, 1898.

MORENI, D., *Notizie istoriche dei contorni di Firenze*, Florence, 1791–5, 6 parts.

——— *Pompe funebri celebrate nell'imp. e real. Basilica di San Lorenzo*, Florence, 1827.

NEGRI, G., *Istoria di scrittori fiorentini*, Ferrara, 1722.

NENCIONI, G., *Fra grammatica e retorica*, Florence, 1953.

NICCOLAI, F., *Pier Vettori*, Florence, 1912.

PARODI, S., 'Una lettera inedita del Salviati', *Studi di filologia italiana*, xxvii (1969), 147–74.

PASQUAZI, S., 'G. B. Guarini', in *I minori* of the series 'Orientamenti Culturali', Milan, 1961, pp. 1339–64.

——— *Rinascimento ferrarese*, Caltanisetta–Rome, 1957.

PELLI, G., *Elogi di uomini illustri toscani*, Lucca, 1772.

PIERACCINI, G., *La stirpe dei Medici di Cafaggiolo* (Saggio di ricerche sulla trasmissione dei caratteri biologici), Florence, 1924.

PIROTTI, U., 'Benedetto Varchi e la questione della lingua', *Convivium*, xxviii (1960), 524–52.

POCCIANTI, M., *Catalogus Scriptorum Florentinorum*, Florence, 1589.

POGGIALI, G., *Serie di testi di lingua*, Leghorn, 1813.

PRAZ, M., 'Rapporti tra la letteratura italiana e la letteratura inglese', in Vol. iv (*Letterature comparate*) of Problemi ed orientamenti critici, Milan, 1949, (ed. Momigliano).

PREZZINER, G., *Storia del pubblico studio e delle società scientifiche e letterarie di Firenze*, Florence, 1810.

Prose fiorentine raccolte dallo Smarrito Accademico della Crusca (Carlo Dati) 6 vols., Florence, 1661–1723.

RAJNA, P., 'Jacopo Corbinelli e la strage di San Bartolommeo', *Archivio storico italiano*, Serie V, xxi (1898), 54–103.

RASTRELLI, M., *Illustrazione storica del Palazzo della Signoria*, Florence, 1782.

RAZZI, DON S., *Vita di Benedetto Varchi*, Florence, 1590.

—— *La Gostanza*, Florence, 1565 (ed. Li. Sal., ded. let. to Isabella Orsini).

RAZZOLINI, L., *Bibliografia dei testi di lingua a stampa citati dagli Accademici della Crusca* (ed. A. Bacchi della Lega), Bologna, 1878.

REPETTI, E., *Dizionario geografico-storico della Toscana*, Florence, 1833–45, 6 vols.

—— *Compendio storico della città di Firenze, sua comunità, diocesi, e compartimento fino all'anno 1849, desunto dal Dizionario geografico-fisico-storico*, Florence, 1849.

REUSCH, F. H., *Der Index der verbotenen Bücher*, Bonn, 1883.

RICHA, G., *Notizie storiche delle chiese fiorentine divise ne' suoi quartieri*, Florence, 1754–62.

RILLI, I., *Notizie letterarie ed istoriche intorno agli uomini illustri dell'Accademia Fiorentina*, Florence, 1700.

RODINI, R. J., *Antonfrancesco Grazzini, Poet, Dramatist and Novelliere*, Madison, Milwaukee, and London, 1970.

ROSADI, G., 'Il Boccaccio e la censura' in *Studi su G. Boccaccio*, Castelfiorentino, 1913.

ROSSI, M., 'Il discorso di Ridolfo Castravilla contro Dante', *Giornale dantesco*, v (1897), Quad. I–II, pp. 1 ff.

ROSSI, V., *Guarini e il 'Pastor fido'*, Turin, 1886.

ROTH, C., 'I carteggi volgari di Piero Vettori nel British Museum, *Rivista storica degli archivi toscani*, i, pt. 3 (1929), 1 ff.

RUD, E., *Vasari's Life and Lives*, London, 1963.

RUGGIERI, R. M., 'Aspetti linguistici della polemica tassesca', *Lingua nostra*, vi (1944–5), 44–51.

SABBADINI, R., *Storia del ciceronianismo*, Turin, 1885.

SALTINI, G. E., *Tragedie medicee domestiche*, Florence, 1898.

SALVINI, S., *Fasti consolari dell' Accademia Fiorentina*, Florence, 1717.

SANESI, I., *La commedia*, Milan, 1954.

SANTI, V., 'Lionardo Salviati e il suo testamento', in *G.S.L.I.* xix (1898), 22 ff.

SANTINI, E., *Storia dell'eloquenza italiana dal Concilio Tridentino ai nostri giorni*, Palermo, 1928.

SANTORO, M., 'C. Landino e il volgare', *G.S.L.I.* cxxxi (1954), 501–47.

SCHEVILL, F., *History of Florence in the Middle Ages and Renaissance*, London, 1937.

SEGRE, C., 'Edonismo linguistico nel Cinquecento', *G.S.L.I.* cxxx (1953), 145–77.

SERASSI, P., *La vita di Torquato Tasso*, Rome, 1785.

SERONI, A., Introduction and Notes to *Le rime di Giovanni della Casa*, Florence, 1944.

SIEBKEES, F., *Bianca Cappello*, Florence, 1868.

SOLDATI, P., 'Jacopo Corbinelli e Lionardo Salviati', *Archivum Romanicum*, xix (July–Dec. 1935), 415–23.

SOLERTI, A., *Vita di Torquato Tasso*, Turin, 1895.

SORRENTINO, A., *La letteratura italiana e il Sant'Uffizio*, Naples, 1935.

SOZZI, B. T., *Aspetti e momenti della questione linguistica*, Padua, 1955.

—— 'Tasso contro Salviati: con le postille inedite dell'Infarinato', *Studi tassiani*, i (1951), 36–67.

SPERONI, S., *Opere*, Venice, 1740, Vol. iv.

SPINGARN, J. E., *A History of Literary Criticism in the Renaissance*, New York, 1899.

SPINI, G., *Cosimo I de' Medici e l'indipendenza del principato mediceo*, Florence, 1945.

SPINI, G. (ed.), *Cosimo I de'Medici: lettere*, Florence, 1940.

Statuti, capitoli et constitutioni del ordine de' Cavalieri di Santo Stephano, Florence, 1562.

TAURISIANO, PADRE I., *Hierarchia Ordinis Praedicatorum*, Pars prima, ii, Series Magistrorum Sancti Palatii Apostolici, 1217–1916.

TOFFANIN, G., *Tasso e l'età che fu sua*, Naples, n.d.

TRABALZA, C., *Storia della grammatica italiana*, Bologna, repr. 1963.

VARCHI, B., *Orazione funerale fatta, e recitata nell'esequie di Michelangelo Buonarroti in Firenze nella chiesa di San Lorenzo*, Florence, 1564.

—— *Due lezioni di M. Benedetto Varchi*, Florence, 1549.

—— *Ercolano*, Padua, 1744.

VASARI, G., *Le vite de' più eccellenti pittori, scultori e architettori nelle redazioni del 1550 e 1568*. Testo a cura di P. Barocchi. Florence, 1966–1972.

VERZONE, C. (ed.), *Le rime burlesche edite e inedite di Antonfrancesco Grazzini, detto il Lasca*, Florence, 1882.

VITALE, M., 'La prima edizione del Vocabolario della Crusca e i suoi precedenti teorici e critici', *Le prefazioni ai primi grandi vocabolari europei*, Vol. i (*Le lingue romanze*), Varese, 1959.

—— 'Le origini del volgare nelle discussioni dei filologi del '400', *Lingua nostra*, xiv (1953), 64–9.

—— *La questione della lingua*, Palermo, 1960.

VIVALDI, V., *La più grande polemica del Cinquecento*, Catanzaro, 1895 (revised after original publication in *Studi letterari*, 1891, Naples).

WEINBERG, B., 'Argomenti di discussione letteraria nell'Accademia degli Alterati (1570–1600)', *G.S.L.I.* cxxxi (1954), 186 ff.

—— *A History of Literary Criticism in the Italian Renaissance*, Chicago, Ill., 1961, 2 vols.

—— *Trattati di poetica e retorica del Cinquecento*, Bari, 1970–2 (3 vols.).

WINSPEARE, F., *Isabella Orsini e la corte medicea*, Florence, 1961.

WITTKOWER, R. and M., *The Divine Michelangelo: The Florentine Academy's Homage on his Death, and Facsimile Edition of 'Esequie del Divino Michelangelo Buonarroti, Firenze 1564'*, London, 1964.

ZAMBALDI, F., 'Delle teorie ortografiche in Italia', *Atti del R. Istituto Veneto*, Serie VII, Vol. iii, Venice, 1892.

ZAMBRINI, F. S., *Lettere di uomini illustri del sec. XVI*, Lucca, 1853.

ZANNONI, G. B., 'Breve storia dell'Accademia della Crusca' in *Atti dell'Imp. e Reale Accademia della Crusca*, Vol. ii, Florence, 1848.

ZENO, A., *Note alla 'Biblioteca dell'eloquenza italiana' del Fontanini*, Venice, 1753.

INDEX

INDEX